Contents

**Attainment Targets
Coverage (AT)**

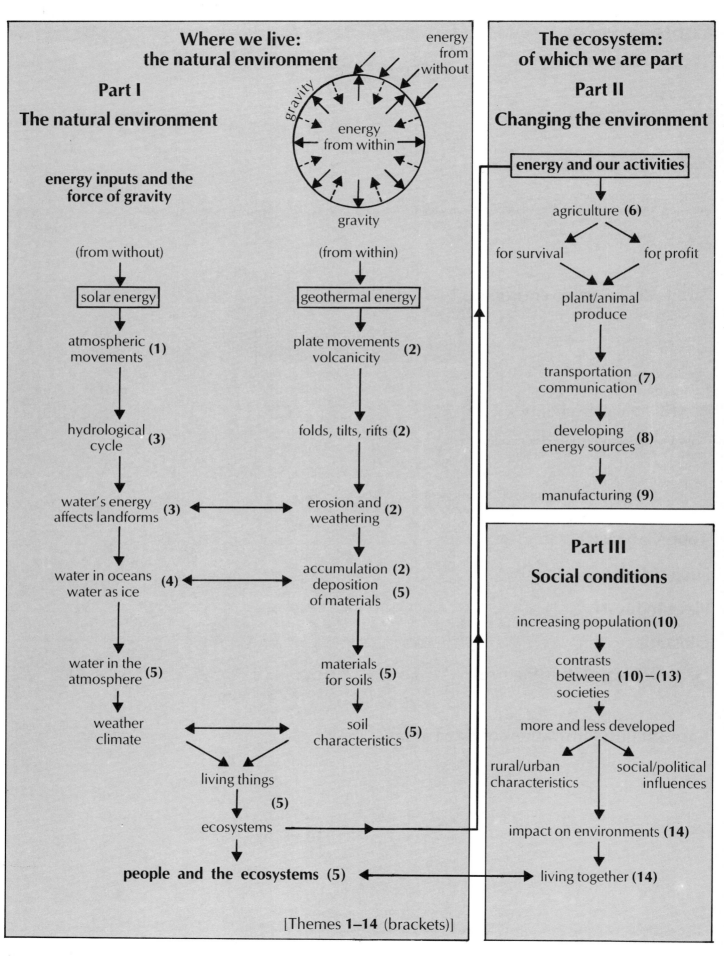

Where we live: the natural environment

Part I

The natural environment

energy inputs and the force of gravity

energy from without

gravity

energy from within

energy from within

gravity

(from without)

solar energy

atmospheric movements **(1)**

hydrological cycle **(3)**

water's energy affects landforms **(3)**

water in oceans water as ice **(4)**

water in the atmosphere **(5)**

weather climate

(from within)

geothermal energy

plate movements volcanicity **(2)**

folds, tilts, rifts **(2)**

erosion and weathering **(2)**

accumulation **(2)** deposition **(5)** of materials

materials for soils **(5)**

soil characteristics **(5)**

living things **(5)**

ecosystems

people and the ecosystems (5)

The ecosystem: of which we are part

Part II

Changing the environment

energy and our activities

agriculture **(6)**

for survival   for profit

plant/animal produce

transportation communication **(7)**

developing energy sources **(8)**

manufacturing **(9)**

Part III

Social conditions

increasing population **(10)**

contrasts between **(10)–(13)** societies

more and less developed

rural/urban characteristics   social/political influences

impact on environments **(14)**

living together **(14)**

[Themes **1–14** (brackets)]

Foundations of Geography

D. C. MONEY

Evans Brothers Limited

Published by Evans Brothers Limited
2A Portman Mansions, Chiltern Street,
London W1M 1LE

Evans Brothers (Nigeria Publishers) Limited
PMB 5164, Jericho Road, Ibadan

Evans Brothers (Kenya) Limited
PO Box 44536, Nairobi

First published 1987
Revised edition 1993
Reprinted 1994

Front cover photos:
(top left) Massive pillars of soft sandstone in
highland Bolivia. Surface boulders protected
the rock beneath them from the beating of
storm rain, and from the small streams which
cut deep channels into the surface. Eventually
these tall columns are left capped by their
shielding rock, until the sides weather away
and the boulder falls.

(top right) The high-rise columns of New
York's financial districts soar up beyond the
ferry terminal of lower Manhattan.

(bottom left) This mural painting represents a
timely tilt at history-book bias and colonial
attitudes. It was photographed on the wall of
the cultural centre beside the river Torrens in
Adelaide.

(bottom right) A London street, with its flats, its
retailing and service functions, and its variety
of people, stresses the scope for geographical
studies in an urban setting.

Acknowledgements

Photographs (by photo number):

Aerofilms: 2.11, 3.6, 4.4, 4.5, 4.10, 4.19, 4.23, 5.17, 6.11, 7.5, 7.9, 8.3, 8.8, 9.2, 12.4, 12.5

British Petroleum: 8.1, 8.2

Business Press International/Farmers Weekly: 6.5, 13.10

Port of Felixstowe: 7.6

Glenrothes Development Corporation: 9.9

Robert Harding Picture Library: 9.6, 9.7, 9.8, 9.10, 12.9

Oxfam: 6.1, 6.2, 6.3, 6.12, 6.14, 6.15, 7.4, 9.13, 9.15, 10.7, 10.10, 12.17, 12.18, 12.21,
13.1, 13.2, 13.3, 13.4, 13.5, 13.7, 13.8, 13.9, 13.11, 13.12, 13.15, 14.1, 14.2,
14.7, 14.8, 14.9, 14.10, 14.11, 14.12

Topham Picture Library: 14.3, 14.4, 14.6

Warrington-Runcorn New Town: 12.14

All other photographs by D. C. Money

Maps, diagrams and illustrations:
Hilary Evans
Ian Foulis
Jillian Luff
Design:
Neil Sayer

Printed in Hong Kong by Dah Hua Printing Press Co., Ltd.
ISBN 0-237-51254-8

Preface

Introducing the subject

Geography should be a fascinating, informative subject for pupils taking a GCSE course. It should also enable them to consider the social problems which confront them, often at first hand, and put them into proper perspective.

The cover illustrates some of the major influences on our lives today; the physical forces, a dramatic example of how they can affect the landscape; the economic forces, represented by the heart of the USA's financial power in lower Manhattan; consumerism, an urban environment, with shops wooing the consumers; and a lively mural from Adelaide, beside the Torrens, which shows us that there is more than one way to view racial problems.

The geography GCSE syllabuses of the various examining boards and associations have a common requirement – **a study of the relationships between people and their environment.** This calls for a clear understanding of the processes which affect the development of particular environments.

Geographers, above all, should have a clear picture of what is concealed in the word 'environment', which is *not* just the physical background to people's activities. Other people and the things they do, and have done, are important parts of our immediate surroundings.

The contrasts between the environment of families in rural England and those in highland Ethiopia, of people in South American shanty suburbs and those in European inner urban areas are the *combined* results of physical, economic, political and social relationships. So, as geographers, we rightly put a great emphasis on people – who they are, where they are, how they behave – and the results.

But this leads some people to regard physical geography as something to be studied purely for its own sake, and to feel that they ought to discard it in favour of social geography. But **physical conditions, and natural energy changes, continuously affect the way we behave.**

In places people clear vegetation and profitably farm the land. In others people clear natural vegetation and, through ignorance or greed, destroy potentially fertile soils. We are much more likely to strike the correct balance if we appreciate the relationships between the living and non-living elements of our environment.

In this case we should understand the processes by which the sun's energy creates movements of the atmosphere, whose moisture helps weather the rocks, whose particles help to form soils which support plants, which are themselves dependent on exchanges with the atmosphere. And so the book deals first with such processes and systems.

Introducing the book

Part I considers the physical processes which every moment of time are acting in the atmosphere and on the landscape, and on the people who occupy it.

The subject matter is presented in Themes. This enables topics to be selected for particular coursework. But the presentation of the Themes follows a firm pattern, as the contents, shown diagrammatically opposite, confirm.

The concept of **ecosystems**, large and small, is introduced in Part I. A system involves inputs, processes and outputs. So here we follow the energy inputs and the flows of energy – from solar inputs, through physical processes, to plant growth and animal consumption. Then in Parts II and III we consider the use people make of the energy they obtain from food and fuels; and finally our dependence on technology to release energy from sources, which may help to maintain our increasing numbers.

Part II shows how people use their own energy to change the physical environment. In fact they interfere with the landscape on a large scale in order to *obtain* energy. They farm for food energy, mine for fossil fuels, build dams for hydro-energy, and so on.

Part III considers who makes up the human race, where we live, how we live, and the results of our social differences and political groupings. It considers the nature of our settlements. It looks at the inequalities and the pressing need to remedy these. It deals with the problems of protecting and conserving the fast-vanishing wildscapes.

The simple consideration of ecosystems brings together the three parts of the book. The concluding Themes of Parts I and III are linked in this way, as shown opposite.

Throughout the book there are inserts to enable the reader to consider what has been stated and its implications. One aim is to lead students to ask themselves the right sort of questions, especially to get used to first classifying things and then thinking what may happen to them in space and time. An example would be: 'What are the characteristics of this landform and the processes acting on it?' (**classification**) 'Where is it? What is its extent? How does being *there* affect the object itself and the processes involved?' (**spatial distribution**) 'How is it being modified with time? Are the processes continuous or intermittent? What secondary landforms are developed with time?' (**dynamics**)

The same sequence of questions may be put when considering people and their settlements.

Additional background material is provided at the end of each Theme, allowing it to be treated in greater depth. Those who wish to follow up particular topics can do so more fully. Suggestions for practical work, methods of investigation and statistical calculations aim at encouraging geographical enquiries and the use of skills needed in the local studies introduced by teachers at appropriate levels.

Teachers now have greater flexibility and freedom to choose and provide illustrative material, and to organise fieldwork. For this reason, there are few detailed case studies. But certain specific rural and urban areas are dealt with in different ways in various parts of the book, so that cross-references will give an overall view of climate, settlement, economic development, transport problems, and so on, as in the case of the Canadian prairies.

Each Theme concludes with various questions and tests to enable a pupil to make sure of the facts presented, and that the ideas behind them have been absorbed. They begin with simple checks and verifications of fact, but go on to problems in greater depth – which should suit those considering further studies in geography.

In place of a general **glossary**, some of the less familiar terms are explained at the end of each Theme. They are presented in the order they occur in the text, or are grouped with related words or phrases, rather than alphabetically...for one term often helps to explain another.

Abbreviations used are also explained in the text, and a comprehensive list is appended on p. 262.

PART 1

The natural environment

Theme 1   Energy for a spinning planet

Introduction – Planet earth

Picture the spinning earth, travelling in its orbit about the sun, as a **system** with an input of energy from the sun, and an output of energy radiating back into space (Fig. 1.2a).

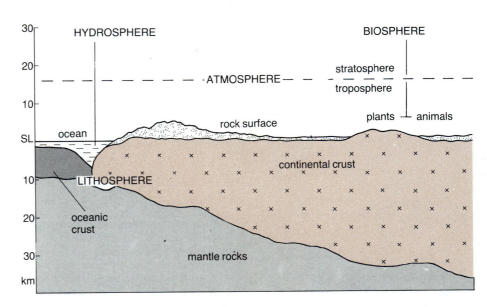

1.3 The four great systems which continually exchange energy and matter.

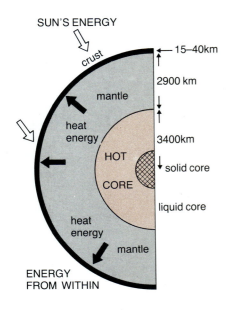

1.1 Energy from the core of the earth affects the surface – see Theme 2.

It is not simply a solid sphere. Even the surface is about 70 per cent water. Above this is a gaseous **atmosphere,** densest at sea-level. Most of the clouds, and the changing weather conditions which affect our daily activities, occur in its lowest layer, known as the **troposphere** – that is, within 14 km from the surface. The atmosphere is held to the earth by the pull of gravity, and rotates with it.

The solid surface is an outer crust of rocks. This is relatively thick beneath the continents (Fig. 1.3), but less thick beneath the oceans. This outer, rocky

part is known as the **lithosphere.** Beneath it is the hot mass of material which forms a **mantle** about the dense, very hot core of the earth.

A continuous input of energy from the sun (solar energy) streams through the atmosphere and onto the surface of rock and water. It also provides energy for all the living organisms which make up the **biosphere.** The total water – in the atmosphere, on and beneath the surface, and also in living matter – comprises the **hydrosphere.**

Later, we see how this stream of energy affects the individual systems, such as the atmosphere and hydrosphere.

At one time half the spinning globe is in sunlight. Our tiny planet is so far from the sun that we may justifiably show the small part of the sun's output of energy which strikes it as parallel rays (Fig. 1.2b).

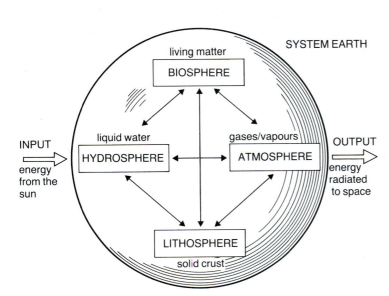

1.2a Energy is gained from the sun and lost to space; and energy passes through and between the great sub-systems.

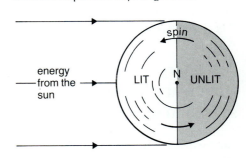

1.2b Solar energy lights up half the globe – see section 1.2.

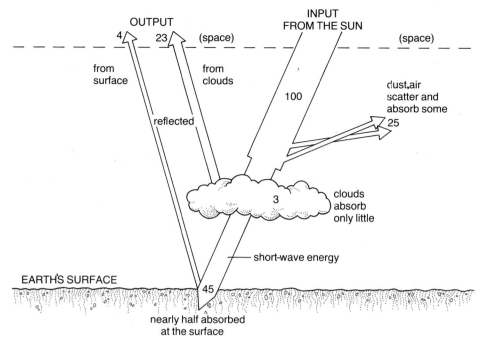

1.4 What happens to 100 units of solar energy entering the atmosphere.

1.1 Energy inputs – energy outputs

This incoming solar energy is also known as insolation. It is a form of short-wave radiation which readily penetrates the atmosphere. A little is absorbed on the way, and some is scattered and reflected by the air – by water droplets and dust particles. When it strikes the surface a small part is reflected back, but about half of all the incoming radiation is absorbed.

The earth's surface, of course, is at a much lower temperature than the sun, and so **radiates long-wave energy.** This cannot penetrate the atmosphere as readily, so it heats the air above it. This is the principal way in which the air gains heat from the surface. Clouds, in particular, first absorb the heat and then re-radiate it. A cloud cover thus acts like a greenhouse: it allows solar energy through to the surface, but prevents much of that radiated from the surface being lost to space (Fig. 1.5 and p. 259).

1.2 Energy received varies from place to place and season to season

The earth spins about its north-south axis once a day, giving us periods of light and darkness. It travels round the sun on its 365¼-day journey as if round the edge of

a plane (the **ecliptic plane**). But **instead of its axis being at right angles to this plane, it is tilted from it at 23½°. This produces contrasting seasons.**

Fig. 1.6 shows that in June the northern hemisphere is tilted towards the sun, but away from it in December. Fig. 1.7 shows how the sun's rays fall on each hemisphere during these months.

Notice that the angle of the *noonday* sun above the horizon varies with latitude. **Latitude is the *angular* position of a place relative to the plane of the equator:** thus in Fig. 1.7 T_1 lies on the southern tropic (Capricorn) at 23½°S, and

T_2 on the northern tropic (Cancer) at 23½°N.

Sunlight falls onto half the globe, while the other half is in darkness. Fig. 1.2b shows how this will appear on two particular days in the year...which days?

Because of the axial tilt, the energy received from the sun varies from place to place and season to season. You can appreciate this by considering the following (answers can be gleaned from Figs. 1.6–1.8):

In Fig. 1.7 A_1 and A_3 lie on the Arctic Circle, A_2 and A_4 on the Antarctic Circle. What it the latitude of each place?

Imagine the earth revolving about its axis on June 21st; for how many hours will the sun be above the horizon within the Arctic Circle and within the Antarctic Circle?

What will be the number of hours of daylight at places A_1–A_4 on March 21st?

Find out why the term **equinox** is used to describe March 21st (see Fig. 1.6). What other date does this apply to, and why?

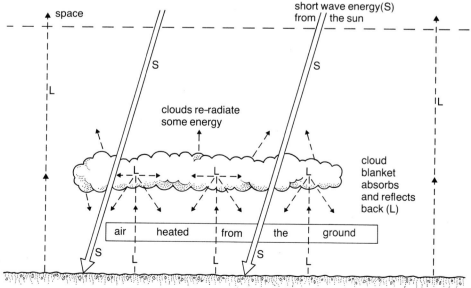

1.5 The 'greenhouse' effect (See also p.259)

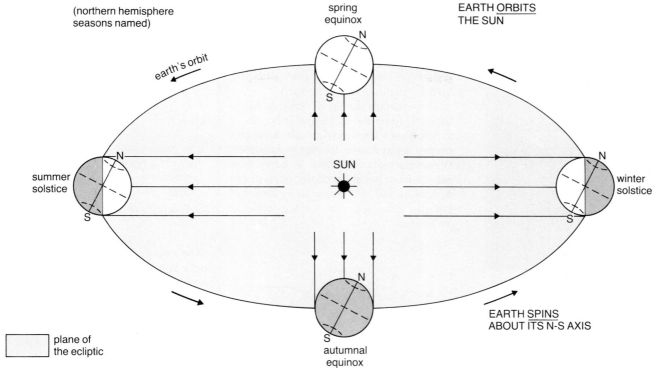

(northern hemisphere
seasons named)

spring
equinox

earth's orbit

summer
solstice

SUN

winter
solstice

EARTH SPINS
ABOUT ITS N-S AXIS

plane of
the ecliptic

autumnal
equinox

1.6 The earth spins as it orbits the sun.

In Fig. 1.8 what is the latitude of **P**? Where is the sun due overhead at noon? What is the date?

You can see that the angle of the noonday sun above the horizon at place **P** is 16½°...(90°–73½°). How does this affect the air temperature there?

Draw similar diagrams for places on the following latitudes for the dates

shown (marking in the angle of the noonday sun above the horizon): 40°N on 21 June; 10°N on 21 March; 23½°S on 22 December.

If at midday you stood a measuring rod vertically at **R**, how could the length of its shadow allow you to find the elevation of the sun?

You can see that in the lower latitudes the noonday sun is high in the sky throughout the year; whereas in winter in the high latitudes it is scarcely above the horizon, if at all.

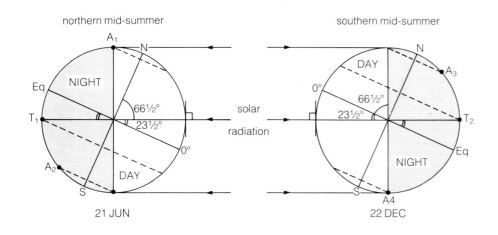

northern mid-summer

southern mid-summer

21 JUN

22 DEC

1.7 Imagine the alternating periods of daylight/darkness as the earth spins about its axis.

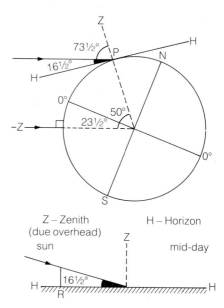

Z – Zenith
(due overhead)
sun

H – Horizon

mid-day

1.8 The sun's elevation (angle above the horizon) at noon.

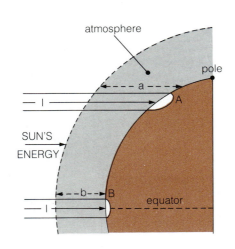

1.9 Effects of the earth's curvature and atmosphere.

The earth's curvature also affects the intensity of heat energy received at various latitudes. Fig. 1.9 shows why the same amount of solar energy is more effective in heating the surface in some latitudes than in others. Notice the different surface areas **A** and **B**, and that **a** and **b** represent the depth of the atmosphere through which the radiation must pass to reach the surface.

> Explain exactly why the intensity of the heat at the surface will not be the same within area **A** as within area **B**.

1.3 How energy is transferred between latitudes

Fig. 1.10 shows the amounts of energy gained and lost during a year at various

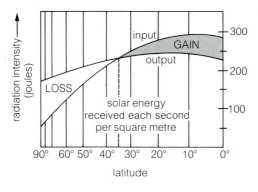

1.10 Notice that lines of latitude are spaced to allow for the area of surface affected.

latitudes. It suggests that places in the higher latitudes *should* get colder and colder with each passing year, and those within the tropics *should* get hotter and hotter. Yet this does not happen.

This is largely due to air flowing (winds blowing) from one part of the atmosphere to another. **The moving air transfers energy from lower to higher latitudes. Water currents also help to carry heat energy from hotter to cooler parts of the oceans** (p. 43). There is also a transfer of energy between ocean surfaces and the air above.

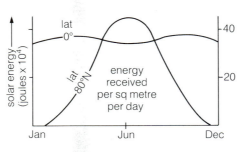

1.11 Energy received per day. Seasonal contrasts in different latitudes.

Fig 1.11 shows that in mid-summer polar regions may receive *more* solar energy per unit area per day than equatorial lands.

> For how many hours a day does the surface receive solar energy on 21 June: (a) at the equator; (b) at 80°N?
> How does this relate to the graphs in Fig. 1.11? What influences may this have on vegetation and crop growth within the Arctic Circle?

1.4 Energy inputs set the atmosphere in motion

The flows of air which transfer energy from one latitude to another (zonally) suggest that **the sun's input is providing energy for a kind of 'atmospheric heat engine'.** The energy gains and losses shown in Fig. 1.10 *should* create an air circulation like that in Fig. 1.12.

This assumes that in the low latitudes surface air is heated, becomes less dense, and so rises. And that at high altitudes it moves away towards the poles, and is replaced by surface inflows of cooler air. At the same time in the cold zones air is chilled, becomes denser, sinks to the surface, and flows outwards.... Yet the *actual wind pattern is very different* (Fig. 1.14).

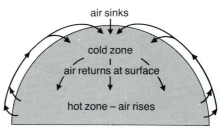

HOW IT WOULD BE if surface were uniform and earth's spin did <u>not</u> affect the air.

1.12 A simplified 'heat engine' effect.

The energy input *does* set the atmosphere in motion, but other factors influence the way the air actually circulates:

1 Because of the rotation of the earth, air travelling towards the poles is deflected eastwards. That moving towards the equator is urged towards the west.

2 This applies to the air which rises in the low latitudes. For as it flows polewards, high in the atmosphere, it is turned to the east (as a westerly wind).

3 The speed of these high westerlies increases as they move away from the equator. For as the distance west to east *around* the earth becomes less and less towards the pole, their momentum carries them around faster and faster...until, at about latitudes 20°–30°, they form a stream of very strong westerly winds high above the surface, known as a **jet stream** (the sub-tropical jet stream).

4 As the upper air cannot continue polewards, as suggested in Fig. 1.12, much of it sinks to the surface beneath the jet stream (p. 62).

5 Part of this sinking air returns towards the equator at the surface. It is deflected towards the west as the persistent easterly Trade Winds.

6 Some of the sinking air flows towards the poles (as westerly winds) and carries energy into regions which would otherwise have an overall energy loss each year (Fig. 1.10).

7 The chilled dense air which sinks over the polar regions flows out, as surface easterlies, to lower latitudes. There it clashes with the warmer air from the sub-tropics, and produces the very changeable weather of this 'zone of conflict' (p. 62).

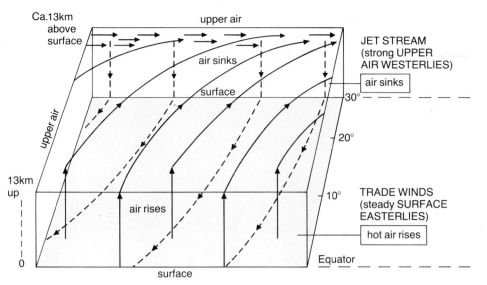

1.13 A three-dimensional look at the way the air circulates. Full lines show air rising, and the upper flows (westerlies); broken lines show air sinking, and the surface flows (easterlies).

The *actual* movements of the winds over the earth's surface at any moment are even more complex; for, of course, the surface is *not* uniform. The large ocean areas and the land masses, with their mountains and plains, affect the air above them. *The effects are considered in more detail on pp 62–75.*

1.5 Sun, shade, and surface features

The sun's energy obviously has a direct effect on rocks, vegetation, and water surfaces. Because of the relief of the land, places close to each other can receive very different amounts of insolation.

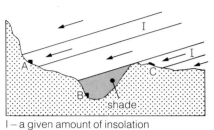

I – a given amount of insolation

1.15 The importance of aspect (the direction a slope faces).

Fig. 1.15 shows the importance of **aspect** (situation relative to the sun's position in the sky).

The amount of energy reflected or absorbed depends on the nature of the surface itself. Figure 1.16 shows the percentage of the incoming energy reflected by various surfaces – a figure known as the **albedo**.

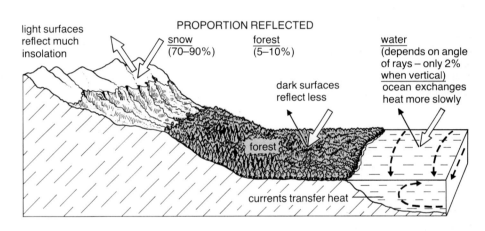

1.16 Different surfaces absorb and reflect different amounts of energy.

> Look at Fig. 1.15 and explain how the different aspect at **A**, **B**, and **C** might affect the local vegetation, crops, and settlement.
> How does Fig. 1.16 suggest that forest clearance would affect the air immediately above?

Intense heat or cold can cause a rocky surface to break up, and so directly affect the soils. While another force is continuously governing the processes which change the surface of the earth . . . **the force of gravity.**

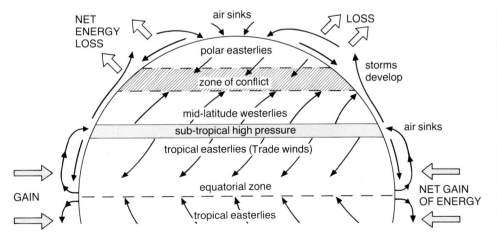

1.14 The wind systems which distribute energy and maintain a balance. In fact the actual flows vary considerably from day to day and season to season.

1.6 Gravity and the results of weathering and erosion

Surface material loosened by weathering or erosion may fall, slide, or roll into new positions under the pull of gravity.

Weathering is caused by the action of atmospheric processes on the surface. Alternate heating and cooling can lead to the break-up of rocks, as the surface minerals expand and contract. Different coloured minerals absorb heat at different rates, and their different amounts of expansion create stresses which may cause a rock to disintegrate. Water also creates stresses by combining chemically with some minerals, and so increasing the size of their crystals (by **hydration**). Oxygen in the air also combines with some surface minerals, producing substances which may crumble away like rust.

The carbon dioxide in the atmosphere forms an acid with water (carbonic acid). This destroys limestone rocks in particular (p. 28). Other gases which pollute the air may also chemically affect the surface, causing **corrosion**.

Water held within cracks may freeze and expand, so splitting the rock; growing plant roots may have the same effect.

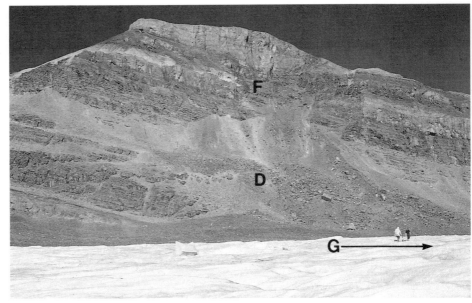

P1.1 Here, in the Canadian Rockies, a glacier (G) (P4.11) moves in a wide valley, eroding the bed and lower slopes. Weathering affects the upper slopes. Angular debris (D) falls from frost-shattered rocks (F) and builds up a scree slope. Some is slowly carried away on ice.

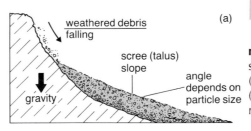

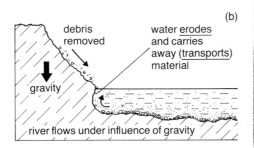

1.17 Landforms are modified by processes of weathering, erosion, and transportation acting together, under the influence of gravity.

When detached fragments fall from the free face of the rock, they tend to build up a pile of debris, known as **scree** or **talus**. The angle of slope depends mainly on the particle size, but tends to be about 32°–38°, unless some other agent removes the fallen material (Fig. 1.17)

Weathered headstones in grave-yards are often of local stone. Why are they particularly useful for indicating rates of weathering?

Erosion is the wearing of rock or loose material by the energy of moving things, such as flowing water, or ice, or air (wind). These often carry with them (**transport**) a load of abrasive materials, ranging in size from boulders to fine dust, which help to batter, or scrape, or scratch the surface. These 'tools of erosion' generally collide as they move, and become smaller and smaller with time – a process known as **attrition**.

The energy of moving water and ice depends on gravity. When the energy slackens, the load of material they carry along may be deposited. Water leaves **alluvial deposits**; ice dumps the debris it transports as **moraine**, or **till**; while the wind may leave coarse particles to accumulate as **dunes**, or drop layer upon layer of fine particles to form **loess**.

P1.2 In north-west Australia the Ord river has eroded (E) a deep valley in an old uplifted plateau. The weathering free face (F) of exposed rocks provides the material of the scree slopes (S)-broken lines – some of which is removed by the river.

Theme 1 Making sure

1 (a) The earth revolves on its axis once every 24 hours; through how many degrees does it turn in one hour?

(b) Locate Manila (**M**), Rockhampton (**R**), Anchorage (**A**) and Barbados (**B**) in your atlas. It is **0900 hrs (9 a.m.) Tuesday** at Greenwich, London (**G**), on the Prime Meridian (**PM**); what is the *time*, related to GMT (Greenwich Mean Time), and what is the *day* at each of these places (Fig. 1.18)?

(c) The shaded area is in darkness. Suggest which day of the year it is.

(d) Account for the path of the International Date Line (IDL) in the area shown.

(e) It is Tuesday in New Zealand. What day is it in Samoa?

(f) Why are large continental areas like Canada and Australia divided into time zones?

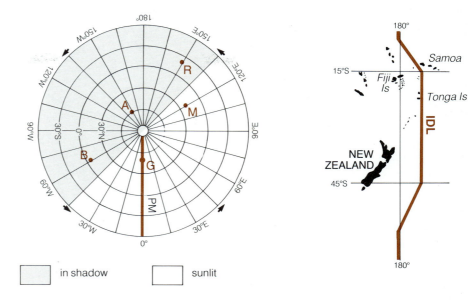

in shadow   sunlit

1.18

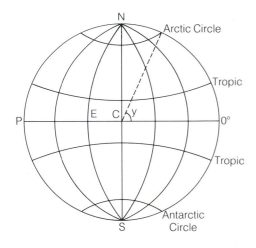

1.19

2 (a) The southern tropic, latitude ...., is called 'The tropic of .....'.

(b) The northern tropic, latitude ...., is called 'The tropic of ....'.

(c) In Fig. 1.19 the angle y is .... degrees. Angle **PCN** is .....degrees.

(d) The latitude of the South Pole is ....

(e) The line **NES** is: (i) a meridian; (ii) a line of latitude; (iii) a parallel?

(f) The east-west distance around the earth at latitude 60° is half that around the equator, and is therefore about 9200/12 800/6400 kilometres . . . which?

3 Is the sun ever due overhead at midday at any place outside the tropics? Explain why.

4 Which absorbs solar energy most readily: (a) dark minerals; (b) shiny minerals; (c) light-coloured minerals?

5 Explain why on a still summer's day a cloud cover may produce a 'greenhouse effect'. Describe what the effects may be.

6 In the tundra lands of the Arctic Circle (p. 97), mosses and small stemmed plants may be found growing on the south-facing side of large boulders, while the north-facing side is bare of vegetation. Draw a diagram to show the reason for this.

7 Why can one play cricket in England up to 2130 hrs (9.30 p.m.) on a mid-summer's day, while at Nairobi (Kenya) play would be impossible at 1930 hrs (7.30 p.m.) without lights?

8 Air sinking to earth from high altitudes both warms and is relatively dry. The barrel of a cycle pump becomes warm while pumping up a tyre. What connections are there between these facts?

9 A belt of dry sinking air persists in the sub-tropics, especially to the **east/west** of the continents. It divides the **easterly/westerly** Trade Winds from the **Easterlies/Westerlies** which prevail polewards of this belt. Delete one direction in each case.

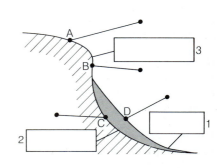

1.20

10 In Fig. 1.20 **A-D** describes the slopes. Copy the diagram and add the appropriate labels: scree slope; convex slope; free face; concave slope. Put the following descriptions in the appropriate boxes 1-3: protected from weathering; largest particles; rapid weathering.

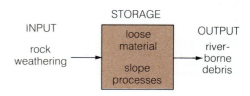

STORAGE

INPUT — loose material / slope processes — OUTPUT
rock weathering   river-borne debris

1.21

11 Relate the system in Fig. 1.21 to processes shown in Figs. 1.20 and 1.17b. How will river action affect (a) the storage; (b) the extent of weathering; (c) the retreat of the free face and angle of slope?

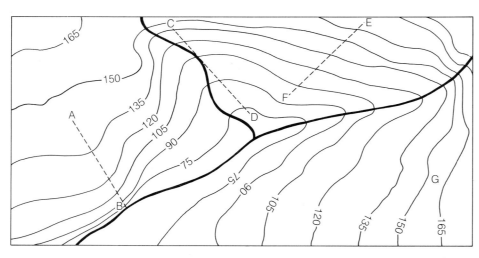

1.22

P 1.3 Landforms are created by different processes acting together. Immense forces once tilted these limy sandstones, until their horizontal bedding planes (B) were vertical. The exposed rock weathers away. Acid rainwater enlarges cracks between the beds into solution hollows (S). Gravity causes detached blocks (D) to fall and build up about the rocky mass.

12 Describe three ways in which water is involved in the weathering of rocks.

13 It is useful to be able to express slopes by contours, and to recognise slopes shown by contours. In Fig. 1.22 the dotted lines **AB**, **CD**, **EF** show concave, convex and uniform slopes; which is which? How may the river be affecting the slope at **B**?

14 In Fig. 1.23 you can see part of a contour map and a cross-section which represent the kind of slope shown in Fig. 1.20. Copy the cross-section, transfer the letters from the map to their exact place on the section, and label them: concave slope; steep free face; convex slope; uniform slope.

15 Draw a cross-section of the countryside between **A** and **G** in Fig. 1.22.

16 Why, when describing the processes now acting on the landforms in Photos 1.3 and 1.4, is it preferable to use the term 'weathering' rather than 'erosion'?

MAP EXTRACT

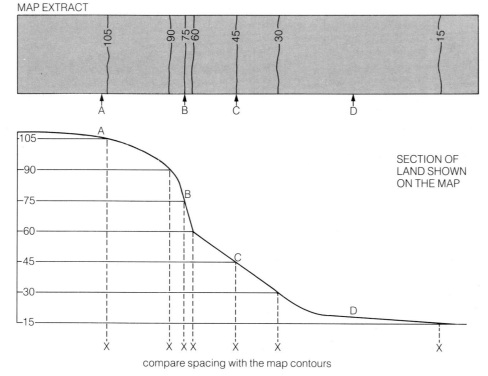

SECTION OF LAND SHOWN ON THE MAP

compare spacing with the map contours

1.23

P 1.4 Frost has shattered these slaty rocks in the valley of a New Zealand glacier. They have split along a plane (cleavage plane) which follows the crystal structure of the rock (not bedding in this case).

Consider the terms used

Short-wave radiation is emitted by very hot bodies (the sun). It easily penetrates the atmosphere.

Long-wave radiation is emitted by less hot bodies. It penetrates less easily.

Energy is the capacity for doing work. Work is done as the energetic force moves a body (mass) some distance, so using up energy. This mechanical energy can be converted (by a generator) into electric energy, and by friction into heat energy.

Momentum is a measure of the mass of a body times its velocity. Why is it harder to stop a cricket ball than a tennis ball struck with equal force?

The force of gravity is the mutual force of attraction between a body and the earth. Every particle attracts every other particle with a force proportional to the product of their masses and inversely proportional to the square of the distance between them. Thus the huge earth (mass **M**) and a surface object like a stone or a person (mass **m**) are pulled together by a force

$$= \frac{M.m.g}{d^2}$$

(where **g** is the gravitational constant and **d** the distance of the object from the earth's centre).

The troposphere is the lowest layer of the atmosphere, extending up to the **tropopause** (with the **stratosphere** above). Virtually all weather – winds, precipitation, etc. – develops in the troposphere.

Solar – related to the sun.

The elevation of the sun is the angle the sun makes with the horizontal plane through the observer (or a particular place).

An eclipse occurs when earth, moon and sun lie in a straight line on the ecliptic plane.

The ecliptic plane is that of the earth's orbit around the sun. (The earth spins about an axis inclined at $23\frac{1}{2}°$ to this plane.)

Equinox – a day when the period of sunlight and darkness (day and night) are of equal length *throughout the world.*

Zonal movement – from one latitude to another.

A jet stream is a narrow band of westerlies at high altitude – just below the tropopause – some 150–500 km wide (and a few kilometres deep). Its speed is often 50–70 knots, but can reach 200 knots – highest in winter when zonal temperature contrasts are great.

Albedo is the percentage of incoming radiation reflected by a surface.

The bedding plane is the plane on which sediments were deposited. It separates a bed (**stratum**) of sedimentary rock from the beds (**strata**) immediately above and below it.

The cleavage plane is the plane along which a rock splits when responding to the way its minerals are aligned.

Hydration is a process by which water is taken up by rock minerals, causing an expansion of the mineral particles themselves.

Corrosion is the disintegration of rocks caused by chemical action.

Corrasion is the wearing away of a solid surface by a material which is being carried (transported) by water, ice or wind (not to be confused with 'corrosion').

Abrasion is the wearing of a surface by rough (abrasive) particles.

Limestones are natural forms (pure and impure) of calcium carbonate. Chalk and marble are forms of limestone. When acted on by acid rainwater (carbonic acid – H_2CO_3), limestones form soluble calcium bicarbonate, and are thus weathered away [$CaCO_3$ + H_2CO_3 = $Ca(HCO_3)_2$]

Attrition is the wearing-down of particles being transported by water, ice, or wind, through collision with other particles. In water they become rounded, in wind angular with smoothed sides.

The International Date Line is necessary because of the accumulated time change of 1 hour for each 15° longitude W and E of the Greenwich Meridian. 180°W of Greenwich is 12 hours slow; 180° E is 12 hours fast. Travellers from E to W lose a day, those from W to E repeat a day.

Theme 2 The ever-changing surface – energy from within

P2.2 The Blue Nile has cut a deep gorge through immensely thick layers of volcanic outpourings (mostly basalt) in the Ethiopian highlands, the down-cutting shown by the broken line. Notice scree slope(S) below the basalt face (B). Tributaries (T) dissect the plateau into steep-sided blocks. Notice also the fields (F) on the ledges of the much eroded valley sides. Curving hollows (H) are valley heads of small seasonal streams.

We can now picture our planet as a system, with inputs and outputs of energy. Its gravity is a controlling force. It holds the atmosphere above the surface. It also speeds up things which are free to move downhill, like falling stones and running water.

But there are other energy sources deep beneath the solid crust which create continuous changes at the surface. The processes powered by this energy have been acting ever since the outer rocks solidified, over four thousand million years ago. What we see today in the natural world – the positions of the oceans and continents, the kind of rocks, the shapes of landforms – reflect what has been happening to the surface over this vast period of time.

2.1 How rocks are formed

When the earth's molten material (magma) first solidified, a crust of **igneous rocks**, made up of mineral crystals, was formed. As the processes of weathering and erosion broke them down, much of the debris was transported by water, ice and wind. It accumulated in depressions and was deposited as sediments on the sea-floor. There their increasing weight, helped by chemical actions, compacted them into thick layers. Those on the sea-bed formed marine **sedimentary rocks** of varying hardness – sandstones, clays, and limestones.

Some of the land deposits, such as dunes and old hardened screes, also survived. Like other early rocks, they have been protected by later deposits – for in

time seas rose above former land areas and left a new covering of sediments.

After living forms appeared on the planet, remains of plants and animals also accumulated. You can see them as **fossils** embedded in sedimentary rocks. Some of the remains created rocks themselves, like the thick shelly limestones. In places successions of plants died and rotted in warm swamps, leaving their carbon content to build up layers which eventually hardened into **coal**. As the sedimentary rocks are weathered and eroded in their turn, their fragments provide the materials

for another generation of sedimentary deposits.

Throughout the long periods of time,

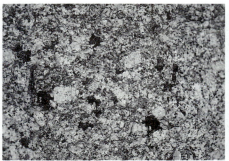

P 2.1 Granite – showing the variety of large crystals of different shape, size, and colour, which formed as the igneous mass slowly cooled.

P 2.3 Gneiss – a coarse-grained metamorphic rock, with bands of crystals reformed from a rock subjected to great pressure and high temperature.

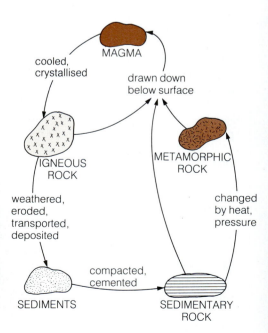

2.1 How rock minerals are changed.

while sedimentary rocks have been created and destroyed, other igneous rocks have been formed from molten materials which have cooled at, or just below, the surface. Where hot **magma** forces its way out of cracks and vents, it flows over the surface as lava. Here it cools quickly and solidifies into rocks with small crystals. One such **extrusive rock** is basalt, which flows freely and has built up extensive, thick, nearly horizontal sheets in many parts of the world (p.14). Some of the magma which escapes at the surface contains more silica. This gives it a glassier texture, so that it flows less freely.

Sometimes magma does not break the surface, but intrudes other rocks as it pushes upwards. Later, erosion may expose this solidified **intrusive lava** (p.23). Because molten masses cool more slowly at greater depth, they contain much larger crystals. Granite is an example of such a **plutonic rock.**

The heat and pressure of intrusive magma can alter the structure of the rocks about it. Even granites may be re-melted, and then solidified into a new, banded crystalline rock, called gneiss. Such change, or metamorphosis, creates a new category of **metamorphic (changed) rocks.** Very great pressures may turn mudstones to slate, or limestones to marble.

Rock types involve many unfamiliar names, but most are descriptive – extrusive, intrusive, sedimentary, metamorphic, plutonic, volcanic. What are the normal meanings of extrude, intrude, and sediment? Biologists use the term metamorphosis to describe the change from caterpillar to chrysalis to butterfly. Some terms are Classical – igneous from *ignis,* Latin for fire; so why is Pluto, the god of the underworld , suitably used to describe a rock like granite, and Vulcan, the god of fire and smiths, appropriate for volcanicity (vulcanicity)?

In some unstable parts of the world the surface rocks are drawn down to a depth where they are melted once again (Fig. 2.6). They are responding to immense forces which are continually changing the face of the earth. These move whole continents about the surface, slowly buckle up new mountain ranges, and create long, widening cracks, or rifts, in the earth's crust.

2.2 The continents wander – plate movements

Beneath the oceans and continents lie a number of plates, made up of the crust itself and the upper part of the mantle. Their thickness varies, but averages some hundred kilometres. Beneath them the hotter mantle material slowly moves. It causes some plates to drift apart, and others to converge, until the edge of one plate is forced under the other.

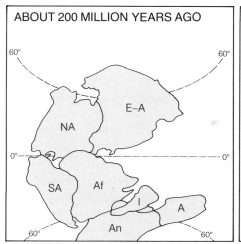
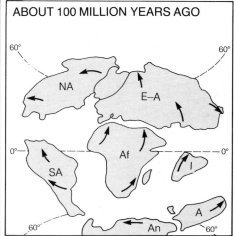

2.2 How the super-continent of 220 million years ago broke up as the plates separated. Notice that about 100 million years ago an ocean separated Africa and India from the Euro-Asian landmass. This has been called **Tethys.** As Africa has closed on Europe, sedimentary rocks deposited in Tethys have been folded, raised, and buckled into the Alps. The Mediterranean is the last remains of the ocean, reflooded from the Atlantic.

The northward-moving Indian plate also collided with Euro-Asia, closing Tethys, and raising and crumpling the Himalayan ranges.

Separations or collisions of the plates bearing the continents have occurred throughout the earth's geological history. Figs. 2.2 and 2.3 show the changes

which have taken place over the last 200 million years or so. Before that period long slow movements had brought the landmasses together to form a 'super-continent'.

Fig. 2.3 shows the shapes and positions of the landmasses today; but, of course, they are still moving. **In Fig. 2.4 you can see the boundaries of the plates.** It shows where they are moving one under the other, where they are moving apart, and where former collisions have created great ranges, like the Alps and Himalayas.

You can see long, spreading **ridges** running through the oceans. A closer look (Figs. 2.4 and 2.5) shows that these occur

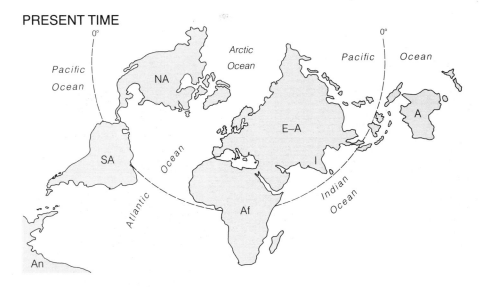

2.3 The continents today with the separating oceans.

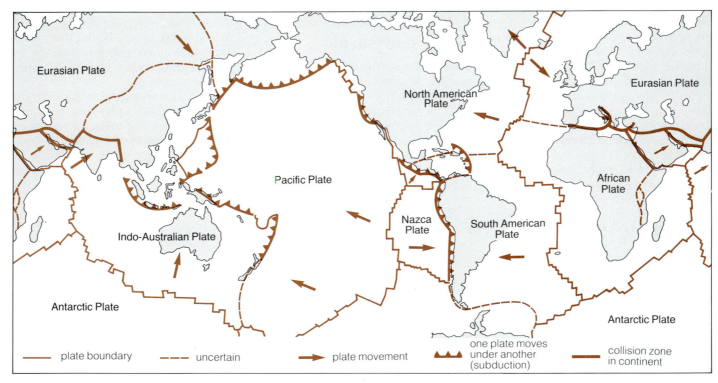

2.4 The plate boundaries. Notice where the plates are in collision and where they are separating.

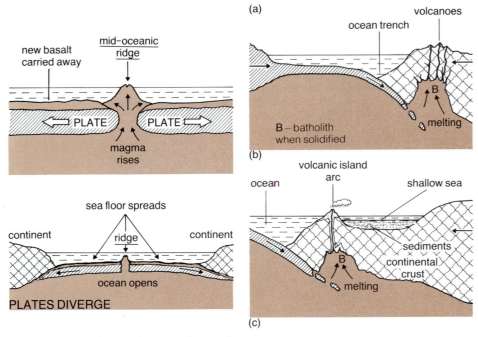

2.5 Magma spreads onto the ocean floor and is carried away by plate movements.

where the plates are moving apart and the oceans opening. Here the emerging magma forms a ridge and spreads out over the sea floor. As the plates move, the solidified magma on the sea bed is carried away, while more magma wells up in the centre of the ridge.

In the Atlantic extrusive material forms **mid-oceanic islands** such as Iceland and

Tristan da Cunha, which are actively volcanic. But the Pacific plates are moving rapidly, and carry such islands away from the uprising zone, so that there are many isolated **sea mounts**.

> What do you notice about the shapes of the mid-ocean ridges? What does this suggest?

Notice how the Pacific is bordered by **island arcs** and deep **trenches** in the west, and in the east by recent mountains with much volcanic activity, such as the Andes. Figs. 2.5 and 2.6 show the processes involved in creating these spectacular features, and Figs. 2.6 and 2.7 stress the relationships between plate movements and volcanic and earthquake activity.

Material worn from the land areas is deposited in deep water between colliding plates. There **sedimentary rocks form. As the plates close, these are thrust up, and slowly folded and buckled into new fold mountains**.

Look at the great plains of northern India in the atlas. They are the surface of deep sediments which fill the trench between the Himalayas and the Indian peninsula.

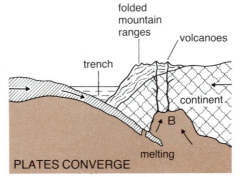

2.6 (left) (a) The ocean crust is drawn down and re-melted; (b) lines of volcanic islands form, separated from the mainland by a shallow sea; (c) collision forces up sedimentary rocks into mountain ranges.

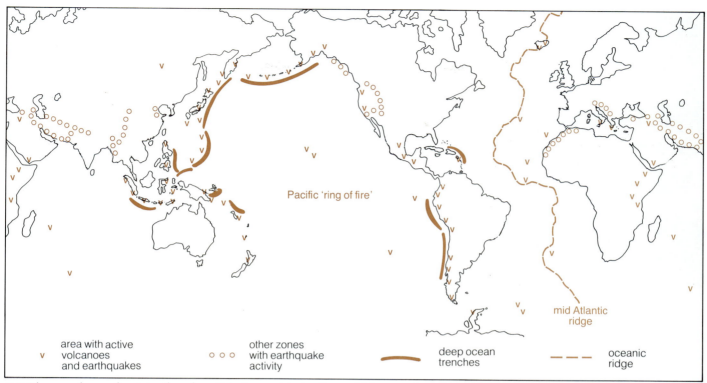

2.7 Observe where volcanic/earthquake activity is associated with new fold mountains, with island arcs, and with mid-ocean separation.

The tablelands of central India were carried northwards on the plate which rammed into and under the southern part of Euro-Asia. Weathering and erosion of the crumpled ranges of the Himalayas have provided the material which fills the trough between, and still extends the great deltas of the Brahmaputra and Ganges.

Earthquakes still shake the Himalayas, and much of the Indian peninsula bears thick sheets of basalt from magma forced up through cracks.

Photo 2.8 shows that volcanic activity occurs where parts of the Mediterranean are still being pinched between the African and European plates.

Thus the earth's internal energy produces movements which create many of the major physical features of the wandering continents. There are characteristic landforms associated with volcanic activity; surfaces displaced along cracks and rifts; and those formed as rocks are upthrust, folded, and tilted. All form part of the present-day scenery.

2.3 Associated volcanic activity

Where the crustal rocks of an ocean plate are drawn down and re-melted, a huge volume of magma rises. It accumulates beneath the folded rocks of the land surface, and on cooling forms a great granite mass, known as a **batholith** ('deep rock') (Figs. 2.6 and 2.8).

Where some of the magma forces its way upwards, it may intrude a vertical crack and solidify as a **dyke**, or form a slab (a **sill**) between horizontal, or tilted layers. Elsewhere, as you have seen, magma extruded at the surface can build up thick sheets of basalt.

It may also be thrown out by spectacular, explosive, volcanic action. The release of dissolved gases often causes successive explosions, which fling solidifying particles (**tephra**) high into the air. Showers of cinders fall back and form an ashy cone about the vent; others may be carried away by the wind. Where molten material continues to push its way through the mound of ash, it helps to build up a steep, layered **composite cone** of a **volcano**. Small secondary cones may appear on its sides.

Occasionally, violent explosions blow out the upper part of a volcano, so that much of it subsides into the central hollow, leaving a great crater known as a **caldera**. Should it fill with water, it forms a crater lake bounded by steep volcanic slopes (Photo 2.7).

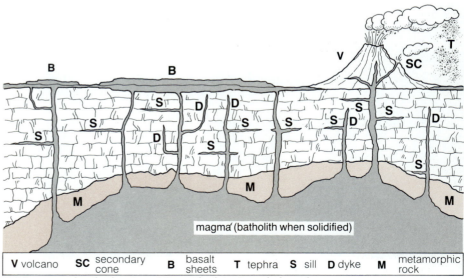

2.8 Some results of volcanic activity, with plutonic rock deep down.

P2.4 Volcanoes cover the landscape with ash, cinders, or hardened lava. Some are acidic, some basic; some fertile, some infertile. Here on Lanzarote people grow vegetables and vines in black ash. Beyond is a wide area of less fertile cindery lava.

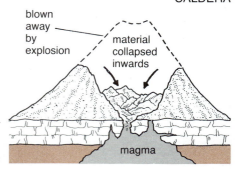

CALDERA

blown away by explosion / material collapsed inwards

magma

2.9 After violent explosions material falls back into the emptying magma chamber.

Not all volcanoes have steep ash cones. From some vents the lava flows less freely. As the magma solidifies into numerous layers, it builds up the gentle slopes of a low **shield volcano.**

Only some 20 to 30 of the world's active volcanoes are erupting at any time. Most erupt violently and then remain quiet (dormant) for periods of varying length. Some, said to be extinct, have erupted after being dormant for thousands of years.

In which part of the world would you expect any volcanic remains to be extinct? Point out where dormant volcanoes are likely to be potentially dangerous.

Active areas may also have hot springs, whose salt-rich waters evaporate and form mineral terraces. Surface water sometimes seeps into underground spaces and becomes heated by the rock. Some may be trapped and super-heated, until increasing pressure suddenly forces out the overlying water as a **geyser** of spray and steam (Fig 2.10).

What conditions would make a geyser erupt at *regular* intervals?

In Photo 2.8 how have weathering and erosion affected the landscape? How have the different types of volcanic layers influenced the shape of the cliffs?

Try to distinguish between the effects of waves at the foot of the cliffs and the processes acting above (see pp. 18–19).

P2.6 Water plunges over ledges in the thick volcanic flows which form much of the forested plateau of south-east Brazil. Basalt poured out of many openings, as over much of peninsular India (the Deccan). In each case it has weathered into fertile soils. This is a small part of spectacular cascades into the deep-cut Iguaçu river. Notice the boulders beneath, and the way the water cuts into the rock face.

P2.5 The sea cave shows the thickness of Lanzarote's lava flows. Beyond, chains of volcanoes rise above the cindery, and in places hot, surface.

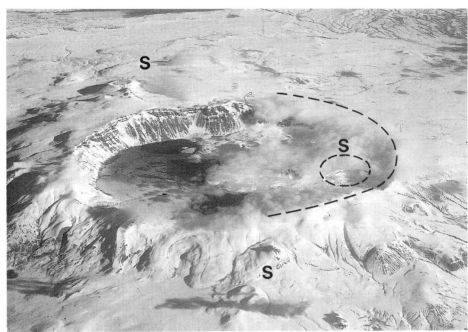

P 2.7 A crater lake amid winter snows in eastern Turkey. Notice the secondary volcanic cones (S) in and about the caldera.

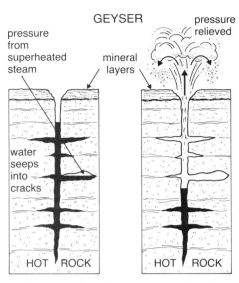

2.10 Pressure is built up as water in the cracks becomes super-heated steam.

P 2.8 Volcanic layers exposed on the inner slopes of a huge sea-filled caldera, formed about 1500 BC by the explosion of the volcanic island of Santorini (in the Aegean).

P 2.9 The remains of a volcano – one of the Glass House mountains which rise above the eucalypt woodland and pineapple farms of coastal Queensland, Australia. The soft ash has been eroded away, leaving only the crystalline lava, which hardened and plugged up the vent.

P 2.10 Pohutu geyser near Rotorua in New Zealand's North Island. Notice the thick salt terraces built up about it. Groundwater converted to steam by hot rock can be harnessed as a source of energy (p. 150).

Even dormant volcanic scenery can be dramatic, with steep, outstanding rock masses. **In some places the soldified cores of old volcanoes have survived the erosion of the ashy cones.** In others, the rugged, rounded cylindrical plugs still show where silica-rich magma *slowly* forced its way out and cooled into crystalline rock.

Look back to Photo 2.2. The Ethiopians have created fields even on the flat ledges of basalt, for these weather to provide very fertile soils. During dry periods, however, water supply is a great problem. Why are there difficulties in obtaining water from the tributaries to the Blue Nile, and from the river itself?

Are all volcanic soils fertile? Are all potentially fertile soils necessarily able to produce crops?

The illustrations suggest that volcanic actions can:

(a) create conditions which favour human settlement;

(b) release dangerous forces and materials;

(c) provide a useful source of electricity;

(d) create tourist attractions.

Point to examples of these in the photographs, and explain how they show this.

2.4 Rifts and displacements

Where the plates move slowly apart, tensions are created in rocks over a wide area. Long cracks, or **faults**, appear, and the rocks on either side of a fault may be displaced by vertical movements.

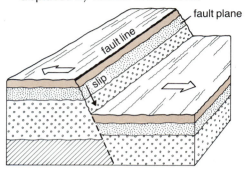

2.11 Slipping along a normal fault, due to rocks easing apart.

Where the land is eased apart along a great crack (rift), the rocks between may subside and form a long **rift valley**. In some places the land between parallel faults is pushed upwards to form a raised block (a **horst**).

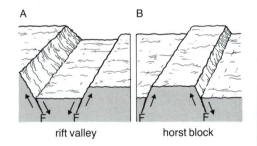

2.12 Movements have caused (A) depression and (B) upthrust between parallel faults.

In East Africa, through the Red Sea and into the Middle East, the earth's crust is being pulled apart. As a result a great complex rift valley system runs for thousands of kilometres and contains many long lakes. There is much volcanic activity. Basalt magma has poured out and covers much of the valley floor in the East African rifts.

How does this resemble what is taking place in mid-Atlantic ocean? Is it possible that the widening rift may become a new expanding ocean?

Unusually hot areas lie beneath the Red Sea. Is this what one might expect if an ocean is opening out?

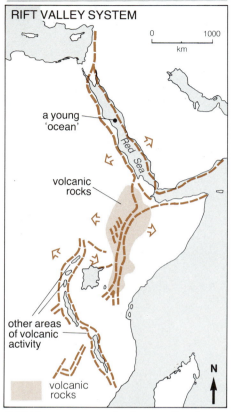

2.13 Here movements of separation have produced immense faults, with much volcanic activity. Notice the scale.

There is a zone with similar spreading in Siberia. Here the long Lake Baikal occupies part of a rift valley system.

Earthquakes result from sudden movements at active plate boundaries. Stress between the moving plates is suddenly released as rocks fracture deep down. Waves of energy (**seismic waves**) pass through the earth and set the surface in motion, or even produce gaping fissures. The energy released is measured on the Richter scale, usually a value 0–9, though there is no upper limit.

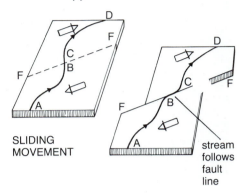

2.14 As plates move alongside one another, tearing movements disrupt a river channel.

In places where the plates slide alongside one another, long tear faults occur and displace physical features, like the river course in Fig. 2.14. Such movements are common in the populous state of California, where the long San Andreas fault shifts from time to time. It can produce high-intensity earthquakes, though many of California's disastrous quakes have been caused by movements along other faults. Stress may be released, and

P 2.11 Looking south-west down Scotland's Great Glen. This was formed by movements along a tear fault, which separated features on the northern and southern sides in the directions shown, by some 100 km. It created a shatter-zone S-S, which ice later eroded into deep troughs – now lochs, linked here by the Caledonian canal.

major quakes prevented, by gradually triggering small movements along a fault, usually by injecting fluid under pressure.

A secondary effect of earthquakes may be a seismic sea wave, or **tsunami**, set in motion by movement of the sea floor.

P 2.12 Movements along a fault F-F across eastern Crete have exposed 8 metres of sheer rock face.

This can travel great distances and drown distant coastlands.

Tremors often give advance warning of earthquakes. They may be picked up by instruments and recorded on a **seismograph**. In China the behaviour of animals and birds who react to warning tremors are effectively observed.

2.5 Folds, tilts and landforms

Earth movements may cause rocks to tilt slowly, or gradually fold them into arches. Those arched upwards are called **anticlines** and the downfolds **synclines**.

P 2.14 Earth movements have forced strata on the shore of Kaikoura, South Island of New Zealand, into tight folds. Make a sketch to show the small synclines and anticlines.

Powerful thrusts may deform these simple folds, and produce the complex, twisted strata we find in mountain chains like the Alps and Himalayas, where plate collisions have thrust up great ranges.

The slopes of the landforms at first correspond to the tilt of the strata. But the erosion of weaker rocks help to produce steep **scarp faces** and **cuesta ridges**, or even a hog's back type of ridge (Fig. 2.16). The shape of landforms thus partly depends on how long the processes of

FOLDING (a)

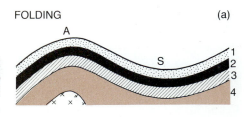

EROSION EXPOSES OTHER ROCKS (b)

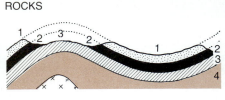

FURTHER EROSION — DIFFERENT LANDSCAPE (c)

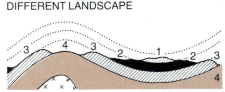

2.15 The erosion of anticline A and syncline S exposes other rocks and so creates new scarps and valleys.

erosion have been acting, for these can modify surface features considerably over a period of time. Fig. 2.17 shows how the sequence of rocks at the surface changes as overlaying strata are worn away, and how the more resistant rocks tend to form ridges.

P 2.13 In eastern Crete massive screes (S) cover the fault line F-F between the uplifted mountain face and the flat valley (V). A narrow gorge (G) follows another fault at right angles to F-F.

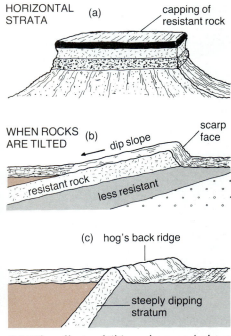

HORIZONTAL STRATA (a) — capping of resistant rock

WHEN ROCKS ARE TILTED (b) — dip slope — scarp face — resistant rock — less resistant

(c) hog's back ridge — steeply dipping stratum

2.16 The effects of tilting where rocks have different resistance to erosion.

P 2.15 *This hard Millstone Grit of the southern Pennines was folded over underlying Carboniferous limestone. Erosion exposed the limestone and left the edges of the grit beds tilted upward and eastward.*

In mountain country folds are often distorted like those in Fig. 2.17. Imagine which rocks would be exposed at the surface if the upper folds were completely worn away. If you walked from **X** to **Y** you would come across the same rocks at intervals along your route, in the sequence shown. As the rocks have different characteristics, this would produce a varied landscape.

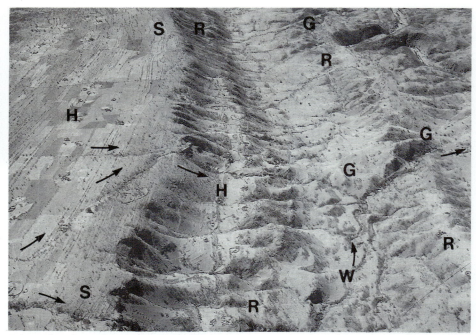

P 2.16 *This shows how processes act together to create landscape features. In high Ethiopia erosion has worn the tilted rocks (at the edge of a great syncline) into parallel vales and ridges (R-R). The scarp edge (S-S) of the flat farmland has been eroded by water from springs (P3.7) and streams, draining to the right. As the land has been uplifted, small rivers have cut gorges (G-G) through the ridges. Notice the water course (W) draining towards the gorge. There are houses (H) and animal compounds even on the ridges.*

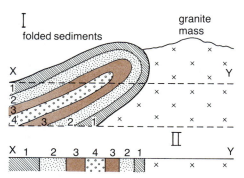

2.17 *Erosion has planed down the landscape, producing a variety of surface rocks. Why would there have been more rugged scenery in the early stages of erosion?*

Erosion on this scale has happened in many parts of the world. Ancient mountain systems have been eroded to almost flat plains. In many parts of the Canadian Shield, their old folds remain only as twisting ridges, for instance.

2.6 Slopes and mass movements of materials

Faults, folds and tilts produce characteristic slopes. But **processes of weathering, erosion, and the movements of masses of material from rock faces continually change the angle of slope.** Sudden mass

movements of material can affect even a hard compact rock (Fig. 2.18).

When loose material piles up, the particles roll and slip forward from an over-steep slope until it becomes stable. We have seen how scree takes up an **angle of repose** according to the size and nature of the fragments. It also protects the lower slope.

Fig. 2.20 shows that where a large **free face** is exposed to weathering, the build-up of scree is rapid. So in time, as more and more of the lower slope is protected, the area of the free face is reduced. Thus the overall slope is altered.

Mass movements vary with the climate

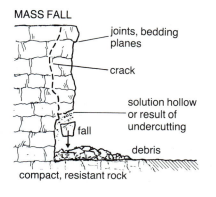

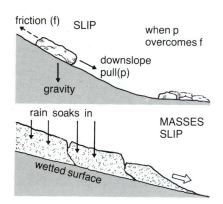

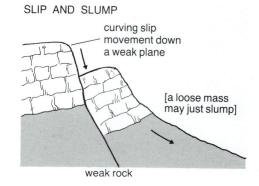

2.18 *Conditions under which mass movements, slips and slumps occur.*

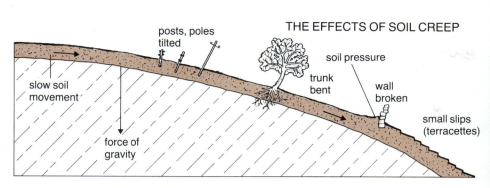

THE EFFECTS OF SOIL CREEP

posts, poles tilted

soil pressure

trunk bent

wall broken

slow soil movement

force of gravity

small slips (terracettes)

2.19 The effects of continuous, and sometimes sudden, soil movements.

P 2.18 Grass has replaced cleared forest near Wanganui, New Zealand, and soil slips have formed terracettes on the steep slopes.

and the type of rocks. Sometimes water seeps through pores and cracks in an exposed rock, or through loose material, and lubricates surfaces beneath. This can cause the whole mass to slip and slide away. This frequently occurs where clay forms an impermeable layer beneath loose rock or debris, causing **mass slips down the wetted surface.** On steep slopes the soil and rock debris can move very quickly. If the mass becomes saturated with water, it may even cause an **earth-flow.**

Gentler slopes usually have a depth of soil and carry vegetation. But gravity urges the soil to move downslope (**soil creep**). On steeper grassy slopes the soil may move in sudden small-scale slumps, producing tiny irregular terraces, or **terracettes**.

P 2.17 Heavy rains turned fine surface materials into a massive mud-flow in this Cyprus valley.

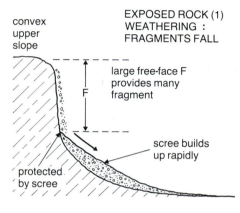

convex upper slope

EXPOSED ROCK (1) WEATHERING : FRAGMENTS FALL

large free-face F provides many fragment

F

scree builds up rapidly

protected by scree

SCREE FRAGMENTS PROTECT (2) THE SLOPE

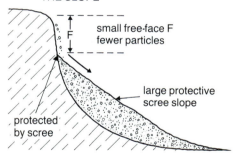

small free-face F fewer particles

F

large protective scree slope

protected by scree

2.20 The proportion of convex, vertical and concave sections of the slope varies with time.

What effects may soil creep have on walls, posts, and poles? See Fig. 2.19; explain the shape of the tree.

Slopes, therefore, are likely to retreat with time. Not all rocks are hard enough to keep a vertical free face, of course; but those that do will tend to be worn back if the fallen material is removed, as shown in Fig. 2.21a. A gently sloping concave area is left extending out from the foot of the main slope – this is the **pediment**.

Other rocks may have gentler slopes and retreat as in Fig. 2.21b. These are convex on the upper slope; but below, where more water washes over the surface and erodes it, they are concave.

In fact, the rate of retreat of slopes may be *very* slow indeed. In resistant rocks this may mean less than 1 mm per year. But

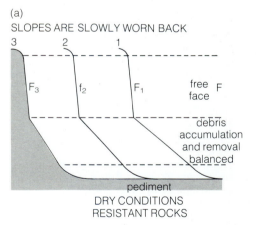

(a)

SLOPES ARE SLOWLY WORN BACK

3   2   1

F_3 f_2 F_1 free face F

debris accumulation and removal balanced

pediment

DRY CONDITIONS RESISTANT ROCKS

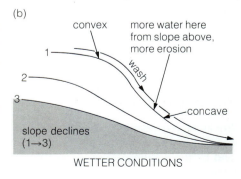

(b)

convex

more water here from slope above, more erosion

1

wash

2

concave

3

slope declines (1→3)

WETTER CONDITIONS

2.21 How slopes change as they are worn back.

we are looking at processes which may continue for tens (or hundreds) of thousands of years (see Q.9, p. 24).

As you have seen, **the shape of a slope and the way it changes with time depend both on the rate of weathering and the rate of removal of weathered material.** We can regard these processes, involving the movements of particles, as parts of a system (Fig. 2.22).

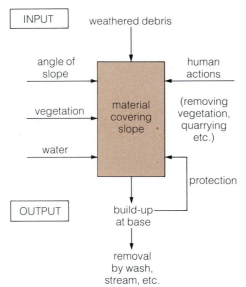

2.22 The movement of material on slopes as a system.

P 2.19 Slumps in loose sandstone create hillside scars in New Zealand's North Island. Describe the inputs and outputs here as part of a system (as in Fig. 2.22).

2.7 When the pressure on rocks is released

Rocks deep beneath the surface are compressed by the weight of overlying rocks and by the accumulations of weathered material. When this cover is removed by erosion, the outer parts of the rock may break away in layers, as the pressure is

DEEP CHEMICAL WEATHERING

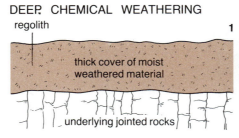

2.23 Tropical rock domes have their origin deep down.

eased, creating loosened sheets or shells (Photo 2.20).

In some rocks the intense pressure, or release of pressure, produces cracks and

P 2.21 These granite tors, with joints enlarged by weathering, were once part of a great batholith, now exposed to form Dartmoor.

joints. When such rocks are buried beneath a mass of weathered material (**regolith**), water may seep down and cause chemical weathering within the cracks. This is particularly so in the moist tropics. There high temperatures increase the weathering rates, and rapid erosion removes the regolith. **Many of the steep-sided, isolated hills of the African table-lands have been formed in this way, as shown in Fig. 2.23.**

Dartmoor in south-west England was once a great batholith. Its granite rocks have been exposed by erosion. Why are the **tors** and granite boulders on the high moorland so broken?

P 2.20 Rocks which were weathered and cracked (C) deep beneath the surface lie exposed on Tanzanian savanna land. Chemical weathering continues to cause **exfoliation**. This peeling of layers (P) creates scars. Notice the inquisitive rock hyrax (H).

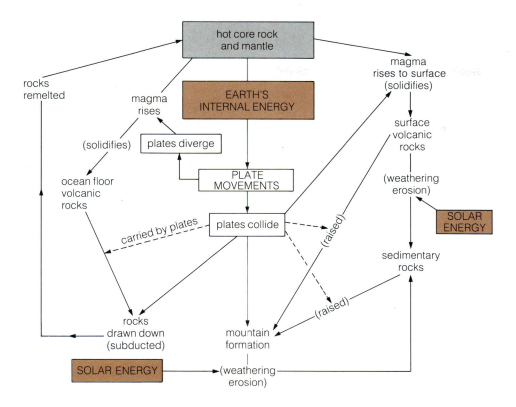

2.24 Solar energy and internal energy create continuous changes at the earth's surface.

2.8 Internal energy and the ever-changing surface

Fig. 2.24 summarises the processes which form, destroy and reform the features of the earth's surface – with continuous movements of energy and matter, as if on an endless conveyor belt.

List as many processes as you can which cause the destruction of igneous and sedimentary rocks exposed at the surface. Consider carefully where the energy which causes the rock to break down comes from, in each case.

Notice that inputs of energy from the sun (solar energy) are involved in various processes in this huge system. How do they help to provide material for the sedimentary rocks?

What other great sources of energy maintain the movements and processes shown above and described on the previous page?

Theme 2 Back-up section

Measuring slopes

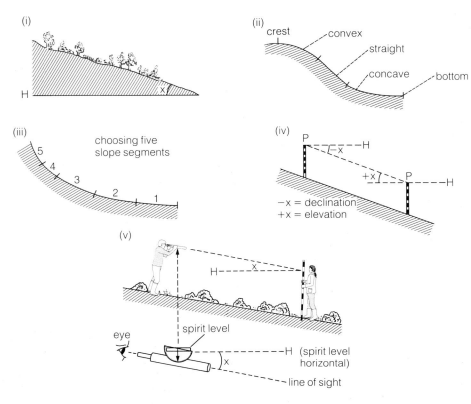

2.25 Measuring slopes – backsight and foresight readings.

Any study of local landforms means investigating slopes and the processes which are continually modifying them. There are ways of making quick, reasonably accurate measurements of slopes, with **simple home-made equipment.**

Fig. 2.25 (i) shows that **steepness** is the angle (x) between the slope and the horizontal **H**. As the angle may be continuously varying over the surface of a particular landform (ii), it is usually necessary to survey small segments (iii), each of which can be regarded as a straight slope.

1 Work in pairs. Use a tape to find the length of the first segment. It usually helps to survey small fixed lengths of, say, 5 or 10 metres at a time.

2 Fig. 2.25 (iv) shows how the line between the top of two poles of equal height, planted vertically, can be used to give the slope angle. You could read the angle from a sighting instrument placed on top of either pole.

It is quicker, however, to sight on a surveyor's pole with a hand-held level; or even on the eye of your assistant, of the same height. The angle between the spirit-level horizontal (**H**) and your line of sight is the slope angle.

3 By changing places you can take a *backsight* reading up the slope (the angle of elevation), either as a check or to average it with your *foresight* reading (angle of declination).

4 From one end of your chosen length,

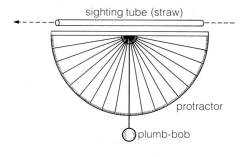

2.26 A simple clinometer.

survey the next 5 or 10 metres up, or down, the slope. Pegs should be used to fix your positions. Number each segment, and record length and angles as you go.

Even small hand-held levels are expensive, but it is possible to make a simple effective **clinometer** from a plumb-bob and line, and a protractor and sighting tube (which can be a drinking straw) glued to a board (Fig. 2.26).

In this case, sight the object; carefully trap the plumb-line against the protractor with a finger, and read the angle between the line and 90° as the elevation or declination.

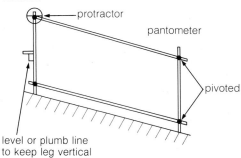

2.27 A pantometer.

For short segments a **pantometer** can be used (Fig. 2.27). Four rails are pivoted, as shown, the short ones vertical and the larger ones parallel to the slope. A protractor is fixed to the forward short leg, which has a spirit level, or plumb-bob, attached to it, to enable you to keep it vertical. After reading the slope angle, the pantometer may be 'walked' along the slope.

Slope movements

Masses of rock, scree or soil may suddenly *slide* downslope, as we have seen. In Fig. 2.28 (i) a boulder (mass **m**) rests on a slope of 20°. Because of the force of gravity (**mg**), the boulder is pulled into the slope (**p**) and has a slide force (**s**) down the slope. It is prevented from sliding by the force of friction (**f**), which depends on the mass and the roughness of the surface. Friction acts up the slope, so that when the boulder is just balanced, on the point of sliding, **f=s**.

In (ii) the boulder is on a slope of 40°. The force causing it to slide is greater than the force of friction, so it moves downslope. If in (i) the surface were lubricated, say by water, **f** would be less and sliding could occur.

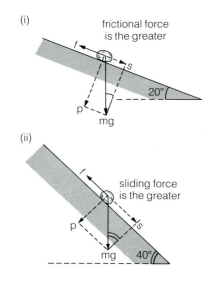

2.28 Sliding as the angle increases.

Soil creep goes on more or less continuously. Its effect can be detected by inserting pegs at measured distances from a reference point, say a scratch on a rock, and remeasuring at intervals of time. T-shaped rods, about 40 cm long and 10 cm across the top, can also be used. They tilt with the movement of the material **(regolith)** overlying the rock.

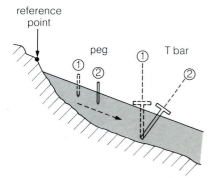

2.29 Pegs and rods show soil movements.

Theme 2 Making sure

1 (i) Attach the appropriate label — **igneous, sedimentary, metamorphic** — to describe the rock formed by each of the following processes (**A-E**).

(**A**) Granite weathers → particles are transported → accumulate → harden → rock
(**B**) Chalk heated by nearby magma → minerals recrystallised → new rock
(**C**) Magma extruded at surface → spreads rapidly → solidifies to rock with small crystals
(**D**) Clay hardened by pressure → forms shale → increasing pressure realigns minerals to lie in sheets → thin hard plates formed at right angles to pressure
(**E**) Shells fall to sea bed → mix with particles → cemented together → with pressure harden into rock

(ii) Which of the following rocks are created by each of the processes **A-E**: **slate, basalt, limestone, sandstone, marble**?

2 Magma solidifies deep down as a plutonic rock. Its crystals are: (a) large; (b) small; (c) sheet-like; (d) powdery — which? Give an example.

3 What practical use do people make of natural geysers; hot springs; granite; and pumice (formed when frothy lava, full of gas bubbles, cools)?

4 How many clues to support the idea of the break-up of a 'super-continent' can you find in Figs. 2.4 and 2.7? What other evidence do you know of?

5 Which of the following is *not* a result of plate *collision*. (a) a deep offshore trench; (b) an island arc; (c) mountain building; (d) a mid-ocean ridge; (e) earthquakes?

6 Look at Fig. 2.30. (a) Name the igneous features **A** and **B**. **B** forms a sheet of igneous rock — a layer spread through other rock strata. (b) Suppose that earth movements tilted the strata in (i). Show by means of a diagram how **B** might appear as a surface rock. (c) **A** sometimes forms a ridge across the landscape, sometimes a trough. Suggest why.

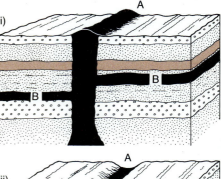

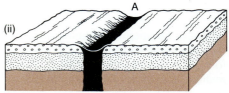

2.30

7 Even 70 million years ago the gaps between the continents were quite narrow. What evidence for continental drift do the following provide?

(a) A small reptile living 250 million years ago is found only in south-west Africa and southern Brazil.

(b) Rocks over 400 million years old of the same type, with similar fossils, are found in north-west Scotland and the St. Lawrence area of North America.

(c) Coal occurs in rocks deep beneath the Antarctic icesheets.

(d) Particles of magnetic substances, such as iron, occur in magma emerging in the mid-Atlantic ridge. Like tiny magnets they orient themselves North-South. Every half-million years or so the earth's magnetic field reverses.

Rocks on the ocean floor, both east and west of the ridge, show a zebra-like pattern with normal poles (N-S) and reversed poles (S-N) alternating (Fig. 2.31). (Remember how the ocean floor spreads.)

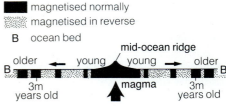

2.31 Seabed minerals show the effects of the reversals of the magnetic poles.

8 Sedimentary rocks accumulate beneath oceans, yet limestones and sandstones form much of the Pennines of northern England. There are also sea-shell fossils near the summit of Mt. Everest. What processes have brought this about?

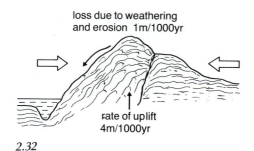

loss due to weathering
and erosion 1m/1000yr

rate of uplift
4m/1000yr

2.32

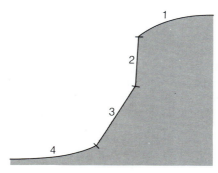

2.34

9 Even as mountains are being formed, they are being worn away. The rates of formation and erosion in Fig. 2.32 are realistic, though they will vary in different parts of the world.

(a) How high is Mt. Everest above sea-level?

(b) From the statistics in Fig. 2.32, how long would it take for the range to reach a height of 6000 metres?

(c) If uplift ceased, how long would it take for the range to be eroded to sea-level?

10 (a) In Fig. 2.33 identify the syncline and anticline: I...... II......

(b) As you walk from **A** to **E** the surface rocks change. Label the surface rocks 1-6 as **R** (resistant) and **L** (less resistant).

(c) Which is the oldest surface rock: 1, 4 or 6?

(d) How do the ages of the rocks change as you walk from **B** to **C**; **C** to **D**; **D** to **E**?

(e) What has happened to the rocks on either side of **B**? What feature do you see at **B**: a joint; a fault; a slump?

11 Copy Fig. 2.34. Label the slopes 1-4 as concave, straight, vertical and convex, respectively. To which slopes (1-4) do the following apply?

(a) weathering causes occasional rapid movements of material;

(b) a slope gradually developed by rain splash and soil creep;

(c) a slope worn (abraded) by material transported over it; the particles are sorted by surface wash;

(d) a slope whose angle depends on new material being supplied.

Give other names for slopes 2,3,4.

13 In hot wet regions there is often a deep covering of loose material formed from rocks far beneath the surface — this is regolith.

(a) Which process causes the break-up of the buried rocks: (i) weathering, or (ii) erosion?

(b) Which process removes the regolith and exposes the rock: (i) weathering, or (ii) erosion?

(c) Which process tends to create loose sheets of rock parallel to the surface: (i) frost action; (ii) rifting; (iii) pressure release? What name is given to the process?

A processes following removal of vegetation

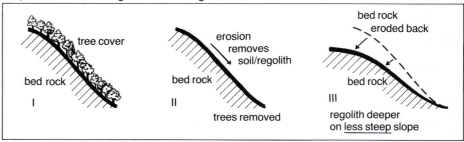

VEGETATION COVER (reduced)

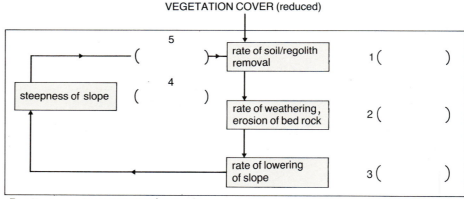

B effects on slope system of removing vegetation

2.35

12 In moist tropical areas deep subsurface weathering is likely in a rock which (a) is folded; (b) has a network of joints; (c) has few joints. Which?

14 Fig 2.35 A shows a slope with its soil/regolith protected by vegetation (I). The vegetation is cleared, so erosion and weathering processes are active (II). This reduces the angle of slope, allowing more material to accumulate (III).

B shows how the slope system is affected by processes following clearance. In each bracket put 'increased' or 'reduced' to describe processes 1-5 in turn .... (brackets 1 and 5 *both* refer to the rate of soil/regolith removal).

Explain how the processes thus adjust to the changing conditions.

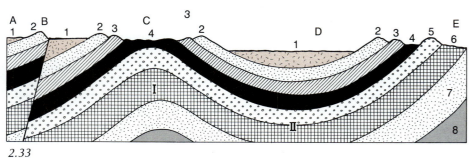

2.33

Consider the terms used

Igneous — fire formed. Mostly applied to igneous rocks formed when magma solidifies.

Sedimentary rocks are composed of sediments which were deposited and then accumulated. Those of mineral particles include sandstones and clays; those from the remains of plants and animals include limestones and coal.

Magma is molten rock material at a high temperature, often containing gases.

A vent is an opening in the earth's surface such as that which allows magma to emerge.

A volcanic process allows molten rock and gases to escape through the earth's crust, often explosively.

Acid lava is rich in silica, has a high melting point, and does not flow easily.

Basic lava has a lower melting point and flows more readily.

Silica is silicon dioxide (SiO_2), the most abundant of earth minerals. One form is quartz, but there are many others. About a third of all minerals are **silicates** (silicon combined with various metals, such as calcium, magnesium and aluminium). Clays are silicates.

Composite cone describes a volcanic cone formed of ash and cinders and lava flows. Also known as a **strato-volcano.**

Dormant (literally 'sleeping') describes a volcano which has not recently erupted, but which may do so.

A metamorphic rock is one formed from another rock through physical or chemical changes.

Seismic — connected with earthquakes.

Tectonic forces are those which deform the earth's crust — plate movement, rock tilting, mountain building, etc.

The lithosphere is the outer part of the upper mantle and solid crust, divided into **plates**.

The lithospheric plates move apart at **constructive plate margins** and are forced one beneath the other at **destructive plate margins.**

Superheated steam, above 100°C, can be formed when water is heated under pressure greater than atmospheric.

A permeable rock is one through which water can pass from the exposed surface to a lower surface. One which does not allow the passage of water through it is **impermeable.** A permeable rock can be **porous** so that water soaks through a mass of tiny pores, or **pervious**, where is passes through joints, cracks, or fissures.

The free face of a rock is an exposed surface too steep for weathered material to collect on it.

An earthflow is the mass movement of waterlogged material down a slope, leaving a scar and spreading out at the base.

The pediment is the gently sloping rock surface away from the foot of an abrupt slope in an arid (dry) or semi-arid region.

Regolith is the weathered waste material lying above the bedrock, including the top soil.

A cuesta is a ridge with one particularly steep face.

A scarp is the steep face of the cuesta, or the steep edge of a tableland — whose surface may dip more gently away from the scarp (a **dip-slope**).

An anticline is an arch of folded rocks, with beds dipping away from the crest.

A syncline is a trough of folded rocks, with beds dipping more or less uniformly to a low point.

A tor is an isolated mass of weathered, jointed rocks often on a hill summit.

Precipitation is a general term for all water transferred from the atmosphere to the surface — rain, snow, hail, dew, etc.

Theme 3 The water cycle and the energy of flowing water

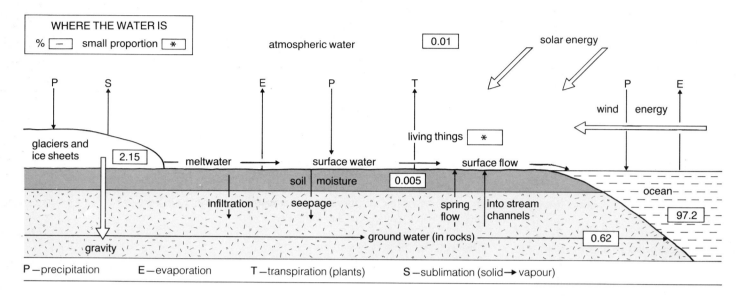

3.1 Energy and the hydrological cycle. Notice carefully where the water is at any moment – and the proportions.

3.1 The water system

We have already seen how water vapour and water condensed from the atmosphere may be part of processes which create and destroy rocks. Water is virtually everywhere, and strictly the hydrosphere extends into the atmosphere with its water vapour.

At any time, however, over 97 per cent of the planet's water is held in the oceans (Fig. 3.1). The rest is part of a great water cycle – **the hydrological cycle** – fueled by the input of energy from the sun. The processes involved include:

(a) **evaporation** – which transfers liquid water from the surface into water vapour in the atmosphere;

(b) **transpiration** from plants – which also transfers water, as vapour, into the atmosphere;

(c) **condensation** – whereby water vapour becomes liquid; often as small droplets suspended in clouds, fog and mist;

(d) **precipitation** – falling to the surface in the form of rain, hail, and snow;

(e) **run-off** – which returns water direct to the ocean via streams, rivers and flood waters.

Fig 3.2 shows the water circulating in this system and the percentage involved, at any moment, in the processes described above. Notice the high proportion returning direct to the ocean as precipitation.

The actual distribution of precipitation over the ocean and land surfaces is very irregular, of course; it varies from place to place and season to season.

At any moment, therefore, the water in this cycle has various forms and circulates at different rates: as vapour in the atmo-

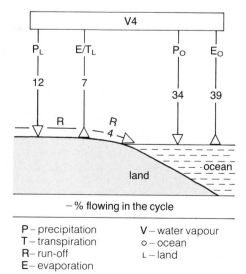

3.2 Exchanges of water between the earth's surface and atmosphere.

sphere, as liquid in the oceans, lakes and rivers, and as solid in snow, glaciers and ice-sheets.

We can look on all this water as being temporarily 'stored' in a particular place, such as a river channel. Some may be stored for a long time – held in ice, until it melts, or in natural reservoirs within the rocks – before eventually returning to the ocean by one path or another. For instance, water which seeps through soils, or infiltrates rock through pores and cracks, may eventually emerge again as a spring. You can study these 'paths' in Fig. 3.1. Notice the energy inputs which keep this great cycle in motion – energy from the sun, and from the resulting winds. And remember that the force of gravity is always acting to cause downhill movement.

Explain how a gain or loss of energy is involved in evaporation and condensation.

How is the force of gravity involved in rainfall and river flow?

How can the wind affect the hydrological cycle?

3.2 Surface water and ground water

Water falling onto the land surface tends to run into existing channels. Many of these will already have been cut by the action of running water (p. 30). During intense storms, sheets of water may run down-slope, covering the surface: this is called **sheet-wash**.

The amount and speed of **run-off** depends on the pull of gravity, the angle of the slope, its roughness or smoothness, and the intensity of the rain. It is also affected by the nature of the underlying

RUN-OFF AND GROUNDWATER

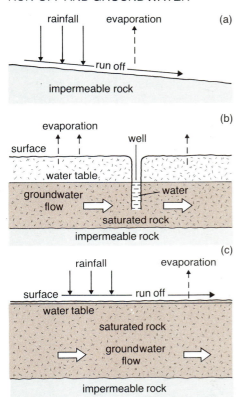

3.3 The water-table rises and falls.

rock and the covering of loose particles and soil. **A great deal of water may soak into the soil and pass downslope through soil spaces.** This **throughflow** is an important contribution to many rivers.

Some water seeps through the soil and then infiltrates the rocks beneath. These may be rocks with many pores (porous), and so **permeable**, or those with cracks and joints which allow water to soak through (**pervious** rocks).

Sometimes the water sinks into the rock and is held (stored) in underground spaces – which may be pores in the rock itself or actual caverns. Most of it works its way slowly downslope, through the

P3.1 A cleared hillside at Mombasa destroyed by rill and gulley erosion before trees could gain a hold (see Fig. 3.9).

pores and cracks and joints, as **groundwater**, before seeping out or emerging as a spring. Sometimes it flows as an underground stream.

3.3 The water-table

Water soaking down through permeable layers or cracks may find its passage barred by an underlying rock which is **impervious** (does not let water through). If water continues to infiltrate, it will fill all the spaces above the impervious rock – up to a level we call the **water-table**. Between the water-table and impervious barrier the rock is **saturated** (Fig. 3.3).

After further rain, more water may soak down from the surface and cause the level of the water-table to rise. When all the

spaces within the permeable rock are filled the water-table is at the surface. Any further rain must flood over the surface as **run-off**.

During dry periods water not only evaporates from the surface into the atmosphere, but also from the water-table into the spaces in the rock and soil above – so that the level of the water-table falls. It will also fall, of course, if groundwater moving downslope through the rocks is *not* replaced by water arriving from higher up.

Where rain falls people may (a) construct dams to hold run-off and store it, or (b) rely on wells, filled by the rising water-table. Which method is most likely where the rock is (i) impervious; (ii) permeable?

P3.2 Overnight storms brought 200 mm of rain to this Queensland farm. Sheets of water washed over the surface, piling the fertile top-soil into ridges. How does the fence show the height of the flood waters?

ARTESIAN BASIN

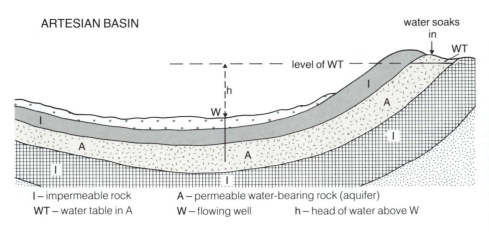

I – impermeable rock   A – permeable water-bearing rock (aquifer)
WT – water table in A   W – flowing well   h – head of water above W

3.4 Artesian water may be obtained from deep aquifers. Consider why this is sometimes brackish and warm. If the well head is above the water-table level the water must be pumped up.

Water held in saturated rocks exerts pressure on water below it; just as water presses down on the bottom of a jug which contains it. Fig. 3.4 shows that when a well is dug to obtain water from a saturated rock, the water will flow out under pressure *if* the water-table is *higher* than the head of the well. The water emerging is known as **artesian water**.

Fig. 3.6 shows how the tilt of a permeable rock, like chalk, with a high water-table, can cause lines of springs to emerge on the scarp face and dip-slope.

3.4 Groundwater and chemical action

Water combines with atmospheric carbon dioxide to produce carbonic acid. This attacks calcium carbonate. It eats away limestone rocks in particular. Many limestones are hard and jointed. As the acidic water passes continuously through a joint or between bedding planes, its chemical action enlarges the space. This can produce dramatically broken scenery.

At the surface, pavement-like slabs (**clints**) become separated by widened joints (**grikes**). Surface water becomes scarce. Even streams flowing from a higher level may disappear down **swallow-holes** in the limestone. Caverns may be formed below ground so that in places the surface collapses.

The acid converts the limestone to a soluble calcium bicarbonate. When this evaporates, it leaves behind calcium carbonate, like 'fur' in a kettle. As drips from the roof of caves slowly evaporate, the calcium carbonate particles become

P 3.3 Over the ages, solution has pitted this limestone surface on Malta. Soil forms in the hollows and supports small plants which tolerate both lime and drought.

P 3.4 In Crete water soaks through the joints in massive limestone (J). It emerges at an underground cave (C), and continues over a small fall (F), cutting into the rock. Notice the fallen blocks.

cemented, and in time build up long **stalactites**. Broader **stalagmite** columns grow upward more slowly, from splashes on the floor.

Limestone countryside broken by surface collapse, swallow holes, and clint-and-grike pavements is known as **karst scenery** (after a region of Yugoslavia).

Why is it generally wrong to describe as 'pure water': (a) freshly collected rain-water; (b) spring water?

Explain how a permeable rock may affect the landscape, and people's lives, a considerable distance from where it occurs at the surface.

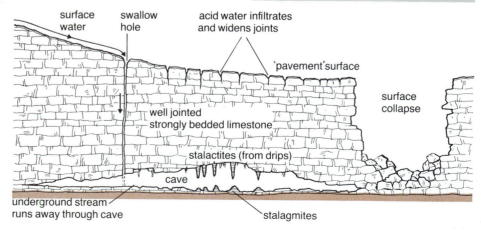

3.5 The effects of acid water on hard jointed limestone.

3.6 Tilted strata with chalk forming a long escarpment above a softer impermeable rock (usually clay in Britain). Water soaks into the chalk and emerges as springs below the scarp face – and sometimes on the dip-slope.

P 3.5 A valley side in eastern Crete shows how water passing through the jointed surface (J) formed caverns beneath (C). An underground stream once ran from left to right (S-S).

3.5 Energy and flow

When water runs in stream channels, or moves gradually through the rocks, it uses up energy in overcoming friction. But what energy has it to start with?

Fig. 3.7 shows a mass of water (**m**) at place **A**. Its height above sea-level is h_a, and the force of gravity (**g**) pulls it downwards. Now **while it remains at A its energy is in a sense stored for future use; it has potential energy** (equal to **m.g.h_a**).

If able to move, it will flow downhill at a velocity which depends on the angle of slope and the friction of its bed, banks, and any obstacles in its path.

As it flows, this energy is used up in carrying along boulders, pebbles and smaller particles, as well as in overcoming friction. Although the slope may be steep, the speed of flow will decrease if the water has to battle its way through a narrow, rough-bottomed channel. **At any point its energy of motion depends on its mass (m) and velocity (v).** Another name for this is **kinetic energy.** (It is equal to **½m.v^2**.)

When the water has reached **B**, its potential energy is now less than that at **A**, for h_b is less than h_a. As it reaches the sea, of course, its potential energy is nil relative to sea-level. However, the energy of its motion may sweep it out into the surrounding sea-water, which slows it up.

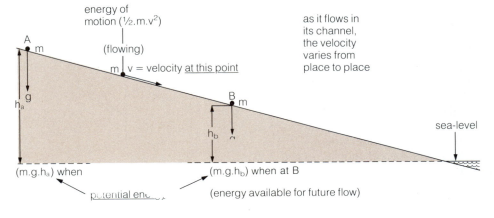

P 3.6 Chalk, porous and with fewer wide joints than hard limestones (P 3.5), gives a smooth, gentler landscape. Here in Sussex the deep dry valleys were formed when the water-table was higher. Spring sapping (P 3.7) may have created the steep valley heads (H).

3.7 Water has a potential energy depending on its height above base level.

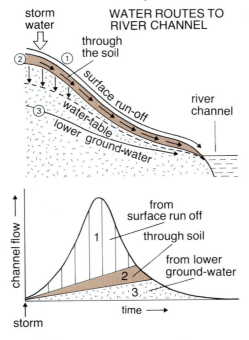

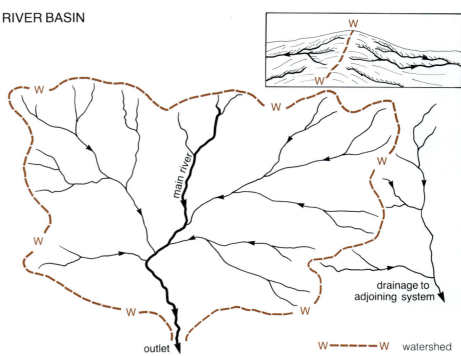

3.8 Notice the time taken for water following each path to make its maximum contribution to stream flow.

Water which soaks in and moves through soil and rocks also has potential energy, of course; but the speed with which it moves through the obstacles about it is slower than that of surface water.

This means that water which falls in a storm, as in Fig. 3.8, will reach a particular river channel after following different paths at different rates. The rapid surface run-off causes a big increase in the stream-flow *before* the throughflow and groundwater have reached the river. The relative ease of movement through these water paths varies from one river basin to another. The graph in Fig. 3.8 shows the effects of these time-lags.

3.6 The patterns of surface flow

Rainwater falling onto a fairly gentle surface usually flows into small channels, or **rills**. Fig. 3.9 shows the water flowing in parallel rills. Heavy storms cause a spill-over into the deeper ones. Small channels are cut in the separating ridges.

In time a deep channel (**C** in Fig. 3.9) becomes the main stream of a small surface water system, with a pattern rather like the veins of a leaf – a **dendritic** pattern. Such tributary patterns are common in river basins.

3.10 A pattern of surface streams in a river basin.

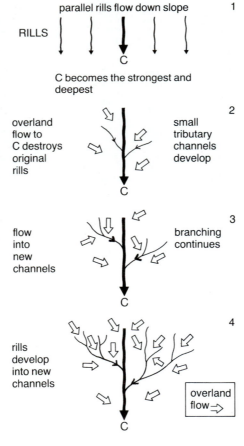

DENDRITIC PATTERN

3.9 Four stages in the development of a dendritic stream pattern.

The extent of a river basin is the whole area drained by the tributaries to the main river channel, above the outlet where its water leaves the basin (on its way to a larger river, lake, or ocean). The boundary separating one river basin from another – the highest part of a ridge – is called a **watershed**.

RADIAL DRAINAGE

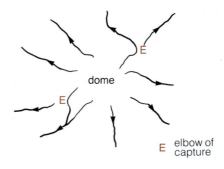

3.11 Drainage from a dome.

Not all river-tributary systems are dendritic. The rock structure and relief can produce other characteristic tributary patterns. For instance, large volcanoes, and rock domes, create **radial** drainage patterns.

A series of parallel scarps guide streams into a **trellised** pattern. In time this may be

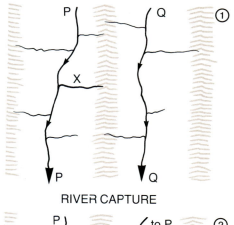

RIVER CAPTURE

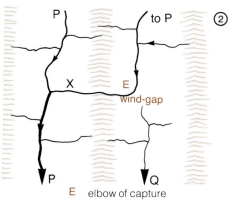

E   elbow of capture

3.12 A trellised drainage pattern, with one river capturing the headwaters of another.

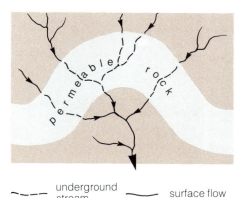

— — — underground   ———— surface flow
           stream

3.13 Where surface streams disappear. In fact underground water may re-emerge far from where it sank in – not necessarily lower down a former valley.

porous rock, or even disappear into **swallow holes** or fissures. After travelling as groundwater, some may emerge further downslope as springs, or streams issuing from caves.

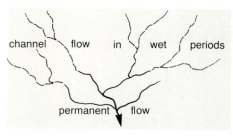

3.14 The upper channels in a basin may flow only after exceptional rainfall.

volumes of melt-water flowed over frozen ground, some during wetter periods than the present.

How will the following tend to disrupt the characteristic dendritic pattern of tributary streams: (a) a very permeable surface rock; (b) alternating scarps and vales?

modified by erosion (Fig. 3.12). You can see how rivers **P** and **Q** followed vales between the scarps. **P** being the stronger, its tributaries cut more actively into the terrain. One strong tributary (**X**) cut down and extended back the head of its valley until it breached the scarp. Eventually it cut down below the level of river **Q**, and diverted its waters, via **X**, into river **P** (which became even stronger). **The process is known as river capture.** Below the **elbow of capture** (**E**) a dry course, or **wind-gap**, separates **P**'s enlarged system from the now much smaller river **Q**.

What signs of river capture are shown in the radial drainage pattern in Fig. 3.11?

How might this have occurred?

Why is 'watershed' a suitable name for the line separating river basins?

Is the watershed a completely satisfactory boundary to show water draining from a river basin? (Consider subsurface water movements.)

The nature of the rocks can disrupt drainage patterns in other ways. If in the upper part of a basin streams flow over impervious rocks and onto very permeable ones, their water may sink into a

Some channels only carry surface water during long wet periods, or after intense storms. Such streams are common on very permeable rocks, such as chalk, and are called **bournes**. Many large valleys in the chalk of southern England are permanently dry. Some were formed during the ice-age, when large

P 3.7 How valley heads are extended: water from snow-melt on Exmoor was dammed by this huge pebble beach around Porlock Bay (P 4.3): springs formed and streams cut valleys into the slope to the sea. You can see how falling pebbles allowed each valley to extend its head back into the ridge.

P 3.8 A steep-sided channel – part of a drainage system eroding sheep pastures in Australia's Murray river basin. Rills are cut into the sides below the hardened top layers.

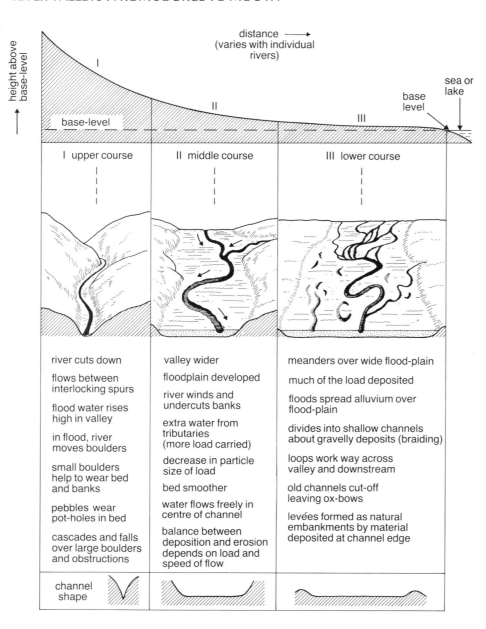

I upper course	**II middle course**	**III lower course**
river cuts down	valley wider	meanders over wide flood-plain
flows between interlocking spurs	floodplain developed	much of the load deposited
flood water rises high in valley	river winds and undercuts banks	floods spread alluvium over flood-plain
in flood, river moves boulders	extra water from tributaries (more load carried)	divides into shallow channels about gravelly deposits (braiding)
small boulders help to wear bed and banks	decrease in particle size of load	loops work way across valley and downstream
pebbles wear pot-holes in bed	bed smoother	old channels cut-off leaving ox-bows
cascades and falls over large boulders and obstructions	water flows freely in centre of channel	levées formed as natural embankments by material deposited at channel edge
	balance between deposition and erosion depends on load and speed of flow	
channel shape		

3.15 Typical changes in the river channel. Not all rivers have three well-defined stages. Some reach base level direct from stage I. Others rise amid lowlands.

3.7 The long profile of a river

Fig. 3.15 takes a sideways look at a river from its source to its mouth, and indicates its **base level. This concave profile is common to many rivers.** There is a steep section, the upper course; a less steep middle course; and a flat lower course, where potential energy is small. The illustrations show some of the main characteristics of the river channel and valley in each course.

These river and valley properties are very generalised. Remember that not all rivers rise in high places. Even where they do, their profile may be interrupted by bands of resistant rock, which create falls.

Sometimes a river flows into and out of lakes or old lake beds. In time, however, such irregularities may be smoothed out (Fig. 3.16).

Should earth movements cause a land surface to rise, the potential energy of the rivers is increased. As uplift continues they tend to cut down into the rising surface. In time some may erode spectacular gorges. Because of the rivers' renewed energy, the process is called **rejuvenation** (being made young again).

Where the rocks are resistant, a gorge, or **canyon**, tends to remain steep-sided as it becomes deeper. There is relatively little widening, especially in dry conditions (Fig. 3.17).

P 3.9 A stream cascades down its V-valley in south-west New Zealand. Swirling stones cut channels in the bed. When in flood, it can shift these larger boulders and tear trees from the valley sides.

WATERFALL

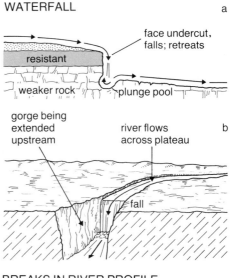

BREAKS IN RIVER PROFILE

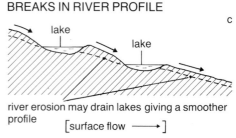

river erosion may drain lakes giving a smoother profile   [surface flow ⟶]

3.16 (a) Swirling water undercuts the resistant rock. (b) This process can create a gorge. (c) As the river deepens its channel, it may drain water from a lake.

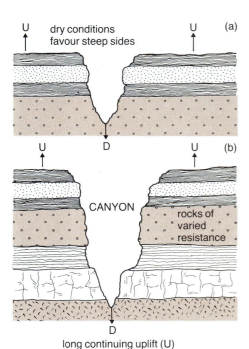

3.17 A deep, river-cut gorge, or canyon, in an uplifted plateau.

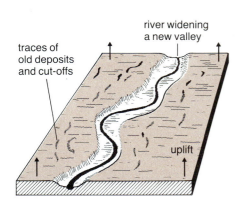

3.18 What happens when the surface, an old flood-plain, is slowly raised.

Fig. 3.18 shows the surface of a low plain which has been steadily lifted by earth movements. Explain why the bends of this meandering river have become entrenched. Consider the change in the potential energy of the river itself.

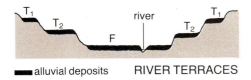

RIVER TERRACES

3.19 A wide valley with alluvial deposits of different ages at different heights.

P 3.10 In western China the river Min cut this gorge as the mountain country was slowly uplifted, in stages (U). The river terraces (T) were formed before the most recent period of uplift. Notice how material (M) from the valley side adds to the load of the river.

Fig. 3.19 shows a river which whenever it overflows deposits alluvium on the flat land beside it – its flood-plain (F). Old floodplains remain as terraces along the valley sides, at different heights and different distances from the river. Work out how this could have come about.

3.8 The effects of channel shape

Various processes which take place in a river channel are shown in Fig. 3.20. A semi-circular channel like this is the most efficient shape; though even in the middle course of a river the channel is usually more like a wide rectangle.

The rushing water drags away loose material (by **hydraulic** action), undermines the banks and causes collapse. A strongly flowing river also becomes turbulent and raises fine sand and gravel from the bed. In general, the faster the flow, the larger the particles it can carry; though very fine particles cling together on the bed and may be less easy to raise than sand (p.38).

Pebbles move forward in leaps and bounds (by **saltation**) as they are lifted, carried and then dropped. When larger pebbles and rocks are dragged along the bottom (by **traction**), they scour and scratch the bed-rock (by **corrasion**) and so erode it. Pebbles may also eddy round

and round in hollows and wear deep **potholes** in a rocky channel.

The water becomes turbulent as it swirls and eddies over the uneven bed.

P 3.11 Swirling pebbles enlarge hollows in the bed of turbulent rivers. Here on a wave-cut limestone platform in northern Cyprus the incoming tide causes pebbles to enlarge the solution hollows.

Most streams have deep pools, separated by shallower riffles.

The relative speed of water flowing in channels of contrasting cross-section is shown in Fig. 3.21. In the wide, shallow channel the effects of friction are felt over the whole cross-section, and so the river is much less efficient at moving its load. **All the material transported by the river is known as the load.** In fact dissolved material, like the calcium bicarbonate from limestones, can make up a large proportion of the load, especially in tropical rivers.

3.9 Channel shape from source to mouth

As the river tears through a narrow valley in its upper course, it is easy to think of it as fast-flowing, especially where the boulders on its bed create turbulent white-water torrents. But there is much friction at the bed and banks, which slows down the actual flow.

During wet periods, however, the river also rises high in the narrow channel, and may be capable of moving huge boulders, or tearing trees from the valley sides (see Fig. 3.23a).

P 3.12 Rivers have cut deep into the uplifted plateau of Exmoor (PP). Here the river Barle meanders through a valley enlarged during wetter periods in the past. It receives and removes debris which falls down the sides.

P 3.13 The lower-middle course of the river Exe. Notice the extent of the flood-plain (F) – a low terrace between the present channel and the valley side (V).

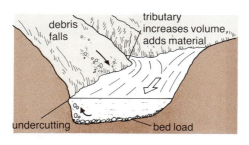

bed. A clear-water tributary may thus increase erosion downstream.

In the lower course friction is greater and the potential energy less, so the river deposits much of its load. As it winds over lowlands, deposits build up on the inside of bends, where it flows more slowly. On the outside of the bends the faster water erodes the bank, narrows the loops, and may create cut-offs, or ox-bow lakes.

land off-shore in the form of a **delta** (Fig. 3.24). The deposits themselves cause the mainstream to separate into a number of **distributaries**. These off-shore deposits are considered also on pp. 45–7.

STREAM ENERGY AND LOAD

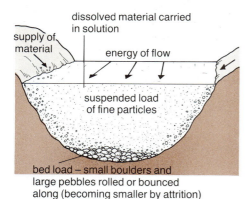

3.20 A stream acquires a varied load from its surroundings, tributaries, and bed.

In the middle course of the river there is more water and the channel has a rounder cross section. Also, as the particles get smaller, through attrition, the bed tends to be smoother and friction less. The flow is stronger and capable of carrying an extra load.

Tributaries bring in additional material, but also, of course, increase the volume of water. The extra flow helps to carry the load along and also to erode the river

CHANNEL SECTIONS – SPEED OF FLOW

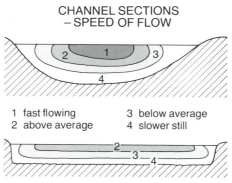

1 fast flowing   3 below average
2 above average   4 slower still

3.21 Friction and stream flow.

Fig. 3.23 shows how heavy deposition builds up the bed of the shallow rectangular channel, causing the river to overflow during wet periods. As the overflowing water loses energy at the channel sides, its deposits become banked up into ridges (**levées**). In normal times these may help to contain the river. But its surface level may be permanently above the flood-plain – a dangerous situation.

Where the river discharges into a lake or shallow sea, there is a sudden loss of energy, so that most of the load is deposited. A muddy river builds up layer upon layer of deposits. These may extend the

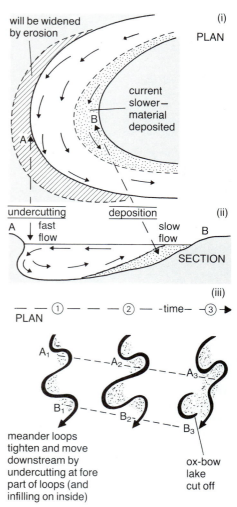

THE PROCESSES THAT CHANGE RIVER BENDS AND LOOPS

3.22 Notice how the processes in (i) and (ii) cause the meander loops to advance and tighten.

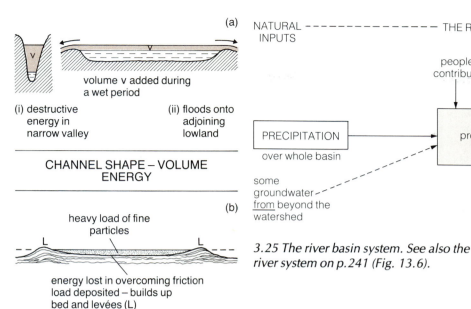

(a)

(i) destructive energy in narrow valley

(ii) floods onto adjoining lowland

volume v added during a wet period

CHANNEL SHAPE – VOLUME ENERGY

(b)

heavy load of fine particles

energy lost in overcoming friction load deposited – builds up bed and levées (L)

3.23 The effects of rising water in contrasting channels.

3.25 The river basin system. See also the river system on p.241 (Fig. 13.6).

NATURAL INPUTS — — — — — — THE RIVER BASIN — — — — — — NATURAL OUTPUTS

people contribute

evaporation

transpiration

PRECIPITATION over whole basin

processes

RIVER DISCHARGE

some groundwater from beyond the watershed

people extract

some groundwater to beyond the watershed

3.10 The river basin as a system

In any river basin, like that in Fig. 3.10, there are plants and animals, and probably human interference. There may be pumping stations and artificial storages; for large settlements and industries use lots of water. People also return water to the river system through drains and sewers (p. 36). Fig. 3.25 shows the natural inputs and outputs of a river basin, and notes what people take out and put in.

The input of a river basin consists mainly of rain and other forms of precipitation. A large part of this input is eventually discharged through the main river. But other processes also release water from the system. There is direct evaporation, transpiration from vegetation, and the loss of some groundwater beyond the watershed – though groundwater may also enter the basin from outside.

The output from the main river channel may be measured in terms of the rate of water discharged from the basin. The **discharge** is the volume passing a point in a given time, usually measured in cubic metres per second (cumecs).

P 3.14 Trees outline the river Darling as it winds across the interior of New South Wales. Notice the cut-off loops and the traces of old meanders over the flood-plain.

P 3.15 The Mackenzie river becomes a maze of waterways, threading through the deposits on the flood-plain, as it approaches the Arctic coast. You can see numerous examples of braiding, cut-offs, and ox-bow lakes.

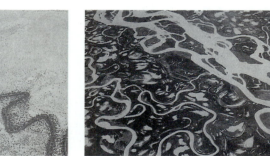

river brings heavy load of clay, silt, sand, gravel

more arrives than currents, tides can remove

horizontal layers of coarse material

fine material settles

DELTA

shallow sea

speed of flow reduced – much material deposited

coarser material settled to form sloping beds

bottom clayey bed of fine particles

lesser distributaries

main channel

△ delta shape

branching 'birdsfoot' delta

3.24 The advance of a delta depends on whether the sediments can settle and build up offshore, without being dragged out by tidal flows or moved alongside by currents.

The mean output and input over a given period can be compared.

Suppose that:
During August **the average rainfall over the basin** (100 km²) is **48 mm** (that is the equivalent of covering it to a depth of 48 mm).

The average discharge from the river during August is 6 cumecs. So the outflow during the month would be: 6 × 360 (sec) × 24 (hr) × 31 (day) = 1 607 040 m³. As the area of the whole basin is 10⁸ m², simple division shows that the water discharged would have covered the basin to a depth of approximately **16 mm**.

You can see that **the output** through the river channel (16 mm) **is only a third of the input** (48 mm). This is not unusual. In south-east England, for example, the output is usually less than 30 per cent of the input.

The shortfall may be due to evaporation and transpiration; storage in vegetation, soils, and rocks, which has not yet reached the main river; retention in dams; controlled use of irrigation; or extraction for homes and industries. Much of this may *eventually* find its way back to the river channel.

3.11 Time-lag in a river system

For certain periods the **output** (discharge) from a river system may be *greater* than the **input**. In winter, for instance, when evaporation and transpiration rates are low, and leaf interference less, the river receives most of the rain which falls. It may also receive water which has been temporarily stored as ice and snow, as well as that from saturated rocks and soils.

Also, of course, people may deliberately regulate the flow.

We need to know as much as possible about natural inputs and outputs in order to regulate river levels against flooding, or to counter low-water periods which might concentrate pollution, or interfere with supplies, or affect fishing or recreation.

WATER DISCHARGED FROM THE BASIN

EFFECTS OF CHANNEL SLOPE

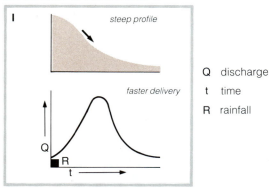

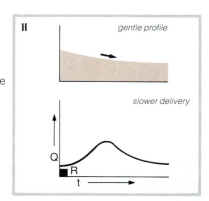

Q discharge
t   time
R rainfall

EFFECTS OF BASIN SHAPE

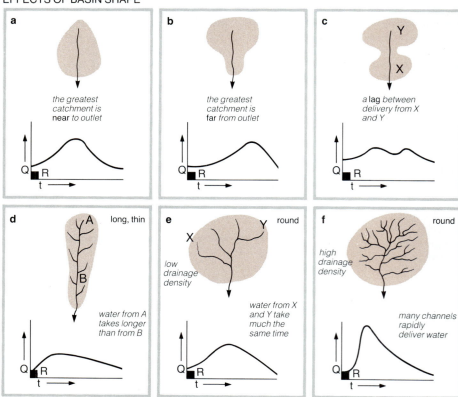

3.27 Facts which make for a fast delivery or slow delivery of water to the main river, and so affect the volume discharged from the basin per second.

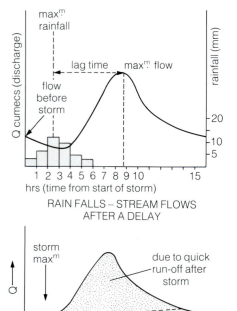

3.26 See how long it takes for the storm water to produce the maximum flow in a river.

The natural time-lag between precipitation falling and water reaching the main river, as shown in Fig. 3.8, is thus very important for practical reasons. **The rate at which water reaches the main river after rain depends on many things:**

1 How heavy the rainfall is and how long it lasts.
2 Whether it falls on pervious or impervious rock.
3 Whether or not the pervious rock is saturated already.
4 Whether vegetation intercepts storm water or checks surface flow.
5 The rates of evaporation and transpiration.
6 Whether spaces within soils/rocks allow rapid down-slope flow.
7 The slope and cross-section of the various stream channels.
8 The density of the channel network.
9 The characteristics of the whole basin — such as its size, shape, and slopes.

> Explain exactly how each of the conditions (1–9) will affect the path of water that falls over the basin as rain. Will it be discharged as channeled river flow from the basin; and, if so, quickly, or slowly, or not at all?

Fig. 3.27 shows a number of basin characteristics which affect the time-lag, together with small graphs which indicate the effects on the volume of water discharged (Q cumecs) during a period of time (t hr) after rainfall.

To understand the shape of these graphs look more closely at the flows in Figs. 3.8 and 3.26. As you can see, Fig. 3.26 shows when the maximum *rainfall* occurred and the time that the river *flow* was at its maximum; the difference is the **lag time**. They also show that *before* the storm the river water discharged from the basin came mainly from the seepage of groundwater into the channel (**base flow**).

After the storm there is a surge of overland flow and an increase in base flow. This dies away until, eventually, base flow again becomes the main source of water in the channel.

3.12 Describing streams and stream density

The effects of run-off vary in different parts of the basin. It is often necessary to look at the flow of streams in the upper and lower parts of the basin separately. One way to describe both the minor tributaries and the larger ones is shown in Fig. 3.28. **The streams are given an order.** Unbranched streams are **first order** ones (1). Where two first order streams join, the down-channel stream is a **second order** one (2); and so on.

The density of streams in a selected area (the **drainage density**) is simply the total stream length divided by the area.

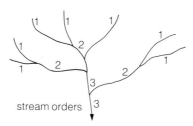

3.28 A main stream of the third order.

Theme 3 Back-up section

Rainfall – interception by vegetation

Before rain can run off or soak into the ground, it is usually intercepted by vegetation of some kind. Some, held by leaves and branches, evaporates and never reaches the soil. Fig. 3.29 shows that the rest passes through the leaf canopy, which will continue to drip for some time, or else runs as **stemflow** down the trunk. It is possible to see what happens over a period of time, using simple apparatus.

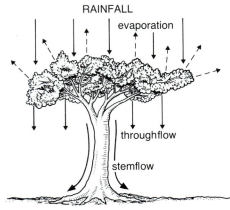

3.29 Rainfall interception.

1 **Construct 5 or 6 rain gauges.** Each consists of a large plastic funnel, a straight-sided collecting bottle, a cork, and a cylindrical tin or plastic pipe to contain them.

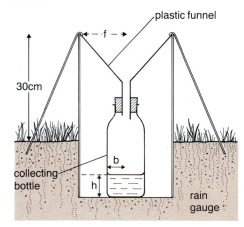

3.30 A simple rain gauge.

They are placed at a selected site (as in Fig. 3.30), so that the funnel rim is 30 cm above ground – to avoid splashes – and

steadied as shown. They need not be dug in if the container is held by a sturdy wire frame.

Simply measure the height of the water collected in the bottle (**h** mm). If the radius of the funnel is **f** and that of the bottle **b**, the rainfall equivalent **R** mm is given by: $R = h\,(b^2/f^2)$.

2 **Place one gauge in an open space** to record the gross rainfall, and **distribute the others under the canopy of a reasonably slender tree.** After a storm, or period of rain when the dripping has stopped, record and compare the amounts in each gauge.

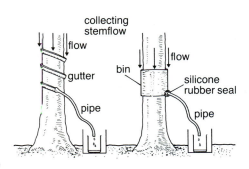

3.31 Stemflow collected by gutter and bin.

3 **A trough can be fitted around the trunk** so that the stemflow is diverted into a collecting vessel. This can be a gutter type (Fig. 3.31), or perhaps a cut-down plastic bucket or bin with a hole made in the bottom to fit the trunk. The side can be split, resealed, and made water-tight against the trunk. A plastic tube takes the water received from a small hole in the side to a collecting bottle. This is not easy to set up, but is effective, and the materials are inexpensive.

Tree canopies vary, so it is interesting to compare interception by different types of tree. It is possible to monitor the changing effects as the trees lose their leaves.

River erosion and deposition

Flowing water may erode particles from a river bed, transport them, and eventually deposit them. **The energy required to lift the particles from the bed does not depend entirely on their size.** Less energy is needed to carry them along. Consider the following:

(a) **A sand grain**, 0.2mm diameter; flow needed to lift it is 30 cm/sec; it will not fall to the bottom until the flow slackens to 2 cm/sec.

(b) **A clay particle**, 0.005mm diameter; the flow needed to lift it is 80 cm/sec; once lifted it will continue to be suspended by a very light flow.

(c) **A pebble**, 100mm diameter; the flow needed to lift it is 350 cm/sec; it falls to the bottom if the flow slackens to 200 cm/sec.

Remember that clay particles are so fine that they cling to one another, and, being smooth, water streams easily over them, so that considerable energy is needed to lift them from the bed.

To understand what is happening in a river we need to be able to measure the rate of flow, the size of particles and the quantity transported.

The river channel

Fig. 3.32 shows part of the channel with water in it – the **wetted perimeter**. It is relatively easy to measure the width of the channel at water level (**w**), and to construct a cross-section after recording the depth at regular intervals. The mean depth (**d**) can be calculated and used to find the **cross-section area (A): A=w.d**.

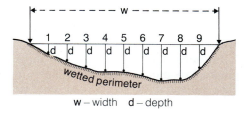

3.32 Plumbing depths (d1 to d9) to find the cross-section area.

How can we determine how fast the river is flowing, when this varies across the section? We can make an approximation from surface readings, as in (a), or find a way of metering the actual flow at distances below the surface (b), at intervals across the section. But, of course, we can only find an average velocity of flow.

(a) **Use a stop-watch to time a float** over a measured distance (say 10m), and so obtain the **surface velocity**. Multiply by a factor of 0.8 to give the approximate **mean velocity**. Repeat a number of times at different points across the width. Average the readings. The float can be a piece of bamboo, or a half-submerged orange.

(b) **A current meter can also be used** at various points across the river. It is usually lowered to 0.6 of the depth. Most manufactured meters have a propeller which revolves at a speed which varies with that of the water; this is indicated on a dial.

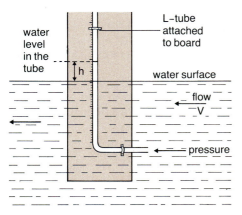

3.33 Measuring stream velocity.

A simple device, used effectively by schools, is the **Pitot tube** (Fig. 3.33). It is basically a calibrated L-shaped tube, of at least 5mm diameter, attached to a board. The stream's velocity (**V**) creates a pressure which raises water in the tube to a height (**h**) above stream level. The velocity (m/sec) can be calculated from the equation: $V^2 = h \times 20$ (**h** = height in metres).

The river discharge

The discharge (Q) can now be found by multiplying the cross-sectional area (**A**) by the mean velocity of flow (**V**): $Q = A.V$

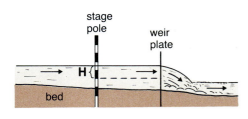

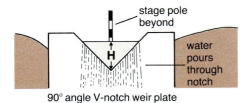

3.34 Measuring the stream discharge.

It is possible to channel the flow of a small stream through a weir with a V-shaped notch of 90° angle to it. The weir may be a plate of sheet metal, or even plywood (Fig. 3.34). The level of water passing through the weir can be shown by a **stage pole** driven into the bed behind it (the water level drops as it flows over the lip of the notch).

The level of a stream is known as the **stage**. The stage pole is marked in metres and centimetres.

The discharge can be calculated from the head of water (**H**); and a graph is made so that a simple reading of height in metres will indicate the discharge in cumecs.

Finding the load carried

The particles carried vary with the flow. They can be trapped in the following way:

1 **Construct a sampler** from a milk bottle and a rubber bung, through which two metal tubes of 5 mm diameter may be inserted. The water flows in through one and air is expelled through the other (Fig. 3.35).

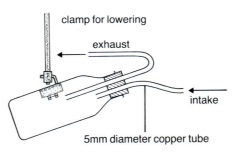

SEDIMENT SAMPLING

3.35 Sampling the load of sediment.

2 Fix a clamp around the bottle. Gently lower it into the stream and raise it: repeat several times until it is full.

3 Transfer the water and sediment to a numbered bottle. Record where taken, and details of flow etc., as needed.

4 Later, weigh a dried filter paper. Shake the bottle, and then filter a measured volume through the paper. Dry again in the oven and reweigh. Subtract to find the weight of sediment. The value can be expressed in milligrammes per litre.

Sediment density – visual comparisons

It is possible to obtain river sediment and weigh out specific quantities. These can be allowed to settle through water onto a filter paper. This is dried, waterproofed with a lacquer spray, and fixed to a card with others of known sediment weight. Their density on the paper gives a visual chart for comparison with your own filtered sample. One snag is that ideally the sediments on the chart should come from the river you are investigating.

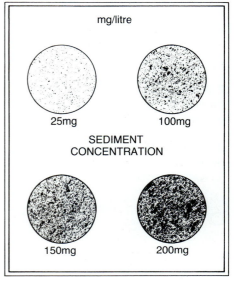

3.36 A visual comparison of sediment content.

The dissolved load may be found by evaporating a large sample of filtered river water to dryness. An accurate balance is needed.

Bed load – the heavy material on the bed – may only move at times of high water and strong flow. Its movements are not easy to follow. Fig. 3.37 shows how a simple box in the stream bed may collect material, which can be measured for its particle sizes and weight.

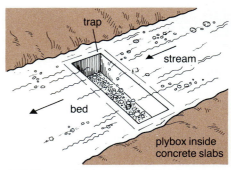

3.37 To trap the heavier bed load.

Theme 3 Making sure

1 Name the processes 1–8, which are all part of the hydrological cycle.

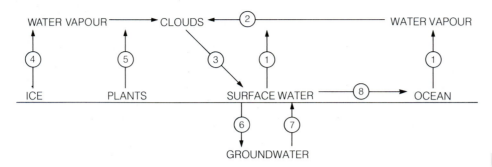

3.38

2 A rock which allows water to pass through its cracks and joints is: (a) porous; (b) impermeable; (c) pervious?

3 A permeable rock is one which: (a) dissolves; (b) lets water pass through it; (c) is easily eroded?

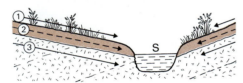

3.39

4 Look at Fig. 3.39. After rain, water will reach stream **S** by processes (1)...., (2)...., or as .....(3) through the rock. (a) Name these processes. (b) What hindrance to flow will there be in each case? (c) Which will produce the least time lag before the water reaches **S**?

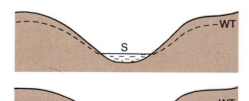

WT – water-table   S – stream

3.40

5 Explain the conditions and processes that make the stream **S** (Fig. 3.40) a seasonal one. What name is given to such a stream?

6 Are the following true or false? Explain.
(a) The particles carried and deposited by a river tend to become smaller downstream.
(b) Rivers always flow fastest in their upper course.
(c) Deposition is most likely where a river's energy is least.
(d) Adjoining river basins are separated by a water-table.

7 Particles which strike one another as they move downstream tend to become: (a) flat; (b) angular; (c) rounded; (d) smaller in size;...which?

8 The process described in question 7 is known as : (a) denudation; (b) corrosion; (c) attrition; (d) hydraulic action?

9 'Rejuvenation' means 'made young again'. Why is the name sometimes applied to rivers during a period when sea-level has fallen?

10 Explain the following:
(a) Gorges cut into resistant rocks are likely to remain steep-sided in dry conditions.
(b) A river receiving clear water from a tributary may be able to erode its bed more easily.
(c) Mid-stream banks of gravel frequently interrupt a shallow, wide river in its lower course.
(d) Sudden floods in a V-shaped valley can be dangerous because of the size of their load, the volume of water, and the effects of hydraulic action.

11 Where might you expect to find the following – in the upper or lower course of a river? (a) potholes; (b) wide meanders; (c) interlocking spurs; (d) levées; (e) high potential energy; (f) a smooth bed.

12 Explain, with a diagram, why hard, jointed limestone rocks in particular give rise to 'karst' scenery.

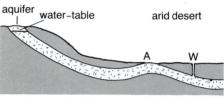

impermeable rock

3.41

13 (a) What is meant by an 'aquifer'? (b) Look at Fig. 3.41. Explain what may occur at **A**, and why this may become a centre of settlement. (c) Would water emerge freely if a well were drilled at **W**? Why? (d) Explain the term 'potential energy' using the water-table as an example.

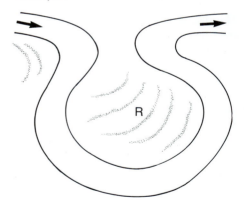

3.42

14 (a) Copy Fig. 3.42. Add arrows to indicate where the river bank is being attacked.
(b) Put **X** at the place where a breakthrough would create a cut-off.
(c) How do the ridges of deposits (**R**) show that the meander loops have been gradually extended?
(d) Extended in which direction?

15 In Fig. 3.43, which plot of discharge against time, **A** or **B**, is likely to represent the drainage system of river **R**? Explain.

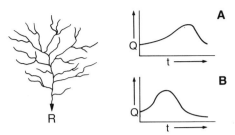

3.43 Q is the discharge, t is the time after rainfall.

16 Flooding after heavy rainfall is likely in a region of: (a) high drainage channel density; (b) low drainage channel density; (c) when the water-table is high; (d) when the water-table is low. Which?

P 3.16 The river Clutha flows across an uplifted plateau.

17 Photo 3.16 shows the Clutha river in the South Island of New Zealand. It flows across the uplifted Otago plateau.

(a) Describe the scenery generally.

(b) Much of the plateau is in a dry rain-shadow region (p. 65). Do the conditions bear this out?

(c) Account for the flat area above the river bank.

(d) Describe and account for the slope and condition of the bank itself.

(e) What is increasing the river's load?

(f) Spring snow-melt in the western mountains greatly increases the flow of the river. How will this affect what you see here (in summer)?

18   RIVER BASIN SYSTEMS

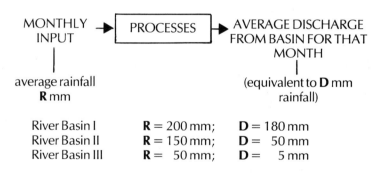

	R = 200 mm;	D = 180 mm
River Basin I	R = 200 mm;	D = 180 mm
River Basin II	R = 150 mm;	D = 50 mm
River Basin III	R = 50 mm;	D = 5 mm

What kind of circumstances might lead to the differences between **R** and **D** in each of these basins?

19(a) plot the river discharge (**Q**) against time from the start of the storm (**t**) using the figures given in Table 1.

(b) Plot the hourly rainfall on the same graph paper.

(c) What is the lag time? Why should this be?

(d) Explain the general shape of the graph.

Table 1

volume of water discharged (**Q**) after time (**t**)				rain during each hour	
time (hr)	discharge (cumecs)	time (hr)	discharge (cumecs)	time (hr)	rainfall (mm)
0	0.6	14	2.3	0–1	0.1
2	0.8	16	1.8	1–2	1.2
4	1.0	18	1.4	2–3	1.9
6	1.7	20	1.1	3–4	2.4
8	2.7	24	0.9	4–5	2.0
10	2.9	30	0.8	5–6	1.9
12	2.6	36	0.7	6–7	1.6

Consider the terms used

Evaporation is the process whereby a liquid changes to a gaseous state (gas or vapour). The rate at which surface water passes into the atmosphere depends on the heat supplied to it; also on the amount of water vapour already in the atmosphere (thus on the water vapour pressure immediately above the surface). Wind helps to prevent air in contact with the surface becoming saturated. So there is rapid evaporation on hot, windy days when the air is dry, and less under cool, damp, still conditions.

Saturation, applied to air, occurs when it contains as much water vapour as it can possibly hold. Cooling will then cause **condensation**, and droplets will appear. Applied to the ground, water fills every space between the mineral particles up to the top level of saturation – the level of the **water-table**.

Transpiration is the loss of water from the stomata of plants (small pores with a mechanism which opens and closes them) – mostly from leaves. This maintains the flow of minerals in solution from the soil through the plant organs – a process checked in many plants when the temperature falls below 6°C. Combined loss by transpiration and evaporation is sometimes called **evapotranspiration.**

Sublimation is the change directly from solid to gaseous state without become a liquid.

Sheet-wash or **sheet-flow** describes water flowing over the surface as a continuous sheet. It can remove surface particles, and when deep its **turbulence** (disturbed flow) can cause erosion.

Throughflow is the sideways movement of water through the soil above the level of the water-table.

Groundwater is all the water in the soil and the underlying regolith and rock. Apart from the throughflow, the groundwater moving sideways (and perhaps reaching a stream, or emerging as a spring) is the **baseflow**.

Artesian (named after a groundwater supply in Artois, France) is used to describe an underground store of water: so an **artesian well** is a vertical channel made to tap artesian water.

Kinetic energy is that which a body has because of its motion.

Potential energy is that which a body has because of its position (like a coiled spring, or a pram at the top of a hill).

Dendritic drainage – tributaries forming a branching drainage pattern.

Wind gap – a dry valley through a ridge, once the route of a river whose waters have been captured by another.

Hydraulic actions are those of moving water alone (without a load).

Saltation (from Latin – *saltare* – to jump): water transportation which causes particles to advance along a bed by a series of leaps.

Attrition is the wearing down of mineral particles by other particles as they are being carried along by water, or wind. Thus they become smaller, and often smoothed, fluted or rounded.

The wetted perimeter of a stream channel is the length of the cross-section of the channel in contact with water of the stream.

Levée – a ridge of alluvial deposits gradually built up whenever a river overflows its bank. They may become large enough to contain a river above the level of the floodplain.

Distributaries are channels which share the distribution of water from the main river, usually across a delta, to discharge it into open water.

The discharge of a river is the volume of flow moving through a cross-section of its stream in a given unit of time at a particular place.

Velocity is used in preference to 'speed' to indicate a rate of motion *in a given direction*.

Aquifer describes a rock which holds water and allows water to move freely through it.

Theme 4 Water in the oceans: water as ice

4.1 The great ocean reservoir

The world's rivers pour their load of particles and chemicals (in solution) into the sea, and so into the inter-connected oceans, which make up 71 per cent of the earth's surface. A great deal of the solid load is deposited on shallow offshore areas of the **continental shelves.** There it builds up coastal deltas, marshes and beaches.

The oceans have a mean depth of 3.8 km. There are thick, fine sediments on the deep ocean floors, but they accumulate very slowly.

Seawater contains about 3.5 per cent of dissolved solids, which include most chemical elements. Some of these, such as common salt, magnesium, and boron are extracted in large quantities. In many parts of the world people extract the salts in desalination plants and obtain fresh water.

In certain conditions huge amounts of calcium carbonate are deposited as small particles, which slowly build up as limestone on the ocean bed. Calcium carbonate is extracted also by tiny organisms which form the coral reefs and atolls.

The volume of the oceans has not changed much over the ages, but the sea-level varies. During ice ages, large amounts of water are locked up in solid form so that the sea-level falls and continental shelves are exposed. In warmer times the melting ice raises the sea-level, so that seawater advances over coastal plains. On the other hand, lands which have been depressed by the weight of the great ice sheets slowly rise again as the ice melts. Therefore the level at which the sea meets the coast varies considerably.

4.2 The movements of the waters

The sun's energy sets the atmosphere in motion and the winds create an ocean circulation (Fig. 4.1). The wind drags along the upper layers of water, so that the **ocean currents** conform to the general wind system, as far as obstructing land-masses allow.

In the North Atlantic the Trade Winds and westerlies set up a clockwise circulation. There is a corresponding anti-clockwise swirl in the South Atlantic. But in the southern hemisphere you can see that the westerlies create a great West Wind Drift of water over the uninterrupted expanses of ocean.

Fig. 4.1 also shows how the shape of the land can create swirls of water. In places these are concentrated into strong currents, such as the Gulf Stream. Notice how this flows from the Gulf of Mexico — and continues towards Europe as the North Atlantic Drift. In general, currents flowing from higher latitudes towards the equator are relatively cold; while poleward-moving currents are warmer than the seas about them.

There are also vertical movements. Dense water sinks and less dense rises. Thus cold, dense water sinking in arctic regions moves equatorwards at great depths.

Surface water in the tropics is strongly heated and has a fairly low density. However, where there is little cloud the rapid evaporation causes it to become saltier, and so denser. In hot dry climates land-locked water surfaces, like the Dead Sea, become very salty (saline) and dense. Layers of salt build up around the shores.

As the wind's energy is transferred to the ocean, surface friction creates a drag. This sets up ripples, which the wind pressure banks up into wavelets. If strong winds persist over a wide stretch of ocean (a long fetch), large **waves** are formed.

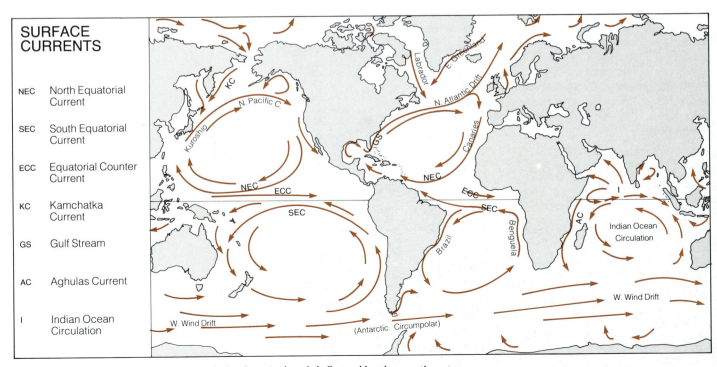

SURFACE CURRENTS

NEC	North Equatorial Current
SEC	South Equatorial Current
ECC	Equatorial Counter Current
KC	Kamchatka Current
GS	Gulf Stream
AC	Aghulas Current
I	Indian Ocean Circulation

4.1 The Ocean Currents – driven mainly by the wind and deflected by the continents.

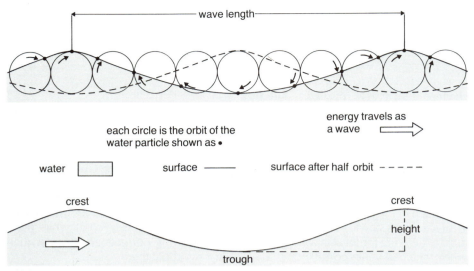

4.2 Energy moves as a wave. The wave form travels forward, but not the water itself (until the wave breaks on the shore).

The wind's energy is thus carried forward by wave motion. But notice that the water particles in the wave simply take a circular path, or **orbit**. The orbits of surface particles are shown in Fig. 4.2. Deeper particles have smaller orbits. The waves which break on the shore are direct descendants of waves generated far away in the open ocean.

Tides are a response to the force of attraction of the sun and moon, and vary as these bodies change their relative position. In general, the ocean waters bulge towards the moon; while at the same time a similar bulge occurs on the opposite side of the earth. As the earth spins, coasts experience a high tide and a low tide twice a day. The actual time these occur depends on the shape of the seas and coasts and inlets.

When sun, earth and moon are in line, **the tidal range** is exceptionally high (**spring tides**). When sun, earth and moon form right angles, the tidal range is small (**neap tides**).

4.3 Where land and sea meet

The waves, currents and tides have great effects on the world's coastal zones. Where the land meets the sea, the processes of weathering and erosion continue to affect the landforms. With the amount of moisture present, weathering processes are often rapid. Some rocks are particularly affected by salt spray. Here and there rivers bring down their load to the sea.

The cliffs

Because of the tidal range, the waves attack cliffs at different levels. A long notch cut at the base of a cliff usually shows the height of most erosion. Storms bring wave attack even higher up the cliff than usual. Waves thump onto the rock face and, with shingle as a tool of erosion, their energy exploits any weaknesses. The wave impact can compress air into cracks, and it expands suddenly on release; processes which can weaken a resistant cliff.

As waves open up large cracks near sea level, caves may be formed, or part of the cliff face may collapse. Weak rocks tend to slip or slump forward, especially if the

loosened material is also saturated by rainfall. The sea sometimes works away at a vertical line of weakness in a cliff and so erodes a long narrow slit (a **geo**).

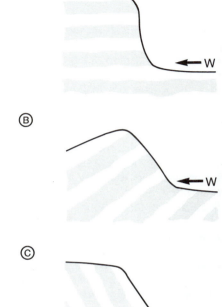

W   wave attack

4.3 Wave attack on horizontal and tilted strata.

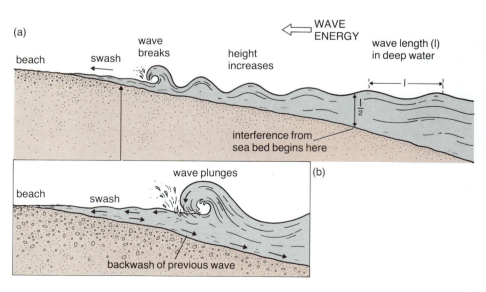

4.4 What happens as the waves reach shallow off-shore water.

P 4.1 The results of wave attack on a headland in southern Tasmania.

The angle of the cliffs and the tilt of their strata affect the rate of erosion. Compare the cliffs, **A, B,** and **C** in Fig. 4.3. Which is likely to collapse most easily? Which will be least affected? Which may slip and temporarily protect the base of the cliff if undercut by wave action? How do the rocks affect the cliff shapes in P.4.1?

Wave action and beach formation

Material falling to the foot of a cliff may be removed by the backwash of water after a wave has broken. It is important to understand the processes which follow the break of a wave, for they affect the whole nature of the cliffs, beach and offshore deposits, and therefore the coastal features as a whole.

Angular material may fall from a cliff face, but most of the large beach debris consists of rounded pebbles (shingle). Why?

As waves move towards the shore and into shallower water, the sea bed interferes with the circular movement of the water particles. The wavelength shortens and the wave height increases, until the crest tumbles forward. Thus the wave 'breaks' and rushes up the beach as **swash**, carrying sand and shingle with it.

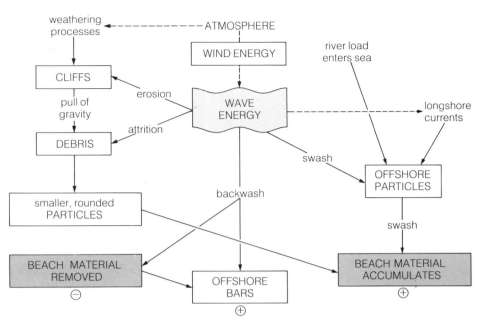

4.5 The continuous processes of construction and destruction. Material is supplied by the cliffs (left) and by currents (right). Swash and backwash rearrange the particles.

As the water pours back down the slope as **backwash**, much of it soaks into beach sand and leaves part of the material stranded on the shore.

When the incoming wave crests are far apart, the backwash from one wave disappears before the next swash occurs. Sand and pebbles tend to be built up on the beach by these **constructive waves.**

During storms the waves, driven by the wind, are steep and the wavelength short. The backwash is so powerful that much of the beach material is removed from the shore and carried seaward. These are **destructive waves.**

P 4.2 A wide sandy beach at Moeraki, south-east New Zealand, protects the cliffs from regular wave attack; but their soft materials weather and fall. What suggests that storm waves occasionally reach the base of the cliffs at high tides?
The hard spheres of limy clay, with veins of calcite, were part of the cliff material, but released by weathering and erosion. They are more complete near the cliff, but broken by erosion nearer the sea's edge.

Longshore drift

The wind usually brings in the waves at an angle to the shore. When they reach shallow water, however, their movement is checked, so that the wave front tends to swing parallel to the shore. Nevertheless, a wave still usually arrives at the shore at a slight angle, and as it breaks and rushes forward, carries pebbles up the beach at that angle. The water, pulled by gravity, returns seawards, *directly down the slope,* bringing some of the material back with it.

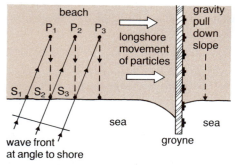

S – Particle picked up by swash
P – particle before return by
    backwash
(1, 2, 3 after each wave breaks)

4.6 Particles are gradually moved sideways along the beach.

A pebble may thus be swept up again and again at an angle, and gradually moved along the beach (Fig. 4.6). It is often necessary to build groynes at right angles to the shore to check the drift of beach material.

Occasionally, storms create waves with sufficient energy to fling pebbles high up the beach. There a **pebble ridge** may accumulate, unaffected by normal processes. Successive storms can leave parallel lines of beach ridges, some a considerable height above normal sea-level. Large waves may also build a ridge of sand and shingle high on the beach, with its crest on the seaward side. This is a **berm**.

Waves may be described as constructive or destructive. Explain. In Western Europe wave actions tend to be more constructive in summer than in winter. Suggest reasons for this.

Strong onshore winds bank up water

P 4.3 Ridges on the shingle beach, running around Porlock Bay from the headland, where storms have piled up the rounded pebbles. What evidence is there that recent storms have flung pebbles to the top-most ridge?

onto the shoreline and may thus cause a current to flow parallel to the shore. With persistent side winds, such currents drift beach material along with them. As Fig. 4.7 shows, **longshore currents** can build up a line of deposits which continues beyond a headland as a **spit**. Acting together, the waves and currents tend to curve the spit into the next bay, though some deposits may extend right across it and form a **lagoon**. Currents may also build enough beach material to link a nearby island with the coast, a feature known as a **tombolo.**

Photo 8.3 on p. 149 shows the striking results of deposition and wave action at Dungeness, over the ages.

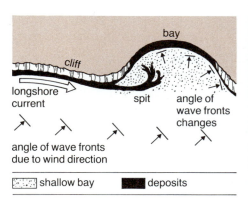

4.7 The changing angle of the wave fronts bend the spit into the bay.

Gentle slopes and cliffed headlands

On gently sloping coasts the waves tend to break some distance off-shore and so bank up sufficient deposits to form a **bar** below the surface. As the bar is built up it may become exposed. Sometimes winds and waves move a bar in towards the shore and finally enclose a lagoon. Such lagoons may be filled with sediment from land sources, or may receive wind-blown deposits, and so become marshy.

P 4.4 The long Chesil beach extends for some 25 km from Portland to West Bay – its rounded pebbles decreasing in size towards the west. When the sea-level was lower it may have started as a barrier beach. It separates the lagoon, the Fleet, from the sea.

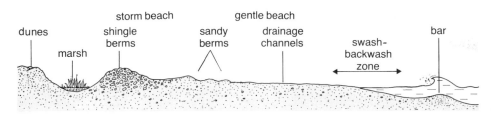

4.8 *The type of beach and its various zones differ according to the constructive or destructive nature of the waves – here constructive.*

Also on low coasts the onshore winds may whip up sand and carry it inland, so that a line of **dunes** builds up from particles deposited behind the beach.

Marram grass with its spreading, fibrous roots helps to bind the dunes, and traps more sand. Eventually, other plants may establish themselves.

Fig. 4.8 shows some of the typical features you may find in the various zones of a gently sloping shore.

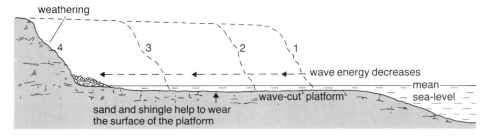

4.9 *As the platform is made wider, the waves' ability to attack the cliff and remove the debris decreases.*

P 4.5 *Constructive waves surge into a shallow bay on the Northern Ireland coast. Notice the angles of the wave fronts in relation to the shape of the bay. Wet sand shows the extent of the swash, and the small arcs of the cusps. Beyond, the wind has built up dunes, partly covered with vegetation. Deposits interfere with the outlet of the river, whose mouth has been given a protective channel. Notice also how the sand held by the protective walling indicates longshore drift.*

P 4.6 *The influence of jointing is seen near Albany in Western Australia, where weaknesses have allowed under-cutting waves to leave this remarkable granite bridge.*

Make a sketch of the coastal features shown in Photo 4.5, and indicate the swash zone, cusps, dry beach sand, dunes, and protective walling.

Explain why the artificial outlet is necessary.

Suggest why the width of the beach decreases along the bay.

In contrast, Fig. 4.9 shows what happens when a cliff is gradually destroyed by weathering and erosion by waves. As it retreats, it leaves a **wave-cut platform**. The waves break and lose much of their energy as they advance over this extending rock platform. So, in time, the retreat of the cliffs become less rapid, although they will continue to be affected by weathering.

Photo 4.7 shows that the results depend on the type of cliff and rock bedding, and also on the ability of waves to erode the face and remove the debris (which temporarily protects the cliff).

Headlands, by contrast, are particularly vulnerable to erosion. Wave energy is concentrated on the sides, as the waves swing in parallel to the shore. As cracks and joints are widened, caves on either

P 4.7 *Waves have undercut horizontally bedded cliffs in northern Malta. Notice the slump behind the debris lying on the wave-cut platform.*

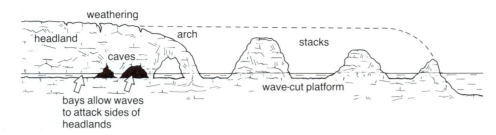

4.10 Features resulting from the energy of waves pounding on an exposed headland.

side of the headland may join and form an arch. When the arch collapses, an isolated block, or **stack**, is left. This is gradually reduced in size by wave attack, so that a headland may have a line of stacks of decreasing size extending from it (Fig. 4.10).

Fig 4.10 shows caves formed in a headland. Sometimes a cave roof collapses and leaves a hole. Waves can surge into the cave with such force that spray is thrown up through this **blowhole**.

How does this indicate the role of wave energy in forming caves and stacks? Why is a headland particularly vulnerable?

4.4 What happens when sea-level changes

If the surface of the land rises, or the sea-level falls, the wave-cut platforms are left well above the level of wave attack.

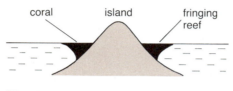
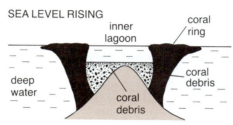

4.11 A fringing reef becomes coral islands.

P 4.8 At Kaikoura, north-east of New Zealand's South Island, uplift has raised the wave-cut platform (WCP). A line of weathering stacks (1–4) show where the headland once extended. Notice vegetation-covered screes (S) below the exposed bedding on the weathering cliff face (F). Why does this suggest a lack of wave erosion? Is this what you might expect?

Stacks may be stranded on the newly exposed surface. Cliffs well inland may show former wave-cut features or sea caves. **Raised beaches** with marine deposits and sea-shells are found along many coastlines at similar heights. They all show the extent to which the sea-level has fallen or the land has emerged.

Coral formations

A general rise in sea-level since the last Ice Age has resulted in thick coral formations in tropical waters. Two organisms, corals and algae, grow together, especially in clear warm waters above 20°C. They need light and so develop just below the

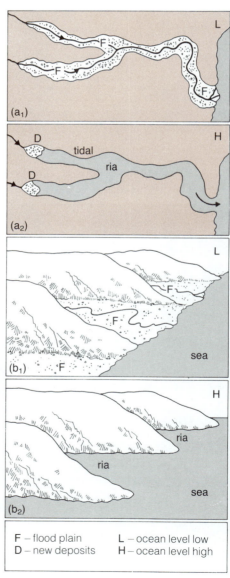

4.12 Rias result from the drowning of river valleys. Their shape may be governed by the landforms (b_1; b_2).

P 4.9 A raised beach (A–B) on Rhodes island. Notice the weathering cliff (W), high above wave attack. What signs are there of present wave action? Cusps (C) have been formed in debris (D) below the beach face.

surface. They secrete hard calcium carbonate which eventually builds up coral **fringing reefs** on shallow off-shore shelves along coasts. Sometimes they form **barrier reefs** on shallow platforms away from the coast.

Reefs fringe many tropical islands. Where the rising sea has covered an island, the reefs may continue to grow upwards and outwards, forming a ring of pure coral. The rings are usually broken into separate coral islands, because of gaps in the original fringing reef. Such an island ring is called an **atoll**, and surrounds an inner lagoon. Seawards, the outer reef often drops to great depths, down the sides of the original island. Many atolls have formed on volcanoes rising from the ocean floor.

Drowned inlets

In many parts of the world the rising sea-level has drowned river valleys, forming **rias**, whose tidal waters extend far inland. As these become deeper towards the sea, and are sheltered by the old valley sides, they frequently make good harbours.

Along some coasts the hills and vales are at right angles to the shore. As the rising waters drown the valleys, they create finger-like headlands, like those in south-west Ireland. Where the sea breaks into valleys parallel with the shore, the ranges between them form lines of islands, as along the Adriatic coast of Dalmatia (Yugoslavia).

The rising ocean has also drowned the deep angular valleys carved by glaciers in coastal mountains and plateaus, as in Norway and the South Island of New Zealand. These long **fiords** provide useful routeways into mountainous country. Valley deepening is usually greatest where the ice is thickest, so that fiords tend to be very deep in their middle valley and become shallower towards the mouth (p. 52).

Fiords illustrate again water's ability to change the landscape in different ways. In this case it was the *energy* of moving ice which eroded these long, steep-sided valleys.

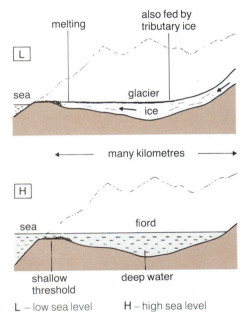

4.14 Rising sea-level creates a fiord.

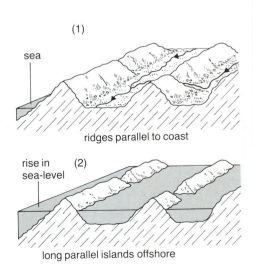

4.13 Rising sea-level creates a 'Dalmatian' type of coast.

P 4.10 The drowned valley system of Milford Haven, south Wales, provides deep water for tankers to berth and supply oil storage depots and refineries (p. 136).

Reasons for sea-level fluctuations

There are many reasons why the sea-level changes. **At the onset of an ice-age water becomes locked in the form of ice, so that sea-level falls world-wide.** During the last ice-age Britain was linked to mainland Europe, and America to Asia, across what is now the Bering Strait.

To some extent, **the great weight of ice depresses the landmass beneath, so countering the falling sea-level.** As the ice melts, the landmass tends to rise again; but so, of course, does the sea-level.

Plate collisions and physical forces in the earth itself also cause both slow and rapid upheavals of the surface. There are thus many reasons why a local coastline may show signs either of drowning or of emergence from the sea.

4.5 Glaciation and the energy of moving ice

Ice accumulates

Under cold conditions, in polar regions and on high mountains, snow collects in hollows and builds up on reasonably level surfaces. If, over a given period, more snow falls than can melt, it will obviously accumulate.

In many places each winter brings more snow than can melt during the year. As it builds up, the new falls press down on the underlying snow and compact its crystals. Some crystals melt under the

P 4.11 The Athabasca glacier in the Canadian Rockies. Moraine from the now shrunken tributary glaciers (T) mingles with the lateral moraine (M) of the main glacier. The snout (S) once extended further forward over the worn debris-covered surface (W).

pressure, and then re-freeze into an ice mass. Increasing pressure removes air from between the crystals, so that the underlying mass becomes pure ice. The less compacted upper ice, with air spaces, is known as **firn** or **neve**.

How glacial ice moves

It takes many years for a large mass of pure ice to accumulate. Like liquid water, **it has potential energy, because of its altitude** (see p. 29). If it can overcome the friction of the rocky surface, it will slide down-slope, with energy of motion sufficient to re-model the hillsides and valleys.

The actual down-slope movement is

slow compared with water. It is mostly a *slipping* forward, though at times sudden surges occur. **Pressure lowers the melting point of ice**, so under the ice-mass there is usually water. However, most of it comes from other sources. In summer melt-water runs over the surface. It finds its way through cracks and down the sides, and feeds streams under the ice. Such water helps the ice slip forward.

Within the glacier, individual ice grains move in such a way that the ice *flows*. As in a river, the flow is checked by friction at the sides and near the bed. The quickest movements are in the centre, near the surface. **Like the river, its great energy, aided by tools of erosion, can tear and wear away surface features and transport material.**

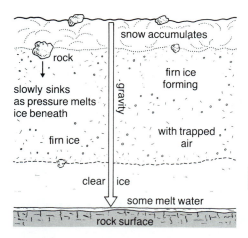

4.15 Snow turns to ice, and firn ice forms. Pressure on the ice raises its melting point: rocks sink in, and melt water is formed beneath the ice mass.

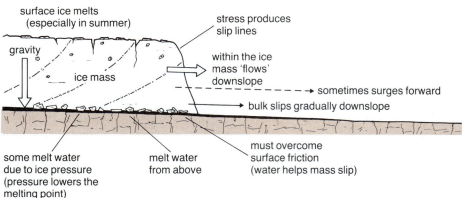

4.16 Glacier ice moves by flowing, though a whole mass may suddenly move along a slip-line.

4.6 Glacial energy and erosion

Speed of movement – rate of melting

Huge icefields can build up on surfaces among the peaks of very high mountains. They feed valley glaciers – great rivers of ice moving slowly down existing valleys. Ice also forms in high hollows and may flow down tributary valleys.

The speed of movement of valley glaciers varies according to the supply of ice, the angle of slope, and the rate of melting. The ice is continually moving forward until it reaches **a point where the rate of melting balances the rate of supply from upstream.** Here the **snout** of the glacier can advance no further.

Ice in Alpine glaciers moves at a mean rate of about 100 m a year, though ten times as fast on steep slopes. There are very steep glaciers in New Zealand's Southern Alps. These move down so quickly and continuously from the high icefields that their snouts lie amid the mild fern forests of the west coast.

Transporting debris

Fig. 4.19 shows the cross-section of a valley glacier. **Frost shattering and rock-falls** from exposed valley sides slither a large amount of angular debris onto the upper surface of the glacier. This is then carried along by the ice. Most of it remains at the sides of the glacier; though where glaciers meet, their lines of debris join to form a mass of material in the middle of the main glacier. Debris transported by the ice is called **moraine**.

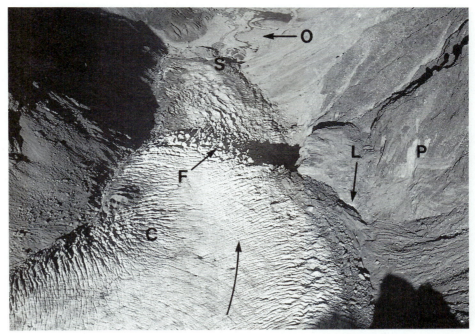

P 4.12 The lower part of the Fox glacier, New Zealand, showing crevasses (C), an ice fall (F), lateral moraine (L), ice-plucked walls (P), and outwash (O) below the snout (S) – once much further down-valley.

Why is there such a large supply of debris from the valley sides in mountain country? Describe the processes which cause this.

Water gets into cracks in the valley sides and in the rocky bed beneath the glacier. This alternately freezes and melts as the ice pressure varies and so loosens rocks, which may be plucked away by the glacier (Fig. 4.19). **Glacial valleys show scars where great blocks have been removed.**

There is also debris beneath the ice: a mixture of angular boulders and rocky material ground down to finer particles. This, too, scratches and abrades the rock surface.

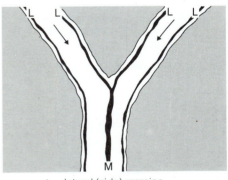

L – lateral (side) moraine
M   medial moraine

4.18 Lines of debris at the sides join to form a mass of moraine in the middle.

Ice tributaries

The high hollows where snow and firm ice accumulate are deepened by erosion as the clear ice rotates forwards. In time, a typical, deep semi-circular hollow, known as a **corrie**, or **cirque**, is formed. The headwall behind it is steepened as rock is plucked away. Eventually adjoining corries may be separated only by steep ridges called **arêtes**. Sometimes corrie headwalls are eroded back into a mountain from all sides, finally leaving a **pyramid peak**, like the Matterhorn in the Alps.

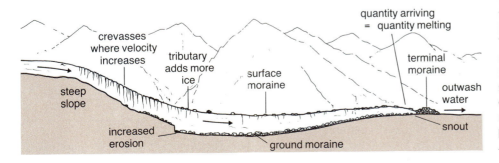

4.17 Profile of a glacier. Notice where a tributary adds to the weight. The ice at the snout is melting so fast that ice arriving from higher up cannot advance further.

P 4.13 New Zealand's Franz Josef glacier. Ice-plucked walls shed debris onto the glacier. In the foreground outwash gravel covers the floor of wide valley, eroded when the glacier extended almost to sea-level.

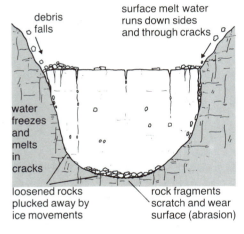

4.19 The energy of the glacier plucks away loosened slabs of rock. Sharp fragments wear the surface.

P 4.14 The pyramid peak of Mt. Tasman in New Zealand's Southern Alps, with snow-filled corries separated by arête ridges. What helps to make such high mountain scenery so angular?

A glacier, fed by a high icefield, begins to slip forward down-valley. Where the gradient steepens, deep **crevasses** open out across the ice. Why is this? What may cause such crevasses to close up further down?

Deep crevasses also open up at bends in the valley. Where would you expect this to happen – at the inside or outside of the bend?

Erosion and deposition

As the large glaciers flow through existing valleys, they transform the upper parts, eroding any interlocking spurs and so creating steep-sided troughs with a broad U-shape (Fig. 4.21). The spurs themselves are worn back (truncated).

After the ice has gone, such valleys clearly show a **break of slope (B)**, where the angle of the previous valley sides was steepened by erosion. The flat valley floor is usually covered by the remains of moraine (**M**). This may be overlain by alluvium (**A**) spread by a river which now occupies the enlarged valley.

The trenches carved by tributary glaciers are left as **hanging valleys (H)** high above the trough deepened by the main valley glacier. From these, streams plunge down as waterfalls (**W**), and build up a fan of alluvial deposits (**F**) where they hit the valley floor.

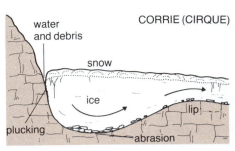

4.20 A hollow deepened by the rotating ice, its back wall steepened by freeze-thaw and plucking by ice frozen to the rock.

Fig. 4.17 shows the long profile of a glaciated valley. It is deepest in mid-valley, where tributaries increase the weight of ice. It then shallows to where, at the furthest extent of the snout, debris piles up as a **terminal (end) moraine**. Melt-water washes much of this angular, crushed material further down-valley.

The profile of a glaciated valley shows that it suddenly becomes deeper *downstream* of a tributary glacier. What causes this?

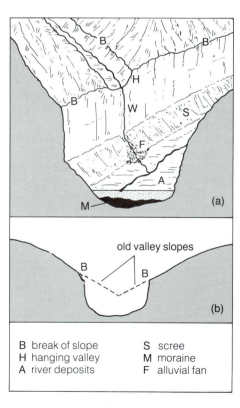

4.21 The slopes of the once-glaciated valley show where spurs formerly projected. Its present U shape is modified by screes, moraine and alluvial deposits.

P 4.15 A deep crevasse in the Athabasca glacier where a tributary's extra energy increased the slope of the floor down-valley.

THE LAST ICE AGE

where the ice accumulated

how it moved

covered by ice sheets

huge end moraines

ice sheet limit

ice sheet limit

4.23 Ice sheets moved outward from their northern source regions, advancing and retreating and finally shrinking. High mountains further south were separate sources of ice; glaciers still linger there.

P 4.16 Outwash and water-sorted gravel below the snout and the terminal moraine.

Why are the middle parts of a glaciated valley usually the lowest?

Under warmer conditions, the snout retreats irregularly, leaving lines of moraine. Mounds may survive to show where the retreat was halted for a relatively long period. **Today long lakes often occupy the deepened middle parts of glaciated valleys**, and in some moraine helps to hold back the water.

In a once-glaciated valley, what would you look for to show how large the glacier was (its maximum height and length)?

P 4.17 Rocks once beneath the Franz Josef glacier show the effects of smoothing and plucking by ice moving from left to right. Similar wrenching and smoothing occur as great ice sheets grind their way forward over rocky surfaces beneath.

4.7 Ice sheet erosion and deposition

During the coldest periods of the last Ice Age, **ice sheets** covered much of northern Europe and North America, where they extended to just south of the Great Lakes. Thick ice sheets still cover much of Greenland and Antarctica.

Great masses of ice accumulate in these polar lands, with an enormous potential energy, and more slowly outwards, down-slope. The force of such thick, moving sheets causes them to override quite large obstacles. In Antarctica the sheets are over 2000 metres thick, and the frost-shattered tops of mountain ranges protrude, as **nunataks**, above the ice. Imagine the weight of this thickness of ice. **Beneath, the surface features are subjected to the great grinding movements of the ice and its mass of debris.**

Lowland areas of hard rock, in Finland and Canada for instance, show how ice sheets once ground deep hollows along the lines of faults and other weaknesses, so that today the surface bears thousands of lakes.

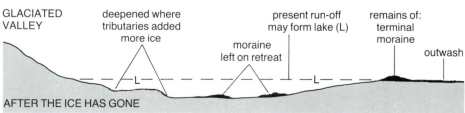

GLACIATED VALLEY — deepened where tributaries added more ice — moraine left on retreat — present run-off may form lake (L) — remains of: terminal moraine — outwash

AFTER THE ICE HAS GONE

4.22 Profile of a once-glaciated valley.

P 4.18 In south-west New Zealand the Waiho river cuts through the now wooded terminal moraine (TM) piled up by the Franz Josef glacier at its furthest extent. It divides into braids as it crosses outwash deposits (D) from the present glacier on the coastal plain. Beyond lies the Tasman Sea.

Streams which once flowed under the ice have left long ridges of rounded gravelly material, which they carried and deposited. Some of these winding **eskers** are over 100 metres high. Other ridges of glacial debris run at high angles to these – the end moraines of the ice sheets, now broken by water channels.

Outwash from ice sheets carried sediments into shallow lakes. When would most material have been deposited on the lake bed – in summer or winter? How would spring melt have affected this process? When would the coarsest material have been washed in?

It is possible to extract sedimentary deposits from lake beds and examine the layers (**varves**) left season by season and year by year. How can this indicate a time-scale for changes in climate and possible effects on the ice sheets?

Find out what you can about the use of tree-rings to indicate past climatic conditions and seasonal changes.

Elsewhere, low rocky obstacles which were over-ridden by the ice show how they were smoothed by erosion on the upstream side and steepened by plucking on the downstream face (Fig. 4.24). These are called **roches moutonées.** Some larger craggy masses protected the softer rocks in the lee. As ice movements steepened the upstream face, this produced a **crag and tail** effect.

During the recent Ice Ages masses of rock fragments were deposited in front of retreating ice sheets and much material was washed forward over the lowland.

The glacial debris forms a thick spread of very mixed particles, ranging from fine clay to large boulders – the deposit is known as **boulder-clay,** or **till**. Some of the till was deposited as swarms of small rounded hummocks (**drumlins**), streamlined by the ice, so that their long axis is parallel to the direction of ice movement (p. 57).

The melt-water outwash sorted out particles by size, so that braided water channels ran across a mixture of fine clay and accumulations of sands and gravels.

Many temperate parts of the world are covered with thick till and outwash deposits. Being of mixed origin, their minerals contain many nutrients for plants and so form rich soils for cultivation. In England the fertile grainlands of East Anglia are evidence of this; though close by are sandy/gravelly outwash areas which are infertile; their soils mostly support heath or coniferous plantations.

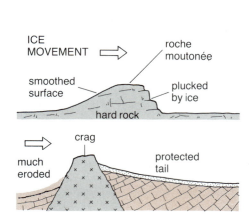

4.24 Low roches moutonées (like sheep lying down) and crag-and-tail hills show the direction of ice movement.

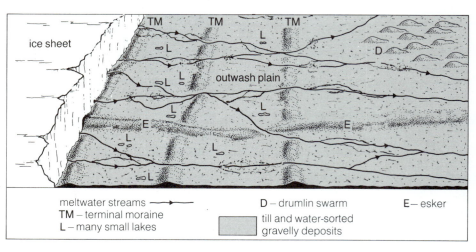

4.25 An ice sheet pours melt-water over the plain from which it has retreated. This sorts and washes forward loose particles. On the plain, winding eskers, lines of moraine, drumlins, and perhaps the features described in 4.24, show where the ice once was.

P 4.19 Ice-sheets, hundreds of metres thick, reach the Antarctic coast. Icebergs breaking away from ice cliffs have some nine-tenths of their bulk beneath the water.

P 4.21 A perched block of conglomerate rock (p. 60) – an erratic left by ice which moved over this now forested landscape of western Tasmania.

4.8 Conditions bordering the ice sheets

The northern lands which now border the polar ice show what conditions must have been like in those parts of Europe and North America *not* covered by ice sheets when the last Ice Age was at its maximum .

Fig. 4.26 shows these periglacial lands, where the ground is frozen throughout the year, except for a shallow surface layer which thaws during the short summer. In autumn this layer freezes again, from above and below. In Siberia the permanently frozen ground (**permafrost**) extends down for several hundred metres.

In winter networks of ice-filled cracks develop in the frozen surface. In summer the surface becomes boggy. Water seeps down cracks and into spaces in rocks. When it freezes again it builds up great **ice wedges**, and forms sub-surface **ice blocks (lenses)** which heave up the surface itself. Stones, too, are forced upwards and litter the ground. **The landscape is thus an uneven waste, with patterns of cracks and bulging mounds surrounded by stones, and summer swamps in the hollows.**

Traces of ice-crack patterns and heaved-up mounds can be seen in those parts of Europe and North America which were not directly glaciated; they often show up well in airphotos of lowland areas.

Vegetation is restricted to low herbaceous plants, using the unbroken sunlight of the short summer to form heath, with rushes and sedges in wet hollows, and mosses and lichens on rock surfaces.

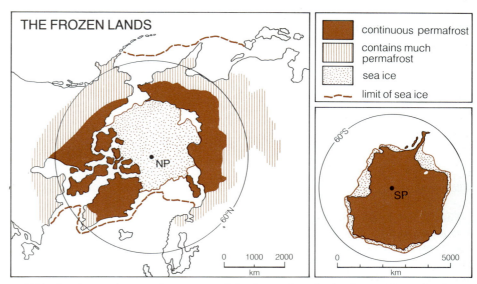

THE FROZEN LANDS

NP

SP

continuous permafrost
contains much permafrost
sea ice
limit of sea ice

4.26 Notice the northern polar ocean and the Antarctic polar landmass. Note also the extent of the permafrost areas in the continental interiors and the influences of the warmer oceans.

P 4.20 Kettle holes left in glacial deposits by the great ice sheet which covered these Canadian prairies, near Alberta.

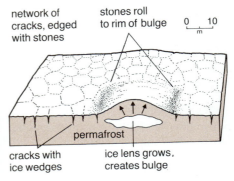

network of cracks, edged with stones

stones roll to rim of bulge

permafrost

cracks with ice wedges

ice lens grows, creates bulge

4.27 Surface bulging, cracks and patterns of stones produce the unevenness of much of the tundra lands.

Theme 4 Back-up section

Information from stranded particles

The shape, size and texture of stones, pebbles and boulders tell us a lot about the rocks they come from and the processes which formed them.

Stream energy causes its load of particles to collide, or dashes them against hard surfaces so that they fracture. In time the angles are smoothed off to a typical roundness . Along the shore pebbles roll and slide together with the swash and backwash. Collisions chip them and smooth corners. Size and roundness vary with the processes involved and the nature of the particles. Flowing water sorts out particles by size.

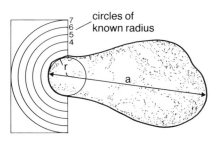

a – long axis
(maximum diameter)
r – radius of sharpest corner

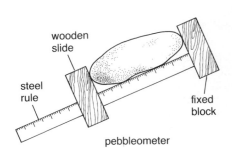

4.30 Rapid measurement of the long axis.

angular   rounded   well
rounded

4.28 Simple description.

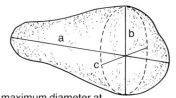

b – maximum diameter at
right angles to a – same plane
c – maximum diameter
at right angles to a/b plane

4.29 Description through measuring shapes.

Glacial ice detaches angular boulders and grinds down loosened materials. It also **transports frost-shattered debris.** The till dumped by ice sheets mantles the landscape long after the ice has gone. **The nature and position of its angular particles provide clues to the movements of ice sheets and glaciers.**

How to describe particles

We usually describe a boulder or pebble in terms of **size** and **roundness**, or **flatness**. We can do this visually, as in Fig. 4.28. For more precise descriptions we measure them.

1 Hold the pebble with its silhouette at a maximum (Fig. 4.29). Measure its greatest length – the long diameter (**a**).

2 Lay the pebble, the same side up, on a chart of concentric circles. Estimate the radius of the sharpest curve (**r**)

3 Find **Cailleux's Roundness Index (R)**:

$$R = \frac{2r}{a} . 1000$$

A spherical pebble will have the maximum roundness index of 1000. Repeat for all the pebbles in your sample and calculate the **mean roundness**.

Two other 'diameters' may be measured:
b the maximum diameter at right angles to **a** (in the same plane);
c the maximum diameter at right angles to this plane.
An **Index of Flatness (F)** may be calculated

$$F = \frac{a+b}{2c} . 100$$

The flatter the particle, the higher the value above 100.

Even the single measurement of the maximum diameter **a** can be useful for comparing pebble sizes at different sites.

Measurements are usually made with a pair of callipers or with a **pebbleometer** (Fig. 4.30). As you might sample more than 100 pebbles at a site, a coloured pen to identify those examined is useful. A tape, or a **quadrat** (a light rectangular wood frame) can be used to fix the sampling area.

How you describe your complete sample depends on what you are trying to find out. Besides the mean roundness or maximum diameter, you might produce **a bar chart to show the percentage of pebbles in chosen classes of roundness or length** (Fig. 4.31).

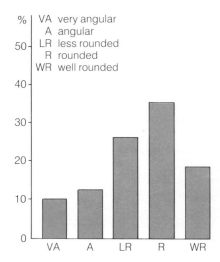

VA very angular
A angular
LR less rounded
R rounded
WR well rounded

4.31 The percentage of different pebble types in a sample.

Processes on a pebble beach

In all your studies identify, if possible, the rock type of your sample. Particles from different kinds of rock are different to start with (a flat shale, or a block of hard sandstone), and respond differently to particular treatment.

First make hypotheses about processes and their results, (a hypothesis is a statement of what seems likely). **Then test them by field observations, recordings and charts.** For instance:

(a) The roundness of pebbles (of the same rock type and size range) will increase in the direction of longshore drift.

(b) The roundness of pebbles (of the same rock type) will vary from the high water mark to the low water mark.

(c) Pebbles on storm beaches (with energetic wave action) will be rounder than those on other beaches.

(d) Pebbles in some size ranges will be rounder than in others (of the same rock type).

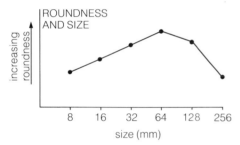

4.32 Roundness in various classes of pebble size.

Fig. 4.32 summarises the findings of several people on different beaches. If your own findings resemble these, you will have to consider why. For instance, will large pebbles be angular because they break into small fragments more easily, and will there therefore be more *small* angular fragments?

In tackling (b), think of how many things might make for roundness or angularity: material newly fallen from the cliff; a wide wave-cut platform; a shingle foreshore where pebbles roll and slide over each other. Is the average size of the waves worth considering?

Different groups can examine the characteristics of a beach profile. They will seek to identify different zones and the types of particle in each zone. Slope

measurements (p. 22) will provide the cross-section. **Particle size can then be related to the zones identified: breaker zone; swash zone; berm crest; storm ridge;** etc. Coarse or fine sand may be described by feel.

The sampling sites must be carefully chosen. To test (a) they should obviously be well spaced. For a beach profile sites might be chosen in the middle of each slope.

When studying the movement of beach material on the foreshore, pebbles coloured with waterproof paint may be placed among other similar size pebbles at low tide, and their position recorded. A search at the next low tide will probably show that many have disappeared, and that some have drifted to new positions.. The latter can be recorded, comparisons made, and causes considered.

Glacial drift

Sites where you can examine glacial drift are likely to be less accessible than the beaches – though glacial till covers very large areas of northern Europe. But glacial deposits can be examined in quarries, cuttings, cliffs, and river banks. Also, it may be possible to find several sites fairly close to one another. Permission is usually needed for digs to expose undisturbed material.

Where boulder clay is exposed, seek out fifty or more large, undisturbed stones. For each use a compass to find the direction of the long axis. For those

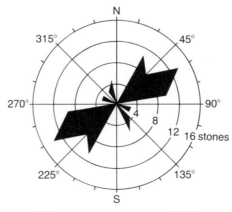

60 large stones lying mainly NE-SW

4.33 A plot shows that most large stones are lying with their long axis NE–SW. So in which directions did the ice move? Do you need further evidence?

exposed in a cutting, a plastic needle may be inserted over the long axis to allow the direction to be recorded more accurately. Of course if one end points north, the other points south. Whatever the bearing, **record the direction of both ends** (180° difference).

Group your measurements into classes of, say, 15°. Plot them on a **rose diagram** (Fig. 4.33), in proportion to the number of stones in each class. As shown, this indicates that most stones are aligned in two classes 180° apart. One of these is likely to be the direction in which the ice moved. Other information, perhaps from recording the orientation of drumlins (p. 54), or finding the origin of erratics, may help you decide.

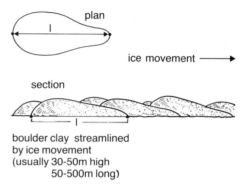

4.34 Moraine dumped by a vibrating ice sheet and shaped by ice movements.

Using sources of information

Investigations of this kind are practical on-the-spot exercises usually in a strictly limited time. So it is essential to have sufficient background information to put the work in a proper context.

Local public libraries, or institutes of higher education, should be able to provide **maps of solid geology and drift geology.** These are most helpful when planning investigations of glacial material, and when afterwards assessing your results, in the light of precise information about glaciated areas.

With shore surveys, **Ordnance Survey maps** of different scales can give much detail of coastal and shoreline features. But turn also to **historical maps** and look for **old photographs** – from History Societies, local newspapers, etc. Such data is useful for dating progressive changes, like the Dungeness deposits (Photo 8.3).

Theme 4 Making sure

1 'The current flows polewards/equator-wards; it is warm/cold.' Apply the appropriate descriptions to the following:

The Canaries Current flows.....; it is.... Also describe in this way the North Atlantic Drift; the Benguela Current; the Peru Current; and the Brazil Current.

2 (a) Where warm and cold currents meet, fog may be formed in the air above the cold waters. Explain why.

(b) Suggest why the seas off New-foundland are notoriously foggy.

3 Low coastlands are particularly at risk from floods due to a combination of (a) neap tides and offshore winds; (b) spring tides and onshore winds; (c) spring tides and offshore winds... which? Explain why.

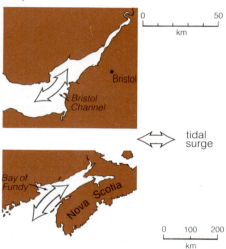

4.35 Two funnel-shaped tidal inlets.

4 Narrow inlets like the Bristol Channel and the Bay of Fundy (Nova Scotia) are funnel shaped. Suggest why they have a very large tidal range.

5 (a) On what kind of cliffs is wave erosion likely to be severe? (b) Under what conditions will erosion be most active? (Consider tides; waves; corra-sion; exposure.)

6 What kind of weathering processes are especially active on coastlands?

7 What kind of cliffs will be particularly affected by solution and corrosion ...those of (a) sandstone; (b) granite; (c) limestone; (d) clay?

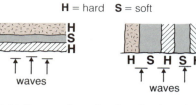

4.36 Coasts where hard and soft rocks alternate . . . either parallel with the shore (concordant), or at right angles to the shore (discordant).

8 'Hard rocks form headlands; soft rocks form bays.' On what type of coast is this most likely to be true, that shown in Fig. 4.36 (a) or that in (b)? Why?

9 Explain how the cove shown in Fig. 4.37 may have been formed. Account for its shape.

10 Look at Photo 4.22. The rock form-ing the headlands and the remains of headlands (**H**) is very different from that inland of it (**R**).

(a) Which is the most resistant to wave action, **H** or **R**?

(b) Explain how this has led to the for-mation of the coves, 1 and 2.

11 Why does cliff erosion lessen as the wave-cut platform increases in size? Explain in terms of energy and cliff pro-tection.

12 Many different shapes and sizes of rocks and pebbles are found on a beach. Where might they have come from originally? Explain why they are often distributed in zones you can recognise.

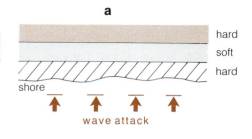

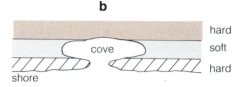

4.37 The results of wave attack on a concordant coast.

13 How does swash/backwash help to sort beach particles?

14 In what ways may a prevailing onshore wind affect coastal features?

15 In Fig. 4.38 a river reaches the sea through a cliffed coastland.

(a) Describe the nature of the deposits at **A**, **B**, **C**, **D** and **E**.

(b) Name features **B** and **E**.

(c) Explain the shape of **B**.

(d) Account for the direction of the current **F**.

(e) What role does **F** have in con-structing any of the features shown?

16 What features distinguish a ria from a fiord?

P 4.22 Coves near Lindos, Rhodes.

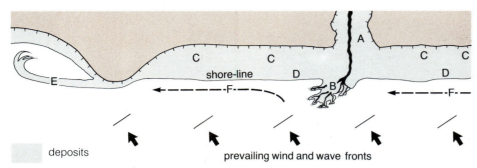

4.38

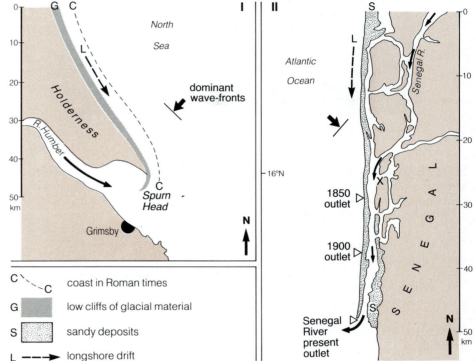

4.41 Water movements and temperature differences off Senegal.

17 Coral rock is a form of: (a) sediment; (b) limestone; (c) salt deposit; (d) sandstone? Which?

18 Is the term 'lagoon' in Fig. 4.11 used in the same sense as 'lagoon' described on p. 46? Explain how they differ in the ways they are formed.

19 Fig 4.39 shows how a groyne affects the amount of beach material. Explain what is happening. What effects may this have on the cliffs at **A** and **B**?

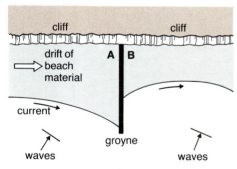

4.39

4.40 Spits form, though on different scales: I along Britain's North Sea coast; II along the West African coast of Senegal.

20 Fig. 4.40 shows two spits of different length – I. Spurn Head across the Humber; II. along the Senegal coast.

I (a) What shows that the Holderness coast is easily eroded? Why do you think this is?

(b) In which direction is eroded material transported?

(c) Sometimes temporary gravel banks appear off-shore. Suggest why.

(d) Explain the occurrence and shape of Spurn Head.

(e) The main Humber river channel has been forced southwards. Why?

II (a) What has been the average annual growth rate of the spit off the Senegal coast since 1850?

(b) **X** marks the fishing town, St. Louis. How will the spit have affected activities there? Suggest why settlements have spread westward over the spit.

(c) The north-east Trades prevail here; but each day westerly on-shore breezes set in. What is the cause?

(d) The westerly breezes boost the north-west wave swell. How will this affect (i) coastal currents (ii) deposition?

21 Fig. 4.41 shows the Trades blowing off-shore from the Senegal coast.

(a) How exactly does this make inshore waters cool?

(b) Fish abound here. What part does wind play in this?

22

INPUT → STORAGE → OUTPUT
The Glacier

(a) What are the nature of the inputs and outputs in a **glacial system**?

(b) **In a steady state**, input = output. What will be happening at the snout if this remains so for a long period? (Consider material transported.)

23 (i) Scratching and smoothing, and (ii) plucking, are processes of glacial erosion.

(a) How does a corrie reveal the effects of both processes?

(b) In what ways may the water beneath a glacier help each process?

24 Increasing pressure lowers/raises the melting point of ice; which?

P 4.23 Loch Avon in the Scottish Highlands.

Consider the terms used

Profile – an outline seen from the side.

Continental shelf – the gently sloping part of the continent covered by the sea; usually extending from the shoreline to some 200m depth, before sloping more steeply to ocean deeps.

Fetch is the ocean distance over which the wind blows to give height and energy to a wave.

Wavelength can be taken as distance between the wave crests.

A geo (hard 'g') is a long narrow inlet opened by wave attack along the line of weakness.

Coral is formed from colonies of innumerable soft polyps, each continuously depositing a hard calcium carbonate skeleton beneath.

Algae are minute, simple water plants with green chlorophyll. Some species help in reef building.

Conglomerate is a sedimentary rock of pebbles mixed with, and cemented by, limy sandstone.

Break of slope is a level on a hillside where the angle of slope suddenly changes.

Till is material deposited by glaciers and icesheets – varying in size from fine clay to boulders.

Drift is a mixture of till and materials sorted by glacial outwash.

Periglacial refers to areas bordering ice sheets, with typical seasonal freeze-thaw conditions.

Permafrost is permanently frozen ground, even though a top layer may thaw during summer.

25 In Photo 4.23 look carefully at the landscape about Loch Avon, in Scotland's northern Grampians.

(a) Identify features caused by ice erosion.

(b) Which features are due to other agents of erosion, now that the ice has gone?

(c) Which features are the results of present-day weathering?

26 After the ice has gone, the shape of the resulting 'U' valley is not entirely due to glacial erosion. What other processes affect its present shape?

27 (a) On what does the rate of movement of ice in a valley glacier depend?

(b) What may happen to the ice where the valley bed falls suddenly downstream?

(c) What may happen to the rate of ice movement where the valley narrows? With what result?

28 Moraine is transported by ice in different ways before being dumped at the snout: as surface moraine; as ground moraine (sub-glacial); as material embedded within the ice (englacial moraine).

(a) Explain the origin of each type.

(b) Why do they differ in quantity, shape and size?

(c) Will each be travelling forward at the same rate?

29 Glaciers can transport masses of rock and leave them stranded far from where they removed them. Such blocks are called **erratics**.

How might an erratic indicate the direction of movement of the ice?

30 What other evidence might you find in a lowland to indicate how an ice sheet moved across the countryside?

31 Many natural features result from (i) a concentration of energy, and (ii) a loss of energy. Which process, (i) or (ii), is particularly involved in the formation of (a) a delta; (b) a berm; (c) a river flowing through a narrowing channel? What occurs in each case?

32 As the rock of a valley floor is eroded away by a glacier it is replaced by ice. The weight of the ice pressing downwards is *less* than that of the rock removed. This causes cracks in the valley floor as the rock beneath *expands*. This may result in even greater erosion. Why?

33 (a) How do the following affect the thickness of snow cover likely to build up in particular parts of the world: latitude; altitude; relief; prevailing wind; distance from the sea; aspect?

(b) Which of these may account for the presence of great glaciers in Norway, the South Island of New Zealand, western Canada, and southern Chile?

Theme 5 Climates, soils, vegetation: the ecosystem

5.1 Energy for the ecosystem

What is an 'ecosystem'? *Eco* comes from the Greek for a 'living place'. So ecology is a study of the relationships between living organisms and everything that makes up the place they live in – the whole collection of plants, animals, and non-living substances. We and they are all part of the **ecosystem**.

The plants are the key, for they use the incoming energy from the sun to manufacture material for their nourishment and growth; from simple non-living substances they produce organic matter. They are **producers**, and may be eaten (consumed) by other living things.

Animals that eat plants – like the herbivores – are **primary consumers**. Those that eat other animals (carnivores) are **secondary consumers.** They are part of a **food-chain**.

If you run quickly, in what ways do you transfer energy to your environment?

The natural cycle is completed by organisms we call **decomposers** (mainly bacteria and fungi), that break down dead organic matter. They make much of it available again as nutrients which can be absorbed by other living organisms.

We ourselves are part of the cycle. We benefit by studying natural processes – what they do to us, and what we do to them.

5.2 People as part of the ecosystem

Later on we look at how people create settlements, farm and trade, and build up societies; and also at how, sadly, they pollute their environment. The parts we

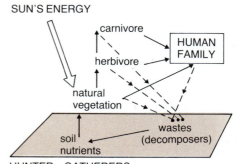

5.2 The soils, vegetation, and animal life absorb solar energy and exchange water and gases with the atmosphere.

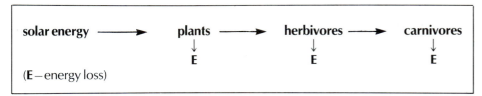

(**E** – energy loss)

Not all the energy absorbed from the sun by plants, and converted to mass, is transferred up the food-chain. **All plants and animals lose energy in respiration and movements (p. 94), so energy is lost at each stage.**

play in the ecosystem depend on how advanced our technology is.

Fig. 5.2 shows a simple system where people live by hunting and gathering natural produce. Those who cultivate the land become part of a more complex system, shown, simplified, in Fig. 5.3.

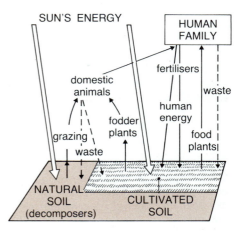

5.3 Even simple cultivation involves more exchanges of energy and chemical elements with the soil.

Plants, as well as animals, compete with each other for space, nutrients, and solar energy. When conditions, the climate in particular, don't change much, the various species achieve a natural balance. But when people clear an area, or their animals graze the vegetation, the balance is upset.

People tend to simplify the plant population. They encourage plants they find useful for grazing. They select particular plants for food. When they interfere with soils, they affect their mineral balance, and upset the relationships between small creatures and the soil they live in. If people are foolish, and take too many nutrients from the soil without replacing them, plant growth suffers. If they are wise, they try to create the most satisfactory balance they can through a suitable agricultural system.

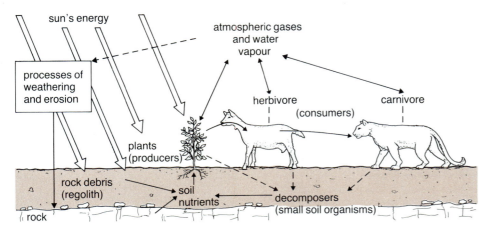

5.1 Continuous exchanges in the nutrient system.

SEA-LEVEL AIR TEMPERATURES (°C)

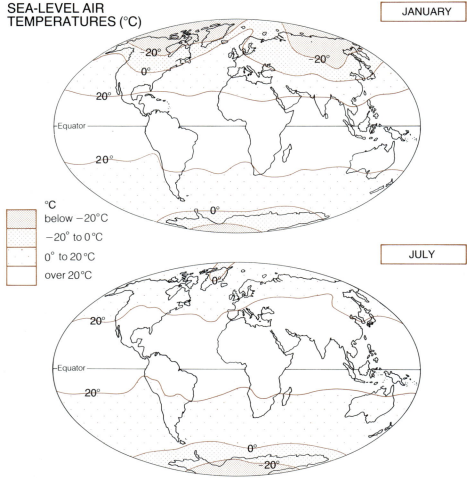

JANUARY

JULY

°C
below −20°C
−20° to 0°C
0° to 20°C
over 20°C

5.4 These mean air temperatures are as at sea-level. The actual temperatures in highlands and mountains vary with altitude. By ignoring the effects of relief we have a clearer picture of the effects of other influences, such as latitude, prevailing winds, and land and sea surfaces.

The use people make of the land depends very much on where they live. The climate is often a deciding factor. You have seen how the energy received from the sun varies with the latitude and seasons; and how the resulting wind system creates contrasting conditions in different parts of the world. As a starting point, therefore, look at the seasonal differences in air temperatures shown in Fig. 5.4.

5.3 Temperature differences in contrasting environments

The mean temperatures shown in Fig. 5.4 respond to the way the angle of the noonday sun decreases, from the low latitudes to the polar regions. They also indicate that land surfaces lose and gain heat more rapidly than the oceans. You can see that places in central Asia have bitterly cold winters; yet their summer temperatures are above average for the latitude. Notice also the contrasts

5.5 (below) Air circulates as part of distinct systems . . . between the tropics and sub-tropics, and in the temperate and polar zones. The Hadley cell is well established and the Trade Winds very regular. Polewards of 30° conditions are more variable. Notice especially the continental effects.

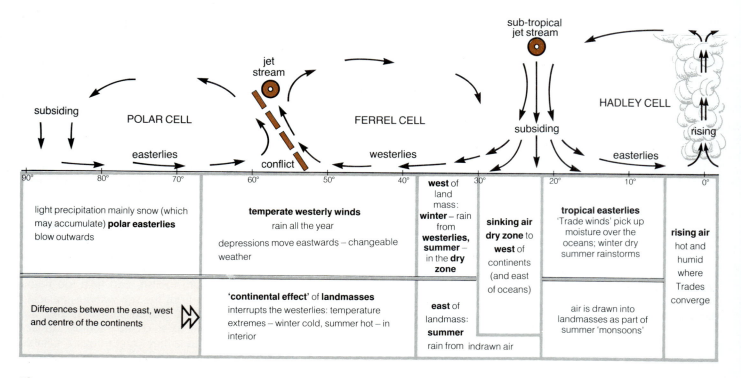

light precipitation mainly snow (which may accumulate) **polar easterlies** blow outwards	**temperate westerly winds** rain all the year	**west** of land mass: **winter** – rain from **westerlies, summer** – in the **dry zone**	**sinking air dry zone** to **west** of continents (and east of oceans)	**tropical easterlies** 'Trade winds' pick up moisture over the oceans; winter dry summer rainstorms
				rising air hot and humid where Trades converge
	depressions move eastwards – changeable weather			
Differences between the east, west and centre of the continents	**'continental effect' of landmasses** interrupts the westerlies: temperature extremes – winter cold, summer hot – in interior	**east** of landmass: **summer** rain from indrawn air		air is drawn into landmasses as part of summer 'monsoons'

between the northern and southern hemisphere. **Consider the following:**

(a) Which surface heats up and loses heat more quickly – land or sea?

(b) Which hemisphere has the greater land surface?

(c) Why do the isotherms mostly run east-west? Find where they do not do so. Consider why.

(d) Look at the January map (*northern winter*): why is there such a great loss of heat from the north-eastern parts of North America and central Asia? What factors affect this besides the low angle of the sun?

(e) Consider the winter temperatures in northern Norway: why are they *above* freezing point on average? See Fig. 4.1, and (a) above.

(f) Look at the July map (*northern summer*): suggest why temperatures in central Asia average well above those of France, on the same latitude.

(g) Why should the greater part of the southern hemisphere show such relatively small differences between summer and winter?

(h) Notice how the 20°C isotherm trends northwards along the west coast of both South America and South Africa. Suggest why this should be. (See Fig. 4.1.)

(i) Where will people have to cope with intense cold throughout the year?

(j) Where will complete winter freeze be followed by a ground thaw above the permafrost (Fig. 4.26)? Suggest what difficulties this may cause.

(k) Can we assume that conditions in the lower latitudes, with mean temperatures above 20°C throughout the year, will necessarily favour agriculture and a comfortable way of life? Consider droughts, excessive rainfall, and other conditions which make life less than easy.

5.4 Wind systems and patterns of rainfall and drought

The circulation of the atmosphere, as you have seen, is closely connected with the temperatures differences shown in Fig. 5.4. Look at the pattern of winds in Figs. 5.6 and 5.7. In general, those which blow across the sea pick up moisture and may

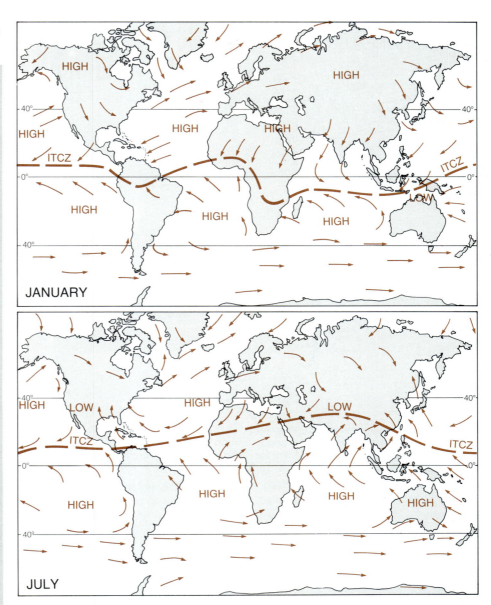

5.6 *Seasonally prevailing winds. Look carefully at the seasonal differences – particularly the movement of the zone (ITCZ) in which the Trade Winds converge towards the hottest land areas. Notice the more permanent influence of sinking air in the sub-tropics, and the pressure conditions due to extreme temperatures (the 'thermal' highs and lows).*

provide rain; while those from dry land areas are less likely to do so.

Moisture-bearing winds, or the lack of them, affect the whole environment – the rate of rock weathering, the soils, the vegetation, the agriculture, and the way people live.

Now follow carefully the circulation of the atmosphere shown in cross-section in Fig. 5.5. Notice how in certain latitudes the surface air rises high into the atmosphere – reaching the upper part of the troposphere – while in others it sinks towards the surface. Rising air expands and cools; sinking air is compressed and warms.

These vertical movements are accompanied by regular air-flows (winds) at surface level. **As shown in Fig. 5.6, winds blow from a certain direction in particular latitudes in particular seasons**. However, they can still vary in direction from day to day, especially in temperate latitudes.

You can also see that there are separate circulations in the tropics, polar regions and middle latitudes.

(a) **Look first at the low latitudes** where the Trade Winds converge. They carry moisture from the oceans. As the air rises, especially over hot surfaces, it expands and cools. But the rate of cooling is checked by the heat given out as its water

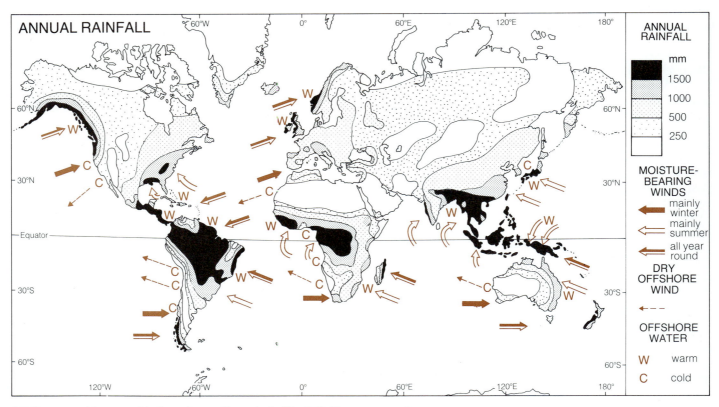

5.7 Compare this map with that of prevailing winds (Fig. 5.6). You can see where
moisture-bearing winds are onshore and where dry offshore winds are dominant.
Notice the effects of distance from the oceans and protection by high mountain ranges.

vapour condenses into droplets (p. 66).
This extra heat energy carries the moist air
even higher. Towering cumulus clouds
develop, and there is frequent heavy rain,
especially during the afternoons.

High in the troposphere this air turns
towards the poles and becomes a westerly flow (p. 5).

(b) **In the sub-tropics** the strong upper
air westerlies (the sub-tropical jet stream
– STJ) prevent further high-level flow
towards the poles. **Here the air sinks
back to the surface.** So, to the west of the
landmasses a blanket of warm, dry air
gives rise to the great deserts. (Look back
to Fig. 1.13.)

(c) At the surface much of this air
returns towards the equator as the easterly Trade Winds, completing the
Hadley cell. These are dry at first, but pick
up moisture from the oceans.

(d) **In the middle latitudes** the surface
air flows polewards, as the westerlies.
These bring much moisture to the western parts of the continents.

(e) **On the western parts of the continents, about latitude 35°**, are the so-
called **Mediterranean lands**. These are in-
between zones – influenced by sinking air
in the summer, but by the moist westerlies
in winter.

(f) **Over the polar regions** the cold,
dense air tends to sink to the surface and
flow outwards, meeting the westerlies
over the oceans. There, in the middle
latitudes these cold polar easterlies clash
with the warmer westerlies. They swirl
about the **lows (depressions)** which move
eastwards, bringing belts of rain with
them (Fig. 5.14).

(g) Within these lows the air rises once
more, high into the troposphere.

Look at the pattern of winds in
Fig. 5.6. In view of the above, which
winds are *not* what you might expect
in their particular latitude?

Account for the description HIGH
and LOW air pressure in specific
places on the seasonal maps (Fig. 5.6).
How do the winds circulate about
these areas? Where do they disrupt the
pattern described in (a)–(h) above?

**There are many reasons why other air
movements interrupt the broad pattern.**
In winter cold dense air flows *outwards*
from the bitterly cold interior of the northern continents. In summer this wind
direction is reversed as moist monsoon
winds blow *into* the southern and eastern
parts of the heated landmasses. Other

parts of the world also experience seasonal wind changes: look at West Africa.

Also, the converging Trade Winds do
not always meet each other in the
equatorial zone, as shown in Fig. 5.6. In
a sense, the meeting place of these tropical easterlies 'follows the sun'. Just as the
latitude of the overhead noonday sun
varies with the seasons, so does the location of the hot zone in which the Trades
converge.

**In Fig. 5.6 the position of this zone of
inter-tropical convergence (ITCZ) is
indicated by a broken line.** You can see
how it trends towards the strongly heated
parts of the continents.

5.5 Where the rain falls; and why

The pattern of all these air flows is shown
in Fig. 5.6, and you can see the distribution of precipitation and the seasonal positions of the moisture-bearing winds in
Fig. 5.7.

Now although moisture may be carried
over land surfaces by the wind, it does not
necessarily bring rainfall.

A given volume of hot air and cold air
may each contain the *same mass* of water

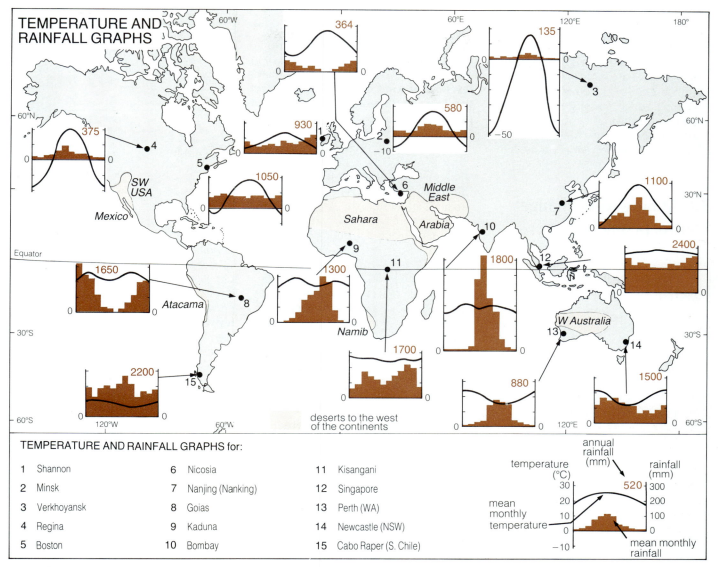

TEMPERATURE AND RAINFALL GRAPHS

TEMPERATURE AND RAINFALL GRAPHS for:

1	Shannon	6	Nicosia	11	Kisangani
2	Minsk	7	Nanjing (Nanking)	12	Singapore
3	Verkhoyansk	8	Goias	13	Perth (WA)
4	Regina	9	Kaduna	14	Newcastle (NSW)
5	Boston	10	Bombay	15	Cabo Raper (S. Chile)

5.8 Look carefully at each graph which shows the mean monthly temperatures and rainfall for selected climatic stations, and their mean annual rainfall. More detailed examples of their climate, soils and vegetation is given in the sample regions on pp. 79–81.

vapour, yet have *different* **relative humidity** (p.88). If the cold air is chilled only slightly, it may become saturated with water vapour, so that droplets condense out (droplets → cloud → rain). This would not happen in the hot air; for this can carry a much greater mass of water vapour without condensation occurring (see Fig. 5.51). Thus moist air blowing into a hot desert region may not be sufficiently chilled to create rain-giving clouds.

But there are other causes of frequent rainfall in various parts of the world:

(a) Over most of the tropics, and in the continental interiors, rain falls mainly in the hottest part of the year. **Convection** updraughts carry moist air high into the atmosphere and heavy downpours occur.

In the convection process air is heated by the surface and expands. It becomes less dense than the surrounding air, so it rises like a bubble or balloon.

(b) Air from different sources, with different temperatures, may clash. Hot moist air will tend to rise over cold, denser air, and, on cooling, cause condensation, cloud and rain.

This is a source of winter rain and snow in eastern China, where cold, out-blowing continental air meets warmer air over the coastlands.

(c) As you have seen, a similar clash between cold polar air and warm tropical air occurs over oceans in the temperate zone, causing swirling **depressions.** These move eastwards over the surface, carrying their rain belts along with them (p. 68).

(d) Where moist on-shore winds rise

over near-coastal mountains, the air expands and cools. Condensation brings heavy **relief rainfall** close to the crests. Places to the sheltered, lee side of the mountains are usually considerably drier (**in the rain-shadow**) – for the descending air warms, and can hold more moisture as vapour.

With these points in mind, look at Fig. 5.7. With the help of an atlas find an example of:

(i) a mountainous coast where prevailing westerlies and eastward-moving depressions bring exceptionally heavy rain.

(ii) a rain-shadow area, inland of a zone with particularly high rainfall.

(iii) a land with little precipitation, but so cold that snow accumulates year after year.

(iv) an arid region which owes its dryness partly to distance from the ocean, and partly to shelter from mountains.

Fig. 5.7 shows that many parts of the world receive less than 250 mm of precipitation a year. Some of these remain arid deserts, while others are green swampy sedge country during early summer. Point to examples of each, and explain why they are so different. Think in terms of temperature and evaporation.

5.6 Where wind changes control people's lives

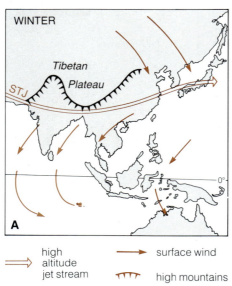

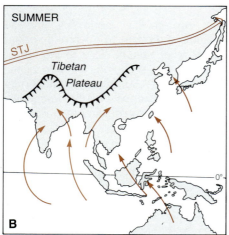

5.9 Notice how the southerly winds of the wet summer monsoons are replaced by outflows of dry, sinking air from the jet stream (now south of the Himalayas) and by air from the cold thermal high over central Asia.

The monsoons

We have already seen that seasonal **monsoon** changes are experienced in several parts of the world. **Fig. 5.9 shows reversals of wind direction which affect the lives of thousands of millions of people.**

A shows that in **winter** the familiar Trade Wind flow is established over India. Notice the position of the subtropical jet (STJ). Why should this mean that there is dry sinking air just south of the Himalayas, and that most of India remains dry during the winter months?

Suggest why Sri Lanka receives quite a lot of rain during the northern winter months. (How do winter temperatures in Sri Lanka compare with those of northern Europe?)

Why are the winter winds over northern China from the west? Why is there often snow as they approach the coast?

B In early summer the northern plains of India and Pakistan are very hot indeed. Even the high Tibetan plateau is much warmer than one might think. The subtropical jet is now north of the Himalayas; so Tibet and neighbouring parts of China remain very dry. **But in the south moist air from the Indian and Pacific Oceans is drawn into the hot land areas**, bringing monsoon rain, especially to sea-facing hills and coastal lowlands. From late May to September series of storms within this great inflow of moist air give periods of very heavy rain.

The whole pattern of life in India depends on these changes and the precise time they take place. The expected arrival of the rain in southern India is within a few days of the end of May. By this time seedlings for the summer crops must be established in the ground, using carefully stored water: if the monsoon is too early, torrential rain can wash them out of the soil; it its too late, they shrivel and die. Summer rice must be followed with crops able to stand the winter droughts – grains such as millet, for instance.

Local winds

Monsoons are large-scale, continental wind changes. But local wind reversals

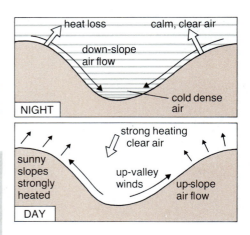

5.10 Valley winds during otherwise calm conditions.

also occur. In hilly country, even on still days, **a downslope night wind** may develop, but give way to an **up-slope, up-valley wind by day**. At night heat is lost from high valley slopes. They chill the air in contact, so that it contracts, and sinks to the valley floor. This can cause cold, misty conditions, or even frosts (which may not suit sensitive plants or fruits). On a sunny day air currents tend to move upslope from the heated valley floor.

The different responses of land and water to heating can produce a strong **sea-breeze** on an otherwise still day, and create a more gentle **land-breeze** at night (Fig. 5.11).

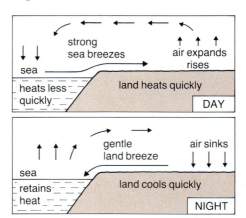

5.11 Sea-breezes and land-breezes.

We have seen that land in the lee of mountains may be relatively dry. This sheltering effect can be exaggerated by the exceptional warmth of any sinking air. **When air moves in from the sea, up and over a mountain range, it expands and cools as it rises.** The rate at which its temperature falls (lapses) is called its **lapse rate**. This is about 1.0°C per 100 m for *unsaturated* (dry) air. But when its water vapour condenses to droplets it gives out

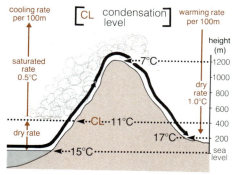

5.12 The Föhn wind. Note that unsaturated air is described as 'dry'.

heat, which slows the rate of cooling. The lapse rate is only about 0.5°C per 100m in *saturated* air. **When the air crosses the range it sinks again and warms at the faster (dry) rate.** Fig. 5.12 shows how this so-called **Föhn wind** reaches the inland plains at a higher temperature.

5.7 Changeable weather conditions

We all know how much day-to-day changes affect our lives. Weather conditions are particularly variable in the broad zone of the westerlies, which lies between the warm, sinking air of the sub-tropics and the cold polar easterlies. The clashes between these warm and cold air masses can create swirls of wind and belts of rain. These tend to move eastwards and affect lands far from their place of origin.

Where depressions form

Where the air masses meet, the lighter, warmer air rises over the cold, denser air, which pushes in beneath it at the surface. The lighter over-riding air causes a fall in air pressure at the surface, so that swirls begin (Fig. 5.13).

Air seeks to move in and fill up this 'low'. But the force of the earth's rotation deflects it, so that it circulates about the centre of low pressure and only gradually moves in towards the heart of this so-called **depression**, where the air rises.

Not all swirls develop into depressions; but in certain places conditions encourage them to deepen. As they do so the pressure contours (**isobars**) appear as in Fig. 5.14. The front of the cold air is shown as ▲▲▲ and the front of the warm air as ●●● . The standard pressure at sea-level is one **bar** (1000 millibars).

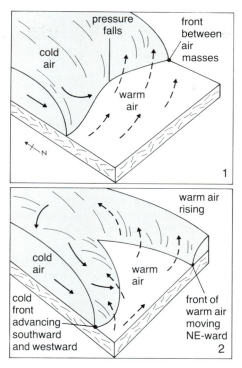

5.13 In 1 the clear front between cold air advancing southwards and the flow of warm, moist air is disturbed. As the warm air rises over cold, the pressure falls. In 2 cold air is rapidly pushing southward and eastward, and in general air is circulating about the centre of low pressure. Warm air rises over cold air at the warm front, which moves eastward, but more slowly than the cold front (see Fig. 5.18).

How the upper air affects surface pressure

The conditions which enable depressions to deepen are related to the flow of the high, strong westerlies, the Polar Jet

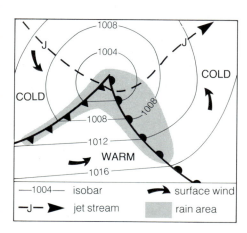

5.14 A surface depression (low) in the northern hemisphere. Air circles anti-clockwise as it flows towards the centre. There it rises high into the atmosphere, and may be drawn into the jet stream.

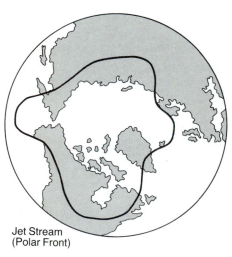

Jet Stream (Polar Front)

5.15 Typical large waves (Rossby waves) in the westerly flow of the polar jet stream. Smaller, tighter waves within the larger ones cause the convergence/divergence seen in Fig. 5.16.

Stream (p. 62). These winds stream around the globe in great waves (partly caused by deflections as they cross ranges like the Rocky Mountains). Smaller loops develop; and on the outer part of a loop the

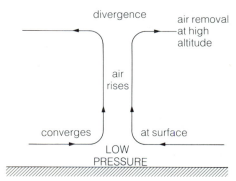

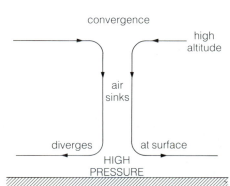

5.16 (top) Upper air divergence favours the development of a surface depression and causes it to deepen. (bottom) High level convergence, with sinking air, creates an anticyclone at the surface.

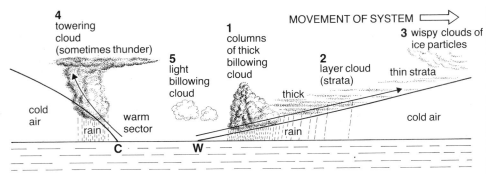

4 towering cloud (sometimes thunder)

5 light billowing cloud

MOVEMENT OF SYSTEM

1 columns of thick billowing cloud

3 wispy clouds of ice particles

2 layer cloud (strata) thin strata

thick

cold air

warm sector

cold air

rain

rain

C   W

5.17 *At the cold front* **C** *warm air rises above colder air advancing at the rear of the depression, causing heavy rain. At the warm front the warm air rises up a slope of about 1:40. Its water vapour condenses at various levels and at great heights forms ice particles.*

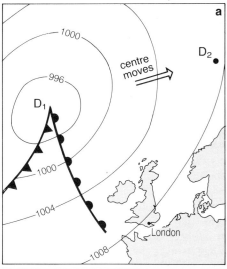

5.18 *In (a) a depression centred at* **D₁** *moves in a few hours to* **D₂***. In (b) a cold front advances so rapidly that it occludes the warm air, giving a single rain belt which dies out.*

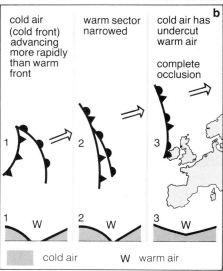

cold air (cold front) advancing more rapidly than warm front

warm sector narrowed

cold air has undercut warm air

complete occlusion

cold air   W warm air

fast-moving air accelerates and draws up air from below. This favours the development of a depression at the surface. Fig. 5.16 shows, in section, how the air moves into a **low** at ground level.

Where the fast-moving upper air stream slows, it allows air to sink to the surface. Sinking air creates a high pressure **anticyclone,** which brings settled weather conditions.

Our surface weather is thus guided by the position of these great waves in the upper atmosphere. They can maintain their own general pattern for long periods, and so affect our seasonal weather conditions.

Weather associated with a depression

As the depressions deepen and move eastwards, they bring cloud and belts of rain with them. Fig. 5.17 shows a section through this weather system.

At the warm front (**W**) the warm, moist air rises over the cold air. Condensation produces thick, towering cloud and rain (1). This gives way higher up to cloud sheets (strata), appearing as grey layers from the ground. Ahead, at a great height, condensation produces long, wispy streaks of ice particles ('Mares' tails').

At the cold front (**C**) at the rear of the depression, the cold air pushes under the warm air, which rises even more steeply. Towering cloud masses develop, often with thunder and heavy rain (4).

As the depression approaches, a person would first see 'Mares' tails' high in the sky; then thickening strata with drops of rain. This would give way to steady rain from lower billowing cloud. The skies would then clear, the temperature rise, and smaller clouds appear.

Finally, the shorter, heavy downpour at the cold front would be followed by clearer, colder air behind the depression.

The clouds have descriptive names: **stratum** – a layer; **cirrus** – feather-like; **cumulus** – billowing (cauliflower-like); **nimbus** – a rain cloud. Moderately high clouds sometimes start with **alto–**.

In Fig. 5.17, which of the cloud types 1-5 might you describe as : alto-stratus; cumulus; cirrus; cumulonimbus?

Fig. 5.18 (a) shows an eastward-moving depression at **D₁**, whose centre will pass just north of the British Isles. What is the wind direction in London? From what direction will Londoners find the wind blowing when the centre has reached **D₂**?

Describe the sequence of weather which Londoners will experience as the depression moves from **D₁** to **D₂**. (Fig. 5.23 gives a more complete picture of an eastward-moving low.)

P 5.1 *Sunshine and clear cold air over Vancouver follow rolls of cumulus and heavy rain at the cold front of a depression passing away inland.*

Sometimes the cold air, advancing more rapidly at the rear of a depression, completely undercuts the warm air, so that it underlies the whole warm sector. The front is then said to be **occluded** and is shown thus ▲▲ ▲▲ . Rain near the front may continue for some time as the depression dies out.

Anticyclones and still conditions

The sinking air which builds up the high-pressure **anticyclones** contains little water vapour. It is heated by compression, and brings periods of hot, dry weather in summer. In winter, however, the sinking air may trap cold air above a moist, or frosty surface. This leads to still, but foggy conditions. In still air water droplets form most readily about the billions of tiny nuclei in the atmosphere, such as dust, smoke, or salt particles.

Until the *Clean Air Act of 1956* controlled smoke released from open fires, British households emitted 85 per cent of the total smoke in the local atmosphere. Why up to that time was London notorious for 'pea soup' fogs? In which months, and under what conditions, would they have been at their worst?

P 5.2 Stable sinking air of the sub-tropical high keeps this part of Eritrea (northern Ethiopia) very dry. Sometimes moist air over the Red Sea causes cloud in the eastern valleys; but, as you see, it disappears inland.

Weather from different airmasses

The British Isles owes its changeable weather partly to the characteristics of air moving in from different sources. The main source of air through the year is the warm, moist *Tropical Maritime* air from the southern parts of the Atlantic. But Fig. 5.19 shows that Britain can receive cold moist air from the Arctic (*Polar Maritime* air) at almost any time of the year. In winter it may be in the freezing grip of cold, dry air moving out of Euro-Asia (*Polar Continental* air). While occasionally during summer hot, dry air comes from the south and south-east (*Tropical Continental* air).

Where else in the world are there similar changeable climates, where one type of air can be replaced by another with quite different properties? Identify one such region and point out where the different types of air might come from.

Where is the source of the *Polar Continental air* that sometimes affects Western Europe? What causes it to build up during the winter months?

What meteorological conditions may cause *Polar Continental* air to spread across the British Isles?

How is the fact that warm, moist *Tropical Maritime* air is the most common source of rainfall over the British Isles connected with:

(a) the frequency with which depressions cross the Atlantic;

(b) the direction of the prevailing winds as shown in Fig. 5.6.

In any season, a thunderstorm may result from the clash between air masses of different temperature – especially if the hotter air is very humid. From which directions and from which sources might such differing air masses clash over the British Isles?

The conditions shown in Photo 5.2 are related to the northernmost part of the Hadley Cell (Fig. 5.5). Explain this.

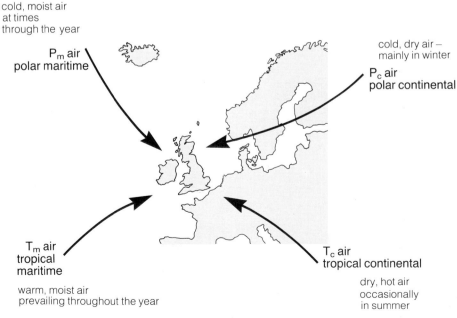

cold, moist air
at times
through the year

P$_m$ air
polar maritime

cold, dry air –
mainly in winter

P$_c$ air
polar continental

T$_m$ air
tropical
maritime

warm, moist air
prevailing throughout the year

T$_c$ air
tropical continental

dry, hot air
occasionally
in summer

5.19 Ever-changing air pressures cause air to flow over the British Isles first from one source and then from another. Warm, moist air from the Atlantic is most frequent, but there are seasonal outbursts of continental air.

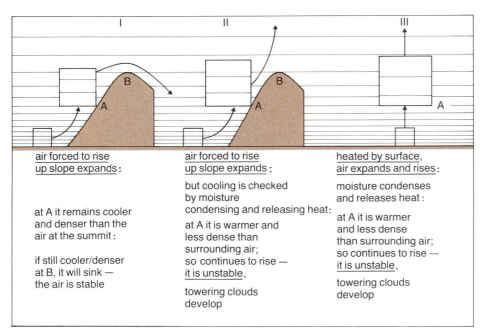

P 5.4 Moist westerly air forced up the sides of volcanic Mt. Egmont, in New Zealand, causes a saucer-shaped layer cloud above the summit.

I	II	III
air forced to rise up slope expands:	air forced to rise up slope expands:	heated by surface, air expands and rises:
	but cooling is checked by moisture condensing and releasing heat:	moisture condenses and releases heat:
at A it remains cooler and denser than the air at the summit:	at A it is warmer and less dense than surrounding air; so continues to rise — it is unstable,	at A it is warmer and less dense than surrounding air; so continues to rise — it is unstable,
if still cooler/denser at B, it will sink — the air is stable	towering clouds develop	towering clouds develop

5.20 Air displaced by relief (orographic effects) and in III by ground heating and convection.

5.8 What the clouds tell us — stable and unstable air

We can tell with some confidence that a depression is approaching by looking at the changes in cloud formation. But even without a depression in the offing, the clouds can tell us whether the air is stable or unstable, and whether rain is a possibility or not.

Billowing clouds and unstable air

If the air is disturbed and forced to rise, either by meeting hills or by gaining energy from a hot surface, it expands and cools. **If it remains cooler than the surrounding air, and thus denser, it will sink back to earth again.** This is a **stable** condition, and rain is unlikely.

If, however, the rising air remains hotter, and so lighter, than the air about it, it will go on rising. It is **unstable**. If it is full of moisture, condensation will occur at a low level and clouds will form.

As heat is given out when the vapour condenses, this *extra* energy helps to keep the air above the temperature of its surroundings — so it will continue to surge upwards. Billowing cumulus clouds, formed in the rising air, point to its instab-

ility, and suggest that rain, perhaps with thunder, is likely.

Fig. 5.20 shows the effects of stable and unstable air being forced to rise over a hill. It also shows how air heated from the surface rises and expands by **convection**.

On fine days, with stable air, separate fluffy cumulus clouds may form, as bubbles of hot air rise from the surface, Their flat bases show the condensation level. Because the air is stable, they do not tower to any great height, and are often called 'fair-weather cumulus'.

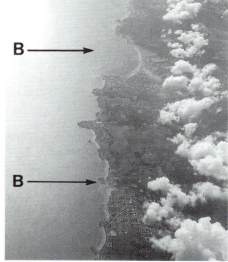

P 5.5 Mid-summer sea breezes (B) with cumulus cloud developing as air rises from the coastland of northern Tasmania. The sky remains clear above the cooler sea.

P 5.3 Cumulus forming in updraughts of hot moist air over a small island off Bali. CL is the condensation level.

Layer cloud in stable air

We have seen how sinking, warming air in the sub-tropics blankets rising air currents from the ground. **Fig. 5.21 shows an example from the Peruvian coastland, which is notoriously dry**, though often cloud-covered or hazy.

You can see that the air above the coast becomes cooler up to about 900 metres (line **s**). Then it encounters the sinking, warming air. Instead of the temperature continuing to fall with height, it *rises* abruptly. This is called **temperature inversion.**

Line a shows what happens when dry surface air, at 18°C, is disturbed and caused to rise. As it rises it expands and its temperature falls (lapses) with height, at a rate called the **dry adiabatic lapse rate (DALR)**. 'Adiabatic' means that it does not exchange heat with the air about it.

You can see that **as it rises it remains** *cooler* **than the air about it (line s)**. Thus it is stable and will tend to sink back.

Even if the air were 20°C to start with, and rose above 650 metres (line **b**), it would still be cooler than the surrounding air.

A layer of cloud tends to be trapped beneath the warmer air, and is thus an indicator of the conditions aloft.

DALR is the 'dry' lapse rate, before the air becomes saturated and clouds form. SALR is the lapse rate in satu-

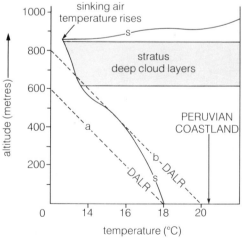

5.21 The full line shows the temperature of air above the Peruvian coastland at various levels. Notice where inversion occurs. The dotted lines represent unsaturated (dry) air. It is forced to rise and cools with altitude – independent of the air about it. Where condensation occurs a cloud layer forms beneath the warmer sinking air above.

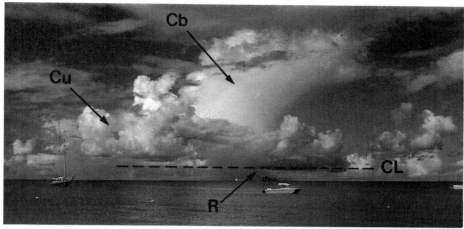

P 5.6 Cumulus clouds (Cu) with anvil-shaped cumulo-nimbus (Cb) giving a rain storm (R) off Antigua. The Trade Winds, starting as dry sinking air over the eastern Atlantic, gather moisture from the ocean. Low pressure troughs further west create these unstable conditions. CL is the condensation level.

rated air; explain why this is *less* than the DALR. See Fig. 5.12.

Which of the examples of cumulus development shown in Photos 5.3–5.5 is due to air-flow being disturbed and forced to rise; which to heating of the lower air?

5.9 Recording and plotting the changing weather

The telecommunications centre at Bracknell, in southern England, continuously collects and processes weather data, and exchanges it with centres such as Washington, Melbourne and Moscow. Coded observations of surface and upper air conditions are received from land-based **weather stations**, weather ships and merchant ships.

Geostationary satellites (some 36 000 km up) scan the surface, and record information every half an hour. **Polar orbiting satellites** also circle the earth every two hours (700–1500 km up). They cross the equator each time at 30° west of their previous passage.

These high-altitude images are of particular value to weather forecasters in the southern hemisphere, where there are fewer land-based weather stations. They increase our knowledge of overall air circulation.

Information from the stations is translated from code to symbols which can be plotted on a weather map. Fig. 5.22 is a simplified **station model.** The circle over the stations shows cloud coverage in

P 5.7 Stable sinking air blankets the western Andes, so that cloud lies in the valleys. Far beyond, high clouds form in less stable air from the Amazon Basin which rises up the Eastern Cordillera.

eighths; the arrow shaft indicates where the wind is coming from, and its feathers show the wind speed (one feather – ten knots; half-feather – five knots). The air temperature and barometric pressure are given, together with a weather symbol and cloud symbol (here showing cumulonimbus giving a rain shower).

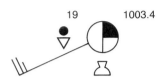

5.22 Conditions at a weather station covered by the circle.

Fig. 5.23 shows a simplified chart of weather conditions at 0600 hrs on a November day, with a depression centred north-east of the British Isles and its warm front approaching Scandinavia. The cold front has cleared northern Britain and most of the west. There is high pressure over the central southern part of western Europe.

1 In which direction is the air circulating about the centre of the low?
2 Comment on the temperature differences east and west of the Danish peninsula.
3 Comment on the temperature differences between London and south-west Ireland, and on their cloud cover.
4 Why are there such contrasting conditions between the west coast of Norway and the interior of Sweden? Describe the weather in each region.
5 Why are the weather conditions difficult to observe in western France? How does this tie up with the higher pressures there? Remember that this is November.
6 Comment on the changes that are likely to affect the British Isles over the following 24 hours.
7 Which cloud symbols would you add to the simplified station model relating to conditions: (a) over Ireland; (b) over London; (c) over Oslo, Norway? (See Fig. 5.24.)
8 Give an exact description of the weather conditions at each of the stations mentioned in Q.7, and of those in Sweden.

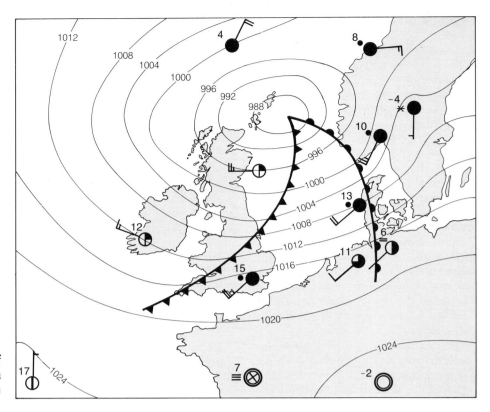

5.23 Weather conditions at 0600 hrs on a day in mid-November.

WEATHER SYMBOLS

WIND (speed in knots)	CLOUD in oktas (oktas = eighths)	LOW-MEDIUM CLOUD		WEATHER
calm	0	cumulus	mist	snow
1–2	1	cumulonimbus	fog	rain shower
3–7	2	stratocumulus		rain and snow shower
8–12	3	stratus	drizzle	rain and snow shower
13–17	4	altostratus		snow shower
	5	alto cumulus	rain and drizzle	
For each additional half feather add 5 knots	6	HIGH CLOUD	rain	hail shower
	7	cirrus		rain and snow
48–52	8 sky obscured	cirrostratus		thunderstorm

5.24 Weather symbols.

5.10 Climate – mean figures and variability

The statistics representing all this varied weather over the years can be averaged out to give figures which represent the particular **climate** of a place. The *mean* monthly, or annual, precipitation can be obtained, or the *mean* temperature range over a given period, or *mean* hours of sunshine for a particular month, or whatever we need. We can then use contours to produce distribution patterns – **isotherms** for temperature, **isobars** for barometric pressure, **isohyets** for rainfall, and so on.

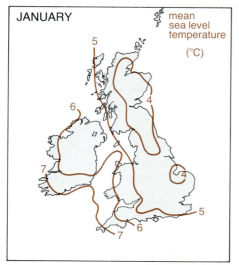

JANUARY

mean sea level temperature (°C)

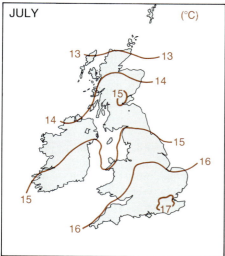

JULY (°C)

5.25 Mean monthly temperatures.

Fig. 5.25 shows isotherms of mean temperature for the British Isles in winter and summer; these are temperatures as they would be at sea-level. Such maps enable us to consider causes of the patterns shown. For instance:

1 In which season does the direct heat of the sun have the greatest influence? How do the isotherms reflect this?
2 In which season is the warming effect of maritime air most noticeable? How do the isotherms illustrate this?
3 How do the July isotherms indicate the different responses of land and sea to solar energy?

Of course some months, seasons or years will prove to be wetter, drier, cooler, cloudier, or windier than the climatic mean. In countries like Britain this may be inconvenient, but not disastrous on a national scale. Whereas **in the less developed countries exceptional**

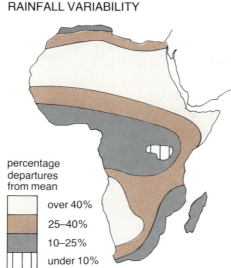

RAINFALL VARIABILITY

percentage departures from mean

over 40%
25–40%
10–25%
under 10%

5.26 Figures of mean annual rainfall do not show the whole picture. Their value is limited. Why does this apply more to some parts of Africa than others?

floods or prolonged droughts can be catastrophic for millions of people.

Fig. 5.26 shows how much the rainfall can vary from the mean in the African continent. Fig. 13.9 considers how frequently the Sahel, south of the Sahara, experiences lengthy periods of drought. Some of the causes of its severe famines are considered on p. 242.

What do the mean monthly rainfall or temperature figures *not* tell us about the heat and humidity of a place? (Look at Fig. 5.26.)

In Fig. 5.26 some parts seem to have much more erratic rainfall than others. In which parts of the continent is the rainfall most unreliable? Suggest why this should be.

Australians also say that the mean rainfall figure is the one amount that never occurs. Why should this apply particularly to inland parts?

5.11 Local climates

We have already looked at local valley winds and sea-breezes, and seen how the aspect of a place, a sunny slope or shaded valley, can affect people and their activities. And, on a continental scale, in spring the Föhn wind's high temperature (p. 67) is of regional importance, for it helps to melt the snows of Canada's western prairies. There the 'Chinook', as they call it, hastens the spring sowing. Also the thin atmosphere of high mountains and plateaus has its local consequences, for the direct heat of the sun can be intense (and a football travels faster!).

Urban climates

But it is not only mountainous and rural areas which have local climatic variations. **Large urban sprawls have quite remarkably different climatic conditions from the nearby countryside.**

Fig. 5.27 shows London's **heat island**, where part of the energy used for heating, and by industries and vehicles, is released

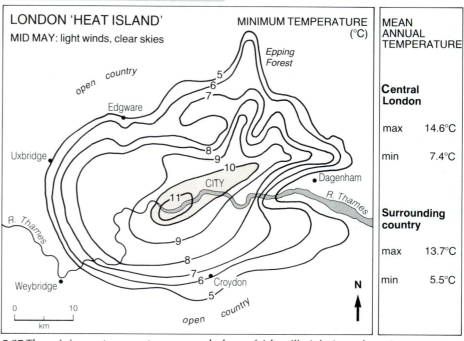

LONDON 'HEAT ISLAND'
MID MAY: light winds, clear skies

MINIMUM TEMPERATURE (°C)

	MEAN ANNUAL TEMPERATURE
Central London	
max	14.6°C
min	7.4°C
Surrounding country	
max	13.7°C
min	5.5°C

5.27 The minimum temperatures recorded on a fairly still night in early spring.

into the air. By day the sun's heat is stored in brick, stone and concrete of buildings and roads. As a result, cities in temperate regions may be degrees warmer than the rural areas, especially on winter's nights when the air is still.

In summer the large cities tend to have more rain, for the extra heat may trigger thunderstorms, and droplets condense on tiny particles in polluted air. Particle pollution can also lead to extra condensation and fog during still winter days.

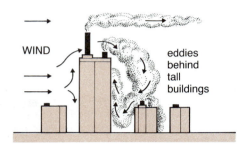

5.28 *Local effects of buildings and the spaces between.*

Narrow streets and alleys concentrate winds and can make corner sites unattractive to shoppers. High-rise buildings can create air turbulence (Fig. 5.28). In large cities east-west streets may receive little sunlight at street level.

Micro-climates in vegetation

In the countryside, where strong winds can erode areas of exposed soil, trees are often planted as shelter belts. Even in the natural vegetation local climatic contrasts abound. **A variety of micro-climates occurs in woodlands and crops.** Sunlight, humidity and air temperatures differ greatly between the edge of a wood and deep within it. The climate of the leaf cover of a tall forest differs considerably from that of plants on the forest floor, in the shade.

Large plants shade smaller ones and deprive them of water. Even the leaves, stem and roots of a single plant exist in different climatic conditions. The heat taken up by a soil raises its temperature and that of the air layer in contact with it, which is often many degrees hotter than the air about the leaves, buds or flowers. Remember that the temperatures usually quoted for a particular place are those taken in the shade in a Stevenson's screen (p. 88) at some 1.2 metres above the surface. They do not show the micro-climate of the plants or soils.

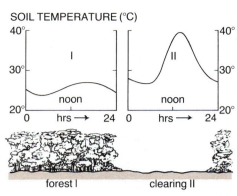

5.29 *How soil temperatures vary during the day in a Surinam forest and where it has been cleared of trees.*

Remember, too, that the ecosystem involves relationships between living and non-living things; so after considering contrasting climates in various parts of the world, we shall look again at the local soils and the plants they support.

Fig. 5.29 shows the changes in soil temperature within a tropical forest (in Surinam), and in soil temperature in land cleared of forest.

(a) Describe the daily changes from midnight one day to midnight the next for I or II in turn.

(b) Account for the hours of the maximum and minimum temperatures in each case.

(c) Account for the differences between I and II.

5.12 World climates

Fig. 5.30 gives a generalised picture of the variety of climates over the earth's surface. It also shows that, because of the north/south differences and the normal wind patterns, described above, there is a recognisable, regular distribution of climates.

There are, of course, innumerable variations caused by local relief. Also much depends on the exact location within the huge areas described. For instance, in what is shown as the tropical wet-and-dry climatic regions of Africa and South America there are very dry areas close to the deserts, and some seasonally very wet ones in lower latitudes and near moist coasts.

Anyone living in East Africa will know how different the climate feels in the highlands near Nairobi and the lowlands about Lake Victoria, let alone the hotter humid coastland near Mombasa. It is not

possible to show local differences on the scale of a map such as this.

On the other hand, **some places lying in similar latitudes and similar continental positions have very different seasonal climates.** For instance, the coastland of south-east Australia between 30°–40° has hot, moist summers, and so does eastern China in similar latitudes. But whereas in winter this part of China experiences very cold winds from central Asia, south-east Australia may have a day or so's 'cold snap' from a southerly wind, but that is all. Compare their graphs in Figs. 5.8 and 5.55.

Be wary, too, of assuming that similar broad climatic regions will have similar forms of vegetation. The tropical wet-and-dry regions may be said to support either 'savanna woodland' or just 'savanna' – that is, tropical grasses with or without trees. But the variety of plant forms is immense, and varies with relief and rock types. It has also been greatly affected by what people have done to the vegetation over the years.

Some regions shade into one another. The cool maritime lands of Western Europe, with rain throughout the year, and a maximum in winter, are not immediately distinguishable from those of eastern Europe. Yet in the interior the summer is hotter; and it is also the rainier time of year (though most of it falls in heavy storms). Then there are the abrupt climatic changes caused by mountains such as the Alps and Carpathians.

Why do places far inland usually have most rain during the summer months?

Many parts of eastern Europe record more rain during summer than in winter – yet there are more rainy days in winter. Explain.

Why are rainfall figures *alone* an insufficient indication of a 'wet' or 'dry' region? What other facts about the climate would you like to know in order to appreciate the condition of the surface and soils?

Climatic characteristics can also vary from the mean values for many years at a time. This is shown dramatically by Lake Eyre, which lies in a depression about the size of Ireland in the arid interior of South Australia.

Until the 1970s most of Lake Eyre was a vast salt flat. Only twice since 1920 had a sizeable area been covered by shallow water. But then, for a number of years,

CLIMATIC DESCRIPTION

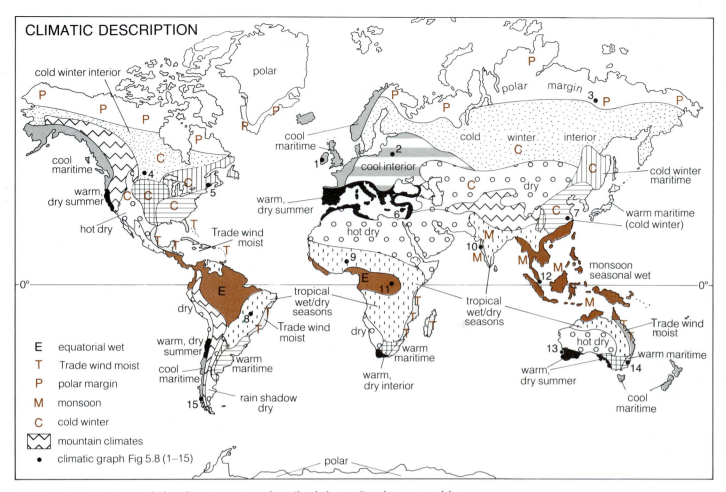

5.30 Firm boundaries mark the climatic regions described above. But there are seldom precise boundaries on the earth's surface. The hot, dry lands of the southern Sahara merge into the tropical wet and dry lands to the south, and within these are many local variations. Turn to Fig. 5.8 to see seasonal conditions at the places 1–15.

central Australia had an exceptionally wet spell.

Photo 5.8 shows that Lake Eyre became a truly large lake, as normally dry channels carried water choked with a load of red particles into the shallow depression. Even so, you can see white salt deposits about the lake and small salt flats (S-S) (*top right*); for air temperatures during summer reach 40–50°C.

Long-term climatic changes are also shown; for the lines of parallel dunes (D-D) were formed in even more arid conditions. They are now fixed by tough drought-resistant plants.

Look at Photo 5.8 and at p.84, and suggest the direction of the prevailing wind when the parallel dunes were formed.

Describe and name the physical features along the lake shores. Suggest how they have been formed.

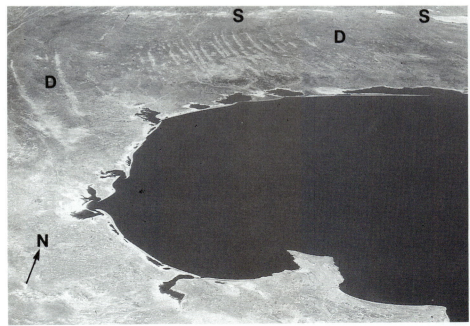

P 5.8 Lake Eyre in the arid interior of South Australia is only a lake in the true sense during particularly wet periods. Mostly it is a vast salt flat. You can see parallel lines of fixed dunes, and a chain of small salt flats beyond. Describe the coastal features formed from debris washed into the lake. This is only a corner of the huge lake depression.

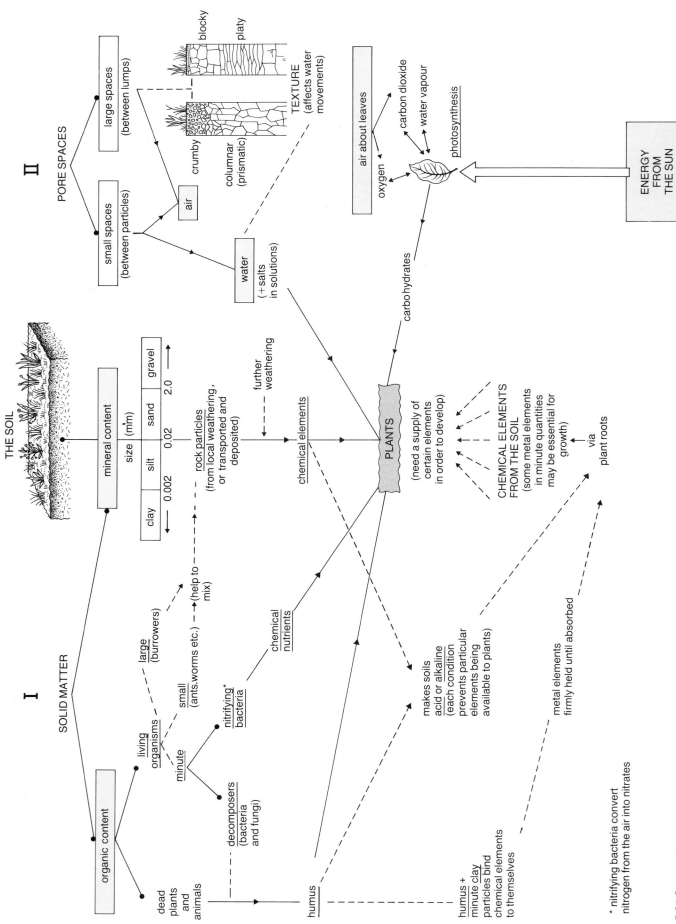

THE SOIL

I

SOLID MATTER

organic content

mineral content

living organisms

dead plants and animals

large (burrowers)

small (ants, worms etc.) → (help to mix)

minute

decomposers (bacteria and fungi)

nitrifying* bacteria

size (mm)

clay | silt | sand | gravel
0.002 | 0.02 | 2.0

rock particles (from local weathering, or transported and deposited)

further weathering

chemical elements

chemical nutrients

humus

humus + minute clay particles bind chemical elements to themselves

makes soils acid or alkaline (each condition prevents particular elements being available to plants)

metal elements firmly held until absorbed

II

PORE SPACES

large spaces (between lumps)

small spaces (between particles)

blocky

platy

crumby

columnar (prismatic)

TEXTURE (affects water movements)

air

water (+ salts in solutions)

air about leaves

oxygen

carbon dioxide

water vapour

photosynthesis

carbohydrates

PLANTS (need a supply of certain elements in order to develop)

CHEMICAL ELEMENTS FROM THE SOIL (some metal elements in minute quantities may be essential for growth)

via plant roots

ENERGY FROM THE SUN

* nitrifying bacteria convert nitrogen from the air into nitrates

5.31 See caption on p. 77.

76

5.13 The soil

Soil is a very complex substance. It contains living organisms as well as non-living materials. These are all continuously involved in processes which provide the plant kingdom, and thus ourselves, with the means for growth and nourishment.

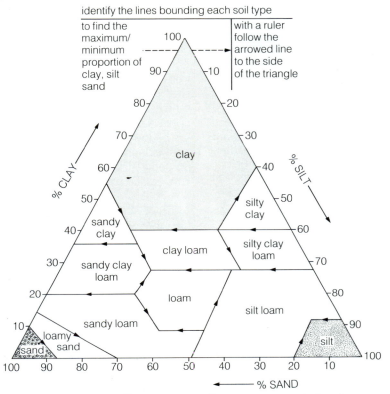

5.32 A mixture of particles of different sizes produces soils of a particular texture.

Fig. 5.31 gives a simple breakdown of soil structure. It enables you to follow the various ways in which nutrients are made available to plants anchored in the soil. Notice, in particular, how important the spaces between the soil particles are.

1 **The mineral content** may come direct from the weathering of local rocks; or it may be deposited as alluvium, boulder-clay or loess. These deposits have probably come from many different rocks, and so tend to be fertile; for their variety of particles can give plants just the minerals they need.

5.31 (left) A soil's fertility depends on delicate balances between living and non-living matter and the solutions and gases which occupy spaces between its mineral particles. Changes in temperature and water supply affect some or all of its constituents and so affect the whole character of the soil.

2 **The solid particles** vary in size, and in the ways they form lumps.
3 **The spaces** between them are important, for they contain air. If the spaces are fairly small they retain water between the particles. The spaces between sand and gravel particles, or between large lumps, allow water to drain downwards too rapidly to supply the plants with dissolved nutrients. Whereas in clay the spaces are so small that water may not pass through at all.

A mixture of silt, sand, and clay produces a **loam** texture, which can hold water long enough for it to dissolve salts and be absorbed through plant roots. The triangular graph (Fig. 5.32) shows how the texture of various soils varies with the proportions of clay, silt and sand.
4 **The dead plant material is broken down by bacteria (tiny decomposer organisms), or by fungi**, and forms **humus**, which recycles nutrients for the plants. Its tiny electric charges also hold metal elements, such as calcium, potassium and magnesium, which the plants need. It prevents these essential metal elements (called **bases**) being washed out of the soil.
5 Tiny clay particles are also able to attract and hold such elements. So a plentiful **clay-humus content** benefits vegetation.
6 Some **soil bacteria** are also active in extracting nitrogen from the air and converting it into soluble nitrates, which the plants can absorb.
7 **Larger organisms**, especially worms, help to mix minerals and areate the soil.
8 **A soil may be acid or alkaline (or neutral)**. This depends partly on which rocks supply its minerals. Sandstones and granites have few bases, so soils derived from them tend to be acidic. Limestones are rich in calcium and produce basic (alkaline) soils.
9 Water can become acidic by absorbing carbon dioxide, or by receiving acids from rotting vegetation. **On passing through the soil, acid water may react with, and so remove, bases.** This leaves an acidic soil. The process of washing out the minerals by water is called **leaching**.
10 **A soil which is strongly acidic or basic may** *not* **be able to supply particular elements needed by a plant** – not even, perhaps, the tiny quantities of zinc or copper some need to survive; so the plant will not thrive in that location.

Some do thrive in highly basic or acidic conditions, like yew trees and cowslips on calcium-rich soils, and fir trees and purple ling on acid moorland soils.

The degree of acidity is called the pH value, and ranges from 0–14. At about 6.5 the soil is neutral. Lower values show the degree of acidity. High values indicate how alkaline it is.

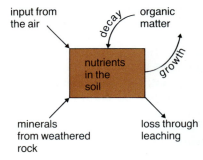

5.33 The soil nutrient system.

Why is the statement **acid + base = salt + water** so relevant to soil fertility?

Suggest why soils on chalk rock (calcium carbonate) are generally thin. How might a farmer improve such a soil?

How might he improve the **texture** of a heavy clay soil?

Use Fig. 5.32 to describe the type of soil containing the following mixtures (%):

(a) clay 35; sand 40; silt 25
(b) clay 18; sand 40; silt 42
(c) clay 45; sand 10; silt 45
(d) clay 18; sand 64; silt 18

5.14 Processes which deplete soils – and deprive plants

Plants require fairly large quantities of nitrogen, phosphorus, sulphur, and such bases as potassium, calcium and sodium. Some also need tiny **traces** of a particular elements, such as iron, zinc or copper.

Nitrogen is supplied in the form of soluble salts by nitrifying bacteria, or is obtained, like phosphorus, from mineral particles or animal manure. **The most important bases for plant development** – potassium, magnesium and calcium – come from the breakdown of rock minerals. But for various reasons they may not *remain* available for the plants:

1 **In wet conditions they are easily washed out of the soil,** for acid water converts them to soluble salts. Even when held by clay-humus (p.77), persistent, percolating acid water can remove them.

2 **Very wet conditions may also cause the actual clay minerals to break down.** These minerals, which form much of the upper soil, are made up of a base (such as potassium) combined with oxides of iron, aluminium and silica. The following conditions cause these compounds to separate:

(a) **In cool, wet, acidic conditions** the bases and the iron and aluminium compounds are strongly washed downwards (leached). This leaves the silica as infertile quartz particles.

(b) **In hot, wet, basic conditions** even the silica may be converted to a form which is leached down.

3 **Persistent rain may lead to waterlogging.** As the soil organisms which cause plant matter to decay cannot get oxygen, the peaty plant remains accumulate. Low temperatures also slow the rate of decay, and directly check plant growth.

5.15 How plants adapt

Plants manage to survive adverse conditions in a number of ways. **There are critical temperatures for plants.** Freezing conditions (below 0°C) can physically damage plant tissues. But most plants cease to grow when temperatures remain below 6°C, for they are unable to draw water from the soil. **Deciduous plants** then avoid losing water through transpiration by shedding their leaves.

P 5.9 In the cool temperate lands the deciduous trees survive the winter months by shedding leaves to preserve moisture. The evergreens with glossy leaves or needle leaves lost little moisture, and can make rapid use of sunlight when the soil temperature rises again.

For any trees to flourish, the mean temperature must be above 10°C for at least two months – otherwise only low tundra plants survive (p. 97). Some, like the **conifers**, require relatively few bases. They can thrive on acidic soils in cold climates. But, of course, they only return a few bases to the soil.

Their needle leaves cut down moisture loss when low temperatures prevent them absorbing soil water. As they are evergreen, photosynthesis starts again as soon as soil temperatures permit.

Other plants develop organs to cope with local difficulties. In dry regions long tap roots reach deep water sources, and small, thick, leathery leaves cut down loss by transpiration. While the grooved 'drip-tip' of leaves of tropical rainforest plants allows them to shed water rapidly.

5.16 How soil horizons develop – illustrated by the podsols

Just as forms of vegetation vary from one climatic region to another, so the **soils too develop characteristics typical of the local climate** (though they are influenced by particular types of rock).

No process acts on its own. The movement of water through the soil tends to create layers (**horizons**) within the soil, each with a different mineral content. This affects the vegetation, as various plants are able, or unable, to obtain the nutrients they require from the soil layers.

In cool, wet regions, under coniferous forest, the soil horizons tend to be well defined (Fig. 5.34). The processes are as follows:

1 The needle leaves fall, form surface litter, and slowly rot to give black acidic humus.

2 Rainwater, itself dilute carbonic acid, acquires more acids from the humus; so any soluble bases are quickly leached out.

3 Acid water breaks down clay minerals. Iron and aluminium compounds are washed down. The silica remains as the sandy, infertile part of a light-coloured upper **A** horizon.

4 The lower soil is less acid: so the iron and aluminium compounds are redeposited. They accumulate in the **B** horizon, creating red-brown iron staining.

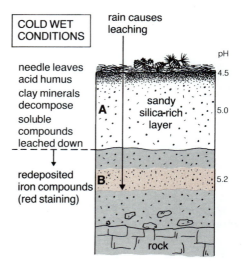

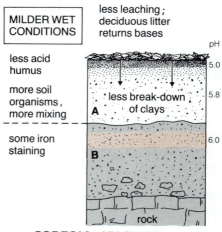

PODZOLS – LEACHING PRODUCES SOIL HORIZON

5.34 Different podzols – whose clay minerals break down in wet, acidic conditions.

5 In the cold and wet there are few living organisms to mix the soil particles; so the horizons show up well. These leached soils, with clear horizons, are known as **podzols.**

Why do such soils not suit *shallow-rooted* grains or vegetables?

In warmer, but still rainy conditions, much of western Europe has deciduous trees and shrubs. Once there were great forests of them. **Here soil processes have produced different results.**

1 The annual leaf-fall provides more bases in the litter.

2 Much litter remains through the winter. But from spring onwards it is broken down by the numerous soil organisms. Earthworms drag down material and mix the mineral and organic matter, so that separate horizons are not so clearly defined.

3 Water soaking through the upper soil is less acidic, so that fewer bases are removed. The **A** horizon is a rich brown, stained with humus, the **B** horizon a little lighter.

These slightly acid **brown earths** are widely used for agriculture – though, because of continuous cropping, the nutrients removed are now usually replaced from fertilisers. Their horizons are seldom as clear as suggested by Fig. 5.34.

5.17 Vegetation and soils – worldwide examples

There are, of course, different types of vegetation and different soils in all the climatic regions shown in Fig. 5.30. Here are examples from some of the places in Fig. 5.8, for which you can find temperature and rainfall graphs numbered as shown. Look carefully at their exact location and notice their seasonal characteristics. The following descriptions will add considerably to what the mean figures can tell you.

A) **Temperate grasslands** of the central Canadian prairies (4)

These extensive grasslands (p. 118) are now part of the great Canadian wheat belt; though **the natural vegetation was once a mixture of tall, and short grasses.** The conditions there and the soil processes are as follows:

1 The grasses die down in winter, for frost penetrates deeply, and a snow cover lasts until spring.

2 The plants have a long rest period, until spring brings a sudden thaw and water moves downwards through the soil.

3 Summers are hot for the latitude, with long hours of sunlight; this is a time of strong evaporation, especially as winds blow freely. Rain comes in heavy storms, sometimes with hail – a hazard for wheat.

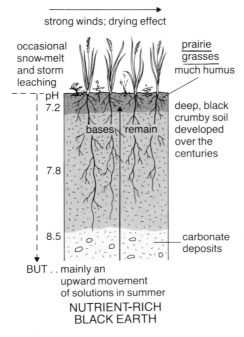

strong winds; drying effect

occasional snow-melt and storm leaching

prairie grasses
much humus

pH
7.2

bases | remain

deep, black crumby soil developed over the centuries

7.8

8.5

carbonate deposits

BUT .. mainly an upward movement of solutions in summer
NUTRIENT-RICH BLACK EARTH

5.35 Deep, rich soils whose bases remain near the surface, available for grasses and cultivated grains.

4 Throughout summer there is a general upward movement of soil solutions, though water percolates down after heavy storms, as it does at the time of snow-melt.

5 The dense mat of grass provides much humus. The low rainfall and the upward movement of solutions therefore produce a deep black, or dark brown, humus-rich **A** horizon. which is naturally fertile.

6 Rising water leaves the less soluble carbonates lower down, as nodules in the soil.

7 The grasses have fine, deep roots, which leave many soil spaces when they die. So the top soil has a crumby structure, and is well mixed by worms and small animals.

This rich prairie soil is known as 'black earth', or by the Russian name for steppe soil – **czernozem** (Fig. 5.35).

B) **The Mediterranean lands** in Cyprus (6)

As in other Mediterranean countries, the land has been affected by thousands of years of human settlement.

1 **The soils vary with the rocks, many of which are limestones.** They are shallow soils, except on coastlands and in valleys. Huge scree slopes are typical, for fallen weathered particles are not readily washed away in these climates.

2 **Both vegetation and soils respond to long hot, dry summers and mild winters, with occasional rain.**

3 With · continuous settlement from ancient times, the vegetation has deteriorated from woodland to a mixture of low shrubs and deep-rooted trees with thick bark. In places there are needle-leaf pines. All are adapted to drought conditions. Many shrubs have woody stems and thick, hair-covered leaves. A number of plants have tiny leaves and protective scented oils – thyme, sage, lavender, rosemary. Some survive by underground storage; their bulbs produce spring flowers which colour the hillsides.

P 5.10 Vegetation on hillside in Cyprus. The variety of thick-leaved, deep-rooted shrubs and needle-leaved conifers are adapted to survive the hot, dry Mediterranean summers.

4 Autumn growth follows summer drought; though spring is the time for most intense growth and flowering.

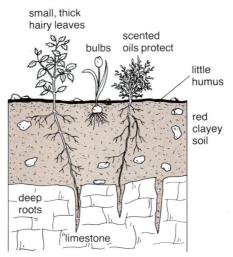

small, thick
hairy leaves

bulbs

scented
oils protect

little
humus

red
clayey
soil

deep
roots

limestone

POOR IN HUMUS –
RED WITH IRON COMPOUNDS

*5.36 Soils without humus staining, so that
the iron compounds appear vivid red.*

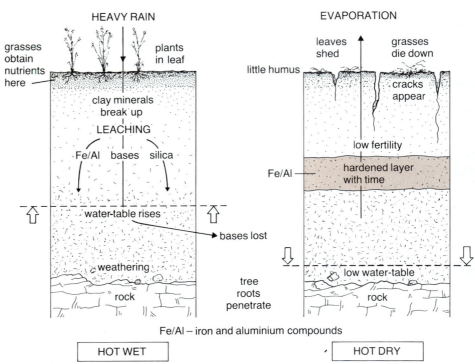

HEAVY RAIN

grasses
obtain
nutrients
here

plants
in leaf

clay minerals
break up

LEACHING

Fe/Al   bases   silica

water-table rises

bases lost

weathering

rock

EVAPORATION

leaves
shed

grasses
die down

little humus

cracks
appear

low fertility

Fe/Al

hardened layer
with time

low water-table

tree
roots
penetrate

rock

Fe/Al – iron and aluminium compounds

HOT WET

HOT DRY

*5.37 Processes which affect soils in many wet-dry savanna lands – though the actual soils
vary with rock types and local conditions.*

5 There is little humus to stain the thin soils; so that where soils are basic, like those derived from limestones, they retain iron compounds, and so are often a vivid red (Fig. 5.36). **Terra rossa** describes the red, deeper soils, formed where impurities from the limestones have slowly accumulated in hollows.
6 On hillsides plants often grow in small pockets of soil, and struggle to survive against the ravages of goats and sheep.
7 Olives and carobs have been part of the landscape for thousands of years; but many of the now typical fruit trees, like the citrus, were introduced more recently.

C) Savannas in northern Nigeria (9)

Here there are contrasting wet and dry seasons, with maximum temperatures of 35° – 38°C through the year. During January, with dry winds from the Sahara, the relative humidity averages only 14%; whereas in July and August, with southerly winds, 100 mm of rain may fall in a day.

1 **Grasses predominate**, with other herbs, and occasional low, deep-rooted trees.
2 During the long drought, when the water-table is low, the grasses die down, and trees and shrubs lose their leaves.
3 These come rapidly into leaf when the wet season starts.
4 The first heavy rains run quickly over the surface. But as leaves develop and grasses grow they intercept the rain, so that water soaks into the soil.
5 **During the rains the heat and moisture**

cause clay minerals to break up (p.78). Iron, aluminium compounds and silica are *all* released and leached downwards.
6 There is little humus. The grasses have to obtain nutrients from the upper soil, which remains clayey and infertile.
7 As the water-table rises with the rains, the **iron and aluminium compounds become concentrated** just above it.
8 When the soil dries, these form hard lumps; and in places a hard concreted layer forms, which may eventually interfere with the movements of soil water (Fig. 5.37).

The balance between grasses, trees, shrubs and soils is easily upset by overgrazing, or attempts at cultivation. **Fire** is often used to burn off old grass and encourage new growth for forage, and this probably helps to maintain a 'grass savanna' at the expense of trees. So **'savanna' may be man-made, rather than simply due to the tropical wet-dry climate.**

There are many variations in soils due to different rocks, slopes and local conditions.

Consider the arguments for and against burning savanna. Which of the following sounds convincing or unconvincing? Explain.

For: (a) It releases potash from vegetation to soil; (b) it destroys grasses and weeds and makes crop seeding easier; (c) it cuts down labour needed for clearing; (d) it removes old grass and causes strong, new shoots to develop; (e) heat cracks the soil and allows water to soak in more readily.

P 5.11 In the wet summer months the savanna grasses are tall and the green leaves of the small acacias provide food for the Maasai giraffe.

P 5.12 In the dry season water is scarce in the savannas. Herdsmen drive their cattle to drink at watercourses which retain sufficient water. Notice the dust of approaching cattle; also the rock debris from the terrace face. How and when will this debris be removed?

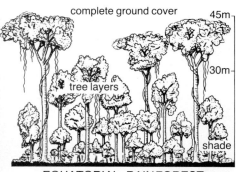

EQUATORIAL RAINFOREST

5.38 The crowns of the trees, young and old, of many species, give almost complete shade. Undergrowth is usually sparse.

Against: (a) If vegetation is destroyed, humus is reduced; (b) carbon, hydrogen and nitrogen compounds are lost as gases and smoke; (c) nutrients from ash are not all added to the soil – heavy rain washes much away; (d) removing vegetation cover leads to erosion; (e) trees destroyed do not easily regenerate, resulting in scrub savanna.

Might burning be more suitable for pastoralists rather than agriculturalists?

root in the junction of branches. There are also parasites, such as orchids, which take nutrients direct from the tree.

2 There are many tree species, and the forest is never without flower. **There is no single leaf-fall season**, though individual species rest at times. Together, the young trees and old trees provide a complete cover of the surface.

3 **The continuous supply of leaf litter is rapidly decomposed, releasing nutrients** which are quickly absorbed by the shal-

low, branching roots. Because of this shallowness, woody flanges spread out from the lower trunk of tall trees and act as support.

4 A red, clayey soil results from the breakdown of soil minerals. Other minerals come from the weathering rock beneath, though leaching quickly removes bases. So **the soils, as a whole, are not very fertile, for most nutrients are rapidly recycled between the soil and vegetation.**

5 The humus does not build up because of the rapid recycling, and the soil is only slightly acid. Nitrogen is made available by nitrifying bacteria and thunder rain.

6 **These tall dense forests suggest great fertility, but the whole balance is easily disturbed**. Clearing soon deprives the soil of leaf litter and exposes it to sun and rain (Fig. 5.39). The original forest does not regenerate on eroded, infertile soils, whatever the climatic advantages.

D) Equatorial rainforest in central Africa (11)

Here there are no long dry periods and little temperature variation. By day the temperatures vary by only 8–10 C°. The air remains humid.

1 **In the rainforest, however, there are many micro-climates**, for the leaf canopy of the tall trees, the lower branches and roots, and the smaller trees alongside, have quite different environments (Fig. 5.38).

The leafy crown intercepts sunlight and rain, and plants beneath are shaded. A host of climbing plants use the tall trees for support as they twine upwards towards the light. Some green plants (epiphytes)

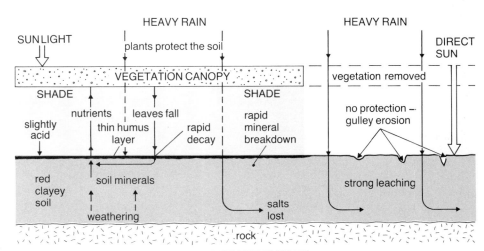

RAIN FOREST CYCLES

5.39 The rapid cycling of nutrients maintains a balance which is lost when trees are cleared.

P 5.13 Riverside vegetation in south-central Sri Lanka. In tropical rainforest small trees and a thick undergrowth flourish where light penetrates in clearings, and along river banks.

Suggest why river water among the great Amazonian forests contains so few nutrients.

We should remember that the **forests are part of a food-chain system**. The plants are producers and are consumed by millions of other organisms. Caterpillars strip foliage from the crowns; termites break down woody tissues on the forest floor; insects reduce the litter; bacteria and fungi cause decay.

Large animals, reptiles, birds and insects are mobile, but find their own places. Bats and birds eat fruit in the canopy, but are preyed on by falcons; squirrels and monkeys eat fruits and insects in the middle levels, at risk from leopard and other cats; frogs, lizards and snakes mostly live near the ground, sought out by many carnivores. Droppings or litter from animal activities among the high canopy are washed down the trunk or drip through leaves. But they, too, are quickly recycled.

The insects, birds and animals all help with pollination and seed dispersal, making for a variety of plant species throughout the forest.

Mountain systems – zones of vegetation

In each broad region the actual plant life varies with altitude, so that mountain systems have zones of vegetation (Fig. 5.40).

On the mountains there are numerous combinations of plants, depending on shelter, shade, soil depth, screes, and so on. Individual plants respond to the fall in temperature with height, and to variations in snowfall/rainfall, water run-off, and aspect.

Soil catenas

Under given climatic conditions, similar rocks and slopes tend to respond in the same way to run-off, leaching and soil movements, so that a regular pattern of soils develops. This pattern is called a **catena.**

Catenas are seen on a large scale, like that in Fig. 5.41, and also on a smaller scale, as shown by the profiles in Fig. 5.58 and on p. 97.

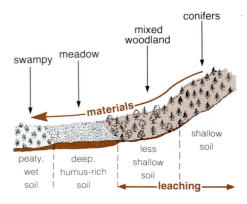

5.41 A regular catena along a low range – from steep hillsides to swampy plains.

P 5.14 Thick flanges help to support tall trees in the moist soils of tropical rainforest. Notice the epiphytes finding nourishment on the trunk itself.

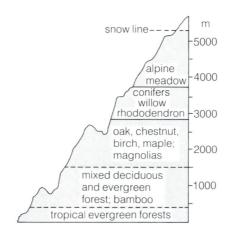

5.40 Altitude zones in the eastern Himalayas; from evergreen forest near rivers to alpine plants near the snowline.

5.18 The deserts – a special environment with familiar processes

Deserts and semi-deserts occupy nearly a third of the world's land surface. Climatic variations cause them to extend or shrink from time to time. But the way people have mismanaged many of the semi-arid lands has converted large areas of these into true desert.

The role of water in creating landscapes.

Where the air is dry and sinking, precipitation is slight (p.71). The combination of clear skies, heat from the sun, and wind blowing freely across surfaces unprotected by vegetation dries up any surface water very rapidly. Yet **desert landscapes owe as much, or more, to water as to wind.**

P 5.15 The floor of this dry valley in the Sinai desert shows traces of the floods which occasionally surge through. These remove and transport debris, like that building up beneath the weathered slopes beyond. A line of deep-rooted trees which tap water beneath the valley bed.

AFTER FLASH FLOODS

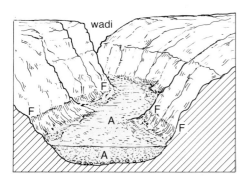

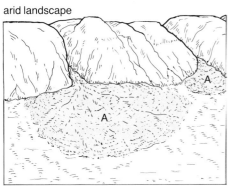

FF – water level in flash flood   A – alluvial deposits

5.42 Flash floods leave thick alluvial deposits in wadi beds and spread materials over adjoining lowland.

1 The occasional convection storms bring intense rainfall. As the water floods across bare surfaces, it picks up debris, ranging from small particles to boulders. These help to scour out surface channels.

Storm waters pour into dry valleys (wadis), churning the deposits on the bed into muddy torrents. A **flash flood** can bring a ten-metres-deep wall of water coursing through a steep sided wadi, eroding the bed and the valley sides.

As it subsides, the flood deposits the boulders and covers them with a thick mantle of finer material. Where it floods out of the wadi and emerges onto a flatter desert surface, it builds up wide fans of debris (Fig. 5.42). As the water spreads outward, it soon evaporates.

Some water collects in desert hollows. As it dries, it leaves dissolved salts behind. White salt flats – **salt lakes** or **playas** – are common desert features.

2 Extensive systems of channels and dry valleys cross most deserts. Many of them were formed in wetter climates, before plate movements brought these lands into a drier zone. Some have been cut during recent periods of exceptional rainfall.

3 Hot desert air can hold much water vapour without condensation. But as the surface chills at night under open skies, there may be heavy dew. Such water causes **chemical weathering.** The dark 'varnish' on many desert rocks is a result of chemical changes, caused by solution beneath the surface. Expansion and contraction due to rapid ˙ temperature changes can also lead to splitting and surface peeling.

Water is therefore an important part of the desert system. **It can also slowly move as artesian water in aquifers beneath the surface.** At natural oases, or where it is tapped, it creates contrasts in vegetation and settlement. Similar contrasts are seen in the valley of rivers such as the Nile, which rise in wetter lands and then cross the desert.

Weathering and wind action

Desert scenery usually includes dramatic angular slopes and isolated rocky masses.

P 5.16 Wave Rock at Hyden. An outcrop of ancient granite with stains of chemical weathering and polished by wind-borne particles funnelled along the face.

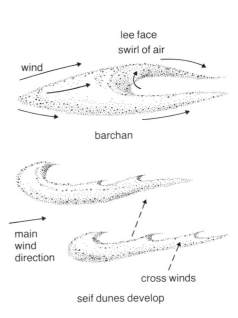

5.45 Wind shaping and moving large dunes.

P 5.17 *Iraq's river Zab carries water to the Tigris through almost treeless desert. Yet water erosion has created a rugged landscape with valleys and channels. Arrows show the uptilt of the rocks. How has this affected the valleys of rivers T–U and V–W? Why does the dry watercourse X–Y fail to reach the river? What has happened on the inside of the river bend near Y?*

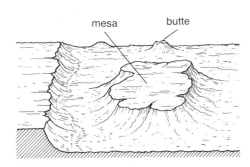

5.43 Weathered slopes retreat, leaving isolated flat-topped blocks.

Bare rock faces weather rapidly, allowing coarse material to fall and build up slopes beneath. Here boulders break down into smaller debris. Some of this is removed by wind, or occasional floods, over the gentle concave slope beyond.

As the processes continue, the slopes retreat, as shown in Fig. 5.43. Sometimes all that remains of a higher surface is a small tableland (**mesa**), or perhaps a detached block (**butte**).

The wind's energy lifts and transports the fine material. The wind-borne particles collide and become sharply angular by **attrition**. They help to erode exposed surfaces. Rock faces become fretted as

these 'tools of erosion' pick out the weaker layers (Fig. 5.44).

Wind erosion is most effective just above ground level where there are many particles. Close to the ground there is surface friction, though turbulent swirls occur. Higher up there are fewer particles.

The particles are deposited where the wind's energy slackens, especially in sheltered places. They also pile up against obstacles, and sandy deposits build up into dunes. Where the prevailing wind

carries sand forward at the dune edges, crescent-shaped **barchans** form. Sand is carried forward from the windward slope and deposited in the lee, so dunes may move forward. Up-draughts steepen the lee face (Fig. 5.45).

Even when the wind comes from one main direction, occasional side winds may drift sand across this and form long lines of **seif dunes**. Swirls of air steepen their sides.

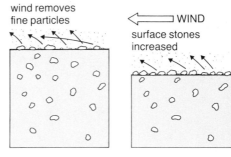

5.46 A stony surface lowered by deflation as wind removes the smaller particles.

Where a mixture of fine and coarse particles covers the surface, the wind tends to remove the finer ones. A process known as **deflation**, which can produce stone-covered surfaces (Fig. 5.46).

Some winds persistently carry very fine materials long distances and deposit them

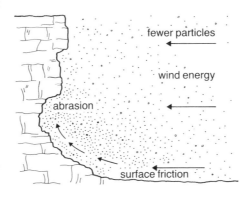

5.44 Wind abrasion picks out weak strata, its effect being concentrated in mid-slope.

P 5.18 Thick accumulations of loess in the dry interior of northern China. Summer rain causes surface gulleying, but the fine particles bind together and provide secure dry walls for cave dwellings and storerooms. In the cold winter the river is frozen, the trees bare, but the fields await spring sowing with wheat, for the loess, derived from many different rocks, is fertile when watered.

P 5.19 A dalek-like species of cactus amid wiry desert grasses. The ridges on the short bulbous green stems bear thorns which are modified shoots.

5.19 Small ecological niches – pond and woodland

A niche is a small area within a larger space. We have seen what a lot can be going on in a small moist location in a desert. But you don't have to go to remote places to find a small ecosystem which shows what delicate balances there are in the natural world. Take, for instance, a pond, small lake, or patch of woodland. Even though it needs an expert to measure precisely the relationships between plant and animal life and their physical environment, a local study, with careful observations and recordings, can be interesting and very informative.

over adjoining lands. Huge quantities, known as **loess**, may be built up over the centuries. Such fine particles cling together, and are sometimes cemented by solutions, forming large areas of soft rock, as in the 'loess lands' of northern China. These are very fertile when watered, but easily eroded when the vegetation cover is removed.

Life in the deserts

The hot deserts are not without vegetation or animal life. Rain may bring colour to apparently bare surfaces, as **ephemeral plants** spring up. These blossom and complete their life cycle in a few weeks, leaving seeds to remain dormant until the next rain, perhaps years later. Other plants have tap roots capable of reaching deep water sources. Some have spreading roots close to the surface, to catch storm water before it evaporates.

Succulents, like cacti, which store water in their tissues, have thick cell walls, and leaves reduced to spines. Some are adapted to salty soils. A few ensure survival by breaking their stem at seed time and allowing the wind to tumble them along, so that at least a few find a moist hollow.

Animals, too, find their own niche. After rains insects seek out flowers, and birds arrive and feed on them. Flies are

abundant; and on the surface spiders and scorpions prey on small creatures such as ants. Rain may bring locusts to feed on ephemerals. They then lay eggs, which produce hoppers, often by the million. In a few weeks the new breed may be flying off as a swarm to neighbouring lands – a threat to crops.

Small creatures lie in shaded burrows by day, and are active at night. They have many adaptations to cool themselves. So do larger animals, like the desert fox, with large ears for cooling. The camel can lose up to half its weight in water, and has a wide range of body temperature. Its nose membrane cuts down moisture loss, but allows moist air in.

(A) The pond

A pond provides an excellent opportunity to examine an ecosystem of manageable size. Such a water surface is apparently contained by recognisable boundaries. But, in fact, a **succession** of plant life often stretches back from the water's edge over what was once part of

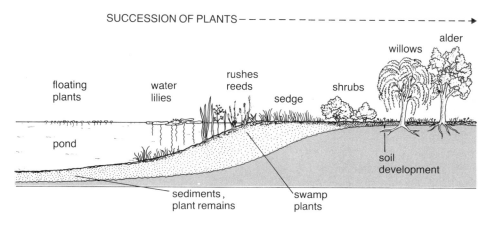

SUCCESSION OF PLANTS - - - - - - - - - - - - - - - - - - - →

5.47 Different forms of plants colonise marshy and dry land. They succeed one another as firmer land is extended.

the pond (Fig. 5.47). So it is usually essential to study its immediate surroundings as well.

Consider a recently formed pond - water occupying a hollow — and what may happen to it. Like all lakes and ponds, it immediately starts to be filled with sediments. Then life forms develop:

1 First comes floating vegetation, including green algae. It adds organic matter to the sediments at the bottom of the pond.
2 As the sediments accumulate, water plants, like pond weeds, root around the edges, under water. They trap more sediment and add more organic matter.
3 As the sediments come to form a rim of waterlogged soil, rushes, sedges and reeds take root.
4 In time the waterlogged area becomes drier. Shrubs colonise it and oust the original plants.
5 These are followed by trees such as alder and willow; and later, perhaps, by oak and birch.

This is what is meant by a 'succession' of plant life with time.

In the water itself there are numerous relationships, which vary with the seasons. Tests can show what is happening.

(a) **Water samples can be taken and filtered**, to isolate algae and other tiny organisms. Simple chemical tests can indicate the amount of chlorophyll present. This gives an idea of the quantity of plant food being manufactured by the small plants (producers).

There are colour-test chemical kits to indicate the proportions of nitrogen and phosphorus in a water sample, and others which test for acidity (pH values) (p. 91). But such precise measurements call for expert work.

(b) **It is usually easier to sample and record the predators**. A fine-mesh net can be used to trap and sample pond life *at various levels*. At the top are insects and larvae, with fish and amphibians moving through the lower levels. A grab can be devised to dredge up bottom sediments, where the mayfly nymphs, crayfish and mussels live.

(c) **Samples of water temperatures** are revealing, for the mixing or separation of top and bottom water depend on them. In summer there are warm top water layers lying over much cooler water, which may thus be deprived of oxygen. When the temperature falls, the water

begins to circulate. This helps oxygen to reach the bottom water and organic material to come to the top, where it may produce a sudden growth of green algae. Mixing occurs again in spring.

(d) **Observations may be made of visiting predators** which affect life within the pond – herons, for example, which seasonally can take large quantities of fish.

The results of human interference can be observed. Some wastes pollute the ponds and directly destroy life. Others, including farm fertilisers, may cause water plants to grow so rapidly that they upset the natural balance. Too much dead organic matter at the bottom, where oxygen is short, means slow rotting and the release of hydrogen sulphide; this makes the pond smelly and harms other life forms.

A good growth of weed may indicate a healthy pond life, but interfere with fishing or swimming. A biologically poor lake with clear water is often preferred for recreation!

Make a **food chain** for a pond, starting with small free-floating water plants.

How does water circulation in a pond affect the ecological balance?

How may a stream which flows into and out of a small lake affect (i) the physical features of the lake itself; (ii) life within the lake?

How would these things depend on the nature of the stream itself? What might it carry in its waters?

(B) A temperate woodland

This is a complex ecosystem, in which plant species compete for light and nutrients. There is a variety of animal life, with species from the large to the minute forming food chains, which together make up a **food web** (Fig. 5.48). To understand how they affect each other calls for careful observation and measurements over a long period of time. Good woodland management depends on such knowledge.

An oak-wood in lowland Britain is a mixture of deciduous trees. In summer the moderate shade of large oaks allows an understorey of other trees, usually hazels, hawthorns and willows. In spring, before trees are in full leaf, anemones, bluebells, wood sorrel and primroses come into flower. Clearance allows other trees, like maple and wild cherry, to invade.

The woods have been disturbed through the ages by cattle and grazing and pigs, by timber cutting, and by coppicing the hazels – cutting back stems and harvesting 10–15 year-old shoots. But a new balance has always established itself, depending on the extra light.

Within the wood there are continuous exchanges of energy. Four-fifths of all the leaves are broken down by worms and spring tails, and are recycled by microorganisms. Periodic plagues of caterpillars – leaf consumers – upset this balance for a while.

Acorns are taken by birds, mice, voles and squirrels, and seedlings are cropped

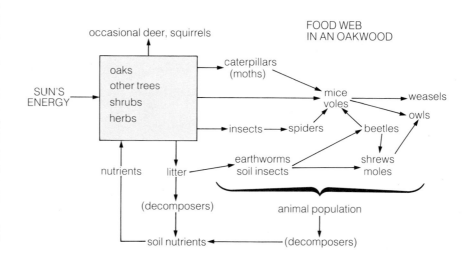

5.48 Numerous food chains are linked to form a food web within a wood. Visiting animals, like deer and birds, may be part of the system, though they do not live there permanently. Severe weather conditions, tree felling, or the explosion of population of a particular species, may affect the balance of the whole community.

by cattle and deer. But oaks are slow-growing and long-lived, and in a century produce more than a million acorns!

Fig. 5.48 gives a simplified view of the woodland food web. Besides the consumers shown, birds and predators such as foxes live in woodland, though many of their activities are related to surrounding territory.

5.20 How we respond to our physical environment

In Parts II and III we shall see how people try to use the physical environment for their own ends. They have found ever more efficient ways of obtaining energy from food via the plants, and of harnessing the power from natural forces and fossil-fuels.

But we also see how we are affected by the results of mismanaging and mistreating the natural environment.

Photo 5.20 helps to put our abilities and actions into perspective. The natural world described in the preceding pages, the rocks and streams and daily weather act now just as they did when this family sat fashioning their implements, nearly two million years ago.

This cutting in the Olduvai gorge revealed the remains of a family, their artifacts, and of animals they hunted near the site. They set up a homestead and lit fires, so they must have felt as we do that they had successfully adapted natural things to serve their own ends.

You can also see in Photo 5.20 the mass of rock layers, the sands and gravels and wind-blown ash that have accumulated over the home of these long-vanished individuals.

We may have made considerable technological progress. But a large proportion of the world population is receiving little *direct* benefit from our advanced technology.

As this newly discovered homestead was being excavated, a group of semi-nomadic herdsmen drove their cattle down over this slope and destroyed one of the skulls. The difference in living standards of these herdsmen and the hunter-gatherers of long ago is not all that great. **So in Parts II and III we look also at the contrasts between the technologically developed parts of the world and those where progress has been slow**. We consider, too, ways in which we are capable of destroying much of the progress we have made.

P 5.20 The living place of a pre-historic family uncovered by excavation in the Olduvai gorge in northern Tanzania.

Theme 5 Back-up section

Recording the weather

A simple weather station requires instruments to measure temperature, humidity, air pressure, wind speed, and direction, rainfall and insolation.

Photo 5.21 shows a **Stevenson's screen** standing 1.2 metres above the ground, well clear of trees and buildings. Its louvred sides allow air to flow freely around the thermometers in its shaded interior.

Separate thermometers record the maximum and minimum temperatures between readings. Fig. 5.49 shows a type of combined **maximum/minimum thermometer** used by many schools.

In the **wet and dry-bulb hygrometer** one bulb is kept damp by a thin muslin cover dipping into water. If the air is saturated no water will evaporate. The drier it is, the more readily the water evaporates. As it does so, heat is drawn from the bulb, causing a fall in temperature (depression). The difference between wet and dry bulb readings shows the **relative humidity** of the air, as in Table 2. From these same readings we use other Tables to find the dewpoint temperatures and **the absolute humidity** (the number of grammes of water vapour in a cubic metre of air).

Table 2
Relative Humidity (%)

Dry Bulb	Depression of Wet Bulb (C°)							
(°C)	0.5	1.0	1.5	2.0	2.5	3.0	3.5	4.0
2	91	82	73	64	57	49	41	33
15	94	89	84	78	73	68	63	58
20	95	91	86	81	77	73	68	64
25	96	92	88	84	80	76	72	68
30	96	93	89	85	82	78	75	72
50	97	95	92	89	87	84	82	79
(Extracts from Table)								

If the wet and dry bulb readings are the same (depression 0.0°), the relative humidity is 100%. How do we then describe the air?

On a spring day (air temperature 15°C) the wet bulb reading is 12°C. What is the relative humidity? Would you describe the air as 'muggy' or 'fresh'?

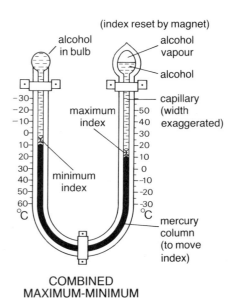

COMBINED MAXIMUM-MINIMUM THERMOMETER

5.49 When read daily, each metal indicator is re-set by a magnet.

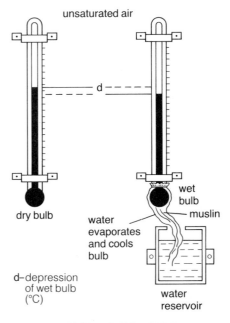

WET AND DRY BULB HYGROMETER

5.50 Finding the relative humidity.

Fig. 5.51 shows the amount of water which can be held as vapour *without* condensation occurring at a particular temperature.

Fig. 3.30 describes a **rain gauge**. Notice that the rain gauge in Photo 5.21 is in the open, on a non-splash surface.

sunshine recorder

Stevenson's screen
● 1.2m above the ground
● louvred at sides
● air space below roof
● white reflects insolation
● contains thermometers:
  1 maximum
  2 minimum
  3 wet and dry bulb (hygrometer)

rain gauge   open site   non-splash surface

P 5.21 Local weather station.

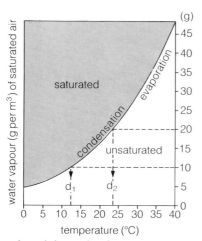

5.51 d_1 and d_2 are the dewpoints – temperatures when condensation takes place. Notice the amount of water held as vapour in each case.

The **sunshine recorder** (on the post) focuses the sun's rays onto a specially treated card (Fig. 5.52). This produces scorch-lines over the periods of time indicated. The times are added together to give the daily total of bright sunshine.

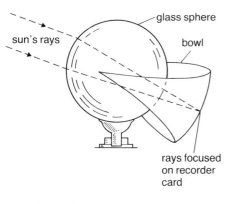

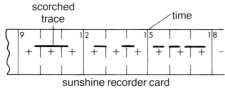

sunshine recorder card

5.52 The Campbell-Stokes sunshine recorder and its sensitised card.

Fig. 5.53 shows how the pressure of a mercury column balances the pressure of the 'column' of air above it. The mean sea-level pressure is taken as 1 bar (1000 millibars) – about 760 mm of mercury.

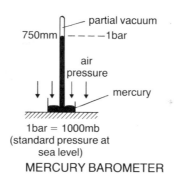

1bar = 1000mb
(standard pressure at sea level)
MERCURY BAROMETER

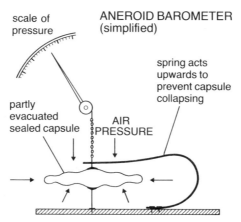

5.53 The principles of the mercury barometer and the aneroid (without liquid) barometer. Note that in physics a standard atmosphere supports 760 mm of mercury at 0°C (= 1013 mb).

Pressure is measured by a **barometer**.

In the **aneroid barometer** (Fig. 5.53) the changes in air pressure on a partly evacuated chamber are indicated by a moving pointer. Increasing air pressure acts against the spring, which moves upwards as the pressure falls. In a **barograph** a pen, instead of a pointer, records the pressure changes, by marking paper on a rotating drum.

An anemometer measures the wind strength and direction. In the pressure-tube type, shown in Fig. 5.54, strengthening wind *increases* the pressure within a float. Also as it passes the holes it causes suction, and so *reduces* the pressure on the surrounding liquid.

The movements are recorded on a calibrated paper on a rotating drum.

Wind direction can be estimated from weather-vane movements, or even drifting smoke – if you know where north is (and if it's not too gusty). For wind strength you can use the **Beaufort scale** as shown in Table 3.

Record other details of the weather when you read the instruments: estimate cloud cover (in eighths); describe cloud types and approximate altitude; report rain, fog, mist, etc.; estimate visibility relative to object at known distances.

Table 3

Beaufort number	description	wind speed (knots)	possible effects
0	calm	less than 1	smoke rises vertically
1	light air	1–3	direction shown by smoke, not wind vane
2	light breeze	4–6	wind felt on face; leaves rustle; vane moves
3	gentle breeze	7–10	leaves/twigs in constant motion; light flag extends
4	moderate breeze	11–16	dust, loose paper raised; small branches move
5	fresh breeze	17–21	small trees sway; crested wavelets on inland water
6	strong breeze	22–27	large branches move; wires whistle; umbrella problems
7	moderate gale	28–33	whole trees in motion; walking into wind difficult
8	fresh gale	34–40	twigs break off; walking into wind very difficult
9	strong gale	41–47	slight structural damage to roofs
10	whole gale	48–55	trees uprooted; damage to buildings
11	storm	56–63	widespread damage
12	hurricane	64 and over	widespread devastation

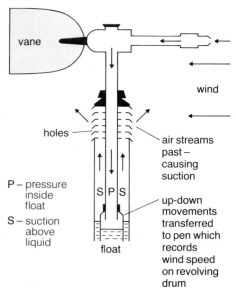

PRESSURE-TUBE ANEMOMETER

5.54 Measuring wind speed. A revolving cup anemometer with a revolution counter is often used.

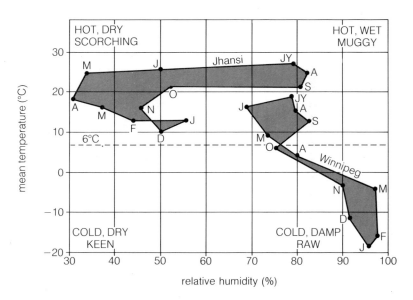

5.56 A combined plot of seasonal temperature and humidity for Jhansi (north-central India) and Winnipeg (south-central Canada).

Information from climatic graphs

By combining two sets of information on a graph (e.g. mean monthly temperatures with rainfall or humidity), the changing seasonal conditions are easier to appreciate.

Thus Fig. 5.55 combines the mean temperatures and rainfall for two places

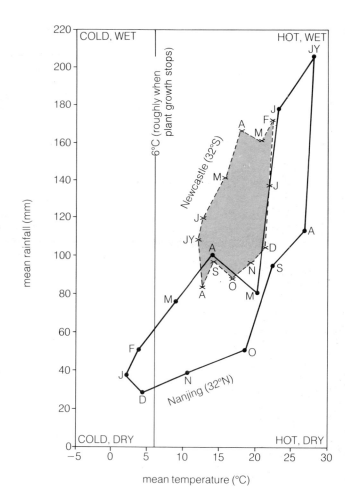

5.55 Hythergraphs for Nanjing (China) and Newcastle (Australia).

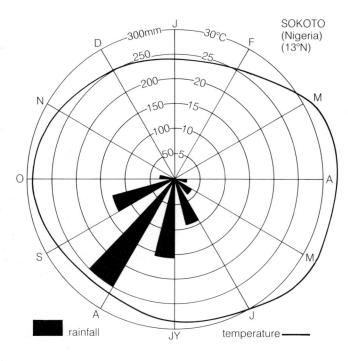

5.57 A circular graph showing temperature and rainfall.

on the sub-tropical eastern coastlands of continents – Nanjing (32°N) and Newcastle (32°S). Their seasonal differences (discussed on p. 74) are much more apparent than in the more usual graphs (Nos 7 and 14 in Fig. 5.8). **This hythergraph also shows at a glance when growing conditions may be affected**; for at 6°C most plants cease to absorb soil moisture.

Fig. 5.56 combines temperature and relative humidity, and gives a 'comfort' description of how local people might find the weather. You can imagine the relief in Jhansi as winter conditions follow the oppressive humid monsoon period, before the heat and drought of late spring. You can also see that while the Canadian prairies escape the mugginess of summer in eastern Canada, their winters are not just cold, but raw.

Fig. 5.57 shows another method of emphasising the distribution of the rainfall and monthly temperatures at Sokoto (No. 9 in Fig. 5.8).

Investigating the soil

This may appear more straightforward than dealing with an unseen atmosphere. But soil processes are complex, and people have been disturbing the top layers for a long time. The *exact* balances between the minerals in a soil is a matter for expert analysis. There are, therefore, limits to what *we* can do. Yet a simple investigation can tell us a lot about the relationships between minerals, moisture, plants and animal life in a given soil.

It is an advantage to visit several sites across a section of relief. Whether the underlying rocks change or not, soil conditions will vary from freely-drained to poorly-drained sites (Fig. 5.58). It is, of course, essential to obtain permission to disturb land.

1 **First describe the soil site:** (a) map reference; (b) date; (c) recent weather; (d) position on slope, angle of slope, elevation, aspect; (e) vegetation and land-use; (f) drainage; (g) parent rock; (h) type of soil.

2 **With a spade, dig a pit about a metre square**. One face should be well lit. Take samples from the face with a trowel. Seal them in polythene bags: label them. If soil is obviously layered – measure, describe, and draw its **profile** in a notebook; comment on the clarity of the horizons.

If a pit cannot be dug, use a **cylindrical auger** to bring up unbroken soil samples.

3 **Examine the texture**. Moisten slightly. Rub between fingers.
(a) **Sand**: feels gritty; particles do not stick to each other; leaves fingers clean.
(b) **Sandy-loam**: gritty; particles do stick; can be rolled into a weak thread; sand grains visible.
(c) **Clay-loam**: sticky; will polish; forms a thread, but not a ring.
(d) **Clay**: sticky; polishes; forms a thread; will bend into a ring.
There are many intermediate types. Particles may stick to each other because calcium carbonate is cementing them. **Test for carbonate** by adding 10% hydrochloric acid – it should fizz. Stones should be recorded by size, shape and kind.

For detail of particles pass a sample through a nest of coarse wire and fine nylon sieves (Fig. 5.59). A **mechanical shaker** helps separate sand, fine sand, silt and clay.

Otherwise pour a weighed sample into a column of water. Sand settles in a few minutes, silt after about 8 hours. Find the amount of particles suspended at a given time by leaving a **hydrometer** in the liquid. It indicates changing density as particles settle, and allows you to calculate the proportion of particle sizes remaining in suspension.

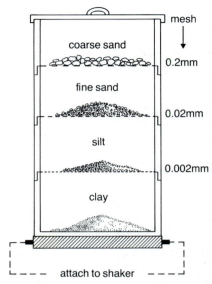

5.59 *The mechanical separation of soil particles.*

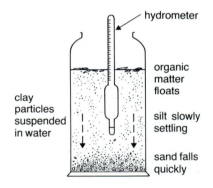

5.60 *Density changes with the rate of settling.*

4 **Record porosity**: many small holes – **porous**; larger, rounded spaces – **spongy**; vertical cracks – **fissured**; no spaces – **closed**.

5 **Describe the structure**: platy; columnar; blocky; crumby (p. 76). Observe the litter, humus, and water content by eye – dry; moist; wet; waterlogged.

6 **Colour may be an indication: red-brown** – well aerated iron compounds; **blue-green** – badly drained iron compounds; **white** (fizzes with acid) – carbonate; **shiny white** (very hard particles; no fizzing) – silica; **black** – humus (much carbon).

7 **Measure acidity/alkalinity** of the horizons with a **soil test kit** or **pH meter**. (a) **pour fresh soil into test tube** (10mm for clay; 25mm for loam; 40mm for sand soil); (b) add 50 mm barium sulphate to aid settling; (c) add 20 mm distilled water;

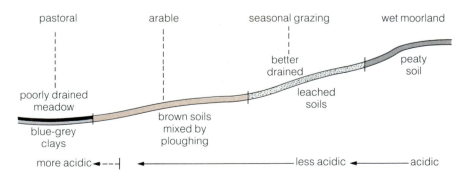

5.58 *Different forms of land-use with changing soil conditions down the slope (see p. 82).*

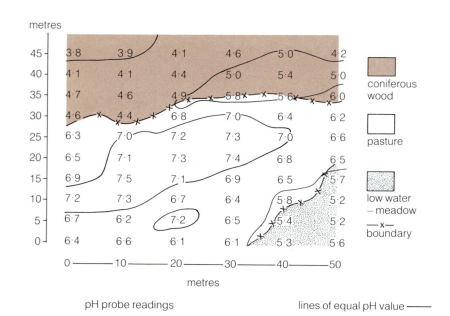

metres

coniferous wood

pasture

low water – meadow

x boundary

pH probe readings   lines of equal pH value ——

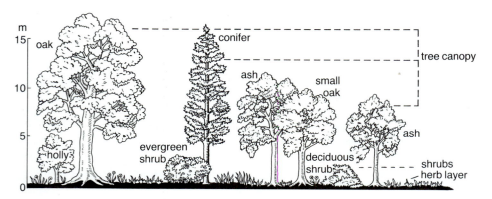

5.62 Vegetation strata (different levels) over a chosen transect.

tree

shrub

herb

needle leaf

broad leaf

deciduous

evergreen

tall tree (>25m)   t

low tree (8-10m)   l

medium tree (19-25m)   m

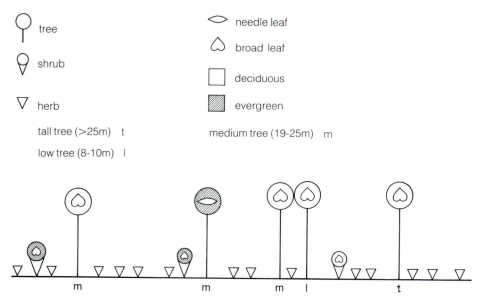

5.63 The use of symbols and codes to describe vegetation along a transect.

5.61 pH values for soils recorded after probing over a grid pattern. What general conclusions could you make about soil conditions in the area surveyed? Suggest reasons for this.

(d) **add 10 mm indicator solution** – a mixture of dyes which react to various pH values; (e) **insert bung and shake**: stand until clear coloured liquid appears; (f) **compare with colour chart of pH values:** pH 1–2 red; 3–4 red/orange; 5 orange; 6 yellow; 7 yellow-green; 8 green; 9 blue-green; 10 blue.

There are relatively inexpensive **pH probes** with a sensitised tip and meter attached. Probe to a consistent depth; wait for the meter to settle; read pH. Clean the tip with fine sandpaper between each probe, and take numerous readings over a selected area marked with a grid. **Fig. 5.61 shows the kind of results which might be obtained from adjacent areas of coniferous woodland, pasture and water-meadow.**

8 **Fauna**: record evidence of the presence and activities of soil fauna, and any larger animals affecting the soil.

Recording local vegetation

This can be recorded both on a plan and on sections which show various layers of vegetation.

1 **Tape a plot** of, say, 500 m². Divide it into a grid.

(a) Select and identify dominant trees. Plot their position on the plan.

(b) Estimate the height of the tree tops and lower branches (or use a clinometer, see p. 22). Record details. Measure the width of each crown by laying a tape on the ground beneath the tree.

(c) Fill in the same information for shrubs, and note the herb layer as you go.

2 **Construct a sample profile**: work out the mean heights and distribution of trees, saplings, shrubs, and ground vegetation, and construct a scale section (Fig. 5.62).

3 **Actual profiles** of the vegetation may be drawn for transects across the area.

There are usually problems, apart from identification, from dense vegetation, and over-lapping layers. For practice, first choose a park or small, open wood and develop the techniques. Divide the tasks between small teams.

4 Valuable studies of the distribution of plants may be done without a detailed knowledge of species. **Codes are often used to describe the plants** – their size, function, leaf shape, and so on. Fig. 5.63 shows a few such symbols, and how they might be used to describe the vegetation in Fig. 5.62.

5 **The transect and quadrat method** may be used in the latter case to study the nature and plant distribution in the lower, herb layer, or for similar studies of other vegetation:

(a) Choose sites on a transect across, say, a moorland (or throw markers from one site to the next to choose locations at random).

(b) Place a quadrat frame, with a cord grid tied on, over the vegetation. It must be big enough to include a selection of units of local vegetation.

(c) Drop a needle from each grid intersect and record either (i) which leaves are hit, or (ii) what is rooted beneath (leaves hide other plants).

(d) Repeat for 50 or more sites. Then calculate the frequency with which particular species occur *at least once* in the frame. Or record the number of occurrences at a site and find the mean local frequency for particular species.

Energy and the ecosystem

A single green plant uses only about 1% of the sun's energy falling on its leaves for photosynthesis. Although it makes new tissue, much of this energy is lost in respiration by the living plant. The increase in new matter is the **net production**.

We can measure the net production of a unit of vegetation, or a crop, in grammes accumulated per square metre per day (Fig. 5.64).

Compare the net production by some of the **natural vegetation** with the high figures for **crops** like rice, wheat and sugar cane in some parts of the world. But remember that big inputs of *extra* energy are needed to achieve these crop yields.

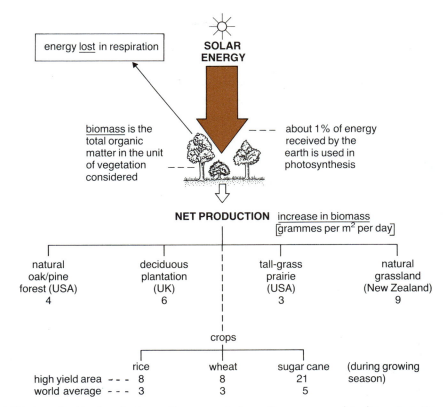

5.64 Net production by plants – or the amount of new tissue accumulated in a given time by photosynthesis. Much of the energy fixed during photosynthesis will have been used up as heat as the plants 'breathe' (during respiration).

In Photo 5.22 the pastures are being irrigated. The food bins near the barns contain extra processed cattle feed. Explain carefully all the energy inputs in this rural scene. Consider the natural inputs, how they pass through the food chain, and the energy used to create and run the farm.

P 5.22 Young dairy stock on one of the many fenced paddocks of a farm on the Canterbury Plains, New Zealand.

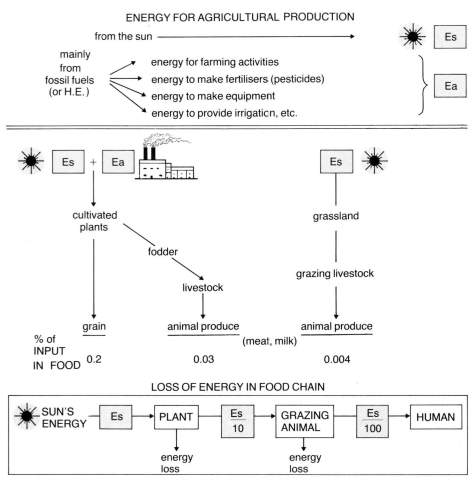

ENERGY FOR AGRICULTURAL PRODUCTION

from the sun ⟶ Es

mainly
from
fossil fuels
(or H.E.)
- energy for farming activities
- energy to make fertilisers (pesticides)
- energy to make equipment
- energy to provide irrigation, etc.

Ea

Es + Ea → cultivated plants

Es → grassland

cultivated plants → grain
fodder → livestock → animal produce (meat, milk)
grassland → grazing livestock → animal produce

% of INPUT IN FOOD: 0.2   0.03   0.004

LOSS OF ENERGY IN FOOD CHAIN

SUN'S ENERGY → Es → PLANT → Es/10 → GRAZING ANIMAL → Es/100 → HUMAN

energy loss   energy loss

5.65 Agricultural production depends on energy inputs from the sun and from fossil fuels and generating stations. Electricity provides direct power (eg. from water pumps) or indirectly via factory products (eg. fertilisers) to increase farm productivity. Notice the different proportions of energy in animal produce from natural grassland and from intensive forms of farming.

Factories use energy to make fertilisers and pesticides; electric energy supplies pumped water for irrigation; and energy is used in all forms of agricultural activity.

Notice the relatively low *world* averages for these crops. Many people cannot afford such high energy inputs, so the yield of their crops is much lower.

You can see in Fig. 5.65 what a small proportion of the energy put in is eventually available to us in food. Energy is lost, at each stage in a food-chain, so we need to keep this as short as possible. It looks as though we would best achieve this by being vegetarians.

However, most people seek a mixed diet for nutrition, so **the role of livestock in farm systems is important.** Farmers try to cut down energy losses by their animals by supplying fodder in sheds; but in doing so must use energy for light, heat, tractor fuel and so on. Agricultural suc-

cess is all about finding a suitable energy balance.

Understanding the ecosystem *can* **help to improve productivity by rural consumers.** In the tropics, where people are often short of high protein food, many ponds are choked by green plants (producers). In China carp have been introduced to feed on, and so keep down, pond weeds. They rapidly put on weight, and their droppings feed very small animal life (plankton), which are consumed by other fish. Thus a bothersome weed is converted to abundant high quality food.

94

Theme 5 Making sure

1 What forms of water are included in the term 'precipitation'?

2 Relief (orographic) rainfall occurs where:
   (a) air heated by the surface cools on rising; (b) air is forced to rise at a cold front; (c) ice particles form in the upper air; (d) hills force moist air to rise and expand. Which?

3 When warm air overlies colder air, there is: (a) convection; (b) inversion; (c) dispersion; (d) turbulence. Which?

4 When moist unstable air rises, it (a) expands/contracts, and so (b) heats/cools, causing (c) evaporation/condensation, which (d) releases/extracts heat to/from the rising air. It thus remains (e) denser/less dense than the surrounding air, and so (f) begins to sink/continues to rise. Say which is correct in each case.

5 Rainfall contours are called: isohyets; isobars; isopanes. Which?

6 Make a station plot to show the following conditions: temperature 6°C; wind north-east, force 3; sky three-quarters covered; rain showers; barometric pressure 996 mb.

7 Is stable or unstable air more likely to give rise to the following:
   (a) thunderstorms; (b) fog? Explain why.

8 What kind of atmospheric conditions are likely to cause fog to affect a large airport such as London Heathrow?

9 Frontal rainfall affects a wide area; relief rain is of more local importance. Explain why.

10 Much of western Britain in highland. How does this influence the amount and distribution of the annual rainfall over the country as a whole? Consider the prevailing wind (Fig. 5.19).

11 Much of Britain's highlands are of hard resistant rock, with thin soils. (a) How does this affect rainfall run-off? (b) Why are upland reservoirs so important?

12 Why do even short droughts lead to water rationing in a country with a high mean annual rainfall, like the United Kingdom? Consider the facts in Q.9, and also demands.

13 Suggest why at Perth (Western Australia) an off-spin bowler, who likes to float the ball into a breeze, is seldom put on to bowl before noon.

14 Fig. 5.66 shows a surface weather map and the cross-section of a westward-moving hurricane (tropical cyclone).
   (a) What is the wind strength at **A** and **B**? (b) Why is it calm in the 'eye' of the hurricane? (c) Why are the skies clear in the 'eye'? (d) Describe how a household at **X** will be affected by the changing strength and direction of the wind as the hurricane approaches and passes. (e) Where does the heaviest rain occur? (f) Describe the clouds at **Y**, their type and height. (g) Suggest why they flatten out at a certain altitude. (h) Why does condensation in hot, moist air boost these great updraughts?

15 Hailstones get larger by melting and refreezing as they fall by gravity and rise on convection updraughts. What conditions may cause such a strong convection?

16 What is meant by 'the ITCZ'? How do its annual movements affect the climates of tropical continental lands?

17 Explain why the world's highest air temperatures occur near 30° latitude, rather than near the equator.

18 In equatorial lowlands, at what time of day are the following most likely: (a) heavy storms; (b) clear skies; (c) mist? Explain why.

19 'Mountains make their own climates.' (a) What is meant by this? (b) Why should altitude affect vegetation? (c) Where in equatorial latitudes might you find natural pastures of short grassland, with sheep farming?

20 Africa's tropical wet-and-dry regions are sometimes described on climatic maps as having 'savanna-type' climate. Why is this a particularly poor description? (See p. 74.)

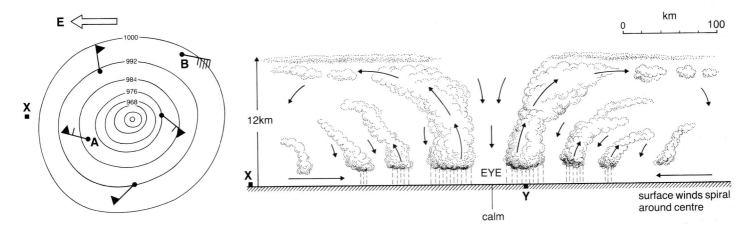

5.66 In the outer tropics such hurricanes form over hot surface water and move eastward, many during late summer, over the Caribbean and into south-east USA. Notice the separate towering columns of cloud, with colder air sinking between them.

21 The mean annual temperatures for London and its surroundings are as shown:

Table 4

location	mean annual temperature (°C)		average altitude (m)
	maximum	minimum	
central London	14.6	7.4	25
inner suburbs	14.2	6.4	60
surrounding country	13.7	5.5	85

(a) Why do these mean annual figures vary as they do?

(b) Which value, maximum or minimum, shows the greater contrasts? Suggest why.

(c) Why would still, clear winter nights lead to particularly great contrasts between the various locations?

Table 5

river	mean monthly discharge over ten-year period (cumecs $\times 10^2$)											
	Jan	Feb	Mar	Apr	May	Jun	Jul	Aug	Sep	Oct	Nov	Dec
Middle Kolyma (Siberia)	1	0.8	0.6	0.6	28	97	54	44	35	24	3	2
Lower Ganges (India)	29	23	16	17	17	48	219	480	382	184	71	39

22 (a) Plot the figures shown for each of these large rivers in Table 5. Using an atlas, follow the course of each river.

(b) Give reasons in each case for the variation through the year. Refer to the appropriate climatic graphs in Fig. 5.8. Consider the effects of freezing, thawing, change in prevailing wind, convection, time-lag, and any other facts which might affect their flow.

23 Local winds may occasionally have special effects. Fig. 5.67 shows where four strong winds affect Mediterranean countries for days at a time, especially in spring. **The cold Mistral and Bora can ruin fruit and flower crops. The Sirocco and Khamsin bring unpleasantly hot, dry and dusty air from the desert.**

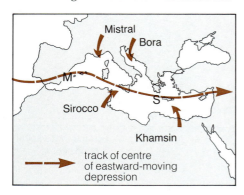

5.67 Depressions create local winds and abrupt temperature changes.

(a) Fig. 5.67 shows the track of a low-pressure system moving eastwards. M and **S** indicate where its centre would be when the Mistral and Sirocco are blowing. Draw a diagram to show how wind circulation about the low will draw air **from** the land areas in each case.

(b) The Mistral is fed by air from high icefields. This tends to reinforce the strong, cold down-valley winds. Explain.

24 (a) In Fig. 5.68 A, B, C, D show air pressures (isobars) over West Africa and south-east Asia for January and July. State which month each refers to.

(b) Copy each map and mark in the wind directions. Put **L** and **H** over centres of low and high pressure. Give reasons for these particular pressures during that month.

25 Put the following in order of **increasing particle size:** sand; silt; gravel; clay.

26 How may the size of soil particles affect their water content?

27 Why is it important for fertile soils to be well aerated as well as moist?

28 A small volume of hydrochloric acid is added to small pieces of: (a) granite; (b) limestone; (c) sandstone. There is no reaction from (a); fizzing from (b); and slight fizzing from (c). Which rock might break down to produce an acidic soil?

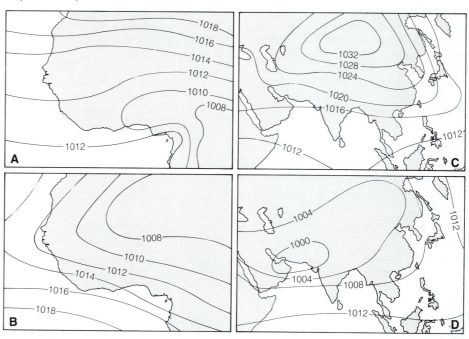

5.68 Seasonal reversals of air flow.

29 For cultivation, a soil with a pH value of 5.0 would probably need additional lime/sand/salt – which?

30 Which characteristics of the soil – particle size; texture; structure; chemical nature; method of accumulation; physical mixture – are indicated by the following descriptions: (a) silt; (b) alluvium; (c) loam; (d) czernozem; (e) platy; (f) saline?

31 What is meant by 'leaching' when applied to soils?

32 Why does leaching by acidic soil water make for infertile soils?

33 What may cause a soil horizon to be: (a) light coloured; (b) very dark; (c) red, or red-brown?

34 Explain what is meant by a 'soil catena', in relation to a sloping landscape.

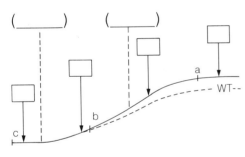

5.69 Groundwater and surface materials.

35 Copy Fig. 5.69, which shows water levels in the rocks and the consequent surface drainage. It also shows movements of soil materials on the slope.

(a) The drainage is described as 'poor' (**P**); 'sometimes waterlogged' (**W**): 'excessively drained' (**E**); 'freely drained' (**F**). Put **P,W,E,F** in their appropriate *box*.

(b) **WT** shows an average profile of the water-table. Explain this, and relate it to the surface drainage.

(c) **a-b** and **b-c** are surfaces which lose/gain material. Write 'receiving' and 'shedding' in the appropriate *brackets*.

36 Copy Fig. 5.70, which shows a chalk escarpment.

(a) Soil pH values of 7.5, 5.8, 8.3, 5.6 were recorded at **A,B,C,D**, but *not* in

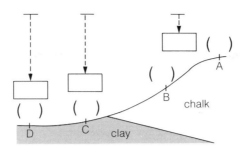

5.70 Changes in soil acidity and land-use.

that order. Put each in its appropriate *bracket*.

(b) The soils are described as: 'crumby marl' (**M**); 'waterlogged when wet, cracked when dry' (**W**); 'thin' (**T**); and 'leached downland soil' (**L**). Put **M, W, T, L** in the appropriate *box*.

(c) The land-use is described as: 'sheep grazing' (**G**); 'best arable' (**A**); 'heavy arable' (**H**). Write **G,A,H** *above the appropriate arrow*.

Explain your choice in each case.

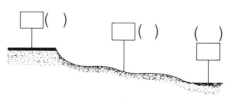

5.71 Soils vary as the slope changes from the old retreating tableland to riverside flats.

37 Copy Fig. 5.71. It shows a soil catena often found in African savanna lands.

Its soils are described as: 'dark, clayey, cracks when dry' (**D**); 'red, sandy, with concrete-like layers' (**R**); 'red-brown, freely-drained, with minerals mixed by erosion' (**M**).

These are said to support: 'poor savanna – little agricultural value' (**W**); 'grazing land' (**G**); 'crops by irrigation' (**C**).

Put the appropriate letters for soils in the *boxes* and those for land-use in *brackets*.

38 Suggest why in equatorial forest thick undergrowth is found mainly on the edge of clearings or river banks. Why can travellers' views be so misleading?

39 A certain type of vegetation may be the result of clearance, rather than simply due to climatic conditions. Give examples of how this might come about.

40 Large-scale forest clearance can lead to a decrease in local rainfall

(a) What might cause this to happen? Think how millions of leaves affect the atmosphere.

(b) Draw a simple diagram to show a chain of events leading from forest clearance to impoverished soils.

41 The lands bordering the world's great ice sheets bear a tundra vegetation of mosses, lichen, sedges, and small shrubs.

(a) In early summer the upper soil temperatures are often *higher* than air temperatures. Suggest why.

(b) Many plants are low and cushiony. How does this help them? (Consider (a) for instance).

(c) There is rapid flowering and fruiting in late spring and early summer. Suggest why.

(d) Some plants are adapted to cope with boggy conditions, others to absorb water at low temperatures. What are the reasons for this?

42 (a) What is a 'micro-climate'? (b) Why are favourable micro-climates so important for plants in a tundra region? Explain in terms of aspect, exposure, and drainage.

43 Photosynthesis results in the production of (a) carbonate; (b) carbohydrate; (c) nitrogen compounds. Which?

44 Which of these statements is *incorrect*, and why?

(a) Photosynthesis takes place in green leaves when light energy is absorbed.

(b) Respiration takes in oxygen, which helps to break down a plant's carbohydrates.

(c) Energy is gained at all stages in a food-chain.

(d) Producers directly use the energy of the sun.

45 In what ways are plants affected by (a) high air temperatures; (b) low ones?

46 Why are the following important for plant development: (a) nitrifying bacteria; (b) humus; (c) soil spaces?

47 (a) Plants which survive desert conditions have special adaptations:
(i) to reduce transpiration;
(ii) to make use of what moisture there is. Give examples of each.
(b) Suggest why desert plants are widely spaced, with much surface exposed between them.

48 (a) Give each of the following its role in a food-chain (e.g. producer, primary producer, primary consumer, secondary consumer).
(i) grass-seed; mouse; hawk; snake;
(ii) lion; grass; vulture; zebra.
(b) Which may be both herbivore and carnivore (omnivore)?
(c) Are places in the food-chain necessarily fixed?

49 Describe the role of flash floods in creating desert landforms.

50 Why and when is dew formed in hot desert conditions? How does it affect rocks and plants?

51 Wind succeeds in altering desert landscapes in many ways. Explain this with reference to: (a) abrasion; (b) deflation; (c) transportation.

Consider the terms used

Ecosystem: a community of plants, animals and their non-living habitat, with energy inputs from the sun. It can be studied at any scale, from the world as a whole to a small defined unit such as a pond.

A nutrient nourishes a living organism, allowing growth and normal functions to take place.

A herbivore consumes herbs (including grasses).

A carnivore is mainly a flesh eater (and an **omnivore** eats subtances of plant and animal origin).

A predator preys on other creatures.

Ephemeral means lasting only a short period – a few days.

Succulent: having fleshy or juicy tissues.

An epiphyte is a plant which benefits from the light, air and moisture around the tree on which it grows, but takes nothing from the tree.

Lapse rate is the rate of decrease of air temperature with altitude. When air is unsaturated with moisture this is called the **dry rate** (DALR) – if it exchanges no heat with its surroundings.

Saturated air holds as much water vapour as it possibly can; as many water molecules enter the air as leave it. Such air cools with altitude at the **saturated rate** (SALR).

Adiabatic means that there is no loss or gain of heat from outside.

To occlude is to shut off or cut off. An **occluded front** occurs when cold air cuts off warmer air from the earth's surface.

Inversion is a reversal of the normal lapse of temperature with altitude (an increase in temperature with height).

Maritime means connected with the sea.

Absolute humidity is the amount of water vapour per unit volume of air (g/m^3).

Relative humidity is the ratio of the amount of water vapour in an air mass and the maximum it could hold at that temperature (usually a percentage).

A hygrometer is used to measure relative humidity.

A hydrometer measures the density (or specific gravity) of a liquid and is designed to float vertically in it.

Dew point is the temperature at which water vapour saturates the air and begins to condense (form dew).

Aneroid means without liquid; and so is applied to the barometer based on an exhausted metal box with a corrugated lid, which air pressure can move up or down.

Humus is a dark coloured structureless mass formed when the plant and animal content of the soil decomposes. In one form it binds itself to minute clay particles (a **clay-humus complex**) and improves the nutrient-holding properties of soil.

Leaching involves the washing downward of organic matter and soil minerals within the soil profile.

A trace element is one which is present in minute quantities yet essential for plant development and growth.

pH is a measure of the acidity or alkalinity (basic nature) of a soil or solution. A strictly neutral solution has a pH value of 6.5; below this it is acidic, above this basic.

Photosynthesis is the manufacture of organic compounds by green plants from water and carbon dioxide, using the energy of sunlight taken in by the green chlorophyll.

Soil horizon: a well-defined layer within a soil profile with different physical and chemical properties from that above and below it.

A catena is a sequence of soil types that occurs from the top to bottom of a hill slope (usually developed from similar parent material); it reflects differences of drainage and slope angle. Similar catenas are seen in areas of similar relief and climate.

A barchan is a crescent-shaped sand dune, with horns pointing away from the prevailing wind direction.

Seif dunes are in the form of ridges developing parallel to the prevailing wind. Cross winds help to build up their height and width.

A flash flood is caused by rapid run-off after heavy rain, and rises rapidly when channelled along a dry valley (wadi) – a high discharge over a short period of time.

Introducing Parts II and III

People as part of the ecosystem

We share the planet with some five thousand million people, and our numbers are increasing by a quarter of a million *a day*! Developing technologies bring us into closer and closer contact with each other. We use rapid transport, and receive instant phone, radio and TV reports of events in distant places.

What we all make of it depends not just on our control over the physical environment, but on relationships between peoples of different racial, social, religious, political and economic backgrounds.

There are wide social and economic gaps between peoples. **Three-quarters of the world's population lives in the less developed countries (LDCs)**, which together produce only about a fifth of the world's wealth. Some have a very small share indeed.

Fig. II.1 shows the broad distribution of the LDCs, most of them in the south. The wealthier, more developed countries (MDCs) are mainly in the north, where an industrial revolution took place during the last century, with coal as its energy source. Industrialisation spread from western Europe into Russia, and westwards to America, with Japan as a latecomer.

There is great variety within the MDCs, but even greater contrasts in the less developed parts of the world. **Many countries achieve only a low agricultural production. For some this becomes increasingly insufficient as their population grows. These are the least developed countries (LLDCs)**, such as Chad and Ethiopia. Whereas others, like Singapore and South Korea, which have been developing light industries and export manufactured goods, are perhaps better described as '**newly industrialising countries' (NICs).**

Fig. II.2A shows that Ethiopia and Somaliland, desperately poor LLDCs, with low incomes and little economic progress, are geographically close to the oil-rich states of the Middle East (which, in fact, contribute financial aid to the poorer countries). There are also contrasts *within* the oil-exporting countries themselves. For while their new commercial cities employ advanced technologies, the ways of life of many of their people have changed little with the centuries.

Here, too, the prosperous core of the Sudan (its northern irrigated lands) contrasts with the expanses of semi-desert bordering Ethiopia, which supports a poverty-stricken population, and with the south, where scattered tribes live among the Sudd swamps.

Fig. II.2B also shows how little the description 'LDC' reveals about a country. In **Brazil** 'average income' is almost meaningless. Statistics of national wealth – GNP per head (p. 168) – put Brazil high

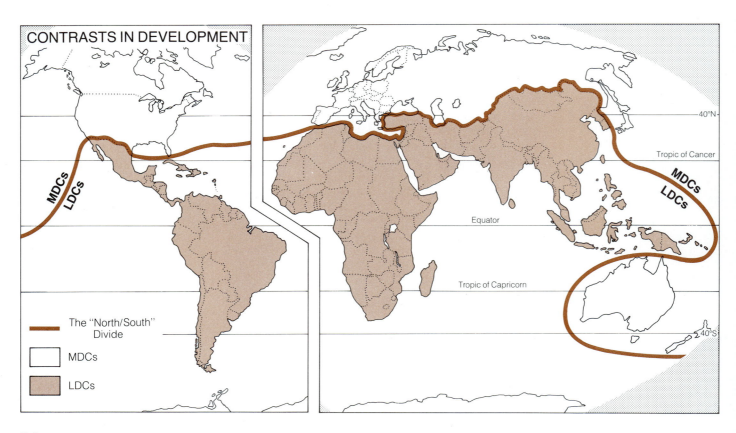

CONTRASTS IN DEVELOPMENT

The "North/South" Divide

MDCs

LDCs

40°N
Tropic of Cancer
Equator
Tropic of Capricorn
40°S

MDCs
LDCs

II.1

"THE LESS DEVELOPED WORLD" – GREAT DIFFERENCES

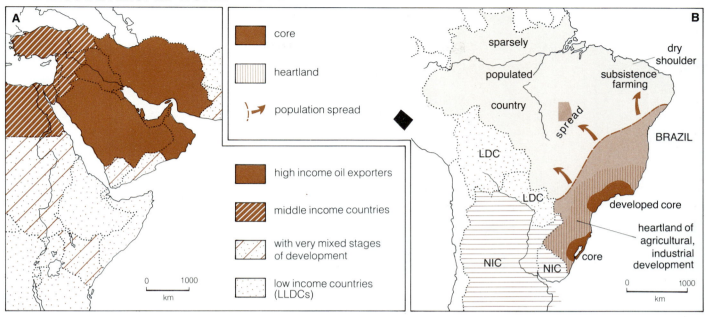

A

core

heartland

population spread

high income oil exporters

middle income countries

with very mixed stages of development

low income countries (LLDCs)

0   1000
km

B

sparsely

populated

country

dry shoulder

subsistence farming

spread

LDC

LDC

BRAZIL

developed core

heartland of agricultural, industrial development

core

NIC   NIC

0   1000
km

II.2

among the middle income group of LDCs. It is often described as an NIC. Yet some regions are overpopulated and underdeveloped, and large areas virtually empty and underdeveloped.

Its agricultural–industrial–commercial wealth is concentrated in its south-eastern heartland, with huge cities at its core. These urban areas, in themselves, contain extremes of wealth and poverty. But beyond are the poor cash crop communities of its tropical coastlands and the dry north-east. These, and the vast empty areas inland, make little contribution to the economy compared with the core region.

The huge, relatively empty Amazonian Lowlands tempt poor families from the over-crowded core regions and commercial developers seeking wealth from timber, tropical produce, or ranching, to clear forest and establish settlements. This occurs particularly where new roads are extended into the interior. And though the extent of destruction, relative to the vast area under forest, is often exaggerated, we see here the conflict between people desperate for new opportunities and the need to preserve the world's most extensive natural rainforests, with their wealth of unique species and inter-dependent communities of plants and animals (p.256).

Bolivia, too, appears as a middle income country. But there is deep poverty in parts of this landlocked state, with its great physical contrasts.

It is obviously impossible to consider every part of the world. But we can look at various constraints which influence what people do, and how they go about it. And just as the physical world reacts to inputs of energy, so do our own activities. **Part II shows how effectively, or otherwise, people harness and use energy for agriculture and industry, for transport, and for communicating with one another.**

In Part III we look in more detail at how people live in their various communities. We consider patterns of social behaviour. And we see how our increasing numbers are affecting the environment.

PART II

Changing the environment

Theme 6 Agriculture

6.1 Energy for survival

Whatever society we live in, we need food, water, shelter and security in order to survive. Above all we must have a balanced intake of **nutrients** to remain healthy. But the **energy** from our food must give us enough strength to obtain that food, and other necessities.

Commercial farming provides food on a large scale, but it's a complicated economic undertaking. So it's better to look first at fairly simple energy relationships between people (**consumers**) and the plant and animal produce (**biomass**) they consume. There are still sparsely populated parts of the world, with space to move, where communities live by hunting and gathering plants, though outside contacts are intruding.

Using energy to gather energy

The bushmen of the dry Kalahari, and various tribal groups in the tropical forests of South America and south-east Asia, are **hunters and gatherers.** They spend several days a week collecting sufficient natural resources to provide energy for their searches, and for daily activities, such as constructing shelters, making clothing from collected plant fibres, and their leisure pursuits. They must provide sufficient for the young and old. **Fig. 6.1. shows the energy balance for those involved.**

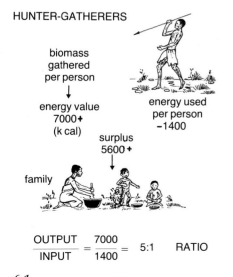

HUNTER-GATHERERS

biomass gathered per person
↓
energy value 7000+ (k cal)

energy used per person −1400

surplus 5600+

family

$$\frac{\text{OUTPUT}}{\text{INPUT}} = \frac{7000}{1400} = 5:1 \quad \text{RATIO}$$

6.1

HUNTER-GATHERER

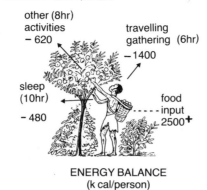

other (8hr) activities −620

travelling gathering (6hr) −1400

sleep (10hr) −480

food input 2500+

ENERGY BALANCE (k cal/person)

6.2

It is estimated that in a favourable tropical woodland **hunter-gatherers** require 40 ha of territory to collect the 300 kg of plant material (leaves, seeds, nuts, fruits, roots) needed to provide a person with the **minimum daily requirement of energy**, about 2400 kilograms-calories (kcal). Their catch of small animals and the occasional large kill would add, say, 100 kcal.

This total biomass would also provide about 60 g of protein, and includes fat (from nuts and animals). **Proteins are needed to build animal tissues.** Protein sources are meat, fish, eggs, milk, and certain plants (e.g. beans). A family of five might thus get a balanced diet from 200 ha of forest, though not all ecosystems would be so favourable.

Fig. 6.2 gives an idea of the energy expended during collecting, and also when resting. (For instance, walking would use energy at a rate of some 600 kcal/hr and running 800–1000 kcal/hr.) They save energy by knowing their territory well, thus cutting down searching time. Sites near water, from which they can collect as much food as possible, may become semi-permanent homes.

The ratio of energy obtained to energy put in

The ratio of energy obtained to that expended by the hunter-gatherer is about 5:1. This ratio is a useful indicator of what happens in various forms of farming. For instance, tribal people growing rice in Borneo, who just use human energy, achieve a ratio of about 7:1. **Yet commercial rice production in California**, which uses large inputs of machinery, fuel, fertiliser, and pesticides, and yields a great deal of grain, **achieves a ratio of less than 2:1.** Much depends on the scale of production, and whether human power, animal-power, or machine-power is used.

In commercial agriculture the ratio of energy obtained to energy put in is *low* by comparison. Why is this? What are the advantages to people *who can afford it?*

Is the provision of high-energy foods – carbohydrates and fats – sufficient in itself for health? Suggest why hunter-gatherers often prove to be in better health than peasant farmers in the LDCs.

6.2 Types of farming – inputs and outputs of energy

Early agricultural societies concentrated on food production. Farming, compared with hunting-gathering, produces more food and fibres, and so enables the whole society to use energy in other ways. They expended energy, of course, on clearing land, planting, weeding, harvesting, and tending animals; but **there was sufficient output for people to do other activities, including craft work.**

When draught animals were used, like the ox and donkey, they freed even more human energy. This led to further craft production, simple manufacturing, barter and trade and more leisure. In the villages and small towns not everyone tilled the soil.

When wind and water power were harnessed the surplus energy increased, and could be used in other ways. In these new societies farmers now had to feed a ruling class, plus administrators, military, merchants, and all the non-agricultural labourers and their employers.

Two basic types of agriculture now existed: subsistence agriculture, where the family farmed to feed itself (but paid dues in produce or cash to a land-owner), and **commercial agriculture**, where people farmed for sale and profit.

6.3 In most parts of the world, at various times, families depending on hunting and gathering have come to live in a settled agricultural society. Domestic animals can then provide extra energy for cultivation and transport, or be reared for food – as they were in this small, fenced hamlet in Saxon England.

SHIFTING AGRICULTURE
energy (kcal × 10⁴)

burning, fencing
7

clearing
10

tools, seeds
4

CLEARED LAND
1ha

planting, weeding
25

carrying
15

harvesting
9

OUTPUT

CROP YIELD

TOTAL INPUT
70

980

people receive
650

pigs, chicken receive
330

meat, eggs
10

OUTPUT
INPUT
= 980 / 70
= 14:1 RATIO

660
food energy

→ supports 7 persons (who need 87.6 per person per yr)

6.4 Energy put into clearing and cultivation is rewarded by a much greater energy output in food for families and feedstuff for animals.

Farming involves many energy exchanges, even where the family cultivates crops mainly to subsist. In tropical forests and savannas many people practise **shifting agriculture**. They fell trees and burn the cuttings and undergrowth to clear the land and destroy weeds. This passes nutrients from the ash to the soil. The cleared plots are cultivated for a number of years, then abandoned as the soil loses its fertility. They are usually left fallow for a long period, so that the soil can gradually accumulate nutrients again.

The energy people use on these tasks can be estimated, and the hours they put in recorded. **Fig. 6.4 looks at the kind of inputs and outputs involved in clearing and cultivating a hectare of tropical forest.** One year's labour provides some 6 600 000 kcal of food energy, and so, as each person needs some 876 000 kcal/yr, it will support 7 persons. So 40 hectares of land scattered about a settlement should support about 280 people. As we shall see, this kind of farming is often combined with more settled forms of agriculture.

Look at Fig. 6.4. What advantage is there in supplying pigs and chicken with so much food energy when their *energy* return is so small?

Why should we be careful when judging farmers' efficiency simply in terms of energy ratios?

6.3 Agricultural systems

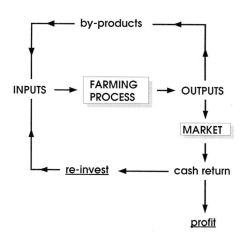

by-products

INPUTS → FARMING PROCESS → OUTPUTS

MARKET

re-invest ← cash return

profit

6.5

Fig. 6.5 represents a settled agricultural system.

In the less developed countries hundreds of millions of families are engaged in **subsistence farming** – farming to survive. They concentrate on feeding the family from the land they occupy. They may sell surplus food, or even a cash crop, but in small quantities.

Most farmers try to get the highest yield from their land. Success and development depend on whether they can afford costly inputs, or can improve their technology. **As the inputs increase, their farming tends to become more intensive.**

This contrasts with the way the shifting cultivators make **extensive** use of large areas, with **few inputs.**

In many of the LDCs this extensive land use applies to animal grazing (pastoralism). In the savannas people slowly move their animals across the grassland with the seasons – a form of **transhumance**. In the dry interior of West Africa the Fulani drive their herds over long-established routes – 'following the rains'. They maintain water-holes, and after grazing burn grass to ensure early growth when the next wet season comes. In East Africa, too, there is **semi-nomadic pastoralism**. Some of the herdmen's relatives remain to cultivate land about a semi-permanent homestead.

Extensive farming also describes the wide commercial ranching of sheep and cattle on the interior plains and foothills of North America. To start with the animals roamed over relatively poor quality pasture. But in time the ranches began to include irrigated fodder crops, as did the cattle estancias of the Argentine pampas, so making their farming more intensive.

At the turn of the century, pioneer settlers converted wide expanses of the Canadian prairies into **extensive grain-growing** lands (p. 118). Year after year the nutrient-rich soils have provided huge quantities of wheat for world markets; though, in fact, declining yields have led to more inputs and careful soil treatment.

This kind of extensive farming gives low yields compared with Britain's intensive wheat cultivation. **But it produces enormous quantities from its huge areas.**

Intensive commercial farming is typical of western Europe and eastern USA, where farmers change the proportion of crops and livestock to suit the market. Here, too, are very intensive forms of farming, such as market gardening.

P 6.1 Hoeing a family plot in Zaïre. After several years' use they rest the soil and clear land beyond for cultivation.

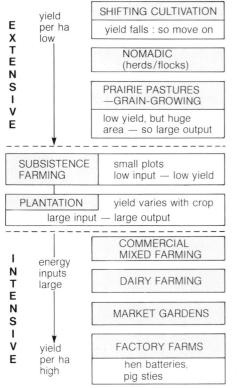

6.6 Agricultural systems which differ greatly in their inputs and outputs.

Plantations, market gardens, 'factory farms', and commercial dairying aim at producing single profitable crops or livestock products, or produce in daily demand. Which type of produce does each specialise in?

6.4 Three contrasting systems

Peasant subsistence farming

Fig. 6.7 shows a typical system practised by millions of families in the LDCs. They farm rented land, or supply produce instead of rent to the landlord. In some countries peasant farmers have a share of communal land and pay dues to the community. In others people belong to a tribal group and farm tribal land.

Their chief input is the family labour. This is used to grow a variety of crops and obtain animal produce from a few chicken, ducks, sheep, goats, or cattle – depending on where they live. Their first aim is to support themselves.

If they own a mule or bullock, it represents another large energy input, in fodder. However, the animal may obtain energy from communal rough grazing or from by-products from the crops (straw and leaves). Its dung can be used as fertiliser – though, unfortunately, in dry lands, where wood is scarce, it is often burnt as fuel.

Tools are usually made locally. So is simple machinery, such as a wooden cart, or bucket-and-wheel. Many families produce plant or animal fibres for their own garments, and perhaps grow an oilseed crop. But, generally, oil and clothing materials are among the necessities they must purchase from their small returns.

This simple system is at the mercy of the climate, the land-owner and health hazards. So often it brings insufficient returns to provide the inputs needed for them to farm efficiently, or to prevent the soils deteriorating.

Give an example in each case. Why is the price of their produce likely to be relatively high?

'The difference between extensive and intensive farming is a matter of inputs and yields.' Explain this.

The actual type of farming in any area is subject to various limitations and constraints, some physical or climatic, some social, some political (see Fig. 6.10). In the end the farmer must weigh them up and choose to act in a certain way. **Continual decision-making is part of farming** – and can so easily go wrong!

We will look in more detail at several contrasting types of farming. Think of the basic agricultural system. Notice the inputs, the processes involved, and what happens to the output in each case.

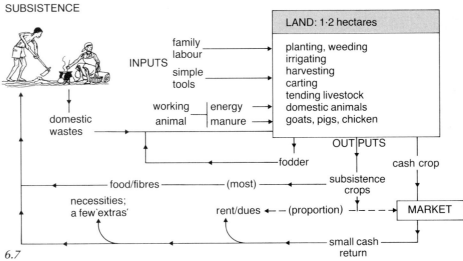

6.7

P 6.2 Subsistence farming in central India, with bullocks pulling a locally made plough.

P 6.3 In southern India village-made machinery crushes sugar cane. The syrupy juice is being concentrated before crystallisation.

Plantation farming

Here a commercial organisation acquires land on which to grow, prepare and package a single crop (such as rubber, tea, or coffee). This is done on a large scale, for a wide market, as efficiently as possible.

Huge capital investment is needed, especially at first – for the crop takes several years to mature. The land must be prepared, the crop established, a factory set up, offices and housing built for a large workforce, and roads and transport facilities prepared.

Most plantations are in the less developed countries. They were established originally with overseas investment, mainly from the former colonial powers. Today many have been acquired by the LDC itself, through government borrowing.

Fig. 6.8 shows such a system. At first it *appears* altogether more secure than peasant farming. Yet there *are* hazards. Where income depends on a single crop (**monoculture**), a fall in world demand can be disastrous. A single crop is also vulnerable to plant disease. Transport costs are usually high, so fuel price increases are a particular burden. There may also be social problems for workers and their families (p. 110). Each farming system has its own difficulties.

Commercial mixed farming

Here the farmer owns or rents several hundred hectares of land. He carefully plans a profitable form of land-use, depending on climatic and soil conditions. He decides which type of crop or stock will give the best returns. **Market prices, or government controls may cause him to change the land-use;** though it takes time to develop new crops.

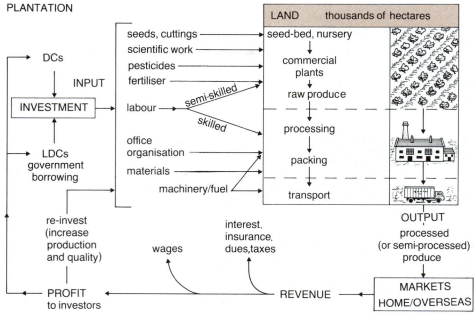

PLANTATION

6.8

P 6.4 Sugar cane from a Jamaican plantation is crushed by massive machinery at a sugar factory.

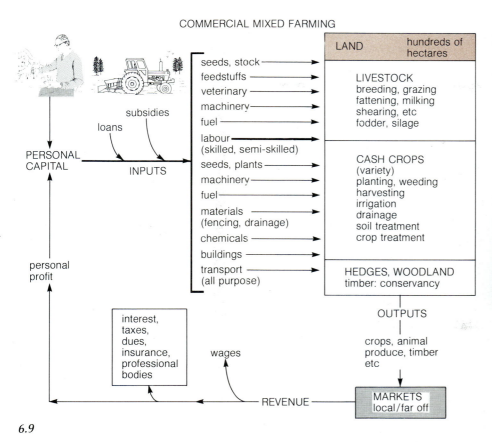

COMMERCIAL MIXED FARMING

6.9

P 6.6 Extensive wheat farming in Western Australia. The combine harvester pours grain into a collecting bin.

He is a businessman, prepared to spend money on fertilisers or pesticides, on animals to improve his stock, on veterinary services, on machinery for a multitude of purposes, and on buildings. His workforce is small, but skilled.

He works out his seasonal activities, often by agreement with large-scale purchasers, who may contract in advance to buy his produce. Sometimes the need for high inputs means temporary borrowing.

P 6.5 Machinery used for disc ploughing and harrowing large fields in East Anglia.

At other times returns are high. His is a **commercial enterprise** which needs careful financing, complying with government regulations, paying wages, taxes and interest, and risking his judgment on future prices and demands (p. 124).

Constraints and decisions

These three systems are just samples of ways in which farming is carried out in various parts of the world. You have seen that there are **constraints** (things which affect what can and cannot be done) in each case.

Fig. 6.10 shows that a farmer trying to make a decision is faced with pressures caused by all sorts of different conditions. The problems facing him depend on what kind of farming he is involved in.

A peasant farmer wanting to get a higher yield may be worrying about extra costs for seed, or fertiliser, or water. A dairy farmer may be wondering about restrictions on the amount of butter he is *allowed* to produce, and the effects of over-production in other countries.

Notice the different groups of conditions which can affect a farmer's decision. The subsistence farmer, with no spare capital, may lose everything through a

lengthy drought, or a hurricane. While a commercial farmer may survive a bad harvest by borrowing, or using funds banked during good years. Each of them, however, is much affected by his legal right to the land, and by the kind of agreements by which he is allowed to cultivate it.

The pressures under which they work may be very great in each case; but for the subsistence farmer failure may literally be a matter of life and death.

6.5 Land holdings – Who owns the land? Who makes the decisions?

Peasant farmers largely depend on family labour. Their prospects for improving both the land and their income depend on the system under which they farm. Most depend on arrangements with a land-owner. Some belong to a communal group, and follow the instructions of a leader or committee. The decisions they can make for themselves are usually limited, and depend on the system of land-ownership, which varies from country to country and place to place.

Absentee land-owners

In many Latin American countries a few wealthy landlords own much of the land. The peasant who cultivates it contributes

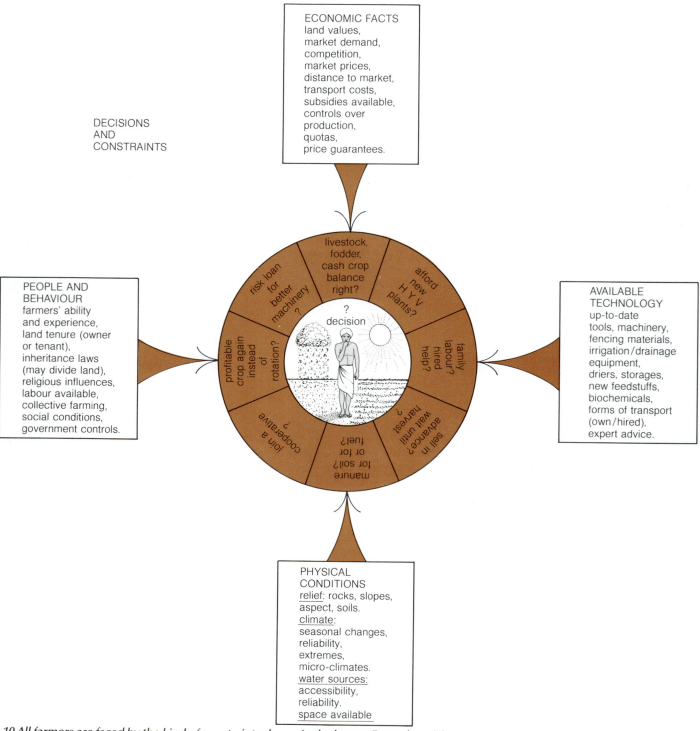

DECISIONS
AND
CONSTRAINTS

ECONOMIC FACTS
land values,
market demand,
competition,
market prices,
distance to market,
transport costs,
subsidies available,
controls over
production,
quotas,
price guarantees.

PEOPLE AND
BEHAVIOUR
farmers' ability
and experience,
land tenure (owner
or tenant),
inheritance laws
(may divide land),
religious influences,
labour available,
collective farming,
social conditions,
government controls.

AVAILABLE
TECHNOLOGY
up-to-date
tools, machinery,
fencing materials,
irrigation/drainage
equipment,
driers, storages,
new feedstuffs,
biochemicals,
forms of transport
(own/hired),
expert advice.

PHYSICAL
CONDITIONS
relief: rocks, slopes,
aspect, soils.
climate:
seasonal changes,
reliability,
extremes,
micro-climates.
water sources:
accessibility,
reliability.
space available

6.10 All farmers are faced by the kind of constraints shown in the boxes. Examples of the decisions they have to make are shown in the sectors: and, of course, there are many others, depending on the natural conditions and the society in which they live.

a large proportion of his produce or earnings to the land-owner. Some cultivate the owner's land for nothing, and subsist off a small family plot. In densely populated areas farms are often too small to occupy the whole family, so some people work as agricultural labourers.

The owner is often an absentee, and may not even live in the country itself. He can receive a large income from vast holdings without making the most of the land. So that while peasant holdings are crowded and over-worked, what could be productive land may remain as ill-managed pasture, or is unused. **These large areas (latifundias) seldom produce the food output they could if the land were redistributed.**

Local land-owners

In south-east Asia most peasants farm small-holdings as tenants of local land-owners, also contributing produce or cash-rent. Their subsistence farming may include only a few commercial crops as a sideline; but because of their numbers the total production by peasant farmers makes a substantial contribution to the country's output.

Changes in world commodity prices are likely to affect peasant farmers and those employed on large estates in different ways. How might this affect the decision of an LDC government – whether to invest in large estates or improve peasant cultivation?

Why are subsistence farmers likely to stick to traditional methods, rather than risk introducing new ones?

In all these countries peasant land tends to become sub-divided into small plots (fragmentation); as when a father's land is divided between sons. Because of increasing rural population, production from small, scattered plots may fall below subsistence level. The family may have to

P 6.7 Mules working one of the many tiny, walled fields near Platres in southern Cyprus, among young vines.

borrow, at a large interest rate, from a moneylender, who may well be the landlord. Many eventually forfeit their land. Thus tenants and small land-owners can become landless labourers, with low wages. Many of the jobless move in desperation to an urban slum (p. 225).

Semi-permanent settlement

In some parts of Africa the population density is low. Here attitudes towards subsistence farming on tribal land can be different from that of the peasant farmers described above. Because extra produce

is often difficult to store, transport, and sell, **families may work to provide for their immediate needs, rather than aim at as high a yield as they can achieve.**

This applies to the **shifting cultivators of the seasonally dry savannas.** But as population increases, many are forced to adopt a more intensive form of peasant farming. Consider how they might do this.

Could they shorten the period the land is left fallow?

If some of their cattle remained near the settlement, could not the dung be used to improve the soil?

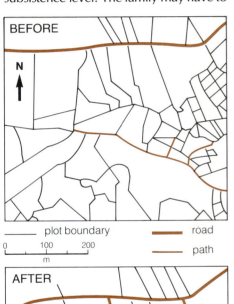

— plot boundary — road — path

0   100   200
m

6.11 During the 1970s fragments of land in south-west Cyprus were made into larger fields, in response to a land consolidation law. Walls were removed and new roads built to give access to the properties. It is now much easier to distribute irrigation water. In the western half of this area how many fields were there before and after redistribution? (After R. King, Geography 65, p. 320)

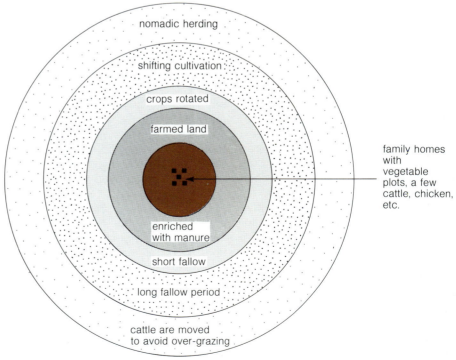

6.12 How land-use zones develop about a small savanna settlement, where families depend on herds of cattle as a main source of wealth.

Could they not adopt a rotation of crops; and alternate beans, or another plant which replaces nitrogen (p. 76) with grains, or a cash crop?

In fact, most of these things *are* introduced in more permanent settlements on the moister savannas. **Zones of land-use (Fig. 6.12) tend to be developed about their homes.**

'Intensity of cropping decreases with distance from the homestead.' Explain this. In which of the zones about the settlement might a cash crop like tobacco or cotton be grown?

The oil palm, a perennial tree crop, is profitable in eastern Nigeria (p.117). In which zone might *this* be grown?

P 6.8 The responsibility system in China allows the old and young to contribute to family income. Here at Jinghong they agreed to raise buffalo.

Collective farming systems

In communist countries, in particular, peasants cultivated the land allocated, but owned by the state. The **collectives** farmed the land according to decisions made by their elected committee and government representatives, who saw that broad policies are carried out.

Recent events in The People's Republic of China show the strengths and weaknesses of this system. Throughout this huge country the land about a village was farmed, until recently, by work teams (usually the active members of the village). A number of teams (villages) formed a brigade; several brigades formed a commune.

The government set each commune a quota for production of crops and animal produce. So each of the teams was set a quota to be produced from the village land. The communes distributed major equipment. They arranged out-of-season labour for teams—work on walling, road and canal construction, and so on. They organised medical services, schools and social centres.

All families received a basic amount in cash and produce, with additions for working effectively. Each family also had a plot of land for its own use. On the face of it, life for the peasant was far more secure than when they were at the mercy of landlords. Yet rural output remained low; and living conditions were adequate but basic, with few luxuries.

How would *you* have reacted, as a team member:

(a) if your team produced twice as much as the neighbouring team (that lazy lot down the road), but their income was much the same as yours;

(b) if individuals in the team did not pull their weight, but got the same basics;

(c) if your extra efforts got some reward, but only a little;

(d) if you could improve production with better equipment, but could not rely on getting your allocation?

Low production showed how a lot of people *did* react. So the government introduced a **responsibility system**.

The state still owns the land, but allows families, groups and individuals to take responsibility for producing and marketing the crops, livestock, timber, and so on. The state buys an agreed amount, and the individual or group works hard to sell extra on the free market. People pay dues for social services, and taxes on what they earn. But they can save to buy new tools, equipment, or fertilisers to improve output.

The system also applies to craftwork, and operates in industry and retailing. It has brought a great increase in production. As people are earning more, they can afford more consumer goods; so there is a market for 'extras' for the home. This encourages local manufacturing and retailing, and provides more jobs.

How *does* increasing incentives for rural people encourage manufacturing industries?

Some land is good, some less good.

So how might the responsibility system cause unfortunate differences in living standards?

Some rural land is near big cities; some is in far distant, difficult hill country. What difference can this make to marketing, and obtaining equipment, and commodities?

Does this suggest that not all people will benefit equally under the new system? If the state as a whole prospers by the system, might not this, in the end, benefit everyone?

Discuss the points above, and argue the benefits or disadvantages of peasant farming under a landlord system, under strict state control, or under a state-organised responsibility scheme.

Peasant small-holdings versus plantations

Plantations are carefully managed on a commercial basis. But there can be drawbacks to their farming methods, and also difficult social problems.

Their labour force is wage-earning, and plantation families may also have small plots to cultivate. Whereas the local population may be mainly subsistence farmers. There can be frictions between the two groups, especially if the plantation workers were initially recruited from abroad: Chinese and Indians working on Malaysian rubber estates; Tamils on the tea plantations of Sri Lanka. There can also be social friction between employees and foreign owners or managers, with different life styles.

The advantage of large-scale production has sometimes been lost by failure to appreciate local conditions. Clean-weeding between Malaysia's rubber trees exposed the soil to tropical downpours. It also prevented plants and leaf-fall returning nutrients to the soil. The fertility dropped, and there was erosion by rapid run-off. Nitrogen-fixing plants are now grown between rows to prevent this.

In fact, peasant holdings now produce a large proportion of tropical tree-crops — rubber, palm oil, cocoa. The tangle of different productive plants on their small holdings prevents soils being exposed.

Recent commercial developments have combined both methods — in a different environment. In the Sudan, factories on new irrigated cotton plantations (in the Gezira) also accept cotton from nearby small-holders, who produce a range of crops.

P 6.9 A Sri Lankan plantation near Nuwara Eliya. Tea bushes cover the hillsides about the factory buildings.

P 6.10 Selling produce from a Sri Lankan family holding – a leafy tangle of trees and bushes yielding fruits and spices.

Commercial mixed farming – conditions of land tenure

A farmer-owner has an incentive to improve his land. He first acquires capital, or credit, to invest in the land, buildings, equipment, seeds, stock, fertilisers, etc. He decides how to re-invest in improvements, and must keep up to date with technical and economic advice.

A tenant farmer, with limited capital, may prefer to acquire the buildings, livestock, machinery, etc., but pay rent. A long lease gives him an incentive to make improvements. When he leaves, the owner may agree to pay for such improvements, though he may first have set a high rent to cover this. Governments, of course, can control rents to prevent tenants being exploited.

How the income from commercial farming should best be used depends on many factors. Farm wages should be much like those in other skilled/unskilled occupations (government controls come into it). But having to pay high wages to skilled employees can affect a decision whether to use mechanisation or employ more labour at lower wages. Much depends on the size and type of farm, and the intensity of land-use.

6.6 New technology – how it affects the LDCs

Many of the ways of making the land more productive are beyond the means of peasant farmers. Introducing new technology may require skills and education they do not have.

In any case, the introduction of new equipment, seeds, or stock, and fresh farming methods does not *ensure* success, even on a large scale. New projects can be fine to start with, and then suffer setbacks. In colonial times huge investments in growing groundnuts in Tanzania's dry savannas were lost because the soil structure was destroyed by agricultural machinery. The relationships between the soils, the variable climate, and the moisture lost during cultivation were not properly researched.

Careful research and planning are essential before introducing new schemes, as the following attempts to improve production will show.

P 6.11 Intensive commercial farming of the English countryside: a pattern of managed woodland, with fields of hay and grain, and pastures with livestock. Large functional buildings and a silo near the farmhouse are reminders of the large inputs.

1 New machinery

It is decided to substitute rotovators or diesel-powered steel ploughs for the peasants' hoes and wooden ploughs. Slow laborious work by men and animals will be replaced by speedy furrowing, **but there may be snags.**

(a) Will this suit the size of the holding?

(b) Can scattered family plots be re-organised, and how?

(c) Have people sufficient education and skill to use and maintain them?

(d) What about the supply and cost of fuel?

(e) Will fewer animals mean importing expensive fertilisers?

(f) How will it all affect local labourers?

(g) Besides the new plough, what other machinery will be needed during the seasons?

(h) A hoe and an animal-drawn wooden plough make a shallow furrow; is deep ploughing going to affect the water content and soil structure?

Comment on each of the above.

2 Using improved strains of stock and seed

By controlling cross-fertilisation, new varieties of plants can be obtained which resist certain diseases, grow at a suitable rate, and give a higher yield. Livestock, too, may be bred to suit local conditions.

In the last quarter-century high-yielding varieties (HYVs) of wheat and rice have heralded in a Green Revolution. In northern India they caused wheat production to rise from 10 million tonnes in 1963–64 to 26 million in 1971–72, and to reach 35 million in 1978–79. **Consider the advantages and disadvantages:**

HYV advantages	HYV disadvantages
1 Respond greatly to fertilisers	1 Need heavy doses of chemical fertilisers
2 Yield per unit of fertiliser much higher than traditional strains	2 Need careful continual weeding
3 Short stalks stand up to weight of grain and to storms	3 Do not stand up to drought
4 Can be planted closer together	4 Need much water and controlled supplies
5 A shorter growing period	5 Need large amounts of pesticides and fungicides
6 Less response to varying day length	6 Some HYVs do not mill well
7 Yield sometimes 2 or 3 times that of traditional strains	

The figures for India suggest that the advantages easily outweigh the disadvantages. But will their use necessarily help the very poor countries, or the poorest regions?

(a) Who is more likely to be able to afford fertilisers, pesticides, irrigation water – the already rich or the poor peasant farmer? Won't this increase the 'poverty gap'?

(b) Well-developed regions with good communications, storages, and mills will benefit more than less-developed ones. Is this what is needed?

(c) Suggest why wheat production is particularly successful in the Punjab – the land of the five rivers (and great canals).

(d) The use of HYVs in the less-developed countries depends greatly on world oil prices. Why?

(e) Many of the least-developed countries (LLDCs) cannot develop great irrigation schemes or import large amounts of fertiliser. Are nations more ready to contribute famine relief than help to provide investment to prevent famine?

(f) Heavy applications of fertilisers may (i) affect soil structure, and (ii) cause excessive algae growth in ponds and canals – why?

(g) Seasonal variations of climate in many tropical countries act against the use of HYVs. Explain this.

(h) The ground beneath the taller traditional crops tends to have fewer weeds. Why is this? What advantage is this?

There are so many factors, large and small, to be considered when making agricultural changes.

3 Biochemical treatments

These can be beneficial in many ways. Vaccines protect livestock; pesticides check insect interference from locust swarms to greenfly; fungicides destroy harmful plant viruses.

But when we interfere with nature, the

P 6.12 Tractor ploughing dry savanna in the Rift Valley in Ethiopia. Deep ploughing is unsuitable for most of the highland soils, and even here there are dangers from the rapid loss of soil moisture.

P 6.13 Crop species are chosen to make the most of the mild winters in south-west China. While winter wheat is harvested, the beds beyond are planted with rice species bred to tolerate these particular light conditions.

results are not always what we expect. Pests can become immune to pesticides; malarial mosquitoes are now producing strains which resist the usual pesticides. Even trapping and killing animal 'pests' may have unforeseen results. Killing birds who eat grain means killing birds who eat insects; so insects harmful to plants may multiply.

Pesticides used against small organisms may also come to harm larger animals and, in time, people. The chemicals pass through the food chain and become more concentrated. The amount may well be very small in a contaminated water plant, but will build up in a fish continually feed-ing on it; and even more in a bird feeding on the fishes (Fig. 6.13).

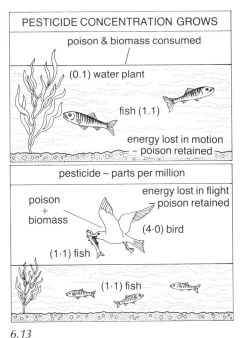

PESTICIDE CONCENTRATION GROWS

poison & biomass consumed

(0.1) water plant

fish (1.1)

energy lost in motion
– poison retained

pesticide – parts per million

poison
+
biomass

energy lost in flight
= poison retained

(4·0) bird

(1·1) fish

(1·1) fish

6.13

4 Intermediate technology

Often the most satisfactory results come from combining old technologies with new. The Chinese call it 'walking on two legs'. The **traditional leg** may be rep-resented by age-old forms of water supply which are effective and still used. People raise water from wells and rivers with a weighted pole and bucket (*shaduf*); oxen and mules still turn water wheels. These are still useful methods.

Much depends on the returns people can get from their methods. It may benefit them to provide energy for electric or diesel pumps and force water through hoses and sprinklers. A profitable crop may justify the high costs. In northern India the extra water needed for the HYV crops comes largely from new tube wells and mechanical pumps. Development may thus depend on the other, **technological leg** – or on using advanced technology in large multi-purpose power and irrigation schemes to supply the energy and water.

P 6.15 A groundnut sheller from simple materials – intermediate technology in Zaïre.

Peasant farmers in the LDCs can benefit by adopting new technology somewhere between the simple implement (hoe) and advanced machinery (tractor). This inter-mediate technology makes use of inex-pensive local materials, or re-assembled parts, to produce effective devices, able to work with as little energy as possible. In this way bamboo, wood, and a few metal parts are assembled to make hand-pumps, rice-planting machines, winnow-ers, or water-diversion channels. **Local energy sources, such as biogas from vil-lage waste, can be harnessed in simple, locally made apparatus** (Fig. 8.4).

P 6.14 Spraying insecticide on individual plants in Sri Lanka.

Make a case for **caution** when introducing machinery, chemicals, and new varieties of plants and species of livestock. Is it misleading to forecast 'miracle results' whenever they are introduced? What should first be done?

Is huge investment in large multipurpose schemes – combined irrigation and electric generation projects – likely to be sufficient *in itself* to give rural families in less developed countries better living standards? Suggest what should go hand-in-hand with such projects. Think of the people's present land-holding arrangements; education; equipment; income; and attitudes. Make a list of **priorities** for an aid project of this kind.

6.7 Land values and how the land is used

Distance from a central market

Early in the 19th century a German, von Thünen, considered how and why rural land-use varies with distance from a market. To simplify things, he pictured one town at the centre of the agricultural area which was its sole supplier. There farmers would all sell particular produce at the same price. The whole area had the same soils, climate and physical features, with no barrier to movement.

His reasoning was that all farmers want to sell their produce at the greatest possible profit (**P**). The cost of production (**c** per tonne) is the same everywhere; but transport (by horse and cart in those days) costs **t** per kilometre. They all receive **s** per tonne at the market. So the **profit** on each tonne is $s-c-(t \times \text{distance to market}) = P$.

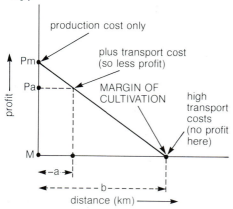

6.14 The cost of producing a commodity is the same everywhere, but profit decreases with distance from the market.

Fig 6.14 shows that a tonne of grain grown close to the market would bring a large profit P_m (no transport costs). But a tonne of grain grown **a** km away would cost $t \times a$ to take to market, so the profit is only P_a. A farmer **b** km away would find that $(s-c-t \times b)$ left him with no profit at all.

The effects of greater inputs (improving the land)

Compare the profits of two farmers X and Y growing the same crop. They get the same yield from the land (30 tonnes per hectare). They each spend £500 in producing it. But **X** is only 2 km from market and **Y** is 20 km away, and the transport cost is £1.50 per tonne/km. At the market they each sell at £50 per tonne. **Case I** shows that **X** makes a profit of £910 and **Y** only £100.

They both decide to increase the yield/ha by spending £800 – using fertiliser and extra labour. The yield goes up to 42 tonnes per hectare. But as you see in **Case II** this more intensive land-use increases **X's** profit while **Y's** goes down. Being 20 km

from the market, it pays **Y** better to have a **less intensive** approach.

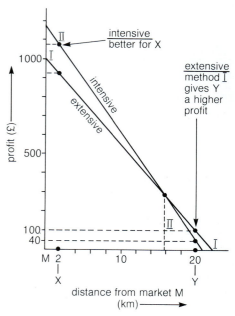

6.15 Why distance from market makes some forms of farming more suitable than others.

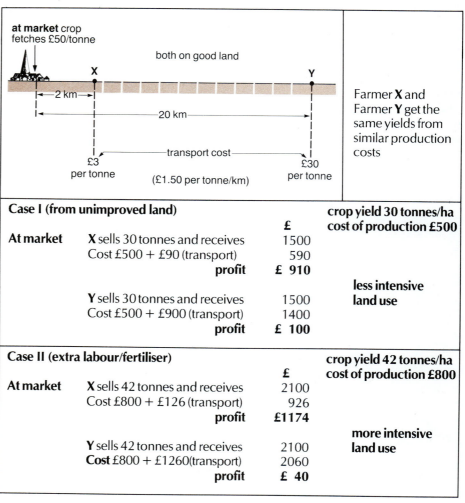

Case I (from unimproved land)			crop yield 30 tonnes/ha
		£	cost of production £500
At market	X sells 30 tonnes and receives	1500	
	Cost £500 + £90 (transport)	590	
	profit	**£ 910**	
			less intensive land use
	Y sells 30 tonnes and receives	1500	
	Cost £500 + £900 (transport)	1400	
	profit	**£ 100**	
Case II (extra labour/fertiliser)			**crop yield 42 tonnes/ha**
		£	cost of production £800
At market	X sells 42 tonnes and receives	2100	
	Cost £800 + £126 (transport)	926	
	profit	**£1174**	
			more intensive land use
	Y sells 42 tonnes and receives	2100	
	Cost £800 + £1260(transport)	2060	
	profit	**£ 40**	

Farmer **X** and Farmer **Y** get the same yields from similar production costs

Fig. 6.15 shows how intensive land-use would give way to extensive land-use with distance.

In Case II why exactly has **X**'s profit soared while **Y**'s has fallen?

Which land would you expect to *bid* the most for, **X**'s or **Y**'s?

If a lot of people bid for **X**'s land, what should happen to its value?

Would you expect land close about a city to be more expensive than land in rural areas? Can you think of several reasons for this?

Bulk and perishability

In the real world varying demands change the market price of crops. Also the yield per hectare can vary, for many reasons. And some crops are bulkier than others, or more perishable.

von Thünen considered such things as well as the effects we have seen. He saw that together they produced a **zoning of land-use** about the market town. Fig. 6.16 shows how the land-use tended to be distributed *in his time*.

Fresh milk and vegetables (**Zone 1**) were in daily demand, and **perishable.** So in those days they were grown on land close to the city, enriched by both cattle and horse manure (townsfolk kept many horses).

Wood for burning was in constant

P 6.16 Intensive cultivation close about the village of Zenia in central Crete. Notice the small plots with vegetables, the windpump, and the animals. Beyond are olive trees on a slope up to rough pastures on the hillside.

demand, but bulky and costly to transport. Beyond the woodland (**2**), grain (rye) was grown intensively, in rotation with a nitrogen crop (**3**). It could stand the cost of manuring and transport. Then came less intensive farming (**4/5**). Far from the market there were livestock whose less perishable produce – butter, cheese, fibres – were sent to market at intervals; and meat animals which could be driven in.

Things which disrupt land-use zoning

Many things could disrupt this neat zoning. **A canal or river enabled cheap bulk transport to extend some zones** (Fig. 6.17).

Explain why the pattern is distorted in this way.

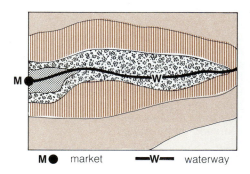

M ● market   —W— waterway

6.17 How water transport can influence forms of land-use.

The presence of other towns, with their own markets, interferes with the pattern. Also some areas are very fertile; others are not and give poor yields. There may be poor land with steep slopes close to a town, or unfavourable micro-climates (p. 74). Mountains, and the routeways through them, also interfere with land-use distribution.

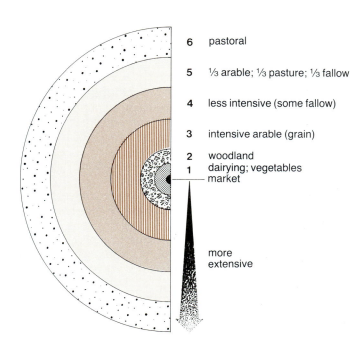

6	pastoral
5	⅓ arable; ⅓ pasture; ⅓ fallow
4	less intensive (some fallow)
3	intensive arable (grain)
2	woodland
1	dairying; vegetables
	market

more extensive

6.16 Zones of land-use about a market settlement served by animal transport, as in Europe in the 19th century.

Today in most parts of the closely settled developed countries, with good communication networks, the simple von Thünen arrangements are masked. Now **transport costs vary with different forms of vehicle.** Several types may be used to market a single product: by truck to a rail halt; then by rail wagon to a cargo vessel at a port. The forms of transport and the competition between them are discussed on p. 129. Nevertheless, the economic ideas simplified above *are* important factors. They can be recognised as influencing land-use about many rural settlements (Fig. 6.18), especially in the LDCs.

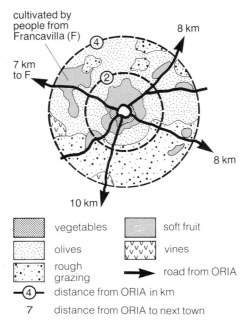

cultivated by people from Francavilla (F)

7 km to F

8 km

8 km

10 km

	vegetables		soft fruit
	olives	vvvv	vines
	rough grazing	→	road from ORIA
—④—	distance from ORIA in km		
7	distance from ORIA to next town		

6.18 Land-use about the small town of Oria in southern Italy varies with soils, distance and communications. Vegetables and soft fruits need much attention, such as watering; olives need pruning and harvesting at particular times; soils and vegetation on limestone outcrops suit only goats and sheep grazing.

Local time-distance responses

Land-use on large farms shows some response to time-distance constraints: crops and livestock needing frequent attention tend to be near the main buildings, and crops needing less attention further away. But such things as varied relief, drainage, soil qualities, and the use of different forms of transport for different jobs act against a zoned pattern.

Simple time-distance considerations affect the marketing of produce. In some cases they can be vital. In Britain, East Anglian farmers may wish to contract to sell their pea harvest to a freezing company. But freezing factories only accept peas harvested *within an hour*; thus they must come from a farm within 50 km of the factory.

What does this assume about the type and speed of the transport and of the road system?

Returning to **land values – we expect a unit of land to bear the crop which gives the best return. But the distribution of crops responds to the combination of market prices, bulk, perishability, and production costs.** If a location near the market is desirable we would expect the value of the land to decrease with distance from the market.

Does a large farm necessarily deal with a *single* market?

What kind of fresh produce would benefit by reaching a large city in a short time?

How have refrigeration, preservatives, packaging, and rapid bulk transport changed the pattern of distribution of farm produce?

How does supplying rural produce to a central place differ from what happened in von Thünen's day? How will this affect land-use distribution?

(a) What about fuel supplies?

(b) How is milk delivered to city dwellers? Where from?

(c) Some foods in daily demand, like dairy produce and vegetables, come from overseas. Give examples, saying where they are produced and how they reach the customer.

(d) Even if some crops seem to occupy 'zones', why does production now tend to be concentrated in certain areas? (Think of favoured sites and modern transport.)

(e) Bulk-handling is cheaper than transporting small loads. How will this affect crop distribution?

(f) Remembering the wish to make the maximum profit per hectare, and time-distance considerations, is it fair to say that von Thünen's ideas still affect land-use at every level?

6.8 Government policies and land-use

One of the facts which might benefit a remote farm is that the government may wish to encourage settlement there and give them financial and other assistance. **A government can have a great influence on land-use.** Its aim is also to make the most profitable use of land – **but** it may also be bound by agreements with other countries or economic blocs like the EEC.

Some governments have closer control over marketing and commodity prices than others. Some marketing boards pay for agricultural research, and improve freight and storage facilities. **Look at how government controls may affect land-use:**

1 **Crop-restriction.** Governments may decide that only a certain amount of land should bear a particular crop. Thus sugar beet production may be cut back to allow LDCs who rely on sugar cane to find markets and make a reasonable profit. So farmers on good beet growing land may be given a **quota** for beet, with penalties for exceeding it.

2 **Purchasing surpluses.** When there is over-production, as with the EEC 'butter mountain', a country, or in this case EEC, may protect its farmers by buying the surplus, storing it, and selling it later at low, **subsidised prices.**

3 **Minimum price guarantees.** Governments may help farmers when world demand and prices fall, by buying a set quota of a product and fixing a minimum price.

4 **Freight subsidies.** These may be given to enable farmers in remote areas to compete on equal terms with other producers, through cheaper transport.

5 **Compensation.** This, for instance, may be given for livestock ordered to be slaughtered to prevent disease spreading, such as foot-and-mouth.

6 **Loans.** Farmers may be allowed to borrow at favourable interest rates in order to make improvements.

These are just a few of the ways in which a government may interfere with the farming system. It is important for the farmer, who has to make decisions and take risks, to keep in touch with government policies.

6.9 How farmers respond – three contrasting systems

Each of the following types of farming illustrates the way farmers respond to the constraints described above and summarised in Fig. 6.10. Look for examples of particular influences – physical, technological, social, and economic. Try to assess which was the most pressing in view of decisions to farm in a particular way. The constraints themselves continuously change, and you can see how each of the types of farming has to adjust from time to time. Notice in the first example how changing conditions alter the methods of farming.

1 Changes in peasant farming in south-east Nigeria

In the forest which covers much of the land east of the Niger delta farmers have long practised bush fallowing. A family, holding some 3–4 hectares, would clear and cultivate land for a year, and then leave it fallow for up to nine years.

A variety of food crops gives a balanced diet – maize and roots (yams, cocoyams, and cassava) for energy, and beans, vegetables and peppers for vitamins and proteins. Each family keeps chickens and goats. There are no cattle, for tsetse flies abound and cause a wasting disease in cattle. But household wastes provide fertiliser.

Unfortunately the increasing population has caused people to shorten the fallow period, with consequent loss of soil fertility. Crop yields have fallen.

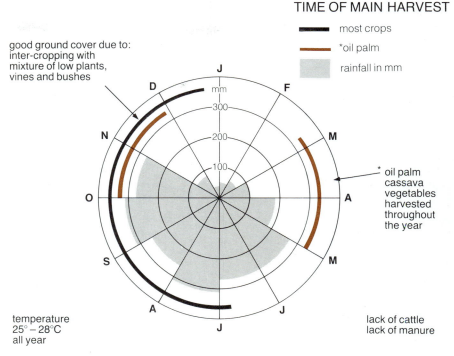

6.20 Mean monthly temperatures and rainfall in south-eastern Nigeria. Notice the main harvest periods, though most crops will yield throughout the year.

Fig. 6.20 shows the climatic conditions. With over 2000 mm of rain and high temperatures through the year, oil palms grow wild in the bush and on family holdings. They yield a variety of products (Fig. 6.22), and oil crushed from the fruit and kernels have long supplied the households, and left a surplus for sale. But the rapidly increasing population has cut down this surplus.

P 6.17 African root crops – taro and cassava.

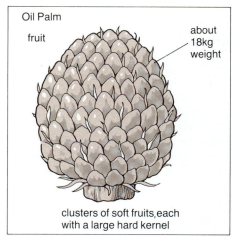

6.21 The fruits and their kernels, when crushed, yield vegetable oil.

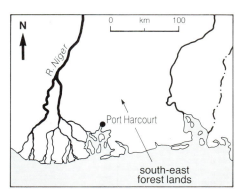

6.19 South-eastern Nigeria is a land of rainforest and watercourses – only the main rivers are shown here.

A government development project now aims to involve all the people in a change of farming style. Farmers are encouraged to take shares in cooperatives, and work on them part-time. These grow new plant varieties and organise small oil-palm plantations. They share the resulting profits.

HYVs of cassava and maize are grown, and pineapples and citrus fruits have been introduced. Fertilisers are bought with returns from the cooperative. Where suitable, a small dam controls streams for rice-growing and forms a pond for fish breeding. Previously there was haphazard fish netting in rivers.

117

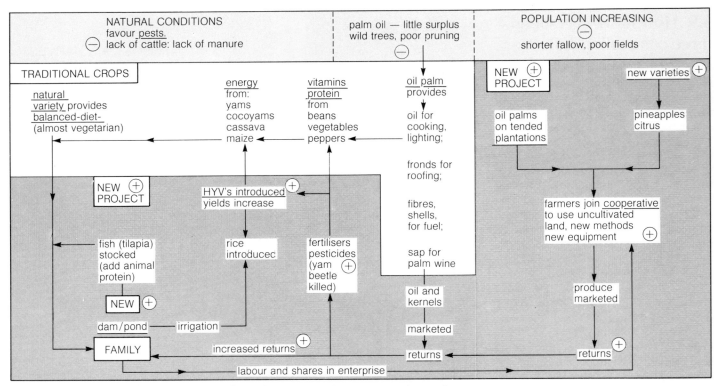

6.22 Traditional crops of the Nigerian rainforest have many advantages, as shown; but there have been drawbacks (–) due to natural hazards, poor farming methods, and demands from an increasing population. The new project (shaded) has created many advantages (+): follow them through.

Fig. 6.22 summarises the advantages and the disadvantages in the old and new systems.

What advantages had the natural climate and vegetation for the family farms? What disadvantages?

What advantage is there in the rapid colonisation and growth of plants on abandoned land?

Was the original land-use a poor one, or have social conditions made it unsuitable?

Progress has been made because people have accepted innovations. Why was outside expertise required to get this going? Would advice alone have been sufficient?

Oil palm trees take four years to bear fruit. Why did the government emphasise, to begin with, that they would give low interest loans as well as practical assistance?

What were the dangers of introducing HYVs? What could government officials do about it?

What are the advantages of establishing cooperatives (p. 128) (a) to the families; (b) to the government?

Photo 14.1 shows a similar example of establishing fish breeding in central Africa.

2 Changes in extensive wheat farming – the Canadian prairies

In 1870 the prairies were transferred from the Hudson's Bay Company to the Dominion of Canada. A great fertile belt of grassland, from the Red river to the Rocky Mountains foothills was opened for settlement. People still saw it as pioneer country, where cattle could range freely and they might grow subsistence crops (Fig. 6.23).

Between 1878–90 the trans-continental Canadian Pacific Railway was extended across the southern prairies. A few branches ran northward into the belt of most fertile soils. The original unit of settlement was a square block of 65 ha, no matter what the terrain. Quarter- or half-sections were granted free to settlers, or sold by railways from their own land grants. The rectangular pattern of fields and roads remains typical of the North American prairies (Photo 6.18).

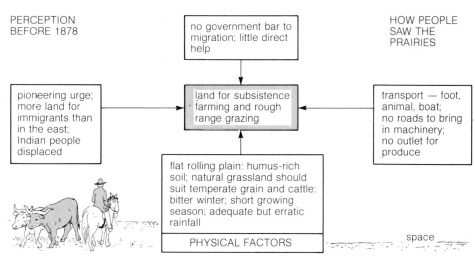

6.23 Pioneer days.

118

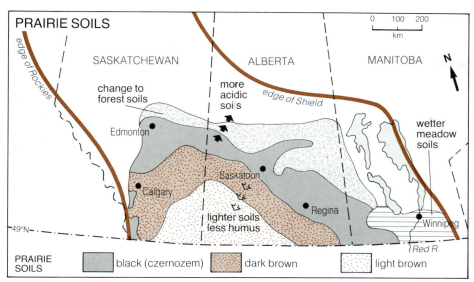

6.24 Soil belts within the Canadian prairies.

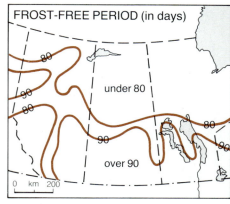

6.26 The frost control.

Even after the railways provided commercial links, **extensive wheat farming** did not take place. The growing season was too short for the soft wheats cultivated in western Europe, the winters too severe for early planting. Then, **in the nineties, early maturing varieties were developed**. These new hard wheats were excellent for bread-making, and were soon in demand by Europe's growing population and elsewhere in the world.

Between 1903–06 an east-west line was completed through the heart of the most suitable farmland. The **flow of immigrants** from the east now reached a peak. Branch lines were built, and by 1910 a million rural people were scattered over these rolling plains.

The many branch lines were essential; for as they used animal transport, it was uneconomic to carry wheat more than 30 km to the grain storages (elevators) built beside the railway. With these technological changes and world-wide demands, people now saw the prairies in an optimistic light, despite occasional climatic setbacks (Fig. 6.29).

Wheat has climatic and soil restrictions which make parts of the prairies very marginal for wheat-growing. The winters are long and severe, so **wheat is sown in spring** and harvested in late summer. Most crops will not grow when the air temperature is below 5.6°C. A killer frost occurs when the Stevenson's screen temperature falls to −2.2°C. There must be at least 80 days without killer frost. There must also be a growing season of at least 110 days. It must be warm enough to give a total of 1200 degree-days. (A **degree-day** is found by subtracting 5.6°C from the mean daily temperature – i.e. 17.6°C–5.6°C = 12 degree-days.)

The short growing season means a lower yield than from winter wheat. As soils are mostly drier than in western Europe, the seeds are planted less densely. **But the huge area produces a large harvest overall. This is extensive farming.**

The prairies have a low annual rainfall. Fig. 6.28 shows that though the best lands

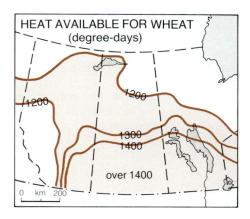

6.27 Where sufficient heat is available during the growing season.

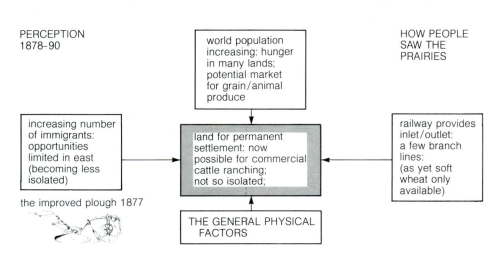

6.25 World demands increase, communications improve, and settlers pour in.

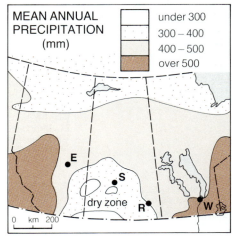

6.28 Notice the extent of the dry zone.

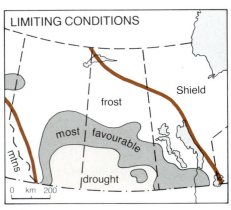

LIMITING CONDITIONS

Shield

frost

most favourable

mtns

drought

0   km   200

6.29

P 6.18 The rectangular pattern of the prairies. The farm buildings near the roads are protected by windbreaks.

average 400–500 mm, a large part of the south-west is much drier. Here the natural grassland did not give the soil such a high humus content as in the rich black czernozems (p. 79) of the main wheat belt. The soils are lighter coloured, with less organic matter, and tend to become dusty when disturbed.

By the 1920s wheat-growing had extended into the drier, more risky parts.

In the dry zone farmers left nearly half their land **fallow** each year, to conserve moisture. They got one crop from two years' precipitation. There was always a danger of wind erosion on ploughed land left fallow.

The rainfall is erratic throughout the prairies, with occasional lengthy droughts. When wheat prices were high (in 1914–18 and 1927–29), settlers who had been attracted to the drier parts by

low land prices prospered. But **prices fell in the world slump of 1929–32; and then came great drought, lasting from 1930–37,** so that thousands of farms were abandoned. The whole prairies were affected, forcing the government to assist farmers with loans, and to research new methods of land reclamation and more secure farming.

Land-use has changed even in the main wheat belt. Now farms of about 1000 ha may have a third of their land under other crops, such as rapeseed and nitrogen-rich forage for animals on pasture. Even when two-thirds of the land is under wheat, about a third of that will be fallow. Crop rotations are used to preserve fertility.

Soils which have long been cultivated are now treated with chemical fertilisers. So **farming has become rather more intensive.** Mechanisation for ploughing, harrowing, sowing, and combine-harvesting has become more efficient. **Fewer men are permanently employed on the farms.** Harvesting means working round the clock; so many farmers, as in the USA, employ teams of harvesters and their machines for the period needed.

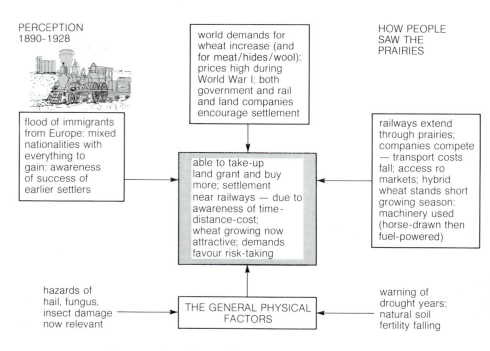

PERCEPTION 1890-1928

HOW PEOPLE SAW THE PRAIRIES

world demands for wheat increase (and for meat/hides/wool): prices high during World War I; both government and rail and land companies encourage settlement

flood of immigrants from Europe: mixed nationalities with everything to gain: awareness of success of earlier settlers

able to take-up land grant and buy more; settlement near railways — due to awareness of time-distance-cost; wheat growing now attractive; demands favour risk-taking

railways extend through prairies; companies compete — transport costs fall; access ro markets; hybrid wheat stands short growing season: machinery used (horse-drawn then fuel-powered)

hazards of hail, fungus, insect damage now relevant

THE GENERAL PHYSICAL FACTORS

warning of drought years: natural soil fertility falling

6.30 Meeting world demands – taking risks.

P 6.19 Grain elevators, with a siding for rail trucks on the Canadian prairies.

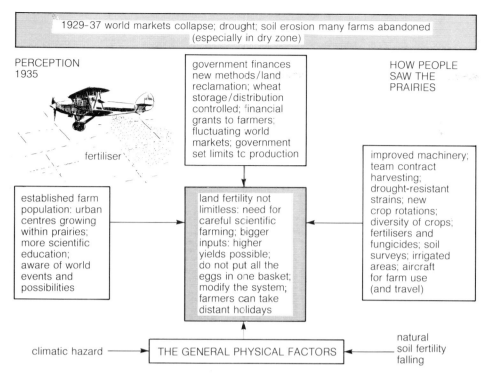

6.31 Economic difficulties and natural hazards call for scientific methods, with government control and financial help for farmers.

The dry south-west is now mainly a ranching zone. About half the land is under pasture, a quarter fallow; only a fifth under wheat. Properties near rivers have mixed farming on irrigated land, and sell fodder to ranches.

In late summer wheat is taken to be sucked up by pumps into the railside elevators. But it is still uneconomic to truck wheat by road more than 35–40 km. The rail wagons take it to huge elevators in collecting centres, like Winnipeg. From there the Canadian Wheat Board directs it by rail to Atlantic or Pacific ports (depending on destination).

The farmers are still affected by events which are beyond their control – not only frost, drought, or hail, but worldwide events which may create a sudden demand for wheat, or otherwise. Though now, in contrast to the early days, the government is closely involved economically.

Make a list of constraints facing prairie wheat growers today, under the headings used in Fig. 6.10.

People have regarded what the prairies can offer in different ways at different times. How does this show that rural land-use is *not* just a matter of the 'right' climate and fertile soils?

How do activities on these wheat-lands illustrate the value of biological research?

What important aspects of climate do the graphs in Fig. 5.8 *not* show?

Some grain from the prairies is sent to Europe via Vancouver and the Panama Canal. Follow this route in your atlas. Describe the transport links from the farm to the flour mills in Europe. What does this tell you of the relative costs of transport by road, rail, and water?

Why is wheat-growing on the prairies said to be 'extensive'? Is it just because Canada grows more than most countries?

P 6.20 A grain ship loading at a wheat terminal in Vancouver harbour.

3 Intensive dairy farming – south-east Australia

In Victoria, south Gippsland has been a dairy farming region ever since it became possible to supply Melbourne's growing population. It then began to export dairy produce through its docks. Most now goes to eastern Asia.

In 1840 the area about Trafalgar, 120 km east of Melbourne, was eucalypt forest. Pioneers took 3 weeks over the journey. When the railway reached it in 1886, much of the land was cleared for dairying. During the next 10 to 15 years, butter factories were established along the line.

6.32 Gippsland, where much eucalypt forest was cleared for dairy farming.

Today the green landscape has farms of about 80 ha, each with some 100 dairy cows – Jerseys, Friesians, or a cross. The milk is collected by 10 000 litre tankers, and taken to the factory which produces the butter, cheese, dried milk, and casein. Not all properties are dairy farms, and country roads are winding. This extends the tanker's daily journey and adds to fuel costs: but a rail halt at the factory gives a rapid outlet for the produce.

Land-use is intensive. On the farms there are often just *two* full-time workers, the farmer and a son. Fig. 6.33 shows that there are many fenced, or hedged, paddocks. Some pastures are rested while others are grazed; some may be growing hay or silage; and others are used for separating animals at particular times. When the grass is growing well the cattle graze strips controlled by electric fencing. This is moved some 20m a day.

Twice a day the cattle are brought in for milking, usually by a six-unit machine. The milk is tested for butter-fat; for income depends on this as well as on volume. The sheds must then be cleaned and equipment sterilised.

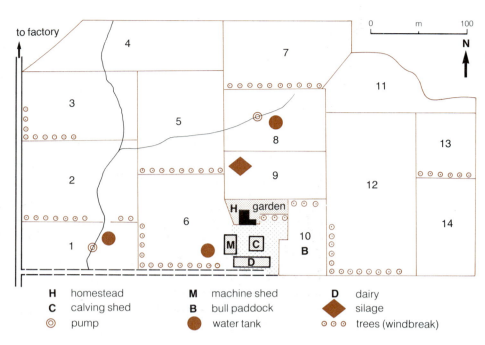

6.33 *The layout of a Gippsland farm, where pastures are rotated among its 14 fields (paddocks), and the actual grazing is controlled by electric fencing.*

Fig. 6.34 shows how the tasks change with the seasons.

Decisions must be made at each stage. After selecting the best yielding cows for calving, which should be sold for meat? (About a fifth are replaced each year.) Should bull calves be sold at three weeks, or be fed for a year and sold off for ten times as much? Are extra windbreaks needed against the cold southerlies (which cause low yields)? Is the pumped water, gravity-fed to the paddocks, adequate? Is expensive spray-irrigation needed for some paddocks (after two years below average rainfall)?

For two men the tasks are daunting. They include autumn harrowing to spread manure evenly over the paddocks; dressing pastures with superphosphate-potash fertiliser; spraying the liquid manure (stored near the dairy shed); seeding with a grass-clover mixture; spraying to eliminate weeds.

So, besides the tractor, a harrow, mower, rake, liquid spreader, seed dropper, and various trailers are needed. **With so little labour, fertiliser spreading may be contracted out** (sometimes light aircraft are used), and also, perhaps, silage making and baling cut grass. **Special services are hired** – veterinary among them.

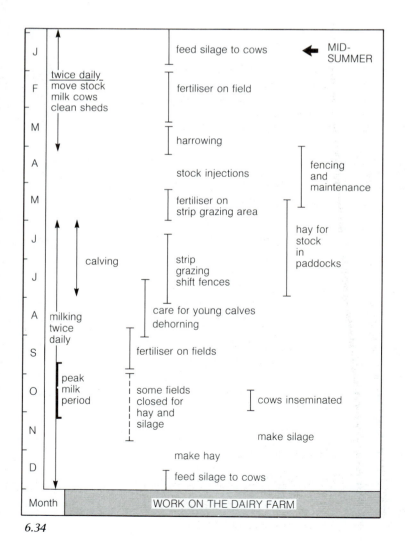

6.34

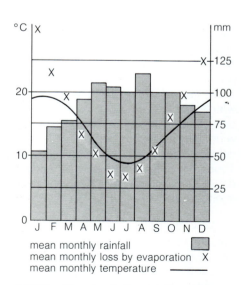

6.35 *The Gippsland climate. Over how many weeks is the mean temperature below 10°C? During which months is the amount of water brought by rainfall at least a third higher than that lost by evaporation?*

P 6.21 Dairy cattle in a paddock on a Gippsland farm.

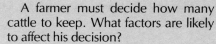

A farmer must decide how many cattle to keep. What factors are likely to affect his decision?

Look at the seasonal activities. Why is peak milk production in October? If the farmer wants a holiday, when would be the best time to take it?

What activities take place close to the farmhouse? Why? Would it be better to have the farmhouse centrally placed amid the paddocks? What would be the advantages/disadvantages?

What else keeps the farmer busy, apart from the tasks described in Fig. 6.34?

Why is this type of farming described as 'intensive'?

The seasonal routines are affected by climate. Pasture growth is low when the mean monthly temperature is below 10°C. It grows well only when the precipitation is a third higher than the evaporation (Fig. 6.35). The rainfall appears favourable, but unfortunately is erratic, especially during the drier months. Over 30 years the January rainfall varied from 0 to 130 mm, and in July from 50 to 190 mm. This can mean a heavy fall in income in some years.

The whole dairy industry is subsidised by the government, which means some security, and helps to maintain exports.

P 6.24 Cheese-making inside this Gippsland factory.

In Gippsland many smaller factories have closed, and milk is sent to larger ones. This involves extra transport costs. Why? What factors might make it cheaper to operate one large factory rather than two small ones?

P 6.22 Collecting milk by tanker.

P 6.23 Dairy factories were set up in Gippsland, with their own railway halts.

Theme 6 Back-up section

Finding out about a farm

Land-use and changing activities

A base map of the field boundaries and farm buildings is needed for a serious study of a farm. It can be prepared from preliminary sketches, or a simple survey, on the spot. If an OS 1:10 560 plan is not available, it could be scaled up from a 1:25 000 map, and amended as necessary. Several copies are needed.

The current land-use can be indicated by shading, with an appropriate key, and details of crops and animals recorded in a note-book.

Details of **relief and soils** can also be filled in on a base map. These could be related to the presence or absence of certain types of land-use; hypotheses should be tested.

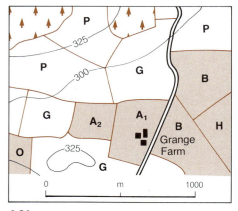

6.36

Fig. 6.36 shows the fields about an English farmstead at a scale of 1:25 000. The land-use at a particular visit is shown by symbols: A₁ arable (rape); A₂ arable (roots); O oats; H hay; B barley; G rotation grass; P permanent pasture. There are two areas of coniferous plantation.

How does the land-use shown tie up with the fact that the farm supported 100 store cattle (for fattening) and 280 sheep?

In which part of England might this be? What types of machinery might you find there?

Changes in land-use can be recorded, either by making several visits during the year, or from information provided by the farmer or farm manager. They would describe work carried out throughout the year.

Besides the distribution maps, calculate the percentage of the total area under arable, pasture, rough grazing, orchards, etc. You can show them on a pie-chart, as on p.128. As 1 per cent is a 3.6° arc, simply multiply the percentages by 3.6. Or you could draw a bar graph.

Routine monthly activities may be shown as in Fig. 6.34, or on a circular chart (Jan – Dec).

Finding out how the farm works

What you have recorded on maps, graphs or charts is the end-product of much planning and many decisions by the farmer. **A simple view of how the farmer must budget helps us understand how the farm actually works.**

He must estimate the return from crops, animals, and woodland as the result of his inputs. **The inputs** are made up of (1) **variable costs** and (2) **fixed costs**. as the following examples show. This is the kind of information to seek from a farmer or manager who is willing to cooperate. **Budgeting of this kind can be applied to any farming system.**

The farmer looks at the fields which will produce, say, winter wheat, potatoes, and beans. He estimates his likely outlay on each of these and his probable return. He also distributes the costs of running the whole farm (his fixed costs) on a *per hectare* basis.

Remember that his estimated profit (Table 6) is the amount *per hectare* and that the area of each crop will be different.

It may appear that beans bring a small return per hectare compared with potatoes. But what advantage is there in having beans in a crop rotation?

You should also consider where the market is, and the cost of transporting beans and potatoes to market. But remember that some crops are grown to be consumed on the farm. Which are likely to be grown for livestock?

Table 6

	winter wheat (per ha)		potatoes (per ha)		beans (per ha)	
VARIABLE COSTS (£)						
seed	(200 kg)	48	(3 tonnes)	540	(250 kg)	170
fertiliser		60		180		54
sprays		25		80		30
sundries		7		120		6
casual labour		–		120		–
total		**140**		**1040**		**260**
OUTPUT (Income) (£)						
5 tonnes grain @ 100 per tonne		500	25 tonnes @ 90 per tonne	2250	4 tonnes @ 120 per tonne	480
3 tonnes straw @ 20 per tonne		60		–		–
total		**560**		**2250**		**480**
margin (estimated gain per hectare)		**£420**		**£1210**		**£220**

Buyers may arrange to collect a crop grown on contract – e.g. potatoes may be grown for a crisp manufacturer. Transport costs are included in the contract.

Now, having decided on the area under each crop, the farmer has a clear idea of his income direct from the soil, though remember what can happen to a crop between sowing and harvest! But then there are his **fixed costs**. These work out at:

Table 7

FIXED COSTS (per hectare)	£
regular labour	120
machinery; repairs, depreciation	60
fuel and electricity	20
contracts	8
rent/rates/mortgage repayments	50
sundries (phone, fees, insurance, etc)	42
total	**300**

Assuming a 200 ha farm, he estimates these fixed costs at £60 000. You can appreciate why **intensive commercial mixed farming must depend on successful business management.**

Planning for labour and machinery

In order to carry out the various tasks through the year, the farmer must plan both for finance and labour. This means knowing the average number of days available for field work. A day is taken as eight hours, though there may well be overtime and working with lights, which extend the period available, but add to the cost.

Fig. 6.37 shows how the days available vary from month to month in eastern England. They vary from place to place, of course.

> What will be the factors which affect the working time available during February and July?

The farmer must be able to estimate

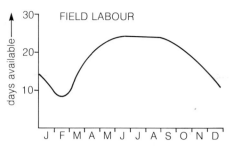

6.37 The average number of eight-hour days available for work in the fields in East Anglia.

how much time can be spent on particular tasks by his **permanent employees:** what effects using machinery will have; and whether he needs **casual labourers** or **contract workers**. Records show, for instance, that hectares worked per 8 hr day are:

Table 8

task	men	ha/day
ploughing (tractor)	1	6
potato planting (2 row)	3–4	1–6
spraying	1	12–16

With this in mind he must consider: cost of tractor hire per hour; contract rate for potato harvesting; aerial spraying contract rates (if a large enough area); casual workers' rate per day; cost of contracting for spraying or harvesting.

> Make lists of those things which may affect the farmer's decision to plant a particular crop in a particular field – under the headings: physical conditions; economic considerations; outside influences.

Wider patterns of land use

Field work should test hypotheses rather than merely describe patterns. They can involve relationships between land-use and such things as slope, altitude, distance, and rock structure.

Suppose we make the hypothesis that **land-use is related to altitude.**

Choose a 1:25 000 Land Utilisation Map of rural land with marked differences in altitude.

Make a 100 point random sample, and record the land-use and altitude at each point. Then plot these on a scatter graph. It is instructive to do this with maps from different parts of the country.

The random points are established from a **table of random numbers**, from which you take a string of six figures which give you a map reference. Then

continue until the next string of six figures give a reference on your map. **The forms of land use** chosen may be numbered (e.g. 1 market gardening; 2 arable; 3 pastoral; 4 woodland; 5 heath) and plotted as shown.

This may reveal clustering, which points to a strong relation to altitude. It also shows the **altitude range** of that particular land-use. In the 50 point sample in Fig. 6.38, the sampling produced a fairly even distribution of the types chosen.

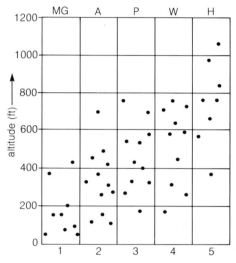

6.38 The distribution of market gardening (**MG**), arable farmland (**A**), pasture (**P**), woodland (**W**), and heath (**H**) at various altitudes.

> What percentage of each form of land use is there?
> Compare the highest and lowest altitudes of each type sampled. Which has the biggest range, which the smallest? Suggest reasons for this.
> Which, on the whole, is most clustered within a narrow range?
> Find the **mean** altitude for each type.
> Now find the **median** value. (The median is the value above and below which are equal numbers of units. Where the numbers are even – as in types 2,4,5 – it's the mean of the two central ones.)
> Add up the amounts by which each point varies from the median (ignoring + or –). Then divide by the number of points in the type. You can now compare the **mean deviation** for each.

A more useful measure of the spread can be obtained mathematically; but, even so, you now know quite a lot about the responses of land-use to altitude. You may also test how the land-use varies with slope, geology, etc.

Theme 6 Making sure

1 What is the exact meaning of 'arable', 'pastoral' and 'horticultural'?

2 Farming System:

A	B	C
INPUTS→	PROCESSES	→OUTPUTS

In which category, A, B, or C, are the following: sugar-beet; combine harvester; fertiliser; capital investment; calving shed; hoe; threshing floor; draught oxen?

3 What are the advantages of shifting cultivation? When and where is it a suitable form of agriculture?

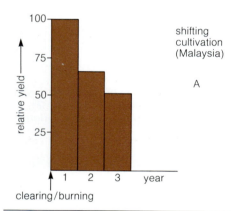

4 Look carefully at Fig. 6.39.

(a) What does the bar graph **A** emphasise about shifting cultivation?

(b) In **B** the soil is being over-used. How have the cultivators responded to the fall in productivity with time? Compare the length of the fallow periods.

(c) Has this proved successful? Look carefully at the periods of cultivation.

5 'Cassava grows in poor tropical soils. Its root, crushed and boiled, produces tapioca (which can be ground for flour). Its energy value is high, but it lacks proteins and vitamins.' What are its advantages and disadvantages for subsistence farmers? What else should they grow?

6 (a) What is meant by 'intermediate technology'? Give an example.

(b) When there is a large supply of rural labour, why might the introduction of agricultural machinery be a disadvantage?

(c) In LLDCs what other reasons discourage the use of advanced machinery in the fields?

7 Technological developments affect farmers at all levels. What particular types of farmers might benefit from the following?

(a) electric fencing; (b) a biogas converter; (c) hybrid wheat; (d) spray irrigation; (e) a tube well; (f) a combine harvester; (g) light aircraft. Explain how.

8 (a) How do the cycles shown in Figs. 6.40 and 6.41 emphasise the importance of improving agricultural efficiency in the LDCs?

(b) Why must improvements in education and technical training go hand in hand with this?

(c) Why are these called 'snowball' effects?

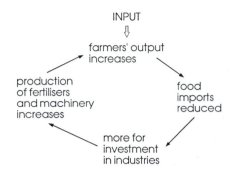

6.40

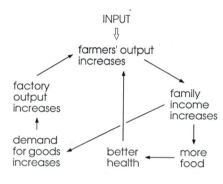

6.41

9 Distinguish between chemical fungicides, insecticides, pesticides and weed killers. Which would be used against: rats; locusts; wheat virus (rust)?

10 Explain why the following movements take place:

(a) **In the West African Sahel** families and cattle move slowly north in summer, then southwards to semi-permanent settlements in winter.

(b) **In Switzerland** cattle move to high mountain pastures (alps) in summer, and down to the valleys for stall-feeding in winter. As a farmer, what would you grow near your valley homestead during summer? Why is this also called 'transhumance'?

(c) **In northern Britain** young beef cattle and sheep are often reared in the hills and sent to lowland areas later.

11 Give reasons why there are many dairy farms on clay soils in the west of the British Isles. Look at a rainfall map. Why may this seem odd in view of the huge demands in south-east England, and von Thünen's arrangement (Fig. 6.16)? How have modern developments allowed the wider distribution of dairy farms?

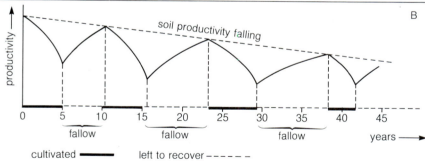

*6.39 **A** Crop yields from a field in Malaysia during the years after clearing the land. **B** Cleared land regains fertility (productivity) during a fallow period. But see what happens as the years go by.*

P 6.25 Intensive vegetable growing in Dutch glasshouses, stretching into the distance.

12 Give reasons why tropical lowlands are usually less suitable as dairy pastures.

13 Explain the purpose of the following rotation: year 1 – barley; year 2 – root crop; year 3 – wheat; year 4 – temporary pasture with clover (ley); year 5 – barley. What is gained during year 4?

14 'As the population density increases so does the intensity of the agricultural land-use.' (a) When and why would this tend to happen? Think of available land and increasing demands. (b) Why may this not happen in LLDCs? Think of the over-use of the land and the difficulties of making improvements.

15 Account for the huge inputs in energy and costs involved in the intensive agriculture shown in Photo 6.25. Consider the buildings, maintenance, day-to-day running, fuel, transport, etc. Describe some of the produce. What justifies such high inputs? Consider also markets – and EEC subsidies (p. 250).

16 How do the figures justify the terms **extensive/intensive** used to describe the types of farming in the following regions:
(a) eastern Canadian prairies (fertiliser input 90 kg/ha: average wheat yield 2200 kg/ha).
(b) Sjaelland (Denmark) (fertiliser input 250 kg/ha; average wheat yield 5500 kg/ha).

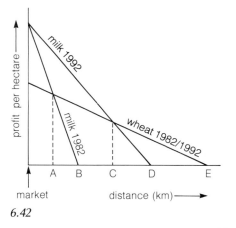

6.42

17 Look carefully at Fig. 6.42.
(i) At which place, **A, B, C, D** or **E**, would you have expected a change from dairy farming to wheat growing (a) in 1982; (b) in 1992?
(ii) The profit from milk production was not the same in 1992 as in 1982. This was because transport costs of milk rose/fell: which?

18 Three crops are grown for sale in Newtown market (Table 9). The market price (£/ha) is shown in column **a**, and the production cost per ha in column **b**. Show in column **c** the profit per ha if there were no transport costs. Column **d** shows the cost of transporting the output per ha (in £ per km). Show in column **e** how far each crop can be carried before becoming unprofitable.

Table 9

crop	a	b	c	d	e
lettuce	80	40	–	4.00	–
wheat	20	8	–	0.50	–
potatoes	50	25	–	1.50	–

Plot a graph showing the profit per ha against distance from the market (as in Question 17) for each crop. At what distance from the market will wheat growing be the most profitable activity?

19 A farmer owns land on the outskirts of a city which would bring a high rent if used for building. Instead he spends a lot on seeds, watering, spraying, continuous weeding, heating, several part-time workers, and occasional casual labour.
(a) What kind of crops is he growing?
(b) Where will he sell them?

Table 10

stage of development	yields (100 kg/ha)		commercial fertiliser (tonnes/100 ha)	area of arable land/tractor (ha)
	wheat	rice		
LDCs	14.6	25.1	0.6	274.5
MDCs	20.4	55.7	11.0	39.4

20 (a) What do the figures in Table 10 suggest about different inputs and their effects?
(b) What other factors should be taken into account when explaining low agricultural productivity in LDCs?
(c) Does improving productivity necessarily depend on an LDC acquiring agricultural machinery or commercial fertilisers? Discuss other ways in which crop yields have been improved in impoverished areas.

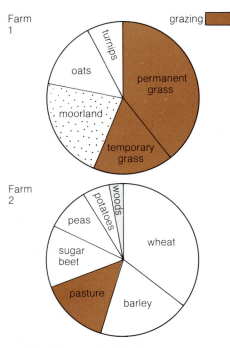

Farm 1

grazing

turnips

oats

moorland

permanent grass

temporary grass

Farm 2

woods

potatoes

peas

sugar beet

pasture

wheat

barley

6.43 Land-use on British farms.

21 Fig. 6.43 shows the proportion of land-use on two British farms. What type of farming is represented in each : **A**–arable commercial farming; **B**–market gardening; **C**–dairy farming; **D**–subsistence farming; **E**–hill sheep farming? Suggest how each crop or field area is used economically on farms 1 and 2.

Consider the terms used

Nutrient – a substance which nourishes. Thus one which passes through the food chain: soil has chemical nutrients for plants; plants pass on nutrients to animal consumers.

Biomass – the weight of living material in an organism (plant or animal), or in a whole ecosystem. An **organism** is an individual form of life, composed of parts which depend on each other.

Protein consists of large molecules of carbon, hydrogen, oxygen and nitrogen, often with sulphur and phosphorus. Proteins are essential in food, for they build body tissues. Cheese, lean meat, fish and eggs are rich in protein.

Casein is a protein of milk. It is curdled by adding **rennet** (a calf stomach extract) and then used for paints, adhesives and plastics.

Algae are green plants which grow mostly in water. Some, like pond scums, grow very rapidly when temperature and nutrients allow.

Biochemical refers to the chemical processes of plant and animal life.

The tsetse fly is a small blood-sucking fly, which breeds in African tropical marshes and moist bushes. It passes a parasite to humans which causes sleeping sickness, and in hooved animals (domestic and wild) causes wasting nagana disease. It thus restricts cattle breeding.

Pesticide is a poisonous chemical used against living organisms (usually small ones) considered to be pests. A **fungicide** is used to kill unwanted fungi. A **biocide** kills plants and animals.

Biogas is a combustible gas (mostly methane) generated by decomposing organic compounds (plant and animal wastes).

Silage is made from a green fodder crop stored in a pit or tall container (**silo**). It is usually chopped, sprayed with molasses, and allowed slowly to ferment. It is fed especially to dairy cattle.

Cross-fertilisation is the fertilisation of the ovules of one plant by the pollen of another, usually by the agency of insects, or wind, or water. But this can be controlled so as to produce new plant varieties.

Fallow land is that which remains unseeded after ploughing and harrowing (uncultivated).

Transhumance is periodic movements of livestock to and from seasonally favourable sites – between lowland and mountains; from drying grasslands to moister ones (seasonal nomadism).

A factory farm is a term used in agriculture where inputs, mechanical processes, and a carefully regulated, uniform output resemble an industrial system.

Latifundia are large estates.

Fragmentation is the process of dividing into smaller pieces – e.g. land holdings into smaller parts.

A rotovator (rototiller) is a machine for turning over soil.

A tube well is one where a cylindrical pipe is driven down below the water-table. A mechanical pump is usually attached to raise the water.

Technology is the knowledge of means used to produce materials necessary for a particular society – a simple tool (elementary technology) or a digital watch (advanced technology).

A constraint restricts freedom and may prevent what one might otherwise do.

Capital is any form of wealth which can be used to finance an enterprise (and so aim to produce more wealth).

A tenant is a person entitled to occupy particular land or housing, often by payment of rent to an owner. **Land tenure** means the terms under which land is held.

Subsist – just to exist and support life. **Subsistence farming** just keeps the family going.

Quota is a proportion, either assigned to a person or group, or to be contributed by them.

A cooperative is an organisation in which people work together to achieve what they might not have been able to do on their own: e.g. groups of farmers set up cooperatives as buying and selling agencies (sufficiently large to influence the market). Bulk buying of seeds or fertiliser may reduce the cost.

A bloc is an association of groups (often of nations) to further their common interests (p. 251).

Theme 7 Transport and communications

7.1 Carrying things along

We have seen how the energy of moving water and air can carry along (transport) solid particles. **Transporting people and goods and messages also uses up a great deal of energy.** The amount depends on distance and speed, and on the bulk carried (a crate of machinery or a letter).

In choosing which form of transport to use you think of the destination, the urgency, and whether you can afford it. For you pay for a proportion of the fuel (energy), the labour, and the costs of keeping truck, train, or aircraft in service. However, many of the world's people are without, or unable to afford, mechanised transport and so have little choice but to use human or animal power.

The energy used varies with the form of transport. Table 11 summarises a number of their particular advantages and disadvantages.

P 7.1 Pick out the means of transport and communication in this busy city scene in Xian, northern China. . . pedal cycles, motor cycles, trolley buses, diesels, telephone wires, newspapers (wall posters), hand signals.

Table 11

carrier	energy source	limitation	advantage
human	daily food	low speed; low bulk	adaptable; mobile
draught animal	fodder	low speed; low bulk	adaptable; mobile
railway train	coal; oil; electricity	fixed route	rapid bulk transport
road truck	fuel oil	moderate speed; lowish bulk	relative mobility adaptable for short haul
powered barge	coal; oil	low speed; limited range/route	cheap bulk movement
ship	wind; coal, oil, nuclear fuel	moderate speed; limited transfer points (docks)	bulk movement; mobile
aircraft	fuel oil	low bulk; high cost; limited transfer points (airports)	speed mobile
pipeline	fuels for pumping; gravity	single route; vulnerable	continuous operation
rocket/space vehicle	gaseous fuel; solar	low bulk; high cost; elaborate base	speed; range; high technology

There are, of course, other considerations when deciding which form of transport to use. **Perishable goods** need either rapid transport or special containers (e.g. refrigerated chambers), as do **liquids and gases** under pressure (e.g. tankers).

Relatively slow transport is not necessarily a disadvantage where delivery is continuous (e.g. ships bringing ore to a coastal steelworks dock and unload one after another).

Very **valuable goods** need security, but can use expensive forms of transport (e.g. diamonds can stand high air fares, being both valuable and small).

The cost of transporting goods increases with distance, but the *rate* **of increase becomes less.** Carriers charge high rates for transporting goods a short distance (p. 136). There are also the effects of the competition between the various forms of transport available.

7.2 Routes of communication

In communicating with each other we convey objects, messages, and ideas over a distance, along a route. When talking, the routeway is mouth to ear (though we may first have travelled some way to convey our message). By harnessing electric energy, we can pass messages by phone, radio, or TV – using wires, cables, and the air as **routeways.**

We often use other people as links in

129

our communications – passing a message or object through someone (or something) in between. We post a letter and allow it to follow the kind of route shown below.

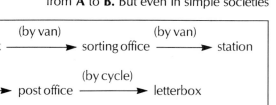

(the links are altered and extended if we send the letter overseas)

Communication of information by newspaper involves the same relations between collecting points, routes, and delivery points.

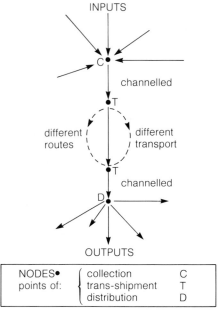

7.1 Lines of communication and transport.

Fig. 7.1, a general model for people, goods, and messages passing along lines of communication (routeways), shows changes from one form of transport to another (trans-shipment) and choices of route.

Make a model of this kind to represent the posting, sorting and delivery of letters (as above). Name the nodal points on the routeway.

This focuses the attention on the concentration of routeways on particular points. You can find examples of this on most 1: 50 000 maps. You will also see that the actual paths of the roads and railways seem to wander about a great deal. So let's consider why.

7.3 Routes deviate from the straight line

Fig. 7.2 (i) shows the ideal way to travel from **A** to **B.** But even in simple societies the ideal is seldom feasible. Things get in the way – a stream, broken ground, someone else's property. A routeway between two villages on a level surface may well appear as in (ii).

Such routes tend to become imprinted on the landscape. Modern transport running over sealed roads, like the B 660 in north Bedfordshire, often follow old patterns (iii). Even the ancient Roman roads

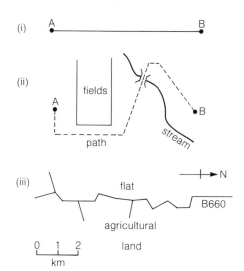

7.2 Routes deviate and become fixed.

and modern motorways deviate from the straight line to some extent.

Even with modern transport, **physical features still influence routes.** Marshy ground and rivers can be crossed by causeways and bridges. Hairpin bends wind up steep slopes to lessen the gradient. Hills are pierced by tunnels. Railways needing gentler gradients, and motorways carrying fast traffic, make use of cuttings and embankments.

But all these things are expensive. So routes may deviate to follow gentler courses and avoid major obstacles. Canals follow lowland where possible, for locks are expensive to construct and cause delays.

The reason for deviating may not, in fact, be **negative** (avoiding an obstacle): **positive**, deliberate, deviations may allow the routeway to serve more people, or collect more traffic.

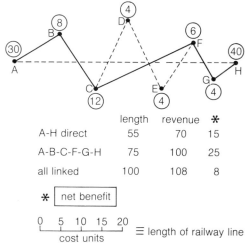

	length	revenue	✳
A–H direct	55	70	15
A–B–C–F–G–H	75	100	25
all linked	100	108	8

✳ net benefit

7.3 Positive deviations to serve people and/or make a profit.

In Fig. 7.3 a railway is to be built between towns A and H. Extra revenue could be obtained by serving smaller places between them. There are no major obstacles, so the line could be made to deviate. The cost of construction and maintenance would increase regularly with distance. As the cost depends on the length of line, we may use this length to represent the cost.

The expected revenues from passengers and freight over a given time are shown for each town (in the same units).

Notice that the line direct from **A** to **H** would cost 55 units to construct and maintain, and bring in a revenue of 30 + 40 = 70 units. Would a line linking all the places be more profitable than this? Experiment with other routes to see if there is a more profitable one than the line **A–B–C–F–G–H.**

7.4 Route networks and accessibility

Settlements and route densities

As villages and towns become collecting and distributing points, they may not only act as markets, but provide services and entertainment. People travel to and from them from different directions. So the density of main routes becomes greater near towns. In the countryside a network of minor roads and paths links clusters of villages. The lowest density is usually in hilly or marshy areas.

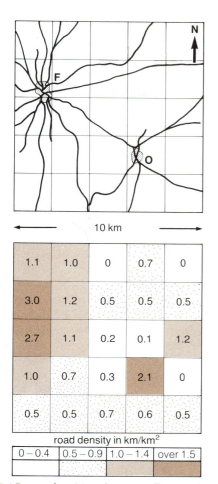

road density in km/km²

0 – 0.4	0.5 – 0.9	1.0 – 1.4	over 1.5

7.4 Route densities about small towns in southern Italy – Francavilla (F) and Oria (O) – (see Fig. 6.18). The road patterns are converted to a density grid.

Fig. 7.4 shows the density of roads near the market town of Francavilla in southern Italy, and about the small rural centre of Oria (p. 116). If we find the total length of road in each square (4 km²), we can present the **route density** in a grid form.

> You can apply the method to any map showing settlements and roads, using a suitable overlay grid. It is easy to find the density of the main roads, but the minor ones may take time to measure. So sometimes the number of road junctions in each square is taken as a rough indication of route density.

The pattern alone is often revealing. In Fig. 7.5 the rural towns of Thetford and

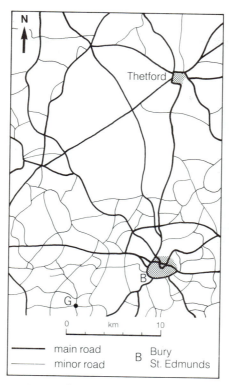

main road
minor road

B   Bury St. Edmunds

7.5 A part of East Anglia where route densities respond to soils and land-use; but a route map does not necessarily show how easy it is to get to a place (accessibility).

Bury St Edmunds each stand out as a major route focus. While the minor roads form a dense network in the areas where the soil has favoured intensive cultivation, they are almost absent where glacial outwash sands and gravels (p. 54) support only heath and planted conifers.

Accessibility – links between places

The country about Bury St Edmunds has a high route density. But this does not necessarily mean that a place like the village green **G** is easy to get at (**accessible**). It depends what form of transport you use. The tiny roads serve family cars but not the large inter-continental trucks, which use the main road network.

A map may show a close network of communications, but it does *not* show the state of repair of the roads, the timetable of buses (or trains), or the traffic density (which varies from hour to hour). It can only give a *partial* view of the accessibility of a place.

Political events or natural disasters may immediately change the accessibility of a place, in some cases permanently.

This, of course, applies to any routeway shown on a map. At any time a railway like that in Photo 7.2 may cease to function.

P 7.2 A narrow-gauge railway in the Peruvian Andes, blocked by a landslide after heavy rain – notice rocks poised on the steep slope.

Nevertheless it is often useful to find out the **relative accessibility** of places; and consider how, by improving routeways, places can be made more accessible.

We can regard the main freight-carrying roads, motorways, and railways as **links** between places (**nodes**). **It is possible to map these links yet ignore exact details of distances, directions, and detours.** In fact the London Underground map is a good example of this (Fig. 7.6).

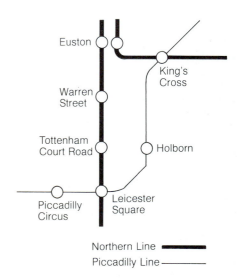

Northern Line
Piccadilly Line

7.6 Part of the London Underground system. This describes connection (links) between stations. Distance/time considerations depend on the frequency of trains.

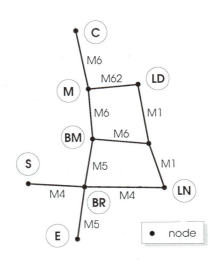

7.7 Links between selected motorways.

Fig. 7.7 shows the transport network formed by the M1,M4,M5,M6 motorways and the M62 link. A junction between two motorways is taken as a node. **Which of the cities** – Carlisle (**C**), Manchester (**M**), Leeds (**LD**). Birmingham (**BM**), Bristol (**BR**), Swansea (**S**), Exeter (**E**), or London (**LN**) **is most accessible in relation to all the others?**

One way to test this is to take each place in turn and **count the links between that and every other place.** The nodal point with the *lowest* total is the most accessible *on this basis.* Fig. 7.8**A** shows the results plotted in a matrix.

But you can get on a motorway and drive, via another motorway, from one town to another: so why not simply **record the distances and add these up?** Fig. 7.8**B** shows the results of doing this. Notice the difference in ranking of Exeter and Leeds in each case. Nevertheless the advantages or disadvantages of those at the top and bottom are still emphasised.

Again **this gives only part of the picture. It shows nothing of traffic, or climatic problems** (fog zones, or wind closing the Severn bridge (M4)). It ignores access difficulties – threading through industrial suburbs to get onto the motorways – especially a problem in huge cities like London.

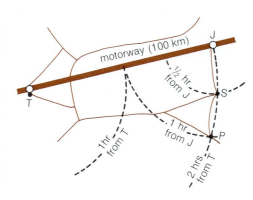

*7.9 Road links from town **T**, and also travel times (isochrones) by minor roads from the town **T** and the motorway junction **J**.*

Accessibility, then, is related to other time-consuming factors. It can also change as communications are improved. Fig. 7.9 shows how a market town **T** is made more accessible to a supply depot **S** by the development of the motorway. (It assumes an average speed of straight-line travel from **T** as 100 km per hour by motorway, and 50 km per hour by other roads.)

You can see radii of 1 hr intervals along side roads from the town, and of ½hr intervals from the motorway junction **J**. How long would goods take to reach **T** from **S** (i) via the motorway; (ii) via other roads? (**T** to **J** takes 1 hr.)

How long would each journey take if the depot were sited at **P**?

What other considerations might affect the choice of routes?

Contours of equal time (isochrones) can be used to show the effect of advantageous routes (Fig. 7.10).

How does the shape of the isochrones in Fig. 7.10 reflect the pattern of the major motorways completed by the mid-seventies?

Relative accessibility changes with time. Consider the M62 and M4 London-Bristol links, which were completed during the 1970s. Remove these from Fig. 7.7, construct a new matrix, and point to the differences between this and Fig. 7.8**A**.

A					links to other places					
	C	M	LD	BM	S	BR	E	LN		
C		1	2	2	4	3	4	4	20	8
M	1		1	1	3	2	3	3	14	3
LD	2	1		2	4	3	4	2	18	5˭
BM	2	1	2		2	1	2	2	12	1˭
S	4	3	4	2		1	2	2	18	5˭
BR	3	2	3	1	1		1	1	12	1˭
E	4	3	4	2	2	1		2	18	5˭
LN	4	3	2	2	2	1	2		16	4

B					distance (km)					
	C	M	LD	BM	S	BR	E	LN		
C		189	195	310	544	440	555	491	2724	8
M	189		69	141	323	267	382	318	1689	3
LD	195	69		184	434	346	461	314	2003	4
BM	310	141	184		240	136	251	187	1449	1
S	544	323	434	240		104	355	294	2294	6
BR	440	267	346	136	104		130	190	1613	2
E	555	382	461	251	355	130	·	272	2406	7
LN	491	318	314	187	294	190	272		2066	5

7.8 A – The number of motorway links between each city and the others
B – Distances to other cities.

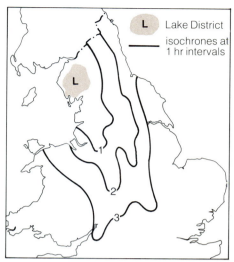

7.10 Travel times within which car drivers could reach the Lake District.

Isochrones may also be used to show times of journeys to and from a given site, such as a school. Some pupils living relatively close may find it takes longer to get to school than those who live further out. The latter may be near a rapid transport route – close to a station served by frequent commuter trains, for example.

Travel times may be found for a large number of pupils, and isochrones plotted. **Choice of forms of transport** may complicate findings – for some nearby may by travel by foot, or cycle, or car, or public transport. Comparisons can be made for particular forms of transport.

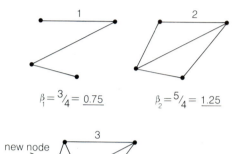

$$\beta_1 = \frac{3}{4} = \underline{0.75} \qquad \beta_2 = \frac{5}{4} = \underline{1.25}$$

$$\beta_3 = \frac{8}{5} = \underline{1.60}$$

7.12 The β-index reflects the extent to which places in a route network are interconnected.

nodes. As the nodal points become more inter-connected, the value increases.

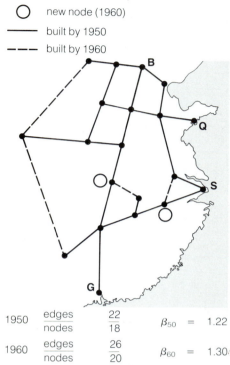

1950	edges / nodes	22 / 18	β_{50} = 1.22
1960	edges / nodes	26 / 20	β_{60} = 1.30

7.13 Railway construction during the 1950s gave eastern China a more integrated network of routes. Today the system includes many more links and extensions. Identify the ports.

Fig. 7.13 shows greater integration of China's railway system between 1950 and 1960. Today the railways of eastern China are much more integrated, and branch lines extend to other ports and to far western oases. (The north-eastern (Manchurian) system is not included in this diagram.)

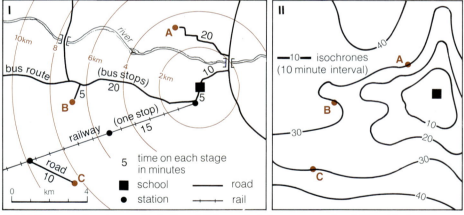

7.11 **I** Routes taken by pupils **A, B** and **C** from their homes to school (**S**), with the average time for each stage in brackets. The broken lines show straight-line distances from the school. In **II** the Isochrones represent travel times from pupils' homes to the school. Compare the actual distances travelled by **A, B** and **C**.

In Fig. 7.11 I, **A** lives closer than **B**, who is near a bus route, and **C**, who is near a station. But **A** is on the 'wrong' side of the river, so follows a devious route. This takes **A** 30 minutes. Both **B** and **C** have a short walk from the bus/railway station. The times for their stages are shown.

Notice that the isochrone representing 30 minutes from the school passes through *each* of their homes, as in Fig. 7.11 II.

7.5 Advantages of better integrated networks

As the networks become denser, with more links, they are better integrated, so they serve the whole area more effectively.

We can express this closer network by means of an **integration index** (or **ß index**). To get this we simply divide the number of **edges** (links) by the number of

LDCs – Networks extended from route centres

Many LDCs have inherited transport systems from colonial times which link the main commercial centres. Today they are struggling to create a transport network to spread manufacturing and increase trade throughout the country. Most have to seek foreign loans and investments to build up new links (p. 170).

In most LDCs the railways and well-surfaced roads have been extended from early colonial centres of control. The first major routes were built to carry commodities to a port or frontier post, or to

133

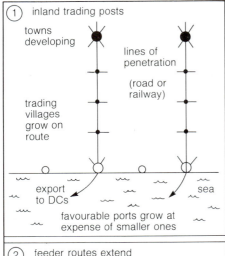

1 inland trading posts

towns developing

lines of penetration

(road or railway)

trading villages grow on route

export to DCs

sea

favourable ports grow at expense of smaller ones

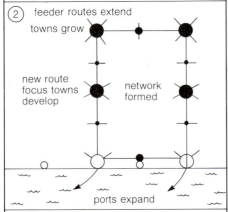

2 feeder routes extend

towns grow

new route focus towns develop

network formed

ports expand

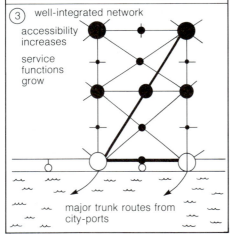

3 well-integrated network

accessibility increases

service functions grow

major trunk routes from city-ports

7.14 1 Colonial routes from export ports to towns controlling the interior; 2 ports expanded and local routes feed developing inland centres; 3 local route networks become inter-connected; trunk routes link major centres.

make it easier for administrators and troops to control the interior.

Fig. 7.14 shows how a network may develop from feeder routes focusing on these ports and inland centres, which grow accordingly. Lesser places on the main routes develop small networks of their own, and begin to link up with the

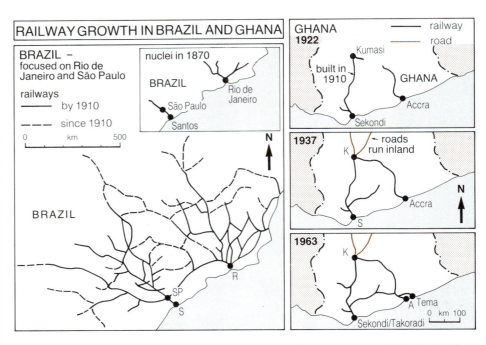

RAILWAY GROWTH IN BRAZIL AND GHANA

BRAZIL – focused on Rio de Janeiro and São Paulo

railways
— by 1910
- - - since 1910

0   km   500

nuclei in 1870

BRAZIL

Rio de Janeiro

São Paulo

Santos

BRAZIL

N

R

SP

S

GHANA 1922

—— railway
—— road

Kumasi

built in 1910

GHANA

Accra

Sekondi

1937

K   roads run inland

Accra

S

N

1963

K

A Tema

0   km   100

Sekondi/Takoradi

7.15 Separate railway networks which focus on particular ports become linked inland.

others. **Finally there is a completely interconnected network, with trunk routes built to link the largest places.**

Fig. 7.15 shows two instances of early routes of penetration joining up as the years go by. Railways from the Brazilian ports of Santos and Rio de Janeiro have first to climb to the interior plateau (where São Paulo has grown). You can see that the separate, spreading rail networks have joined, encouraging scores of new towns to develop in the hinterland.

In southern Ghana the rail route inland from Sekondi enabled the colonial power ready access to Kumasi, the large Ashanti tribal centre. The eastern railway was extended more slowly into the inland cocoa-producing areas. Eventually the two lines of penetration were joined.

While such railways may encourage development at various places along their length, roads allow transport to be more flexible and can serve local needs.

A really efficient transport system needs railways and trunk roads to carry long-distance traffic, backed up by feeder roads for local passengers and commodities.

Ghana's central network of roads runs

P7.3 A port built to serve colonial developments. Mombasa dockside with rail lines, road transport, cranes and a ship loading pyrethrum oil and tea for Canada.

P 7.4 In many LDCs transport problems lie in the hinterland of city-ports. Highways link Brazil's large ports; but, as here, road making of a different kind is needed to extend the transport system further west.

to the northern parts of the country, and links settlements along the coast. The road networks in eastern Brazil are also joined by highways; and regular flights link Rio de Janeiro, Santos, and São Paulo.

In tropical LDCs seasonal disruptions are a problem. Floods and landslides can make roads expensive to maintain. Bridging is costly, and ferries time-consuming.

7.6 Transport systems are continually changing

Britain – canals, railways in the 19th century

By the early 19th century Britain's canals, though narrow, shallow, and hampered by locks, **were vital industrial links**, carrying materials for coal-powered manufacturing. **Yet by mid-century an integrated railway system already served the expanding industries and ports.** Trunk routes linked the great cities and branch lines spread among the scattered rural population. Competing companies sometimes duplicated lines.

In 1840 it took 4½ hr to travel from London to Reading by road, but only 1¼ hr by rail (45 min by 1900). **The time-distance effects are strikingly shown in Fig. 7.16**, pointing out diagrammatically where so many minutes of rail travel might take you (from London).

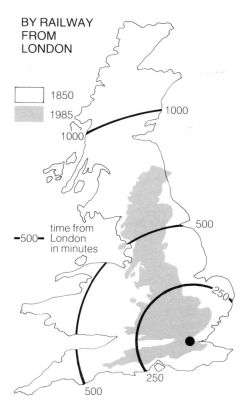

BY RAILWAY FROM LONDON

□ 1850
▨ 1985

time from London in minutes

7.16 Showing how much quicker it became to travel by rail from London to other parts of Britain.

Point to those parts of Britain which appear to have shrunk and those which are elongated. Account for this in particular areas.

Roads compete with railways

Fig. 7.17A shows the great density of railway routes remaining in 1950. However, road transport had been taking freight and passengers from the railways for over 30 years. Many lines were under-used and the system over-manned. **The result was a great pruning (Fig. 7.17B). Then came steps to make railways more competitive:**

(a) concentration on main rail routes; (b) electrification; (c) faster trains (especially passenger inter-city and freight liners); (d) container transport (compact bulk quickly transferred between ship-rail-road); (e) special carriers (car transporters, waste containers, etc); (f) automation and computer control; (g) a reduced labour force.

Despite this, the government has had to subsidise the railways to keep freight rates and passenger fares competitive.

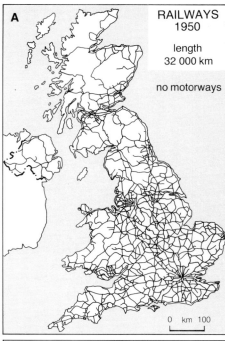

A   RAILWAYS 1950
length 32 000 km
no motorways

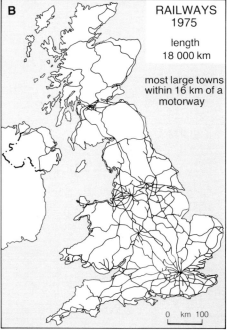

B   RAILWAYS 1975
length 18 000 km
most large towns within 16 km of a motorway

7.17 The effect of line closures.

Since the sixties, the growing motorway network and better trunk routes have benefited road transport. But the road system also has difficulties, for most of it developed haphazardly before the days of heavy traffic and large vehicles.
Problems for road transport include:
(a) congestion and bottlenecks; (b) narrow streets; (c) old buildings (shaken by vehicles); (d) pollution in confined spaces; (e) continual resurfacing; (f) re-aligning roads not built for long-distance traffic.

P 7.5 The West Midland motorway interchange at Gravelly Hill (Spaghetti junction), with factories nearby.

The motorways have the advantages of directness and speed, with few bends and easy gradients. They free other routes and ease urban congestion. But they, too, have drawbacks:

(a) costs of construction and maintenance are high; (b) they take up much land; (c) they form a barrier for much of their length; (d) infrequent access points; (e) hazards in fog, frost and rain; (f) congestion where they end.

Changes in technology continually act on existing forms of transport. The decline in coal-carrying by rail was partly offset by developing rail tankers to carry the growing volume of oil and oil products. But road tankers still have the advantage of mobility.

Now competition comes not only from road transport but from the development of **pipeline networks** for oil, natural gas, and petro-chemical products (Fig. 7.18).

Before looking at the more widely ranging sea and air transport, we must take notice of **costs** – for a combination of time, distance, energy needed, and costs of contruction and operating, affect the ways we actually use transport.

7.7 Transport costs

Charges for services

When goods are to be moved over a distance there are charges to cover a number of services. **The costs vary with the factors shown in brackets:**

1 **loading** (ease of handling; specialists employed)

2 **movement** (weight/bulk; distance/time)

3 **trans-shipment** (unloading/reloading; storage-see 1)

4 **final unloading** (see 1)

5 **insurance** (nature of journey; type of goods).

On top of these will be fixed costs and profit for the carrier.

A fixed (terminal) cost covers a proportion of the expenses of the carriers (maintenance of vehicles, office work, etc.). This is charged anyway. Then the cost of moving the bulk over the actual distance is added.

Suppose there is a fixed charge of £1 per tonne moved; and then a rate of 5p per tonne per km to cover loading and unloading, movement, and insurance. **Fig. 7.19 shows how the total cost increases with distance**. But you can see that the **average cost** per tonne **falls with distance**. It is relatively more expensive to carry goods over short distances.

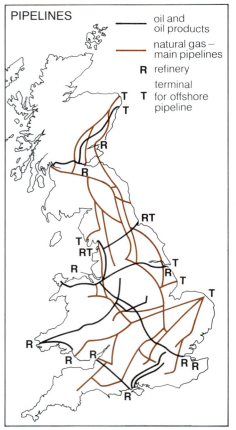

7.18 Pipelines form effective transport networks.

7.19 **A** shows how the average cost of carrying a tonne of goods one kilometre falls with the distance transported. How, and why, does the fixed cost affect this? **B** shows charges made for three stages (steps) according to distance.

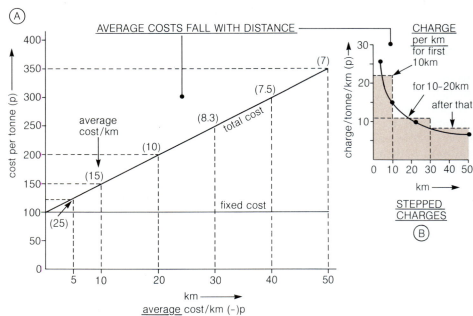

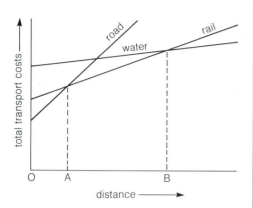

7.20 Look carefully at the fixed cost (before the journey begins) and the cost of the actual movement of goods by each form of transport.

In order to avoid complicated calculations, there is often a **stepped scale of charges** – e.g. 22p per tonne per km for the first 10 km; 11p per tonne per km between 10–30 km; and 9p after that. In some cases there is a fixed rate whatever the distance (like the Post Office's letter rates).

Terminal costs are lower for road then rail or sea or air transport. Why do you think this is? Which will be the highest? Explain.

Fig. 7.20 shows transport costs of road, rail and water. Notice the fixed (terminal) costs on the y-axis. Which have the higher **movement** costs, road or rail; rail or water?

Which is the most competitive within distance **OA**? Which in **AB**? Which over long distances?

Freight rates are affected by many other things. Very expensive goods can bear higher transport charges. With general

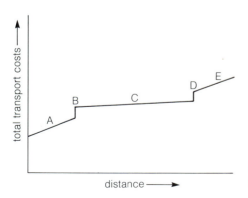

7.21 The effects of trans-shipment.

P 7.6 Felixstowe harbour, with row after row of stacked containers.

goods low rates are often quoted for a return journey, to try to fill an otherwise empty vehicle.

Which are likely to have the higher freight rate – a new car or the same weight of component parts? Why?

Fig. 7.21 shows goods travelling by road, then being trans-shipped by sea, then on again by road. Explain the slopes of the five parts of the graph **A-E**.

7.8 Sea and air transport

Ocean vessels have a wide choice of routes. They provide slow transport, but can carry a large load per trip. They are a cheap way of moving bulky goods, but need to carry as much as possible each time. **Bulk cargo**, like crude oil and ores, is not packed and can be shipped in large quantities. **General cargo** is mostly packaged.

Large vessels are *relatively* cheaper to build and maintain than small ones. Fuel cost is lower *per tonne carried,* and they need fewer hands to operate them (per tonne).

The size of a ship using a port is limited by the depth of water and berthing facilities. There may be jetties for large vessels, or pipelines to tankers anchored offshore (Photo 8.2). As the size of vessels

has increased, some ports have declined in importance. Others have developed **outports** close by, where water is deeper.

Bristol (Fig. 7.22), 10 km up the tidal river Avon from the Bristol Channel, was once Britain's second port. Give three reasons why Avonmouth has become its outport, with an important industrial area about it. Why are there locks at the entrance to its docks?

Port charges are high, so a quick turn-round is essential. Here, again, containerisation of the load helps (Fig. 7.23). There are specially designed **container ships** (Photo 7.7).

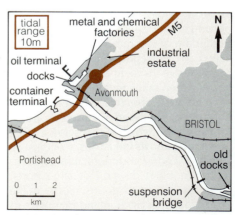

7.22 Notice the activities focused on the outport.

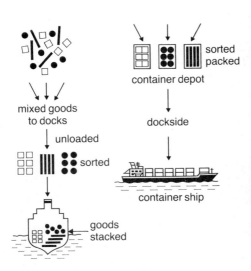

7.23 Different methods of delivering, sorting, and loading.

P 7.7 A container ship docked at the main terminal in Sydney harbour.

Explain the advantages in load handling shown by Fig. 7.23. The containers are large standard-size metal boxes. What will be the differences in storage facilities at a container depot and a non-container port dealing with general cargo and bulk cargo?

What other advantages are given by container transport? Consider security, labour force, time taken in packaging and trans-shipment.

What disadvantages could affect a port converted as a container terminal? Think of employment and local industries.

Felixstowe, a container port, is also used by **roll-on/roll-off** heavy goods vehicles (HGVs) – see Q.16, p.145. What advantages have HGVs for overseas deliveries? Why do HGV owners offer special rates for return freight picked up abroad?

Smaller vessels may collect and deliver cargo at large well-located ports which serve a wide hinterland and handle ocean-going vessels. Such a port, like Rotterdam at the mouth of the Rhine, is called an **entrepôt.** Some, like Hong Kong, serve as a financial-commercial link between many nations.

To be really effective, a port needs not only deep, sheltered waterways, but a location from which it can serve a large population and its industries, so it must be linked to a good communication system. Industries often develop at large ports, based on imported goods. Some make use of materials from inland manufacturing regions.

Specialist ports may handle particular exports; for instance, the iron ore passing through Port Hedland in Western Australia (Photo 7.8).

Use an atlas and sketch the location of Montreal, one of the major outlets for Canadian wheat (p.121). Trace the St Lawrence Seaway through to Thunder Bay on Lake Superior. There are hydro-electric stations at many of the locks, which allow the water to fall in steps from the Lakes.

Montreal's population has increased by a third since the Seaway opened in 1959. Point to its advantages as a city-port. Think of one particular drawback (see p. 65).

Air transport has the advantage of speed. Planes carry a small load, but can make frequent trips in a short time. They are expensive to develop, construct, and maintain. Commercial airports are complex. They take up a lot of land, and need careful siting.

Large aircraft may *appear* to have a wide choice of routes, unhampered by ground relief. **In fact, they are subject to many constraints:**

1 Flight paths are controlled for safety reasons.

2 Routes are planned to keep the aircraft full. This can mean direct long-distance flights, or routes with positive deviations to serve airports on the way.

3 Physical constraints on and near the ground are important. Fog, frost, and the relief near the airport may be hazards for take-off and landing. Airport siting takes these into consideration.

4 Countries may prevent aircraft using their national airspace, for political reasons.

Aircraft routes relate to wind systems at ground level and in the upper air. A jet flying out from Heathrow (UK) to Miami (USA) followed routes **A** and **B**

P 7.8 Long trains deliver iron ore to dumps besides the docks at Port Hedland, a specialist port of great economic importance on the mangrove coast of Western Australia.

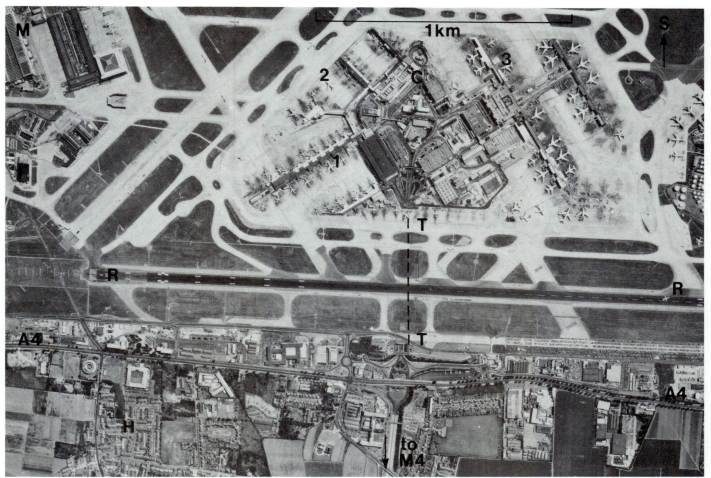

P 7.9 Heathrow Airport with planes standing at Terminals 1, 2 and 3 grouped about the control tower (**C**). Notice the northern runway **R–R**. Terminal 4 lies beyond a parallel runway to the south. **M** indicates maintenance buildings. **T–T** is the road tunnel leading to the M4 motorway. The housing (**H**) is very close to the airport.

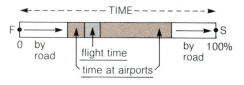

7.25 Transport by air. Consider the percentage of the journey time taken up by movement and by waiting.

shown in Fig. 7.24. Which was the outward route; which the return? Give your reasons for this.

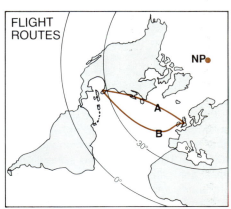

7.24 Outward and return routes of a passenger plane between Heathrow and Miami.

Small planes, or helicopters, are used for short transport flights, or for other commercial purposes (e.g. crop-spraying). But, generally, long-distance jets have become larger. This means longer runways, and airport facilities to deal with lots of people leaving and arriving simultaneously.

The airport itself must have good access by main road and rail routes to prospective customers. It should be clear of urban areas, for safety and noise reasons. It needs a large area for the runways (wind direction may affect the actual lay-out), and space for the great number of operational and storage services.

The distance of the airport from urban areas, and from other transport terminals, adds to the overall time of travel by air. So do the procedures and wait at the airport. Air freight, too, may spend a long time at each airport before onward transport by road or rail.

In calculating **overall travel times,** such additions to the main journey must be taken into account.

Fig. 7.25 shows the transfer of freight from a London factory (**F**) to a town in Scotland (**S**), with the proportion of the journey-time spent in the air.

(a) What therefore needs to be considered when thinking of freighting by air?

(b) Draw a similar chart showing the stages, with the percentage journey-time, for moving freight by air from a London factory to a Sydney suburb.

(c) Compare the two charts. Under what circumstances is air freighting likely to be most favourable/least favourable?

7.9 Energy and transport – conclusions

Whatever forms of transport are used, they all require an energy input. Foodstuffs supply human and animal transport; fossil fuels, hydro and nuclear sources provide energy for machines.

In comparing the **energy efficiency** of various types of transport, we need to think about what they can carry (their carrying capacity). We may decide to use them because of cheapness, or on conservation grounds. But we also consider such things as speed, comfort, and mobility.

Look carefully at Table 12:

(a) how many cars are needed to carry 100 people? How many coaches?

(b) a rail train uses more energy per km than a car. Why is *less* energy consumed when 100 people travel 100 km by train than when they go by car?

(c) which is the most economical for long-distance travel – coach, car, or train?

(d) what might be the advantages and disadvantages for the 100 persons travelling by aircraft?

P 7.10 Elaborate transport systems and high energy consumption are features of cities in the MDCs: illustrated by development adjoining Toronto's harbour on Lake Ontario. . . factories and commercial buildings, expressways, city roads, car parks, railways, shipping, oil storage, and the incinerators and sewage plant beyond.

(a) Which car-less families will be at the greater disadvantage – rural or urban? Why?

(b) Suggest why so many rural bus services have been reduced.

Table 12

carrier	average capacity (persons)	energy input per vehicle-km (litres)	energy input to carry 100 persons 100 km (litres)
high speed train	470	2.00	200
car	4	0.17	420
coach	53	0.45	90
aircraft	100	9.20	920

Whether people have a choice of transport or not depends on where they live and what they can afford. The statistics in Table 15 on p. 144 tell us a lot about the circumstances within a country. They highlight contrasting conditions between MDCs and LDCs.

Even in the MDCs the provision and use of transport varies between urban and rural areas, as these average figures for the UK show (1990):

Table 13

location	% families with 2 cars	% familes without a car
rural areas	39	4
urban areas	21	35

7.10 Bottlenecks and rush hours

However efficient the forms of transport or trunk routes, they are hampered whenever there is a bottleneck in the transport system. Most large cities are fed by multi-lane highways. But these end in a network of smaller roads threading through the inner city.

Daily commuters are delivered to mainline stations by a rapid succession of rush-hour trains. They are dispersed to places of work, as quickly as possible, by city buses and underground (metro) railways. The number of trains arriving and departing is carefully scheduled to cope with hourly changes in the volume of passengers.

Multi-storey car-parks and parking meters in the inner city prevent stationary vehicles jamming the streets. Through-roads and underpasses can maintain normal flow; but they can still be choked with rush-hour traffic.

Alternative schemes include: (1) banning inner city private motoring; (2) arranging suburban parking for long-distance commuters – who then go by bus or rail to the city centre; (3) staggering working hours and shop opening/closing times in the central areas; (4) ring roads to take traffic from converging motorways and distribute it round the city; it is fed into the centre at suitable junctions.

Already large cities have extended rapid underground (metro) services to the outer suburbs. This allows commuters to leave their cars far out. Airports, which generate road traffic, are also served this way – as by the underground extension to London Heathrow.

Fig. 7.26 shows mainline railways, and an inner city underground network running out through the suburbs (but omits suburban surface lines and stations). All these link with trunk roads, motorways, and inner and outer ring roads – **an integrated system.**

What options are open for the long-distance commuter at his home, wishing to drive, park, and continue by train?

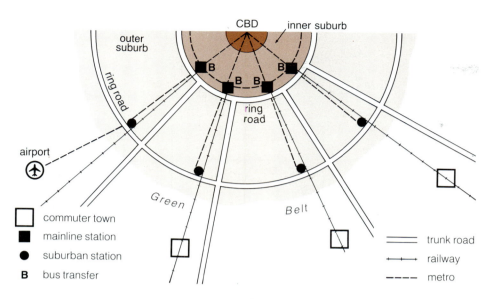

7.26 Daily access routes from the suburbs and commuter towns to places in the city centre.

How will this kind of network influence the location of offices, light industries, large shopping centres, and hypermarkets? (See p. 220.)

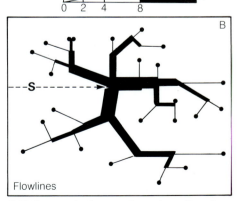

7.27 **A** records the number of pupils using each road link. **B** shows the same movements as flow-lines

Back-up section

Simple studies of mobility and routes

Flow-lines depicting the daily movements of pupils to school are easy to construct. Locate homes on a map and draw the routes from home to school. These will converge at certain points. Pencil in the number using each section of the routes.

Use a directly proportional scale to give the width of flow-lines (Fig. 7.27). Decide on the maximum width for the highest number. Complete a scale triangle. Draw the appropriate width of line on either side of that representing the route. Rub out the pencilled numbers.

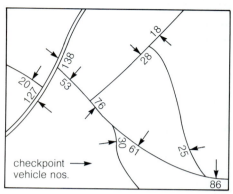

7.28 The number of vehicles passing each checkpoint in a given time.

To study traffic using a route network over a given period, checkpoints are established close to intersections where flow changes may occur (Fig. 7.28). Prepare a map of the network.

Record the number of vehicles passing in either direction during a period sufficient to give an average flow per hour. Pencil in numbers on each link. Peak and off-peak periods may be chosen, and flows compared.

Fig. 7.28 shows vehicles recorded over an hour at checkpoints 1–11. A few turned off within a link; but the overall figures enable a flow diagram to be constructed.

Space–time–distance transformed

Space–time map transformation can also be simply demonstrated by timing a journey into and out of two urban areas and over the space between.

Distance travelled in a given time may be read from a car (or minibus) **odometer**.

Table 14

time (hr)	odometer reading (km)	distance (km)	comment
1400	12050.6	–	in the centre of A
1405	10251.8	1.2	2 lights, long delays
1410	10254.2	2.4	through suburbs
1415	10256.0	1.8	roadworks, long tail-back
1420	10261.4	5.4	clear of suburbs
1425	10268.1	6.7	climbing,
1430	10275.3	7.2	little traffic,
1435	10286.1	10.8	fast road across
1440	10297.2	11.1	top of moor
(continued to the centre of B ....)			

The time-distance graph (Fig. 7.29) **illustrates differences during the journey from A to B**, with observations recorded at the time. This is based on the readings recorded in Table 14:

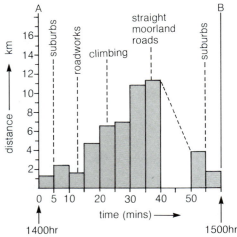

7.29 Comparing distances travelled in equal intervals of time.

Two methods may be used: (1) by recording the distance travelled during, say, 5 minutes (Table 14); (2) by recording the time taken over successive distances of, say, one kilometer.

Fig. 7.30 shows 4 kilometres of road on a map, from the T-junction to the second church. This is given a **topological change** in (ii). In (iii) the journey is represented by a **time map**. Compare the spacing of the check-points with those in (ii) and account for the differences.

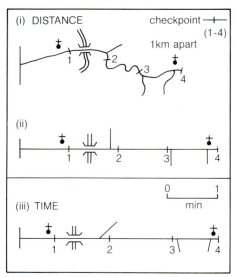

7.30 (i) Route distances and directions; (ii) distance scale only; (iii) time scale. Look carefully at (i) and give reasons for the time variations in (iii).

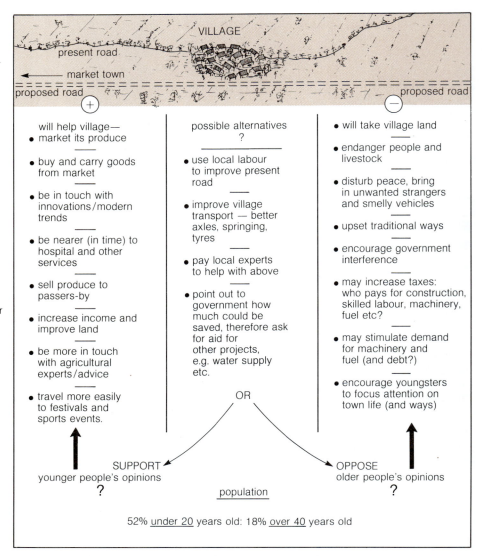

VILLAGE

present road

market town

proposed road   proposed road

(+)   (−)

will help village—
- market its produce
  ___
- buy and carry goods from market
  ___
- be in touch with innovations/modern trends
  ___
- be nearer (in time) to hospital and other services
  ___
- sell produce to passers-by
  ___
- increase income and improve land
  ___
- be more in touch with agricultural experts/advice
  ___
- travel more easily to festivals and sports events.

possible alternatives
?
___
- use local labour to improve present road
  ___
- improve village transport — better axles, springing, tyres
  ___
- pay local experts to help with above
  ___
- point out to government how much could be saved, therefore ask for aid for other projects, e.g. water supply etc.

- will take village land
- endanger people and livestock
- disturb peace, bring in unwanted strangers and smelly vehicles
- upset traditional ways
- encourage government interference
- may increase taxes: who pays for construction, skilled labour, machinery, fuel etc?
  ___
- may stimulate demand for machinery and fuel (and debt?)
- encourage youngsters to focus attention on town life (and ways)

OR

SUPPORT
younger people's opinions
?

OPPOSE
older people's opinions
?

population

52% <u>under 20</u> years old: 18% <u>over 40</u> years old

7.31 Villagers in an LDC country might see advantages (+) and disadvantages (−) in a proposed new road. People with different interests are likely to have different ideas – whether to accept it, protest against it, or suggest alternatives.

Apart from the fieldwork, useful information about transport networks may be obtained from railway, bus, and airline **timetables**. These can be used for topological comparisons (Fig. 7.38), and for comparing times taken by different forms of transport, and competition between them. These vary in countries of different size and at different levels of development.

Improving communications – viewpoints in an LDC

It is easy to imagine that improving connectivity will benefit all concerned. Planners may have good reasons; but local people in an LDC may think otherwise.

Fig. 7.31 gives some idea of the reactions of villagers to a proposed new road. Weigh up the arguments for and against. Consider what you as a villager would feel about it. Would the alternatives be acceptable? Intermediate technology has been a great help to rural communities in Asia and Africa (p. 113).

It is worth considering how other innovations – new systems of land-use, a large local dam, communal farming, and so on – would be viewed by those concerned, and drawing up a 'balance sheet' as in Fig. 7.31. This is best done by acquiring a background knowledge of particular people and their local circumstances.

Theme 7 Making sure

1 Which form of transport is best suited to the materials **A-E**: aircraft; ocean bulk carrier; container vehicles; ocean tanker; road truck?
A-exported metal ore; **B**-gravel; **C**-packaged goods; **D**-crude oil; **E**-intercontinental mail.

2 Explain why distance can be thought of as physical distance and also in terms of cost and time.

3 Railways are most competitive when small/bulky freight items of high/low value are moved occcasionally/regularly over distances of 5km/50km/250km. Which? Say why.

4 Suggest why in Britain railway freight traffic has declined more than passenger traffic in the last thirty years.

5 A 'freightliner' long-haul train carries containerised manufactured goods at high speed on regular services between cities and container ports. Why is their journey usually overnight? What form of transport will be needed at their destination?

6 Turn to Photo 7.9
(a) Why is Heathrow some 25km away from central London?
(b) In which direction does the main runway shown here run? Suggest why.
(c) How may Heathrow have affected the choice of location of the growing high-tech industries along the M4?
(d) Closeness to the airport is an advantage for many, but a disadvantage for others. Point to some groups of people who may have problems created by Heathrow.

7 (a) Compare the ß-index of the route networks on the islands I and II in Fig. 7.32.
(b) In II which place is the most accessible, which the least? Give your reasons.

8 Why are transport networks compared when considering the extent of development of various countries? Why should one state the exact nature of the routeways linking settlements?

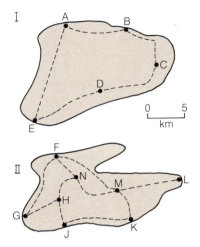

7.32 Roads linking island settlements.

9 Fig. 7.33 shows settlement on the Canadian prairie at the turn of the century.
(a) Explain the pattern of the railways in **A** and the roads in **B**.

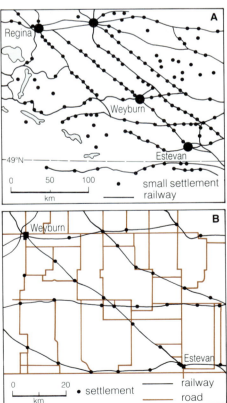

7.33 The Canadian prairies in 1900.
(**A**) railways and small settlements;
(**B**) part of the road network.

(b) How do the small settlements relate to the rail network?
(c) Divide **A** into quarters. Calculate the route density in each quarter.
Give reasons for the low density in the south-western quarter.

10 Canadian wheat reaches Europe not only through the east coast ports, but also via Vancouver and the Panama Canal.
(a) What does this reveal about relative costs of transport by rail and sea?
(b) Describe the stages of transfer and storage on the way.
(c) Why is Vancouver an all-year-round port, whereas Montreal's is closed from November to March?

11 Fig. 7.34 shows three stages in the development of the East African railways.
(a) what was the purpose of the first stage?
(b) How does stage two suggest development in the Kenya highlands and northern Tanganyika (Tanzania)?

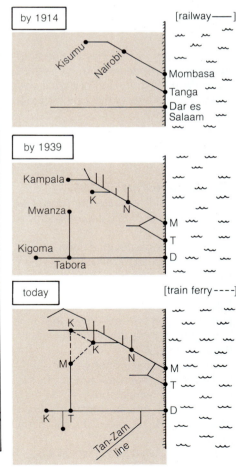

7.34 A developing railway system in east Africa.

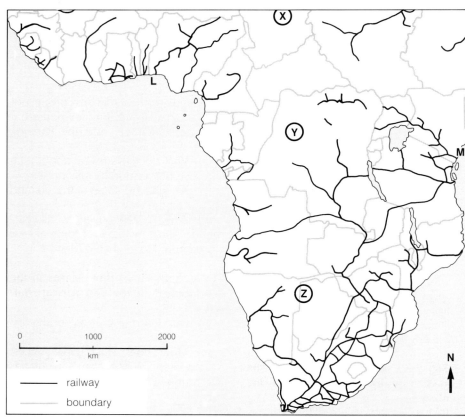

7.35 Railway systems in Africa south of the Sahara.

(c) Explain what has helped to increase the connectivity of the system since World War II. Find out what you can of the building of the Tan-Zam railway.

(d) Draw a map to show how the East African railways have become part of a wider system.

12 Look carefully at Fig. 7.35.

(a) Why did separate transport systems develop in Africa, each based on a large port?

(b) Most long-distance links to the interior have been by railway rather than road. Suggest why.

(c) Which of the countries shown in Fig. 7.35 has the densest and most integrated railways system? Why is this?

(d) Why is there a lack of railways in the areas **X, Y, Z**?

(e) How many countries are landlocked? Have they railway links to the coast? If so, to which ports?

(f) A trans-African highway, from Mombasa (**M**) to Lagos (**L**) has been proposed.

(i) Roughly what length would it be?
(ii) Which countries might it pass through?

(iii) What main *physical* difficulties would there be?

(iv) What other hindrances might affect it?

(v) Would it necessarily carry much traffic throughout its length?

(vi) Where might most of the traffic be?

13 (a) Table 15 shows great differences in the transportation of passengers by rail in a year. Is this just because of the size of the population? Does the density of population have anything to do with it, or the density of routes? In some countries people are scattered over a wide area, in others clustered. What effects will these things have on passenger transport?

(b) **In Fig. 7.36 the mean density of population (δ) is plotted against (e), a figure obtained by dividing col 1 by col 5 which roughly indicates the extent to which the population uses the railway.** On the scatter graph a best-fit line shows the general relationship.

(i) What does this suggest about countries like the UK and Netherlands?

(ii) Calculate (δ) and (e) for the USA; enter its position on the graph. What does this indicate about passenger use of its railways? Suggest reasons for this (see col. 3 of Table 15 and Fig. 7.38).

(c) Why is the density figure misleading when it comes to actual population distribution and location of railways? Consider China, for instance.

(d) Ought not the stage of development of the countries (p. 169) and their economic prosperity to be considered? Why?

(e) Suggest reasons for the low passenger and freight figures for Mali.

(f) How do the statistics in columns 2 and 3 indicate the stage of development of the country concerned?

(g) Suggest why China's rail freight figure is so much greater than the commercial motor vehicle figure.

(h) What other factors – physical, climatic, social – may influence these statistics?

14 A firm wishes to build a new factory in the UK. It has **distribution centres (D)** at Glasgow, Bristol, and Leeds, and a **head office (H)** in London. You have a map of main road routes (Fig. 7.37).

(a) Where would you recommend

Table 15

country (1985)	1 rail passenger (person-km) (m)	2 rail freight (tonne-km) (m)	3 motor vehicles ('000) passenger	commercial	4 area ('000 km²)	5 population (m)
Mali (M)	173	241	15	10	1240	8
Colombia (C)	193	726	723	368	1139	29
Thailand (T)	9122	2718	687	395	514	51
China (C)	241 600	812 600	790	2200	9597	1060
India (I)	240 810	196 488	1351	1450	3288	770
Netherlands (N)	9266	3269	4772	353	41	14
USA	17 649	1 377 264	13 148	39 583	9363	238
UK	30 084	12 720	17 272	2424	245	56

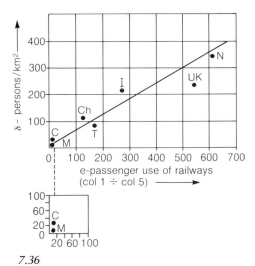

7.36

(c) How might the time of year affect your choice of transport?

(d) Apart from the time differences, what other reasons are there for passengers to choose one or other of these forms of transport?

(e) Why does a *choice* of this kind apply to people in the USA rather than those in the other countries mentioned in Question 13?

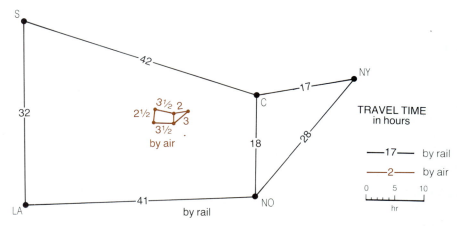

7.38 Distances and travelling times by train and plane.

the factory to be built, for reasons of transport and communications? Give your reasons.

(b) Why is a head office in London an advantage for many firms?

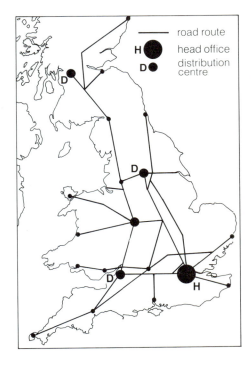

7.37

15 Fig. 7.38 compares distances travelled and times spent on the train and in the plane between cities in the USA.

(a) Look at an atlas and account for the considerable differences in the length of rail/air journeys in each case. (Consider rail service as well as physical conditions.) Which shows the least difference? Why?

(b) What else would affect the journey-time between offices in two of these cities?

16 How do Table 14 and Fig. 7.38 help to explain why long-distance passenger transport in the USA has declined, whereas in Britain it can stand competition more successfully — even though line closures and government subsidies have been necessary?

17 Felixstowe, the large general cargo port, can handle threequarters of a million containers a year. Two-thirds of Britain's general cargo is shipped by containers. Felixstowe opened a container terminal in 1967, and now has three container and two freightliner terminals with ro-ro facilities.

(a) What advantages has Felixstowe in relation to trade with Europe?

(b) Why is Rotterdam's role as an entrepôt important to Felixstowe?

(c) Why was priority given to building dual-carriageway links from Felixstowe to the M1, M11, A1, and M6? Make a simple map to show these roads, and the major centres linked to Felixstowe.

(d) Liverpool is a large port, but its trade has declined. Compare its situation relative to Europe and to the UK's main centres of populations with that of Felixstowe.

Consider the terms used

A node is a point in a network where lines (edges) meet. **Nodality** is the degree to which lines (routes) concentrate on a point.

Connectivity is the degree to which the nodes of a network are directly connected to each other. The *B*-index (nodes÷edges) measures this; the greater the connectivity, the higher its value.

Accessibility is the extent to which a place is 'get-at-able'. It varies with the routeways and the forms of transport available. A village served only by narrow lanes might be inaccessible to a 60-seater coach.

An isochrone (Greek, *chronos* – time) is a line joining places which can be reached in equal time from a given starting point.

A positive deviation is one which is chosen for a particular purpose (usually for an advantage). **A negative deviation** is forced on one by some particular constraint (a hill in the way).

To integrate is to bring parts together into a whole.

A commuter is a person who regularly travels a considerable distance to a place of work, usually daily (from an outer suburb to city centre, for example).

Hypermarket (Latin, **hyper** – beyond) describes a large shopping centre situated in the outer suburbs – usually to serve car-borne shoppers.

An entrepôt is a place to which goods are brought for redistribution to other places. Well-located ports (like Rotterdam and Hong Kong) perform this function, transferring goods between world shipping and smaller, shorter-haul vessels.

Hinterland describes the whole area which has close ties with a central place. For a port, it is the area inland over which it distributes, and from which it receives goods.

An odometer shows the distance travelled by a vehicle, by recording the revolutions of a wheel.

Topology is concerned with the position and relationships between points, lines and areas – but *not* with distance between points, the straightness of lines, or size of areas – as on the London Underground map.

Roll on/roll off (ro-ro) describes facilities for a heavy goods vehicle to be driven onto a ship and driven off again to continue its journey abroad (without its load being disturbed).

Theme 8

The commodity which so strongly affects national interests.

P 8.1 A North Sea oil platform. Off the Shetlands the oil comes from strata 4000m below the sea bed, itself some 150–200m beneath the platform.

Theme 8 Sources of energy

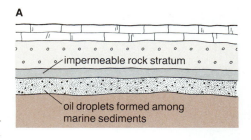

8.1 Renewable and non-renewable sources

Energy from the sun, via plants, via food and fodder, gives people and their draught animals the power to do work – in a limited way.

To increase our power to do work, we release energy by burning (combusting) the plant material which formed **coal** and the fatty parts of billions of tiny marine organisms which became **oil** and **natural gas. These are fossil fuels containing energy waiting to be used**, like the potential energy of water held at a high level, which we harness for **hydro-electric** power.

Now we have begun to harness processes which release energy within the sun itself – nuclear fusion and **nuclear fission**, using suitable elements from the earth's crust, such as uranium.

Coal, oil, gas and uranium are minerals which are **non-renewable** in the short term. In time even large reserves become exhausted. By contrast, hydro-electricity can continue to be generated as long as water flows through the turbines. There are other **renewable** sources, such as wind, waves, tides, and the direct use of solar energy – though as yet, these are minor sources on a world scale.

8.2. Releasing and distributing energy

Coal and refined forms of oil and gas are burnt directly to provide heat. Fossil fuels and nuclear energy provide heat to produce steam, to drive turbines which generate electricity. Oil and gas are also combusted in engines to drive machinery, and move forms of transport.

Electric energy is transmitted through cables, which can be linked to form a wide network, or **grid** (Fig. 8.5). Energy is supplied to the grid at places where it is considered best to operate a power station. How complex the grid, and where the stations are, depend on the demands for energy, and how it is generated. They also depend on national politics and public opinion; for each of the sources has advantages and disadvantages which can affect whole communities of people.

Energy from coal

1 Certain coals suit particular purposes – anthracite for heating spaces and steel-making; steam coals for generating electricity.

2 They come from specific locations – coalfields.

3 Coal is bulky, expensive to transport, and leaves waste material when combusted.

4 Comparative costs of land/sea transport are important. Low-cost water transport can favour the use of coal mined near a coast and delivery to near-coastal sites.

5 Power stations require assured supplies of fuel, as cheap as possible:
(a) Thick, unbroken coal seams suit mechanical working, and favour high productivity and lower production costs.
(b) Production costs are usually high in old, long-used coalfields, with small collieries and depleted reserves.
(c) Thick seams near the surface may be opencast mined. Coal is exported very competitively from those located near the coast (as from eastern Australia and eastern USA).

6 Large power stations near productive, long-life coalfields, with direct delivery from collieries by 'merry-go-round' trains, are particularly efficient.

7 Even low-energy fuel, like **lignite** (brown coal), which requires energy to compress it before use, may be better for *local* power stations than more distant steam coals (p. 150).

8 **Government actions may influence the fuel used, the sources of supply and the location and type of power station. Policies change from time to time.**
(a) The work-force of a large modern colliery may achieve the same rate of output as five times that number of smaller collieries. Yet whole mining communities may depend on high-cost pits – not just the miners themselves. So they may seek government subsidies to keep collieries open.

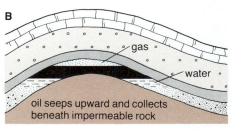

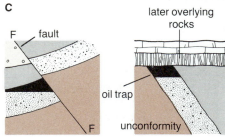

8.1 Oil deposits and overlying gases become concentrated and trapped beneath impermeable layers of rock, through folding, faulting, or later deposition.

(b) Coal and oil compete as energy sources. A government may restrict conversions of power stations from one source of energy to another. It may tax fuel oil, or subsidise stations using coal.
(c) Imports of cheap coal, or coal of particular quality, may be controlled.

9 Coal-burning pollutes the atmosphere. It varies with the type of coal, and is expensive to control. Sulphurous coals may add harmful acid to rainwater.

10 Thermal power stations require much water for cooling purposes.

Energy from oil and natural gas

1 Oil and gas are from precise locations, and often occur together (Fig. 8.1).

2 They are easier to store and move than coal – passing through pipelines, and carried by tankers between terminals in exporting and importing countries.

P 8.2 Tankers of 300 000 tonnes berth at these jetties at the Sullom Voe oil terminal in the Shetlands. This receives oil from two pipelines linked to a cluster of oilfields 150–250 km to the north-east.

Energy from nuclear sources

Fig 8.2 shows how the nucleus of an atom can break up (by fission) to release an immense amount of energy. Uranium, as mined, is mostly a stable form ^{238}U, whose nucleus has 238 particles (92 protons and 146 neutrons). But it contains 0.7 per cent ^{235}U, which is less stable. Before use in a power station, it is enriched to increase the proportion of ^{235}U.

When struck by a slow-moving neutron, the ^{235}U nucleus breaks up. This releases a huge amount of energy and also **two** neutrons. The latter go on to strike other ^{235}U nuclei, so creating a **chain reaction.** If uncontrolled, this releases a vast surge of energy, as in an atom bomb (**A**).

In generating stations this *is* controlled by using a material which slows the neutrons (for their next collision). Rods of other materials are used to absorb the excess neutrons. This keeps the chain reaction under control (**B**).

Fission products are bulkier than the original fuel. After a time they are transferred to be reprocessed. Unburnt fuel is recycled, and waste disposed of in various ways.

3 Costs of oilfield exploration and development, and building terminals and refineries, are high.

4 Fields must have large resources to be worth developing. Even so, their lifetime is limited, usually to tens of years.

5 The possession and exploitation of large oil and gas reserves has a great effect on a nation's economy, especially in less developed countries.

6 Countries relying heavily on oil exports are at risk when demand slackens, prices drop, or reserves fall, or when conflicts disrupt production.

7 Wealth from oil needs to be invested in projects which will benefit the country in the long run – including alternative sources of energy.

8 Importing countries suffer when oil prices are high; and also when the currency used to buy oil is strong on world markets, for their own purchasing power drops. But see p. 245.

9 Oil and gas create less atmospheric pollution than coal, but spillage of oil and oil products is a hazard.

10 Valuable chemical products are obtained from oil and gas.

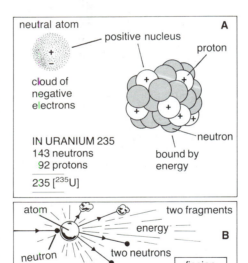

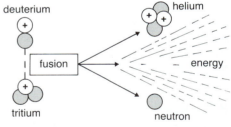

8.3 A large input of energy is needed to cause fusion, which releases much greater amounts of energy.

8.2 (right) Energy from the nucleus of an uranium atom (A) is released by bombardment (B), starting an immense uncontrollable release of energy from other nuclei (C). A substance must be introduced to absorb neutrons and control the rate of energy release (D).

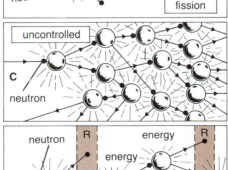

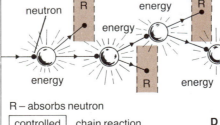

When the nuclei of light elements are made to combine (by fusion) large amounts of energy are released. The forms of hydrogen ^2H and ^3H are called 'deuterium' and 'tritium'. Fig. 8.3 shows what happens when they fuse together.

In sea-water one in 6500 hydrogen atoms is the heavy deuterium. The potential energy content of $1m^3$ of sea-water is that of 2000 barrels of oil; the reserves are unlimited!

The problem is to make two positive nuclei (which repel one another) combine. It can be done at very high temperature, creating a mass of positive nuclei and free electrons. As the temperature is some 40 million °K, no material can contain

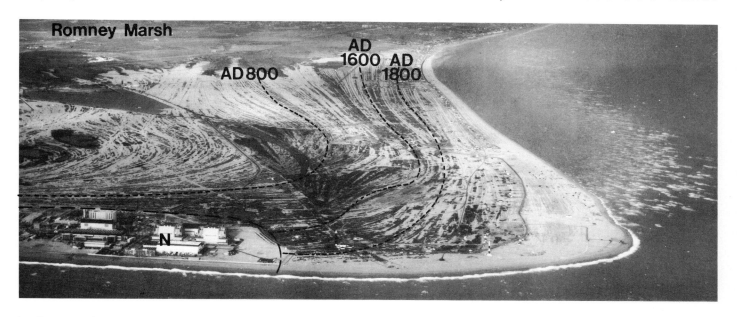

Romney Marsh

AD 800   AD 1600   AD 1800

N

it. But an electro-magnetic field can. Using fusion to harness almost limitless energy is an attractive prospect, but research is proving expensive, and its practical use is a long way off.

1 Uranium ores are precisely located, and non-renewable.

2 Precautions against radioactive leakage are expensive, and disasters have already occurred.

3 Radioactive waste must be disposed of safely. Reprocessing plants can greatly reduce the volume and produce plutonium – used in weapons.

4 Construction and closure are very costly.

5 Operating costs are low.

6 A large volume of water is needed for generating and cooling purposes.

7 After a boom in the 1970s, relatively few stations have been built.

P 8.3 Consider the advantages and disadvantages of siting the Dungeness A and B nuclear power stations (N) in this area of deposition, backed by Romney Marsh. Notice how the deposits advanced over a period of a thousand years, and the recent increases.

P 8.4 In Tasmania six huge pipes carry water from a lake storage to generators at Tarraleah power station. On the right are the transformers.

Hydro-electric energy

1 A continuous flow of water through turbines is provided by controlling the natural flow of a river by a dam or barrage; or by creating a water storage (lake) behind a dam in well-watered highland. A head of water and a reliable flow are the main things.

2 Continuous low-cost energy production, with low maintenance costs.

3 No pollution, except visually, by pylons and cables.

4 May be combined with control schemes, for water supply or flood protection.

5 Construction costs are high.

6 Storages may silt up.

7 There is a great loss of water from evaporation in hot, dry regions.

8 A storage may disrupt existing settlement.

9 A dam may disrupt fish migration and breeding upstream; but the lake may become a controlled fishery/nature reserve or be used for recreation.

Alternative energy sources

Wind-driven turbines are a cheap source with visual and noise drawbacks. The UK, with favourable weather conditions is increasing production at selected sites. California has large clusters of such turbines in 'wind farms'.

Solar energy can be concentrated by reflectors or absorbed by panels. The effectiveness varies with cloudiness and length of day. Large-scale production and length of day. Large-scale production is well developed in California and Utah. Small solar reflectors and panels provide heat for domestic use in many tropical developing countries.

Biogas is produced when farm and household wastes are rotted down in

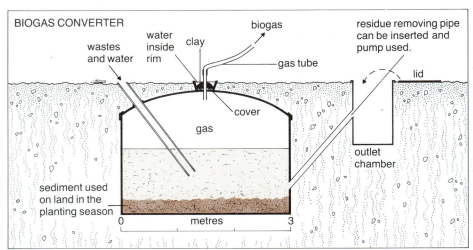

8.4 A locally made concrete structure (to a pattern), in which animal and plant refuse decomposes and releases gas. This can supply rural households and machines. Added chemicals allow the sludge to be removed and used safely as a fertiliser.

P 8.6 A grab works part of these lignite deposits in southern Victoria. Notice the thickness of overburden beyond the exposed coal.

special converters (Fig. 8.4). It can supply energy to rural households and small machines in the LDCs. Its use is widespread in China and parts of India.

Wave energy is little harnessed as yet, but **tidal energy** is developed in some estuaries which concentrate the flow. It generates electric energy as the water surges in, and as it drains out. In Europe, the Rance estuary in northern France is a locally important source. In the UK plans have been considered for a Severn Tidal Barrage. But such projects are very costly, and other energy sources are available.

Geothermal energy from heat beneath the earth's surface drives steam turbines in several volcanically active areas as in P 8.5, and on a large-scale in northern California. Deeper sources of heat are being considered elsewhere.

In every case there is the problem of locating the generating plant so as to serve domestic and/or industrial needs. Look at each of these minor sources and consider how difficult it might be to do that.

8.3 The location of power stations

Thermal stations

1 The cost of transmitting electricity through power cables is high. So there is an incentive to locate generating stations near large energy markets – big cities and large industrial complexes (Fig. 8.5).

2 Again, high transport costs mean that most coal-burning stations are on or near a coalfield; or where water transport can deliver coal cheaply.

3 With an electric 'supergrid', as in Britain, large stations on economically productive coalfields are more efficient than many smaller stations (p. 147).

4 Oil-fired stations can operate where demand is high and transport costs would make coal expensive. Some near major oil refineries, such as Milford Haven in South Wales, have a large market close by.

5 A source of cooling-water influences the precise location of thermal stations.

6 Preservation of the landscape, and pressure by conservationists, can influence the development of coalfields and oil-fields. They also affect the location of power stations (Fig. 8.5).

P 8.5 In New Zealand's North Island the central plateau is volcanic. Heat from the rocks (geothermal energy) creates steam to drive turbines at Wairekei power station.

P 8.7 The great Yallourn power station in Gippsland, sited close to vast accumulations of brown coal (lignite).

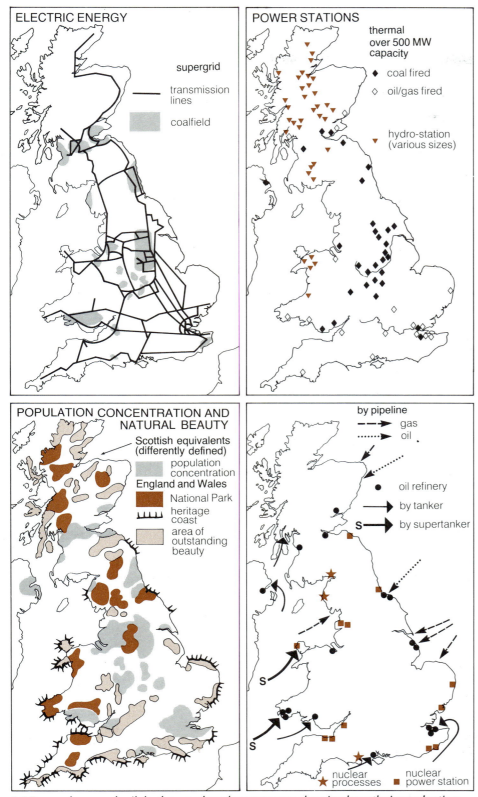

8.5 *Energy from coal, oil, hydro-, and nuclear sources; showing how their production and distribution relate to concentrations of population and areas of natural beauty.*

Comment on the following statements, using information from the maps in Fig. 8.5.

(a) It is cheaper to supply electricity to large markets (centres of population/industrial concentrations) via the grid, rather than send fuel from the coalfields to generate electricity there.

(b) The large coalfields are still densely populated, and coal-burning stations are still important there.

(c) There are oil-powered stations which can obtain fuel from refineries located close to where electricity demand is high.

(d) Oil refineries are mostly located near terminals where large tankers can berth, or are linked to these by pipeline (see Fig. 7.18).

(e) Britain's gas supplies pass through a small number of shore-line terminals (see Fig. 7.18).

(f) Most nuclear power stations are coastal, but relatively near the areas of greatest demand.

(g) Most nuclear power stations are in southern Britain because of demand/because other energy sources are less available there/because other sources there may run out.

(h) Hydro-electricity supplies less than 4 per cent of Britain's energy because stations are restricted to the wetter, more mountainous parts/because they are far from areas of greatest demand.

(i) The river Trent is a useful source of water for thermal power stations.

(j) The high density areas of the super-grid are in areas of highest consumption.

Nuclear stations

1 These tend to be on the edge of areas with a great demand for energy. They must be clear of concentrations of population (public concern about safety), but are attracted by the market.

2 Coastal locations and estuaries ensure the large supplies of water required.

3 A large site excluding the public is needed, in case atmospheric concentration of gaseous wastes occurs under inversion conditions (p. 71), as well as for accident safety reasons.

Coal, as a source of energy, combined with industrial raw materials has been a locating influence on industrial development. The great Shanxi coalfields of northern China have the same combination of textile and metal industries as Britain's northern coalfields during the 19th century. Heavy industries supplied by thermal power stations cluster on China's north-eastern coalfields and oilfields.

4 Some regions, as in Italy and California, USA, are likely to experience seismic activity (earth movements) which increase the risk of accidents.

5 Disposing of nuclear wastes is a problem. A few plants like Thorp in Cumbria process imported wastes. Burial where rocks prevent sideways and downward movements is a feasible alternative. Deep-sea dumping is another, most controversial method.

Hydro-electric stations

1 Certain regions are eminently suitable for generating energy from falling water: glacial lakes amid highlands, and large, permanent rivers in deep-cut valleys which are readily dammed. But these are often in wildscapes, far from dense populations or industries with a high demand for energy.

2 Long-distance high-voltage transport is expensive.

3 Production at a multi-purpose dam is advantageous (p. 180).

4 Not all HE stations are large. In wet, hilly parts of south-east China, thousands of small water-powered generators provide electricity for rural peoples.

5 HE stations near deep coastal water may attract industries with bulky raw materials and particular need for electric energy, as with aluminium production in British Columbia and northern Tasmania.

8.4 Demands on the grid

Energy demands vary at different times of day, from season to season, and on special occasions (Fig. 8.6). Demands for industry and domestic purposes are low at night but increase as people get up, switch on lights, cookers, heaters, and reach their places of work. However, large factories may operate 24 hours a day on a shift basis.

The seasonal changes in daylight hours are predictable; the occurrence of very cold weather, with increasing energy demands, less so. Breakdown at some stations means adjusting output from others.

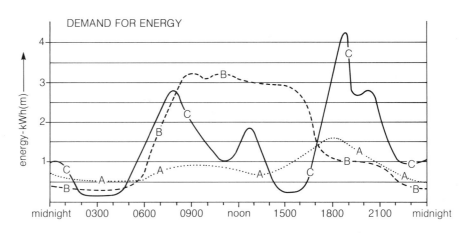

8.6 Energy demands by households, factories, and offices vary from hour to hour throughout the day and night.

The sudden demand for energy as Auckland city viewers switched on to the televised *Scotland v All Blacks* rugby match from Murrayfield (U.K.) in 1972, resulted in a temporary blackout. What time was it in Auckland at the start? Would the *normal* demand at that time be – average/high/low?

Fig. 8.6 shows a typical electricity demand during a winter's day in Britain's industrial Midlands, from domestic, industrial and commercial consumers.

(a) Which plot (**A, B** or **C**) represents domestic, industrial, commercial demands?

(b) Explain in each case how and why the demand changes during the day and the reason for 'peak' periods.

(c) Draw graphs to show how the demands by **A, B** and **C** might occur on a summer day.

What can be done to encourage domestic users to even out their demands during the 24 hours?

In some places hydro-electric generation can be adjusted to cope with peak demands by means of pumped-storage, as at Ffestiniog in north Wales. Electricity is used during off-peak periods to pump water to a higher reservoir. It is released to generate extra electricity during hours of peak demand.

Much energy is wasted at power stations. It is lost to the atmosphere, and in the hot water discharged. But this water is too cool for long-distance supply. So many power stations in Scandinavia and other European countries are adapted to pipe it, together with other, hotter, water, for domestic uses.

8.5 Energy demands – by the developed and less developed countries

The consumption of energy in industrially developed countries is huge compared with the less developed ones (Fig. 8.7). Many of the LDCs have sources they *could* develop. But they lack capital to invest in such projects. The low demand, and the shortage of skilled, educated technicians are all part of the cycle of poverty (p. 170).

Large development projects in LDCs are usually financed from abroad, by foreign companies or international organisations. But this does not necessarily break the overall cycle of poverty.

In Zambia, building the Kariba dam provided electricity for the Copper Belt, which relied until then on coal from Rhodesia (Zimbabwe). It supplies the mines, refineries, and towns on a strip of some 120×50 km on the northern border. But it has done little directly to benefit the rural areas from which most of the labour comes.

Wages in the copper belt and taxes on minerals exported *are* assets. But there has been little effect on rural underdevelopment.

Yet development projects can improve general living standards in the LDCs. The large Gezhou dam on China's Chang jiang (Yangtse river) combines energy generation with flood control and water-supply systems. Further upriver huge investment in the Sanxia dam (Three Gorges project) will bring economic development to central China, where living standards are already rising rapidly.

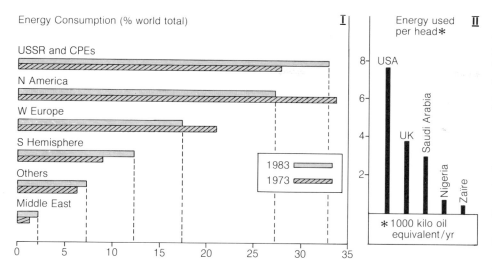

8.7 I Compare the energy consumed in various parts of the world in 1973 and 1983. II Striking differences in the energy consumed per head of population in 1983 by MDC and LDC countries. (CPE – Centrally Planned Economy).

The proportion of energy consumed (Fig. 8.7), **and of oil in particular, shows a downward trend among the MDCs and an upward one in the LDCs.**

Table 16

oil (% of world consumption)				
Year	1973	1978	1983	1988
MDCs	87	84	80	78
LDCs	13	16	20	22

Some LDCs, notably the oil-rich states of the Middle East, are high energy consumers. Their economy depends almost entirely on non-renewable petroleum. Time will show how their investments at home and abroad, and plans for alternative energy sources, will affect their future development. Meanwhile they tend to raise the oil consumption figures for LDCs, with which they are classed.

Even so, as the populations of the LDCs are rapidly increasing, and more and more people are living in towns, there is a general rise in energy consumption.

Look at the location of Iran, Iraq, Kuwait, Qatar, Saudi Arabia, the United Arab Emirates, Algeria, Libya, Nigeria, Gabon, Ecuador, Venezuela, China and Indonesia. They are members of a group of oil-producing LDCs, known as OPEC (Organisation of Petroleum Exporting Countries).

There are great differences among these oil-producers in their location,

climate, population, and stage of economic development. Choose three contrasting countries in this group, and point out the ways in which they differ.

The effects of changing oil prices

In 1973 and 1978–79 OPEC sharply increased oil prices. There was a ten-fold increase in under ten years. The economies of MDCs and LDCs alike were affected, though in different ways. Many of the industrialised countries, the world's

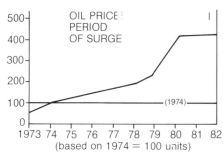

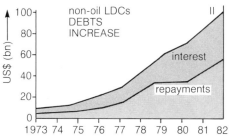

8.8 I Shows what happened to world oil prices between 1973 and 1982.
II The effects on oil-importing LDCs .

largest consumers, began to cut back demand – by greater efficiency in power stations, factories, home heating, domestic appliances, and so on. By contrast, consumption increased in the centrally-planned economy countries (CPEs), for the USSR supplied their oil and gas at below world market prices.

Oil supplies are vital to MDCs and LDCs alike. Japan imports virtually all its oil. Being industrially developed, it wants assured supplies even more than low prices. **All but a few LDCs use oil as a main energy source.** So they are particularly hard hit by price increases of this kind, which they cannot afford.

The fates of the MDCs and LDCs are closely linked. When MDCs feel the pinch, their demand for produce from the LDCs falls. They are also less likely to lend the LDCs funds for development, or to do so at low interest rates.

Fig. 8.8 shows the effects on non-oil LDCs of increased oil prices and high interest rates together. As a result the prospect for development became bleak. Many have to find money for interest charges rather than for projects to help their economies. They need oil for agricultural programmes – for mechanisation or fertiliser factories – so that energy crises may deepen their food problems.

The sudden fall in oil prices in 1986 brought some relief for the oil-importing LDCs. But oil-exporting LDCs like Mexico, Venezuela and Nigeria were hard hit. Mexico, which has huge interest payments to meet (on loans for its development), found these an even greater burden.

8.6 Energy resources and the future

Energy consumption will continue to rise as world population increases and as demands from the LDCs grow with development.

High oil prices slow the drain on reserves to some extent, as the main industrial countries conserve energy and turn to renewable sources as far as possible. Fig. 8.9 forecasts the use of energy sources by the IEA countries. These high-consuming European countries, together with Canada, Australia, USA and Japan, cooperate with members of OPEC over energy matters.

The relative shares of world oil production are shown in Fig. 8.10. Remember that **oilfields have a relatively short life.**

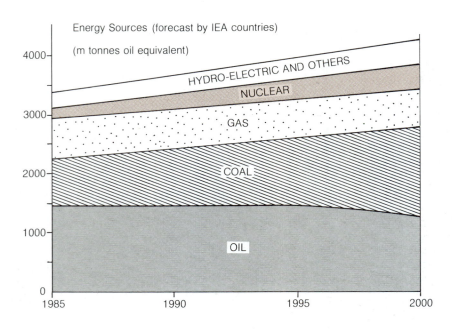

8.9 Notice which sources are expected to have a larger or smaller proportion of the world's energy consumption in the next quarter of a century.

The reserves of the OPEC countries should last about 80 years at present levels of consumption. Many of the non-OPEC sources will have a much shorter life.

Look again at Fig. 8.9. Which was the major energy source in 1985? Which sources are likely to have a greater share in the future?

Also bear in mind that energy problems for thousands of millions of people in developing countries are concerned with day-to-day subsistence. **Firewood is a vital energy source for cooking.** For the large numbers who live in the savannas and lands cleared of monsoon woodland **there is always a shortage of wood for burning. So the use of dried animal dung for fuel continues, and much-needed fertiliser is lost.**

The daily search for firewood takes up time and energy. The circumstances described above put oil for burning beyond the means of millions of people.

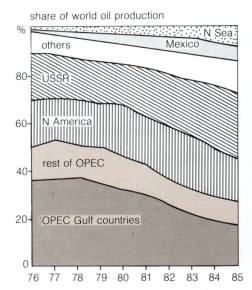

8.10 (right) Notice the relative contribution of each of these sources in 1976 and 1985 and which increased their share of oil production over this period

OIL SUPPLY ROUTES

→ primary
→ secondary
• oilfield

8.11 Movements of oil from the main oil producing areas.

Theme 8
Back-up section

The world's energy scene has changed so rapidly and faces such an uncertain future that it is worth taking a closer look at how industrially developed countries respond.

The changes in Western Europe

1 The main manufacturing countries in Western Europe developed industrially with the help of their own cheap coal. Even Sweden and Switzerland (which didn't) referred to their hydro-electricity as 'white coal'.

As late as 1962 they were using more coal than oil – except for Italy and the Netherlands (Europe's main centre for oil imports).

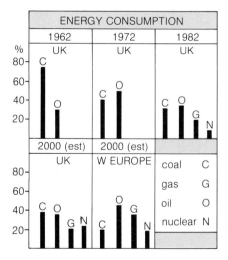

8.12 The extent to which various sources have supplied UK energy demands since 1962, with forecasts for 2000 AD (and for Western Europe as a whole).

2 By 1972 imported oil had become the main energy source (Fig. 8.12), except in the Netherlands, where it was second to gas (from its own great reserves).

3 Almost all their oil was supplied by a few oil-exporting countries (Fig. 8.11), whose resources were prospected and developed by international oil companies. Subsidiaries of these companies refined, distributed, and marketed the oil products.

4 About 60 per cent of all Western Euro-

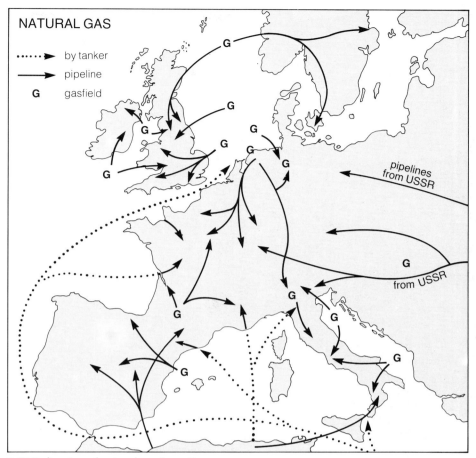

8.13 Deliveries of natural gas from Euro-Asia and north African fields in 1985.

pean energy was coming from foreign oil, from foreign suppliers.

5 As in the UK, coal production declined. The Netherlands and Italy ceased production. Almost all West Germany's deep-mined coal now comes from only 25 mines.

6 Then in 1973 and in 1978 came the huge OPEC increases in oil prices. In response Western European countries began to:

(a) cut down waste and take conservation measures

(b) restrict demand – discouraging big schemes which use too much energy

(c) look for alternative supplies, if possible in their own country – nuclear energy, natural gas (Fig. 8.13), coal for oils and chemicals. (This boosted research into new power sources.) Many nuclear power stations were constructed, others projected (Fig. 8.14).

7 The down-turn in oil prices in the mid-1980s affected national economies, but has not reversed these long-term plans.

A closer look at energy in the UK

Coal declined as the main energy source for a number of reasons:

1 Gas for heating ceased to come from coal used in gasworks.

2 Railway engines turned from coal to diesel.

3 The steel and electrical industries came to use coal more efficiently.

4 Competition from alternative fuels – and in recent years from cheap coal exported from South Africa and Australia.

5 In 1964 natural gas from Algeria was imported into Thames-side gas terminals. In 1967 the first North Sea gas came ashore. **By 1975 95 per cent of UK gas was from the North Sea.**

6 **In 1975 deliveries of North Sea oil began**, and soon oil supplied the major proportion of the UK's needs, **with surplus for export.**

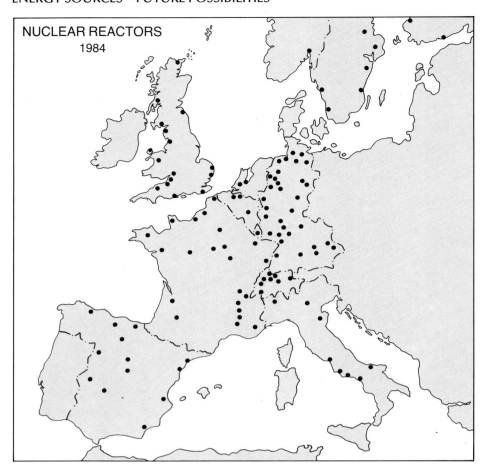

NUCLEAR REACTORS
1984

8.14 Sites of nuclear energy production or the processing of nuclear wastes.

7 **As prices rose, oil became a greater source of national income.**

All this led to **a move of coal-mining away from the high-cost mines.** It began to be concentrated in a few large, productive ones, with considerable social consequences.

Future plans must accept that the life of oil reserves is limited. There are a number of possibilities.

(a) In 1990 nuclear power stations produced about 18 per cent of the country's energy. The capacity is being increased over the next few years. There is, however, great public concern over safety, especially after USSR's Chernobyl disaster in 1986.

(b) The huge gas fields in the North Sea, and elsewhere in Europe and North Africa, are being used more extensively in manufacturing industries.

(c) It is possible to process coal as a substitute for crude oil and natural gas – South Africa, in particular, distils much oil from coal.

(d) Fossil fuels should last at least until the mid-21st century. By that time new technology may be releasing energy from other sources. This cannot be taken for granted – so research and development must be funded.

Theme 8   Making sure

1 What exactly is meant by: a **fossil** fuel; a **thermal** power station; a **nuclear** power station?

2 Why do we consider coal a **primary** source of energy and electricity from the grid a **secondary** one? Name other primary sources.

3 What are the main considerations in choosing a site for (a) a nuclear power station; (b) a large coal-fired power station? Consider advantages and disadvantages.

4 Any system that converts a primary energy source into a secondary one involves a loss of energy, which lowers its efficiency. What losses are involved (a) at a thermal power station; (b) in transmitting electricity to the consumer; (c) in using electricity to (i) cook a meal; (ii) heat a home?

5 (a) Which energy sources may be looked on as **renewable?** (b) Which of these is most developed at present? (c) Which show considerable possibilities for the future? (d) In what ways are these sources limited by natural conditions?

6 In Brazil sugar cane is converted to alcohol for use as a combustible fuel. There are plans for farming plant life from the ocean for similar purposes. 'The short energy chain is an advantage in each case.' What is meant by this? Would these projects do more than solve local shortages?

7 Draw up an energy chain to show the stages by which solar energy is transferred to the biogas used to cook a meal for an Indian family.

8 Fig. 8.15 shows the water used in a power station. Why is the volume of fresh water needed to produce steam for energy generation less than that of water used for other purposes? How do the two supplies relate to one another? What does this indicate about the efficiency of a power station?

9 It is relatively cheap to transport coal by water. Why in Britain is less coal transported by water than by other means?

10 What factors may cause the output of coal per man-shift to vary from one coalfield to another?

11 Compare the energy requirements during the year of householders in Stockholm (lat. 59°N) with those in Brisbane (lat. 27°S).

12 A large drainage basin helps to give the regular flow needed by hydro-electric stations on the main river. Egypt's Aswan dam on the Nile generates electricity in a desert area.

(a) Draw a map to show the extent of the drainage basin which maintains the flow. Look at your atlas and draw the main tributaries to the lower Nile.

(b) Find out why the Blue Nile and White Nile contribute their maximum amounts at different times.

13 Oil and gas are transferred vast distances from their source to countries which are large energy consumers but lack such resources. Give two examples of such movements of (a) oil, (b) natural gas. Explain exactly how each is transferred from source to customer.

14 Explain why super-tankers are used to reduce shipping costs, and why this helps to lower the delivered price of oil. What disadvantages are there in using such large vessels?

15 In 1988 the energy consumed per head (in the equivalent of kg of coal) in various countries was:

A USA 9517; Japan 3741; Australia 6848;

B India 282; Kenya 102; Uganda 24;

C Kuwait 9191; Venezuela 3018; Mexico 1697.

Consider the energy consumed for different purposes: by manufacturing industries; by refineries; during daily domestic life; for leisure activities; by vehicles; for heating/cooling buildings; and so on.

(a) Suggest what the countries in each of the groups have in common, and which of these many factors affect their energy consumption in each case.

(b) In the countries in Group **C** there are contrasting levels of energy use by different consumers – one high, one low. Find out why this is so in each case.

16 Suggest reasons for the different proportions of energy generated by Thermal (**T**), Hydro (**H**), Nuclear (**N**), and Geothermal (**G**) sources in each of the countries in Table 17:

Table 17

source of electric energy (%)

country 1990	T	H	N	G
Canada	20	65	15	–
France	10	20	70	–
Italy	76	22	*	2
New Zealand	25	73	–	4
Norway	0.5	99.5	–	–
Saudi Arabia	100	–	–	–
Sweden	5	50	45	*
Switzerland	2	61	37	–
U.K.	80	2	18	–

* very small

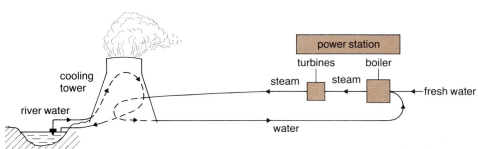

8.15 The supply and recycling of water at a thermal power station.

P 8.8 Trawsfynydd nuclear power station in north Wales.

17 Photo 8.6 shows how the world's largest accumulation of brown coal is mined. Several huge, local power stations (Photo 8.7) burn the crumbly brown coal, and feed transmission cables with about half the electricity used in the state of Victoria.

(a) What method is being used to mine the coal? (b) High voltage transmission is expensive. Why not send the coal 100 km to the main market for electricity, Melbourne? (c) Compression and heating reduces the moisture in brown coal from 66% to 15% and forms briquettes. Its heating value is more than trebled, and it is now used state-wide – why?

18 People look on energy production and supply from different viewpoints. Most want a non-polluting source, easy to handle. Some want supplies which enable them to manufacture competitively, run transport cheaply or provide regular employment. Some see particular sources as polluting the environment or producing dangerous waste. Some see a useful source of national income an asset not to be wasted. Others see energy imports as a waste of foreign currency, or likely to lead to dependence on a foreign power.

What would *you* hope for regarding energy supplies, and what might *you* fear, if you were: (a) a conservationist; (b) running a transport firm; (c) a domestic consumer; (d) controlling a manufacturing industry; (e) an environmentalist; (f) developing industries in a country with few worthwhile energy sources; (g) planning national supplies for the next 50 years?

19 The nuclear station beside Lake Trawsfynydd (photo 8.8) stands amid the beautiful North Wales countryside, inland of Harlech. Like other Magnox reactors it has been shut down, but controversy rages over its future. It would be hugely expensive to demolish safely and clean the site. It could be cased in concrete and buried beneath a man-made hill, but would not be safe for 135 years.

Discuss the problems of siting nuclear power stations, and why this site was used.

Consider the terms used

Fossil fuel refers to a solid, liquid, gas or vapour formed naturally from ancient plant or animal remains which will combust (can be burnt as a fuel) – and so includes coal, lignite, peat, petroleum and natural gas.

Lignite, or **brown coal**, retains some of the woody texture of the original coal-forming plants.

Anthracite is a hard form of coal, with little bitumen. It burns with an intense heat, but almost smokelessly.

Thermal energy, and **thermal power**, describe that obtained by burning fossil fuels – usually by making steam which drives electric generators.

Opencast mining uses machinery on a large scale to extract minerals deposited close beneath the surface, by removing the layers above (the **overburden**).

Fission is the act of splitting into parts. Hence **nuclear fission** involves splitting the nucleus of a heavy atom into smaller particles, with the release of energy.

Fusion is the act of making things unite to form a whole. Hence **nuclear fusion** is the use of intense heat energy to make the nuclei of atoms combine and release even larger quantities of energy.

Nuclear reprocessing uses radioactive waste from nuclear power stations to turn it into a form which will also release electric energy under controlled conditions. The operation usually involves long-distance transport of wastes in specially constructed containers to specific re-processing plants.

On the absolute temperature scale (the Kelvin scale) – **°K**, the interval between the ice point (water freezing) and steam point (boiling), at normal atmospheric pressure, is 100° (as in the Centigrade scale). Absolute zero, 0°K, is −273°C; and so to convert °C to °K add 273°.

Theme 9 Industries

9.1 There are many forms of industry

1 **Primary industry** means getting raw materials direct from land, sea, or air – mining an ore, catching salmon, or felling a tree for timber.

Which of these resources can be called 'renewable'; 'non-renewable'; 'extractive'?

2 **Secondary industry** involves processing raw materials, or assembling parts, to manufacture a product. It can be a simple **home** or **cottage** industry, but is usually carried out by a firm in its plant, factory, or works.

Some manufacturing is described as 'heavy', some as 'light'. Which would you imagine describes: steel-making; ship-building; TV manufacture; biscuit making; brick making? (Which of these use bulky materials or heavy parts?)

P 9.1 Primary industry provides the logs floating in booms on Canada's Ottawa river. They are raw material for the factory (top left). Timber and paper manufacturing are secondary industries.

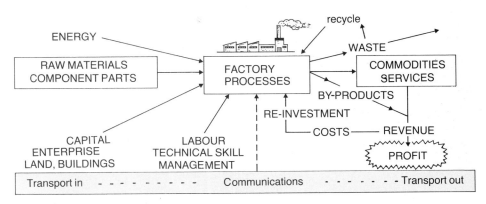

9.1 An industrial manufacturing system.

3 **Tertiary industry** provides services. Its labour force works in banks, schools, tea-shops, government offices, hospitals, theatres, and so on.

Which of these works in a tertiary industry: a window cleaner; a fisherman; a musician; a potter; a postman? Explain why.

Let us first look at industries in the MDCs, and in Britain especially; where, during the 19th century, mass manufacturing began to produce great wealth. Today many of the MDCs have old, heavily populated industrial regions, with factories and processes which have become outdated.

But unlike the LDCs, most of the MDCs readily find ways of acquiring capital to invest in more modern industries using new technologies, some more successfully and rapidly than others.

9.2 Systems, chains and links in manufacturing

A factory has first to be constructed in a suitable place on a suitable site. Among other things, this requires capital (money), land, labour, energy – and enterprise on someone's part. These are all **initial inputs.**

The factory can then operate as a system, as shown in Fig. 9.1. There is an **input** of purchased materials to the factory, whose various processes involve **manufacturing costs.** The **output** of finished, or semi-finished products is transported (at a cost), and when sold

brings in a **revenue.**

revenue – total costs = profit

Look back to the 'factory farm' (p.128) and suggest other costs which will be involved. How might the profit be used to benefit future production?

Manufacturing can be done by a **small firm** at a particular place, or by a **large corporation,** like a motor company, with many activities at various places all linked together. **One car plant may draw parts from tens of thousands of other factories, some from abroad.** There are also offices for development, research, marketing,

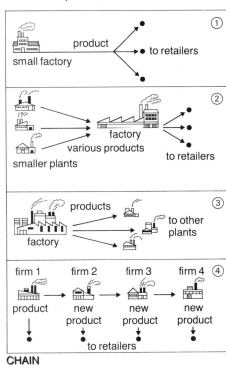

CHAIN

9.2 Factory links and where the products go.

P 9.2 A factory needs space for manufacturing (**F**), offices (**O**), car parking (**C**), materials (**M**), and loading (**L**). It needs ready access to markets via road transport (**R**) and rail trains (**T**), and, if possible, room for expansion (**E**).

and so on. These may be separate from the head administrative office, or the main factories.

> Why do you think the head office of a manufacturing plant is often in the centre of a large city – sometimes in another country?

Some factories are part of a chain which extends from the primary producer to the sale of the consumer product. There are successive stages of manufacture by different firms, each doing a particular task.

> Consider the links in the chain extending from sheep shearer to the carding, spinning, dyeing, weaving

processes which produce cloth, to the garment manufacturer, and the tertiary retailer in the shop. Explain what goes on at each stage.

Construct another set of links from lumberjack through manufacturing processes to the reader of an evening newspaper.

In each of these, different factories and different firms may be involved. They are often clustered, not far from each other, in the same region. What

advantage is this? But why has the development of (a) the electric grid; (b) motorways, made clustering less necessary?

The links between factories and with their markets (through retailers) are summarised in Fig. 9.2. Which of these (1–4) represents the manufacture of the following commodities: (a) motor vehicles; (b) raw silk, woven silk, silk dresses; (c) steel; (d) biscuits?

9.3 Manufacturing in a particular place

Fig 9.5 shows that many factors affect the location and siting of the factory, and whether or not it will operate efficiently at a particular place.

Bulk and weight

The nature of the inputs and outputs is of prime importance; not just their availability and costs but their actual weight and bulk. Some products are less bulky than the materials used: as in the conversion of iron ore, coal, limestone, and other ores into steel; or sugar beet into sugar. In other industries the weight and bulk are increased: as in a brewery, where a large quantity of water is added by manufacturing, and the cans and bottles make the product bulky to distribute.

The cost of transporting materials and products increases the price of the final commodity delivered to the customers or to other manufacturers. Here, too, bulk is a factor.

P 9.3 Tertiary employment in Granada TV Rental in Bedford.

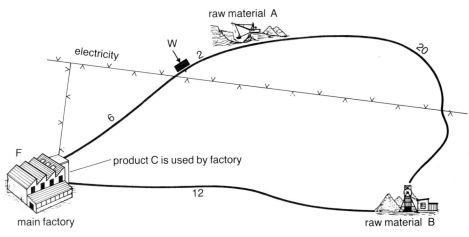

2 tonnes A + 1 tonne B → 1 tonne C

9.3 Where to manufacture **C**?

Location of materials and markets

In Fig. 9.3 it is intended to build a works to manufacture a commodity C, to supply to factory F. One raw material, A, is 8 km from F; the other B is 12 km from F and 20 km from A.

It takes 2 tonnes of A and 1 tonne of B to manufacture 1 tonne of C. The cost of transport of materials and product is the same – 12p per tonne/km.

> Where should the works be built to keep the costs of transport as low as possible? Four places are considered: at the main factory F; at mine A; at mine B; and at an available, well-drained site (W) near an electricity transmission line.
>
> The cost of transporting raw materials to the works and the product to the factory would be:

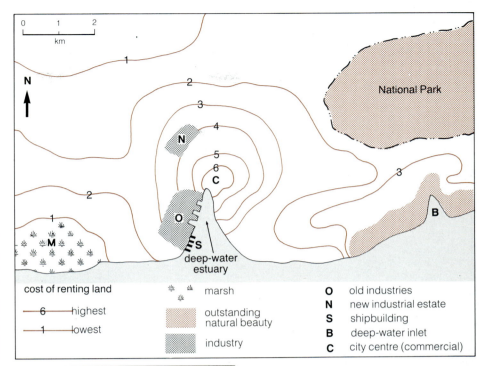

9.4 Some factors affecting land rent values.

cost of renting land

| —6— | highest |
| —1— | lowest |

marsh

outstanding natural beauty

industry

O	old industries
N	new industrial estate
S	shipbuilding
B	deep-water inlet
C	city centre (commercial)

Works at A		cost (p)
mineral from A		0
mineral from B	(1×20×12) =	240
product to F	(1×8×12) =	96
		336

Works at B		cost (p)
mineral from A	(2×20×12) =	480
mineral from B		0
product to F	(1×12×12) =	144
		624

Works at F	cost	(p)
mineral from A	(2×8×12) =	192
mineral from B	(1×12×12) =	144
product to F	=	0
		336

	Works at W	cost (p)
mineral from A		=
mineral from B		=
product to F		=

> Insert the calculations for the works if sited at W 2km from A.
>
> Which site is obviously unsuitable from the point of view of transport costs?
>
> Of the other sites, suggest how the choice might be made on grounds *other* than costs of transport.

In this example there is a single market, F. But, of course, **many firms distribute their products over a wide area**, in competition with other producers. So a site near a motorway, or near a port, may be considered. And remember that other considerations, such as cheap labour costs, may outweigh transport cost factors.

Investing in land, buildings, and machines

Large corporations can usually obtain funds, or credit from other enterprises they control; or they may issue shares on the stock market to raise capital.

They can invest in the whole infra-structure – the term which describes buildings, drainage, access roads, etc.

Small firms have to look for loans or local investors, and are much influenced by land values and costs of buildings and labour (which vary considerably between regions).

The space required varies with the industry. Some need large stores, waste dumps, and extensive car parks; others require only a few rooms.

The cost of renting land tends to increase towards city centres and decrease towards rural areas and waste land (p. 221). But **permission to develop industry in the countryside may be restricted** (and forbidden in National Parks). Even with government approval to develop waste land, the site may require expensive improvements.

Private developers, and government and local authorities lay out **industrial estates** on the outskirts of many towns. Sites are prepared and access roads provided for a cluster of various light industries. But, of course, **heavy industries require more specific locations;** and some, like shipbuilding, have a restricted choice.

Fig. 9.4 compares values of renting land about a large port and in the rural and coastal areas beyond. There are two main industrial concentrations in the city-port, though smaller industries are scattered through the urban area.

> (a) Suggest why there are few manufacturing industries within a kilometre or so to the north of the estuary.
>
> (b) Many industries developed about the docks and shipyards. What kind of firms might you still find there?
>
> (c) New firms might find advantages in renting old buildings in this area. Why would this be?
>
> (d) The new industrial estate has advantages of lowish rental values. What other advantages would there be? Consider, for instance, accessibility, traffic congestion, and employees.
>
> (e) A large manufacturing industry might consider a site at M. What cost advantages/disadvantages would there be? If its chimneys emitted

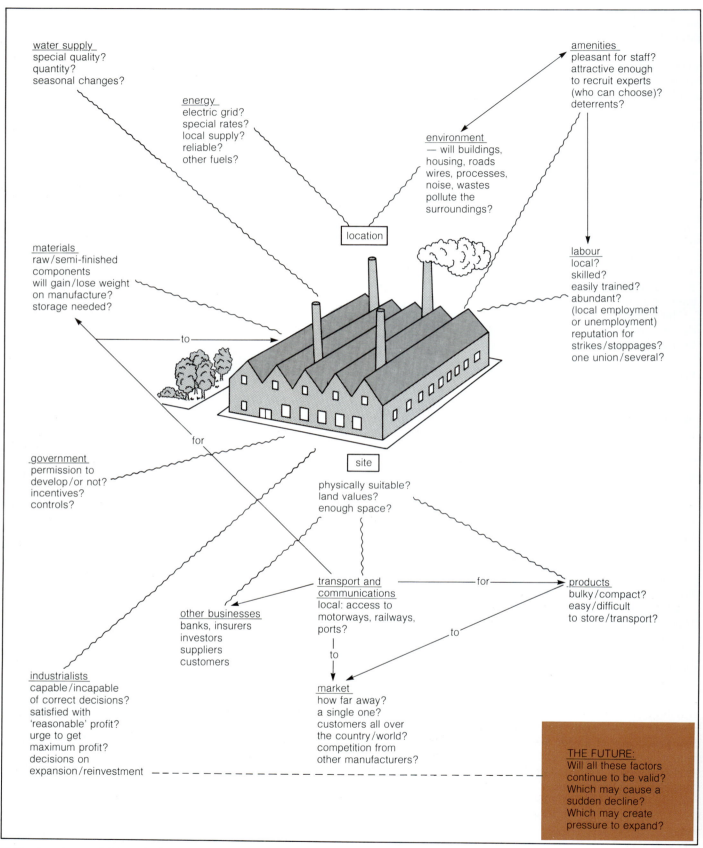

water supply
special quality?
quantity?
seasonal changes?

energy
electric grid?
special rates?
local supply?
reliable?
other fuels?

amenities
pleasant for staff?
attractive enough
to recruit experts
(who can choose)?
deterrents?

environment
— will buildings,
housing, roads
wires, processes,
noise, wastes
pollute the
surroundings?

location

materials
raw/semi-finished
components
will gain/lose weight
on manufacture?
storage needed?

labour
local?
skilled?
easily trained?
abundant?
(local employment
or unemployment)
reputation for
strikes/stoppages?
one union/several?

to

for

site

government
permission to
develop/or not?
incentives?
controls?

physically suitable?
land values?
enough space?

transport and
communications
local: access to
motorways, railways,
ports?

for

products
bulky/compact?
easy/difficult
to store/transport?

other businesses
banks, insurers
investors
suppliers
customers

to

to

industrialists
capable/incapable
of correct decisions?
satisfied with
'reasonable' profit?
urge to get
maximum profit?
decisions on
expansion/reinvestment

market
how far away?
a single one?
customers all over
the country/world?
competition from
other manufacturers?

THE FUTURE:
Will all these factors
continue to be valid?
Which may cause a
sudden decline?
Which may create
pressure to expand?

9.5 The location and siting of a factory. Look at each of the factors in turn. This will give
you some idea of the many different considerations involved in the location. Then look at
Fig. 9.7. As you see, decisions are often made because of personal views. Photo 12.14
shows what an interested corporation feels are the things which will persuade a firm to
re-locate in its particular area.

unpleasant fumes, what climatic considerations might affect the decision to allow it to develop there or not?

(f) Suggest why land values are relatively high inland of the inlet **B**.

(g) Permission is sought to build an oil-terminal at **B**. Who might consider it suitable/unsuitable, and on what grounds?

The work force

A firm needing many workers may find a large urban area better for recruiting people with different skills than a small town. The ease of recruiting depends partly on whether there is much general unemployment, and partly on the particular skills required and the numbers available. Sometimes skills are concentrated in a certain area.

In some industries a large proportion of the total costs are made up of labour costs – they are **labour-intensive** – as in dressmaking. In others the capital costs are particularly high, as in oil-refining. They are **capital-intensive**.

Suggest why most tertiary industries are labour-intensive. Give examples.

The introduction of machinery and automatic processes tends to reduce the need for employees, but may increase the demand for better educated employees.

Explain why this is so in tertiary, as well as secondary, industries. Consider clerical work and administration, and the introduction of computers and other capital items.

When manufacturing declines – industrial inertia

Sometimes new inventions and new production methods cause existing factories, or whole sections of an industry, to decline. Lancashire's cotton textile industries suffered in this way; partly because new foreign factories competed successfully, but also because synthetic textiles, using chemical raw materials, were produced elsewhere.

In areas with declining industries largescale unemployment creates great social problems. **New industries may come into the area to replace the old** (p. 167). But if they don't, redundant workers may have to move elsewhere, and perhaps re-train.

P 9.4 From a main trunk link to the A1, trucks enter and leave an industrial estate on the outskirts of Bedford, where local and national firms take up prepared sites and buildings.

Local ties are strong, however; and distant jobs may mean getting a new, expensive house. So it is the younger who tend to move and look for jobs with prospects and good living conditions.

But the past continues to influence the present. In Britain both textile and steel industries flourished on the northern coalfields, so that a large industrial population is rooted there. New technologies have made the original industries out-of-date; but the infrastructure, like buildings, roads, railways and housing, remains. Hopefully, it may come to serve newer forms of manufacturing. **The inability, or** **reluctance, to move is part of industrial inertia.** People, like the infrastructure, remain; a workforce which must adapt to new industries, if these can be attracted.

Many Lancashire textile works have been converted for firms making such things as car upholstery, light engineering products, rainwear, foodstuffs, and fabric toys. Which of these shows links with former industrial skills?

Fig. 9.6 suggests remedies for old industries unable to compete. Describe the snags in each case in your own words.

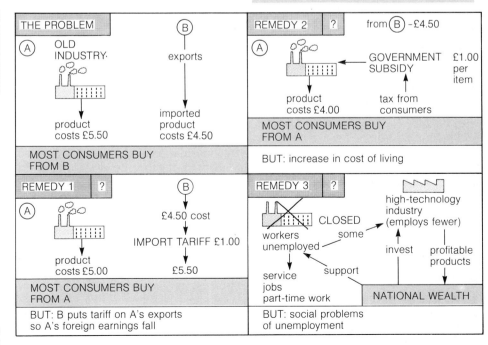

9.6 The old industries can no longer profitably compete. Remedies 1, 2, and 3 are possible, but there are drawbacks to be considered.

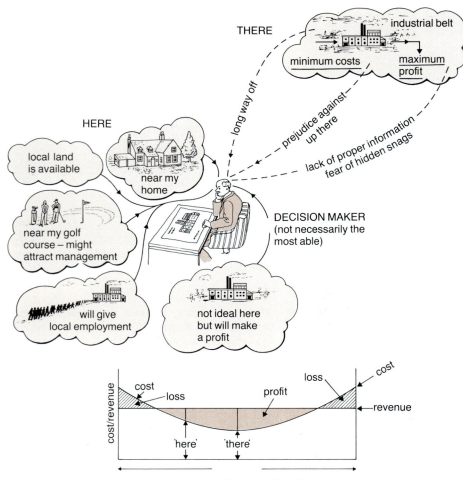

9.7 Where should the new factory be . . . here, or there?

Pleasant places to work in

For those willing to move, a pleasant setting for a factory in an attractive environment for workers and families are obvious pulls. This is a major consideration for firms which need **highly skilled employees,** who can select well paid jobs to suit themselves.

In countries with a variety of climates and natural environments, like the USA, **many firms advertise to attract such employees on the basis of 'sunshine hours' or outdoor sporting activities.** A large number of new electronics industries are in the sunnier parts of California.

9.4 Best location? Maximum profit?

Looking at Fig. 9.5 you will see that, apart from energy and water supplies, which are considered separately, there are two vital controls over the factory and its processes. These are the industrialists who set the whole thing up, and government

policies which affect their decisions (p.167).

We have been looking at how a factory may be sited to ensure minimum costs and maximum profit. But in fact many businessmen do not actually seek this. For various reasons they aim simply to make **satisfactory** profits. The way they may look at it is summarised in Fig. 9.7.

This is an example of how people's behaviour affects development. The businessman (decision-maker) may reject an industrial area as unattractive, even though the factory he wants might do exceptionally well there. He may not even know that area well, but his **perception** of 'there' is an unpleasant one.

Most people have prejudices for or against particular places (or people). These are often based on hazy images, or TV jokes; 'flat-capped industrial northerners' (in a grim environment), or 'toffee-nosed southerners' (in soft suburbia or Sloane-ranger country).

The businessman may know that the factory will make *some* profit if sited locally ('here'). So why move from a pleasant environment, which may, any-

way, attract a skilled workforce? He thinks he can find capital locally and would be pleased to provide local jobs.

His decision is a **satisfactory** one, but not an **optimum** one. The graph shows that the goods manufactured will produce a steady revenue, but the costs only allow a profit within a certain area. Notice that the area 'there' would produce a maximum profit, rather than his own location – 'here'.

9.5 Where are the actual industries?

Certain industries are most likely to be near sources of raw material (especially if this is bulky compared with the product) – brick-making and potteries near clay sources; cement works near limestone quarries. **Others are where there is the greatest demand; they are market-oriented,** like the service industries. Some have inescapable needs for a particular site like shipbuilding (though with possible choices of location).

A few industries need very large amounts of electricity. They are best located close to major generating plant. If the raw materials are imported, a deep-water site is an advantage. Aluminium production illustrates both constraints.

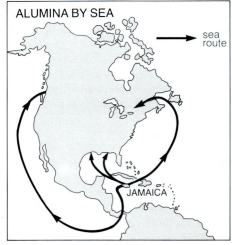

9.8

Aluminium comes from its ore bauxite. This is converted chemically, with heat, into alumina, then smelted to give aluminium metal. The latter process requires huge quantities of electricity. Fig. 9.8 shows the movements of alumina from Jamaica to smelters in Canada's St. Lawrence valley and to a fiordside plant in British Columbia, 80 km from a large HE station.

P 9.5 Aluminium on the dockside at Bell Bay, beside Tasmania's deep-water Tamar estuary.

Why does Jamaica simply convert its bauxite to alumina and not produce aluminium itself?

What advantage is there in sending alumina to Canada rather than bauxite?

Photo 9.5 shows aluminium produced at Bell Bay in northern Tasmania. Find why Tasmania is considered suitable for processing alumina sent from coastal Queensland. What particular advantage has Bell Bay by being on the deep Tamar estuary?

Suggest why electro-chemical and electro-metallurgical products form a large proportion of Norway's industrial output.

Most industries can now strike a balance, and find a location between sources of material (which could be partly or entirely imported), the main market for their goods (which could be overseas), and a source of labour (which could be attracted from elsewhere). The electric grid system supplies energy over a wide area and, with improved transport and communications, **many light industries are footloose (not tied to one place).**

And yet there are clusters of industry in certain places. In some areas industrial inertia and local skills have continued to attract particular types of industry; though the materials and products may change form – the *type* of shoes manufactured in the East Midlands, for example.

Certain industries tend to pull in others, producing a cluster of linked factories. Thus, as Fig. 9.9 shows, a rubber and plastics firm serves neighbouring electrical instrument and radio component firms, and also footwear manufacturers. Local sectional building and printing firms serve one another and several of the others. These, with their workers and families, from a market for the local tertiary industries, retailers, and professions.

Competing, rival firms are often close together in a good, accessible location, which gets a reputation for that type of industry. They can benefit from local specialist suppliers and because of their number, get advantages from local services and amenities.

Such **agglomerations of industry** may cluster where land values are low, and where there is space to develop, and uncluttered roads. As the population and services expand, and factories multiply, what may happen to the land values, and the road traffic? In time, may not some consider moving (see p. 167)?

The newer high-technology industries differ from the older declining industries in their requirements for materials, energy, labour, markets and the locations they prefer.

Industries making such things as electronic components, instruments, and computers are footloose. Yet they tend to form close clusters. Their products can

become obsolete very quickly. Many researchers and specialist suppliers are involved not only in 'the latest' products but in planning for the next. Skilled labour

P 9.6 Mass employment of metal workers in the 19th century . . . razor grinding in Sheffield, with the aid of belt-drive.

P 9.7 In 1865 a Sheffield factory makes steel wire for the Atlantic Telegraph Cable . . . a period when so many inventions and innovations created booming employment in metal industries.

P 9.8 Specialist employment in a 'high-tech' industry – a woman inspects microcircuits in an electronics factory in Milan.

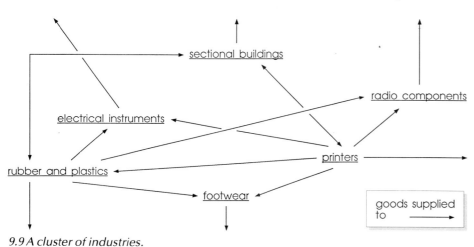

9.9 A cluster of industries.

sectional buildings

electrical instruments

radio components

printers

rubber and plastics

footwear

goods supplied to ⟶

GLENROTHES

- highly skilled workforce
- excellent industrial relations record
- wide variety of industrial premises and sites
- comprehensive and balanced industrial profile

47 Electrical and Electronic companies, 2 Freight Forwarding agencies, 6 Printers and Publishers, 3 Haulage companies, 10 Computer companies, 22 Business and Secretarial services, 4 Packers, 2 Robotic Engineering companies, 25 Mechanical Engineering works, 15 Precision Engineering groups . . . and a man who makes printed circuit boards.*

COMMUNICATIONS

ROAD: Linked by the M90 to the national motorway network. The East Fife Regional Road, currently under construction, will further improve communications.
RAIL: Markinch, on the eastern boundary of the town is on the main London–Aberdeen line.
SEA: Close to the major deep water ports of the Rivers Forth and Tay.
AIR: Fife Airport in Glenrothes, is fully equipped for private and business flying. Edinburgh Airport is only ten minutes away by light aircraft.

Helicopter landing facilities are also available.

GLENROTHES

Glenrothes was designated a New Town in 1948. Since then the town has experienced steady growth and is now the administrative capital of Fife Region, as well as a recognised centre of industrial excellence, particularly in the electronics and engineering industries.

Glenrothes now has a population of some 38,000 people. This is projected to increase to over 45,000 by 1996 with an eventual increase to 48,000.

HOUSING

The town has been built in precincts or "villages" to retain an element of local character and individuality. There are many house types suitable for most needs. The owner-occupation rate is now almost 40%.

SHOPPING

The Kingdom Centre is one of the largest enclosed shopping complexes in Scotland encompassing an extensive range of retail outlets. Each precinct has its own neighbourhood shopping centre with community facilities.

LEISURE AND RECREATION

Extensive facilities to suit almost every sporting taste.

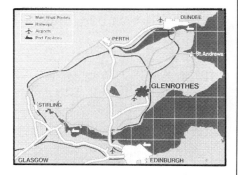

• GLENROTHES

*With support from Glenrothes Development Corporation Michael Conway has set up his own company C. B. Circuits to produce printed circuit boards.

EDUCATION

Glenrothes has 14 primary schools, 3 secondary schools and one College of Technology, noted for its close links with industry. Of the eight Scottish universities, 5 are within easy travelling distance of Glenrothes.

P 9.9 The New Town of Glenrothes advertised to attract firms and skilled workers who can choose their place of employment. It stressed the high-technology nature of many industries in Glenrothes, and the advantages of a location adjacent to major communications.

and special materials are concentrated in **agglomerations** – the best known being the so-called 'Silicon Valley' in Santa Clara county, California.

Many of these and other high-technology industries are located in a belt along the M4 from Oxford to Slough and in that from Milton Keynes to Cambridge. There are particular growth areas near Cambridge. Another lies between Glasgow and Edinburgh; and in Fife Glenrothes is attracting specialist electronics-computer firms.

Many electronic firms have headquarters in the USA. Suggest how this relates to the high-tech Western corridor along the M4? Consider Heathrow airport.

Why does Glenrothes Development Corporation stress both industrial possibilities and social attractions?

Urban to rural movements

In most of the MDCs manufacturing activities have been shifting from large urban areas to small towns and to locations in the countryside. The reasons seem to be that:

1 In big cities space for industrial development is scarce, and land expensive.

2 City firms have high operating costs.

3 City congestion makes access difficult.

4 Rural areas have room for development; labour costs are lower (and perhaps union controls are less).

5 **There has also been a growth in small independent local firms, as well as branches of larger ones, in rural areas.**

6 Rural areas have environmental attractions and are improving accessibility (though that may endanger the environment).

9.6 Government controls and assistance

Governments can act in various ways to assist areas of high unemployment. They can also help deprived regions far from the main industrial areas. In post-war Britain they have concentrated on two broad types of area:

(a) where major industries are rundown and unemployment high.

(b) those far from the most productive industrial–agricultural regions, often scenically beautiful, but remote (some, like parts of Devon and Cornwall, have attracted people from elsewhere, but have high unemployment).

Governments have taken three main courses:

(i) **Direct financial help:** Companies which move into (or expand within) the area may receive grants for new plant and machinery. Firms may receive a subsidy for each person they employ. **Tax relief** may be given on profits, to encourage re-investment.

(ii) **Investment** in communications, buildings, industrial estates, and means of improving the environment within the area.

(iii) **Control** by checking the development of certain new industries *outside* these areas; and **encouragement:** by per-

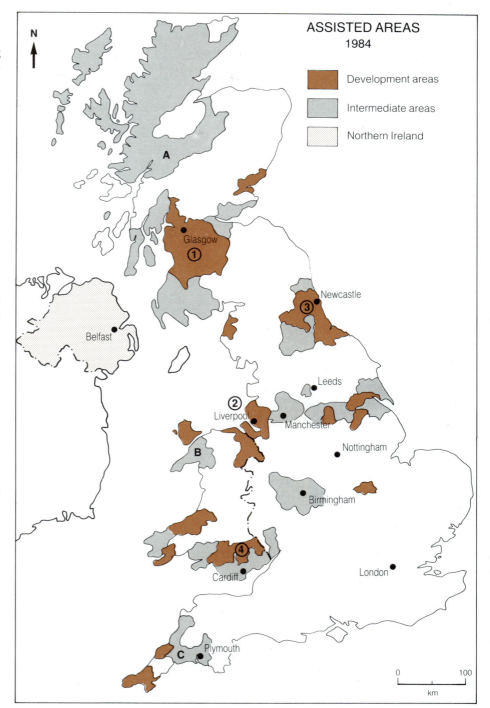

9.10 Government assisted areas in 1984

suading service firms to set up branches, or relocate themselves within the area.

Fig. 9.10 shows **development areas** seen as needing special help; and some needing assistance at a lower level. Both qualified for help with factory rents, transferring workers, training, research, and development. Later, firms were encouraged to seek profitable locations in the south-east. But, with recession, this, too, is a region of high unemployment and firm closures.

The development areas **1–4** have characteristics and problems in common; as do the intermediate areas **A, B** and **C**. Explain what these are, and why each needs particular assistance.

What kind of primary, secondary or tertiary industries might be encouraged in area **A**? Which kind of industry would be unsuitable?

What would you stress to encourage an industrialist to move a factory to a site in region **C**, concerning (a) the

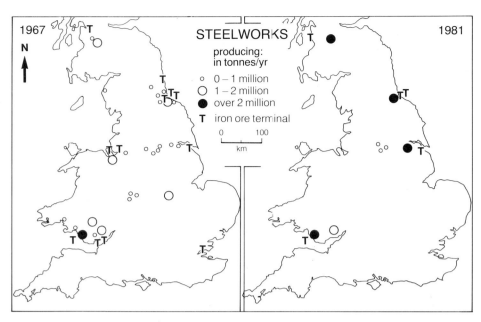

9.11 Steel production . . . 15 years of change.

risks large increases in the cost of living, without necessarily improving long-term manufacturing prospects.

Discuss these possibilities. Argue the government's case for and against this course of action.

How would you reply to the statement that 'industrial geography is about energy, materials, products, and places, not about politics and unemployment'?

9.7 Industries and economic growth

A country's income

The economic growth of most of the LDCs has been affected by 19th century colonisation by European powers. Before that most of them had certain traditional craft industries – cloth weaving, leather working, carpentry, metal working – as did the present MDCs before industrial manufacturing began.

The goods manufactured, services rendered, and income from investments all increase a country's wealth. Their total value in a year is the country's **Gross National Product (GNP).**

Dividing the GNP by the number of people in the country gives the **GNP per head.** We can use this figure to compare how productive particular countries are, and to assess their progress year by year. **If the investment income is not included, the value is known as the Gross Domestic Product (GDP).**

land, (b) the environment, and (c) government policy?

What kind of questions might you ask if you were considering moving a factory to **C**?

There is thus much government influence on industrial location in the MDCs. And, of course, in communist countries the aim has been to centrally direct overall development and location of industries, for political reasons.

Many MDCs are now seeing their older manufacturing industries decline. Which to let go, which to revive, and which new ones to encourage are difficult problems. There are social as well as economic considerations.

Capital invested in manufacturing industries may bring only a small return compared with that put into service industries. However, export of manufactured goods brings in foreign currency – needed to pay for imported goods no longer manufactured – but so do some of the service industries.

What kind of tertiary industries may earn much foreign currency?

Britain's iron and steel industry has been reorganised over the last quarter of a century. Examine Fig. 9.11.

(a) What changes have been made in (i) the number of steelworks; (ii) the proportion of small steelworks to large ones; (iii) the location of steelworks on the coalfields; (iv) the number of ore terminals?

(b) In which areas will employment

in the industry have fallen considerably, or, indeed, vanished?

(c) Suggest reasons for the redistribution of the industry in this way.

Fig 9.6 has shown possible ways of dealing with industries unable to compete with foreign manufacturers.

In addition to these, a government may decide to create employment by building more houses, better roads, power projects, social centres, etc. This may save on unemployment benefit payments and improve social conditions for those taking work. But it

P 9.10 A Pennine valley scene at Halifax in the 1930s, with factories and long lines of terraced houses established when Britain's textile industries flourished on the Yorkshire coalfields. A scene which owed everything to previous generations, but with close settlement which has remained part of the industrial conurbation shown in Fig. 11.15. Towns have been restructured, but new industrial encouragement is needed to combat unemployment.

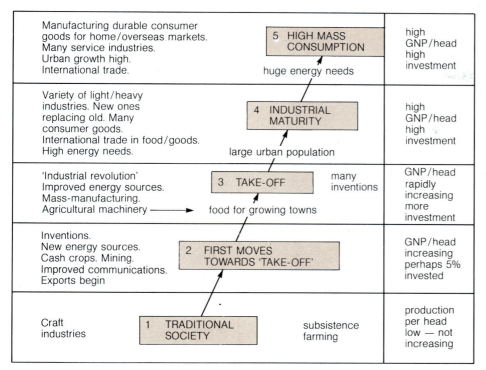

9.12 Stages of economic growth in the more developed countries.

In the MDCs where industrial manufacturing brings a high income, the GDP is vastly greater than that of most LDCs.

In Germany, for example, over 40 per cent of the country's GDP comes from primary and secondary industries and only 2 per cent from agriculture. Whereas in Ghana only 9 per cent comes from primary and secondary industries and 61 per cent from agriculture. In the 1980s the GDP per head for Germany was more than fifty times that of Ghana.

Stages of development

In 1960 W. W. Rostow introduced a model which showed how the MDCs moved from the craft industry stage to their present one, with many service industries and factories manufacturing consumer goods (Fig. 9.12).

Consumer goods are partly those we buy off the shelves of stores and supermarkets for daily use, and partly **durable (lasting) goods** which include such things as cars and washing machines.

Like all models, this gives us an insight into what has happened and can happen. **It also allows us to consider** *why* **the movements from stage to stage do** *not* **appear to be happening in many of the LDCs.** Even in the MDCs the rates of movement from stage to stage vary considerably (Fig. 9.14).

It is useful to see how this matches with other models. Consider **stage 5** together with predictions made by Fourastié in 1964 (Fig. 9.13). Notice how the proportion of people engaged in primary, secondary and tertiary industries has changed as economic development has proceeded.

Why do you think more and more people are working in service industries at **stage 5**?

Does the drop in the numbers working in secondary industry necessarily mean that the wealth produced by manufacturing industries is falling in proportion? Or are there new types of industry which employ fewer people? (Look back to Photos 9.3 and 9.8.)

Fig. 9.14 shows how countries have moved from **stage 3** to **stage 5**. Discuss what was happening in each country during each stage. Find out what caused the movement from one stage to the next. Suggest why the other countries have passed from **stage 4** to **5** more quickly than Britain?

How do recent energy crises and problems of declining industries suggest that **stage 5** is not a very stable one? Suggest a possible **stage 6**.

Rostow investigated a limited number of MDCs. **It is certain that the kind of growth he shows in the model is** *not* **happening in many of the less developed countries**, even in those which have received large investments.

The countries which industrialised first obtained the world's raw materials and supplied industrial goods to world markets very freely. Times have changed: today the LDCs have not the opportunities to do such things.

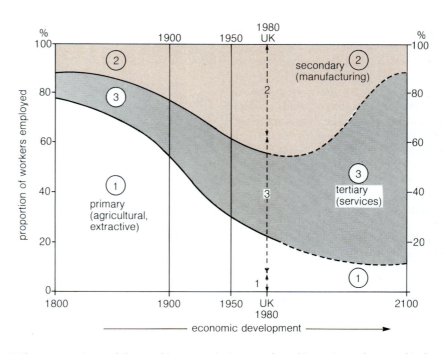

9.13 The proportions of the working population employed in various classes of industry, with a forecast (after Fourastié).

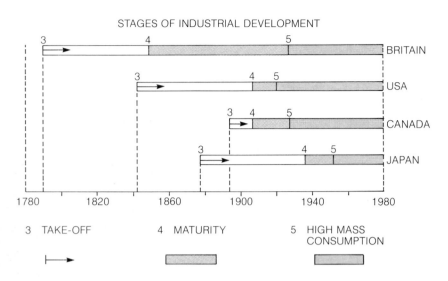

STAGES OF INDUSTRIAL DEVELOPMENT

3 TAKE-OFF   4 MATURITY   5 HIGH MASS CONSUMPTION

9.14

9.8 Industries in the less developed countries

The cycle of under-development

We have seen how subsistence farmers in the least developed countries may be caught in a cycle of poverty (p. 152). **The LDCs themselves are trying to escape from a cycle of under-development.** In most of them less than a tenth of the people work in manufacturing. There is a shortage of capital to invest in new industries, energy sources, and the infrastructures – roads, and railways.

With subsistence farming and poorly-developed manufacturing offering low wages, few can afford more than essential items of food, clothing, and household pots and pans. So **there is a lack of demand for consumer goods (which would itself encourage manufacturing).** This means there is little prospect of creating the capital needed to invest in improving agriculture, let alone establishing profitable industries. Fig. 9.15 shows this cycle of under-development.

Capital *can* **be acquired in several ways:**

(a) **from the MDCs** through government grants and loans; or from private investment by companies.

(b) **from grants and loans from official organisations** like the Western countries' Organisation for Economic Cooperation and Development (OECD), or from OPEC (p. 153), or from specific UN funds.

(c) **from compulsory savings**, or by in-creasing **taxes** within the country itself (though hardly possible with widespread poverty).

(d) **by exporting** cash crops or natural resources.

Sadly, funds from overseas do not necessarily break the cycle of under-development. Too often the grants and aid are hasty contributions in times of disaster. Some have political strings attached. Also private investment may aim to set up industries simply to *process* raw materials for final manufacturing in the MDCs. So the capital is not used to bring manufacturing to areas which lack industrial employment.

Even when capital *is* available there are problems if the workforce is unskilled, under-educated, and perhaps in poor health. **Improvement in education and health services have to go hand-in-hand with other investments.**

Most LDCs need foreign investment but are cautious about accepting it from any foreign power which might come to dominate them. On the other hand foreign investors may be unwilling to risk capital in a country which has social problems and is tied to a different political system. World politics, therefore, have considerable influence on the progress of the LDCs.

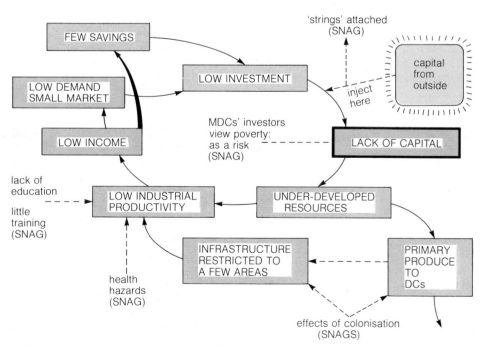

9.15 The cycle of under-development in LDCs with insufficient capital. So many things (snags) act against improvements. Even when capital is available, financiers may be reluctant to invest in such a poor country, while the LDC may be wary of being tied economically, or politically, to a foreign power.

Stages of growth – some effects of colonialism

Western European nations had colonial control over most of the present LDCs from the late 19th to mid 20th century. They established industries, roads and railways, where none existed. But these were mostly designed to ship raw materials, or semi-manufactured ones, to the growing mass-manufacturing industries in Europe.

This set a pattern of industrial growth which differs from that of the MDCs, the Rostow one. **Many of the people have remained at Stage 1**, practising traditional craft industries, alongside those introduced in **Stage 2**.

Stage 2 has mostly consisted of industries processing primary products (sugar milling, sisal for rope, etc.), **or extractive industries** such as timber-cutting and mining ores. It was not in the interest of the MDCs to have textiles, or metal and engineering products, manufactured in their colonies – for colonial peoples were a large market for cheap goods made in European factories.

Even after gaining independence, the economies of many LDCs follow the old pattern. There remains a 'hidden' control by the MDCs – sometimes called **neo-colonialism**. The industrially developed

P 9.12 India, a vast country with developing industrial regions, advertises home manufactured machinery for air conditioning, irrigation, and clothing. Many of the minicabs, here used as a tertiary industry, are now made in the country.

countries still require primary or semi-finished products; so they invest in the LDCs to that end. They also provide expert know-how, advisers, and sometimes management. Many LDCs now draw on increasing numbers of their own educated executives and technicians — though by no means all of them.

P 9.13 Rubber exported from LDCs returns in the form of manufactures . . . such as these tractor tyres in Kenya.

If many parts of an LDC remain poor and inaccessible, should not investments in transport and communications be put *before* industrial development? What about costs, distances, and demands for industrial products? Would the risk be too great?

If the remote interior is well populated, what kind of local industries might benefit *them* most?

Look at Zambia's metal industries (p. 152). Are they mainly supplying demands in the country itself? What *is* their main purpose?

Does Zambia's GNP figure ($US320 per head in 1990) reveal anything about development within the country as a whole?

From southern Zambia many have found employment in Zimbabwe and South Africa; what dies this indicate?

Look again at the development of communications and cities in Ghana (p. 134).

Why in colonial times did industries develop near the major ports? Suggest why most of the country's firms producing consumer goods are also there: think of demands and labour requirements.

There are three industrial concentrations in the three urban areas of Accra-Tema, Secondi-Takoradi, and Kumasi. Why particularly there?

If you wished to locate a firm in an LDC what would be the advantage of choosing the largest place? Wouldn't this continue the old 'colonial' pattern of industrial location, rathern than spread manufacturing through the country?

P 9.11 Processing crêpe rubber in a Sri Lankan factory. Crude crêpe sheets are exported to large overseas manufacturers of rubber products.

P 9.14 Factory employment on a large industrial estate near Nairobi. As in many LDCs, much of the work is assembling rather than manufacturing complete products.

Further stages of development

It is unrealistic to **generalise** about further stages of development and economic progress for the LDCs. **Some have developed very rapidly in recent years. The oil-rich states** in the Middle East have jumped straight from the traditional craft **stage (1)** to a society with high mass consumption (**stage 5**) – though in most of these countries traditional rural activities exist alongside the most advance technology.

There are contrasting levels of industrial development among the LDCs. Compare tiny countries like Chad, scarcely beyond the craft industry stage, with a huge country like China, with its centrally-planned economy. As China progresses, it is developing light rural industries as well as introducing advanced technology into mass-manufacturing.

P 9.15 Home industry, using a cycle wheel and spindle. Hands both provide the power and control the fibre.

The newly industrialising countries (NICs), such as Hong Kong, Taiwan, and South Korea, manufacture electrical and electronic goods and textiles which compete successfully in world markets. They owe much to the initiative of numerous small firms, with cheap well-organised labour, and capital from abroad.

Countries like India, Brazil, and Mexico have attracted sufficient investments to develop core regions with technologically advanced industries. Yet millions of their families live barely above subsistence level. Like China, they are struggling against huge increases in population (p. 183).

For the LDCs there are a number of stages of industrial growth (though individual countries do not necessarily pass from one to the other):

1 traditional craft industries (often alongside later stages)

2 processing primary produce (colonial patterns)

3 import substitution (decreasing dependence on imports from the MDCs)

4 manufacture of capital goods and consumer durables (for those NICs breaking the cycle)

5 high technology and mass consumption (for a few, like the Middle East oil-producers – though not all their people have reached the 'mass consuming' stage).

In stage 3 countries develop light industries which need only moderate amounts of capital, but which save on the costs of imports – food production, furniture, household goods, textiles, and printing. They can also accumulate capital for re-investment.

During times of economic hardship, the MDCs export less to the LDCs, which may encourage the LDCs to set up their own light industries. However, the MDCs also provide loans for the LDCs, and in hard times they are likely to charge high interest rates, which can hinder development.

Stage 4 is the real 'take-off' for development. Unfortunately mass-manufacturing industries are frequently owned by foreign firms or international corporations. Discuss the advantages and disadvantages this can bring to an LDC.

9.9 The tourist industry

Tourism is a recent and growing industry for many LDCs. In the MDCs a combination of rising incomes and decreases in the real costs of transport has increased demand for overseas holidays. Consider the following:

1 Transport improvements have had much to do with the growth of tourism. Which in particular?

2 The global distribution of most LDCs makes them attractive to people in the MDCs. Give a number of reasons why this should be.

3 There are particular links between LDCs and tourist markets: Canada–

P 9.16 In Singapore most of the old districts with craft industries and small retailing have disappeared with the advance of large commercial buildings and high-rise flats.

P 9.17 Hotels built with foreign capital bring tourists flocking to Caribbean beaches.

Caribbean; Australia–Fiji; West Germany–East Africa; UK–Mediterranean lands. Account for these tourist connections.

4 Tourism is a labour-intensive industry. Who finds employment besides the hotel staff?

5 Only a small proportion of the cost of a foreign holiday benefits the receiving country. Why is this? Where does the money go?

6 Why is it difficult for the LDCs to acquire a greater stake in the industry, e.g. hotel ownership?

7 Tourism may boost local vegetable and livestock production. But in many cases food has to be imported. Suggest why this may be necessary. How does this affect the LDC? Consider costs and competition.

8 What sort of things are likely to strain good relations between tourists and the local population?

9 High-spending tourists can cause the price of local commodities and also land values to rise. How may this affect the poorer members of the population?

Despite many drawbacks, however, tourism does benefit the economy of most developing countries.

Environmental damage, however, has increased with the surge of tourism. There is direct pollution: untreated sewage has affected many Mediterranean shores. There are also secondary effects: the replacement of Alpine vegetation by the roads, buildings, and pistes of ski resorts has led to summer flooding, mudslides, and erosion, especially in the Austrian Alps.

Local characteristics which once attracted holidaymakers have been lost under high-rise hotels, apartment blocks, and amusement arcades. Certainly not all the local people benefit from tourism. Many resent the changes in the landscape and in their way of life, and their treatment by insensitive visitors. Undesirable social behaviour is often introduced.

Remember that these aspects of international tourism can also apply to the home country. Some of the problems involving tourism and visits by car to parks and leisure areas are highlighted on p. 254.

P 9.18 A different life style along the edge of the inlet adjoining the Antiguan beaches shown in Photo 9.17. The islands benefit from tourism, but the spread effect is limited.

Theme 9
Back-up section

How are people employed, and where?

In most countries employment in agriculture, industry, and services is unevenly distributed, being more concentrated in some regions than in others.

To express this concentration statistically we use a **location quotient**. This can be calculated for any activity (**X**) as follows:

$$\text{Location quotient for } \mathbf{X} = \frac{\dfrac{\text{number employed in } \mathbf{X} \text{ in the region}}{\text{total employees in the region}}}{\dfrac{\text{number employed in } \mathbf{X} \text{ in the country}}{\text{total employees in the country}}}$$

A value greater than 1.0 implies that the activity is more concentrated in the region than in the country as a whole.

(c) In the West Midlands there are large industrial clusters. What does the location quotient suggest about farming in the 'rural' midlands?

If figures are available, a location quotient can also show how industries are concentrated in districts, or in urban areas, within the region itself.

Would the numbers employed be a really satisfactory indication of the importance of *an industry* in a region? The workforce of various firms varies with the type and scale of manufacturing. Discuss this.

Table 19 shows the number of employees in England's national planning regions and how many of them are engaged in (1) energy production, and (2) mechanical engineering and vehicle

PLANNING REGIONS

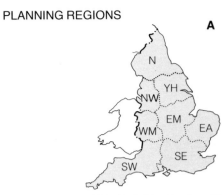

A

YH   Yorkshire-Humberside

MECHANICAL ENGINEERING AND VEHICLES (ME & V)

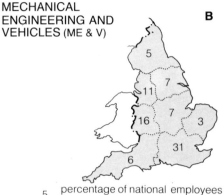

B

5   percentage of national employees in ME & V manufacturing

9.16

Which regions show particularly high proportions of workers in energy and water production? Give reasons for this. Refer to pp. 150–52.

In which region is the largest number employed in such production? Suggest why. Why is its location quotient so low?

Is the distribution of mechanical engineering and vehicle production evenly spread over the country?

Table 18

| employees (1989) '000 | England | | | | | | | | Wales | Scot | UK |
	SE	EA	SW	WM	EM	YH	NW	N			
in agriculture	58	30	41	25	28	25	16	11	22	28	284
in all occupations	7694	765	1715	2029	1556	1805	2411	1078	964	1923	21953
location quotient	0.6	3.0	. . .	0.9	1.4	. . .	0.5	0.8	. . .	1.1	1.0

Consider agricultural employment in various parts of the UK – the regions shown in Fig. 9.16.

manufacture. The *percentage* of the regional workforce employed in those industries is shown in brackets.

Calculate the location quotients omitted in Table 18.

Which parts of the UK had *more* than the national average employed in agriculture? Suggest why in each case.

Say how the figures reflect the following:

(a) Different types of farming employ different numbers of workers . . . consider the arable farms of East Anglia and the high hill farms of the northwest.

(b) In the south-east there are exceptionally large numbers employed in service industries. Yet there is much agricultural employment. Consider London.

Table 19

| employees (1989) '000 | Planning Regions (England) | | | | | | | | UK |
	SE*	EA	SW	WM	EM	YH	NW	N	
total	11292	765	1715	2029	1556	1805	2411	1078	21953
in energy and water	145	13	27	36	57	57	44	38	460
	(1.3)	(1.7)	(1.6)	(1.8)	(3.7)	(3.2)	(1.8)	(3.5)	(2.1)
location quotient	0.6	0.8	0.7	0.8	1.7	1.5	0.9	1.7	1.0
in engineering and vehicles	812	72	193	394	181	180	283	114	2335
	(7.2)	(9.4)	(11.3)	(19.4)	(11.6)	(10.0)	(11.7)	(10.6)	(10.6)
location quotient	0.7	0.9	1.1	1.8	1.1	0.9	1.1	1.0	1.0

* incl. Greater London   (–) % of total employed

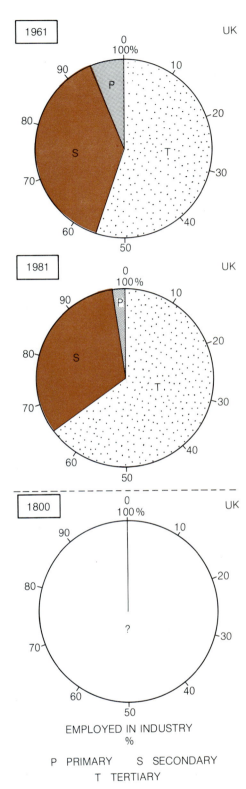

9.17 Changes in the nature of employment in the UK.

Which regions have the highest concentration of workers in these activities? Find reasons for this.

Fig. 9.16 shows that almost a third of the employees in mechanical engineering and vehicle production are in the south-east. Why, again, is the location quotient so low? What is the value of using these two different statistics?

Fig. 9.16 shows regional characteristics by percentages. The regions could be shaded to emphasise particularly high, low, or average values.

Various forms of graphs and charts can stress the proportions engaged in particular industries at a given time. The **pie charts** in Fig. 9.17 give an immediate impression of the changes in numbers engaged in primary, secondary and tertiary industries in the UK in 1961 and 1981.

Look at Fig. 9.17. Complete a similar chart for the year 1800 (based on Fig. 9.13, showing Fourastié's figures for the MDCs at that time). How, and why, does this contrast with the other charts?

A triangular graph may also be used to emphasise the shifts in occupation with time. In Fig. 9.18 **A** and **B** show how agricultural employment declined in Italy, West Germany, the USSR, and the UK within a generation.

To construct a graph like this, mark the value on the edge of each scale (**P, S, T**). From each in turn draw a line parallel with the side of the *next* scale. These lines meet in a point.

In Fig. 9.18 **A** you can see the figures for Italy represented by a point on the graph. Make a list of figures for primary (**P**), secondary (**S**), and tertiary (**T**) employment in each of these countries in 1960 and 1980.

Fig. 9.18 **C** shows how a triangular graph can also be used to indicate the way particular industries vary in costs on wages, energy and materials. In which of the shaded parts of the graph would you look for labour-intensive and energy-intensive industries?

Write down the proportion of the costs of wages, energy, and materials involved in aluminium smelting, butter production, and the clothing industry. Give reasons in each case.

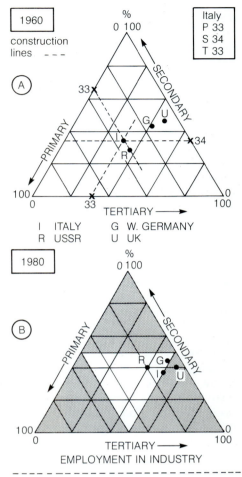

I ITALY   G W. GERMANY
R USSR   U UK

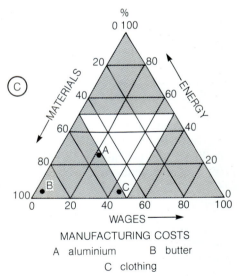

MANUFACTURING COSTS
A aluminium   B butter
C clothing

9.18 How the nature of employment changed in four countries over a 20-year period. **A** shows how to read the proportions. . . A similar graph, **C**, is used to show what proportion of manufacturing costs in the three industries are due to materials, wages and energy inputs.

Using statistics with caution

You have seen how different statistics can give a different picture of the distribution of industries and industrial employees. The same applies to those related to productivity and national wealth.

Table 20

% of GDP (1989)

country	manufacturing	mining	agriculture
Chad	16	1	46
Gabon	10	45	10
Venezuela	16	22	6
Bolivia	11	12	24

Table 20 provides data for the four countries shown in Fig. 9.19. At a glance, Chad might *appear* to be very much an agricultural country; Gabon poor in agriculture, like Venezuela, apparently, but developing its many minerals to give its population the high standard of living suggested by the GDP/head figure in Table 21. Bolivia's manufacturing would *appear* to be on a par with Venezuela's and its agriculture more productive.

Table 21
1989

country	GDP/head ($US)	population (m)	area ('000 km²)
Chad	159	5.4	1284
Gabon	2733	1.2	268
Venezuela	3400	18.8	912
Bolivia	858	7.0	1099

The data in Table 21 tell a different story, however. Chad's agriculture only contributed $73 per head, and Bolivia's $205, similar to Venezuela's $204 (6% of $3400).

> Calculate the actual amounts in $US per head contributed by manufacturing, mining and agriculture in these countries.

Backing figures with facts and descriptions

The figures still cannot tell us about *the actual conditions* **which create these statistics.** Take **Chad**: see how little Chad's agriculture earns for its five million people. But we still need to know that its huge area is largely desert and semi-desert, that livestock make up 20% of the GDP (and that, even then, a large part of their meat is smuggled out on the hoof).

We should know that a relatively tiny irrigated area provides cotton for a small textile industry and cane for sugar refining; and that its mining is for salt, with a small oil output piped from a single field.

And we should certainly realise that the figures are affected by prolonged drought and civil war.

The people of Gabon *appear* **more fortunate.** The country is rich in oil (is chief output) and also in manganese, iron, uranium, and other metal ores. Its GDP/head is one of Africa's highest. It was much higher until oil prices fell, and poor demand for steel in the MDCs cut its manganese output.

But we should realise that Gabon's foreign debts are immense. It receives overseas aid to develop its roads, railways, and power sources. And the figures do not show that half its people are subsistence farmers living amid equatorial forest.

Venezuela is very rich in oil, aluminium and iron. It has a huge eastern industrial complex based on HE development. Its capital city has numerous commercial and financial businesses, and light industries, **yet two out of five Venezuelan families live near a minimum subsistence level**; and, despite the GDP/head figure, shanty suburbs surround the commercial heart of the capital, Caracas.

Much of landlocked Bolivia is cold high tableland amid the mountain ranges of the Andes. Tin and copper in the highlands, and oil from the lowlands, have been exploited with foreign capital. But the country struggles to meet interest pay-

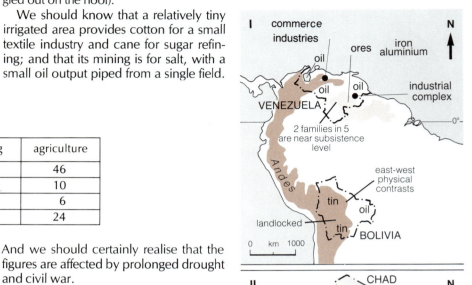

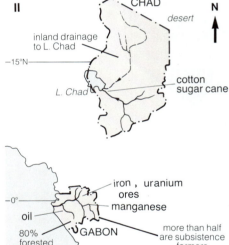

9.19

ments on huge debts. The industrial contribution is mainly from metal treatment and oil refining. Unemployment is high, and the chief agricultural output is from the warmer eastern foothills and lowlands, which are less populated.

These very brief summaries suggest that while statistics are necessary tools for the geographer, **we shall not have a realistic picture of a region or a country unless we find out as much as we can about the actual conditions** . . . physical, social and political. We must also remember that the past has much bearing on the present.

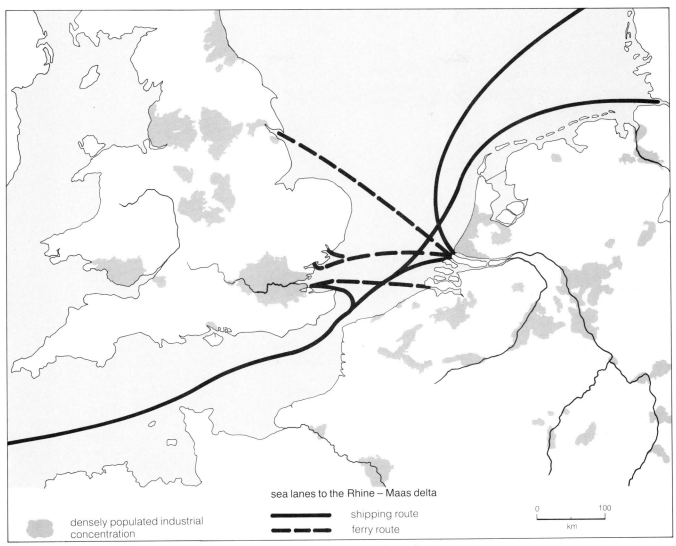

sea lanes to the Rhine – Maas delta

━━━━━━━ shipping route

━ ━ ━ ━ ferry route

densely populated industrial concentration

0   100
km

9.20 The industrial concentrations of north-west Europe. Water routes show the economic importance of the Rhine-Maas delta lands.

Industrial location on a continental scale

Just as there are favourable core areas for industry within a country, so **broader zones of industry have developed within continents.** In Fig. 9.20 you can see where heavy industries and concentrations of industrial employees first developed about the coal and iron ore deposits of Germany, France, Belgium, Luxembourg and the UK. Large populations, especially in huge, spreading cities like Paris, Brussels, and London became markets for manufacturers.

You can see a great north west/south east belt where concentrations of population remain through industrial inertia (p. 163). Throughout this zone, the older mining methods are being restructured, and old industries are giving way to, or being joined by, new ones.

Notice the other great cluster of indus-trial population in a key location in the Netherlands. A ring of urban develop-ment links Amsterdam with the lower Rhine. **Where the Rhine and Maas form a common delta a huge industrial–com-mercial complex has grown up, near Rotterdam and Europoort.**

Fig. 9.21 shows the dock areas which have long transferred imported materials, and exports of ores, coal, and manufac-tures between the world's merchant ship-ping and the inner lands of western Europe. Here is Europe's greatest **entrepôt**, trans-shipping cargoes between strings of river barges and coastal and ocean-going vessels.

Here we have a clear example of **loca-tion** forcing people to triumph over dif-ficulties. The loose sediments of the Rhine delta are not ideal for industrial growth. Buildings need special foundations. In early settlements houses were built on wooden piles. The land needs continuous

P 9.19 Barges such as these carry a huge tonnage of coal and ores along western Europe's great industrial waterway - the river Rhine. Notice how they are propelled, and the way they are linked together as a large single load.

177

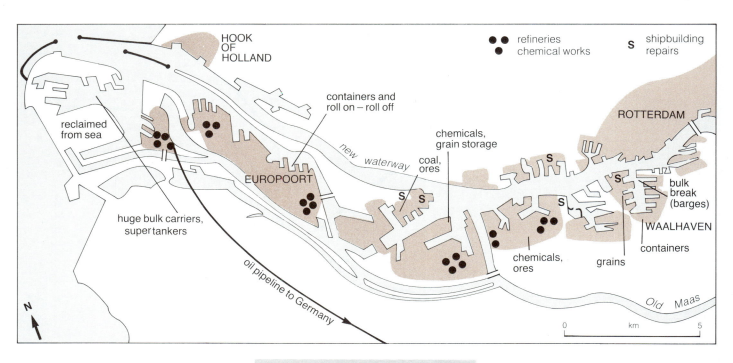

9.21 Industrial developments on reclaimed land between Europoort and Rotterdam.

drainage. Waterways must be kept clear by dredging. But you can see that whole areas have been reclaimed from beneath the sea. If the location is totally right, people will strive to overcome the draw-backs.

Consider how the docks, storage facilities, and industries have changed with the times:

What kind of ships berth at the deep-water outer docks?

What happens to the mineral oil delivered?

How have the docks responded to modern methods of bulk transport?

Find out, in general terms, why *location* has played such a big part in the rapid industrial development of Singapore and Hong Kong, LDCs now better termed **Newly Industrialising Countries (NICs).**

This Rhine-Maas industrial zone has increased its market potential. For it is now linked by various forms of rapid transport to fellow members of the EEC. It can also more easily serve the large number of customers among the populations shown in Fig. 9.20. You can also see the west European industrial core in Fig. 11.21.

Another example of inertia continuing to create a huge market is the pull of the population of New York and the north-eastern manufacturing belt of the USA. Industrialists still see this as **an area where factories and distributors will find the greatest number of customers within a reasonable distance** (thus lowering transport costs). They will be close to materials, capital, and people to employ.

Fig. 9.22 is based on local retail sales. It shows how these advantages fall off as one moves away from the biggest potential market, New York City.

P 9.20 Almost continuous traffic on the waterway between Europoort and Rotterdam. The banks and inlets are lined with industries.

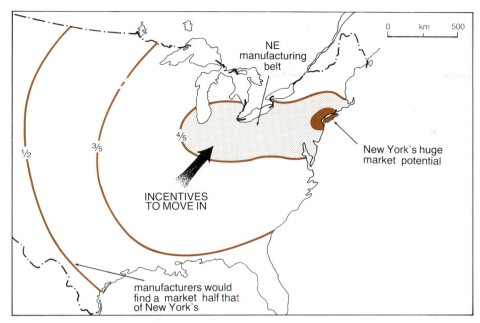

9.22 Manufacturers consider the pull of markets for their products.

Theme 9   Making sure

1 Name an industry in which these materials are inputs, and say which are *raw* materials: clay; upholstery; girders; wool; sugar; manganese; paper; sunflower seeds; sugar cane.

2 Consider the following flows in a factory system: (a) recycling waste products; (b) disposing of waste products. Give examples of industries where (a) is useful and (b) requires care and forethought.

3 (a) Which of these industries can be described as 'footloose': coalmining; electronics; cutlery manufacture; retailing; brickmaking; banking?
  (b) Are there restrictions on the location of those you have called 'footloose'?

4 In Fig. 9.3 transport costs are compared by considering the weight of material and distance moved. Are transport costs always directly proportional to distance? Why? (see p. 136)

5 Various functions in a particular manufacturing industry may be located in different places. Give examples of this.

6 (a) Why may individual businessmen have different reasons for deciding where to locate a particular type of factory?

  (b) Give reasons for *your* choice of an ideal place to work in a manufacturing industry.

7 What is meant by 'agglomeration'? How may this reduce industrial costs?

8 Textile industries originally developed near sources of raw material and energy.
  (a) Give two examples.
  (b) What factors have brought about changes in the distribution of textile manufacturing centres?

9 What is meant by a 'market oriented' industry? Give an example of this.

10 Explain what might influence the location and site in the case of (i) a bakery; (ii) a printing industry; (iii) an artificial fertiliser plant.

11 Fig. 9.23 shows an industrial system.
  What other inputs are important to the location of a manufacturing industry and which outputs are shown as (**?**)?

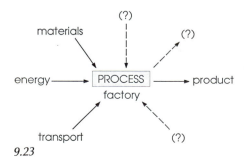

9.23

12 How may a large inland waterway affect industrial location? Give examples.

13 Make a sketch map of a large manufacturing region in which industrial inertia is an important factor. Briefly describe its history and present activities.

14 New 'high technology parks' are being built where the industrial units are close to academic establishments (colleges, institutes), or to existing high precision industries – as in north-west Bristol. What are the reasons for this? Consider 'know-how', new inventions, rapid changes in technology, distance, and mobility of the products.

15 Give reasons why many manufacturing plants have moved from a city centre to a rural site.

16 A government gives incentives for manufacturing in assisted development areas: grants for part of the building and machinery costs; rewards for generating new employment; tax allowances; preferences for government contracts.
  (a) Why is there a need for special development areas?
  (b) Are these all in old industrial areas?
  (c) How might such grants clash with government intentions to *reverse* movements away from city centres?

17 Give reasons why workers in areas of high unemployment may hesitate to move to regions with low unemployment rates.

18 A description of 'infrastructure' may be taken as including site developments, communications, markets, commerce, banking, and planning organisations. Briefly consider why all these things are so closely connected with industry.

19 'Growth in manufacturing depends on investing in both factories and infrastructure; this should include educational establishments.' What is meant by this? Why does it particularly apply to LDCs?

20 (a) Explain the term 'intermediate technology'.
  (b) Describe how it may help the growth of small-scale industries in the LDCs.

21 Why may intermediate and advanced technology *both* be needed for balanced industrial growth within an LDC? Which large country is successfully combining the two?

22 How may labour-intensive industries benefit an LDC? Give examples.

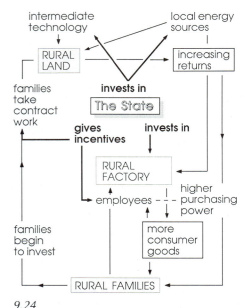

9.24

23 State policies with incentives to make profits are summarised in Fig. 9.24. They aim to develop *both* agriculture and industry in order to improve rural living standards (as in China). Explain how this should come about by following the arrows in the diagram.

24 City-ports in the LDCs develop a core industrial region about them (Fig. 9.25). This contrasts with weak industrial development inland (the peripheral regions).

(a) How is this core region related to the need for: (i) a consumer market; (ii) available labour; (iii) a transport-communication focus; (iv) a centre for investment and decision-making; (v) links between industries?

(b) What kind of inland developments may increase such growth? Consider Fig. 9.26.

(c) Why do people tend to migrate from the interior to the core?

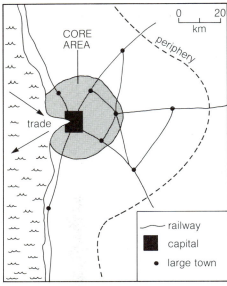

9.25 Concentration of population and industries in a core area about a city-port.

(d) Find an example of this. Make a sketch of the core and periphery. Explain how the core developed.

25 In Fig. 9.26 X shows where mineral resources have been found in a tropical LDC. What kind of problems may hinder their development? Consider location, infrastructure, energy, capital and labour.

26 Fig. 9.27 represents some of the effects of completing a water supply and power project in an LDC.

(a) Why are such developments called 'spread effects'? Give examples.

(b) Explain the links leading to improvements in health and social conditions.

(c) What else would require capital expenditure besides the dam and power plant?

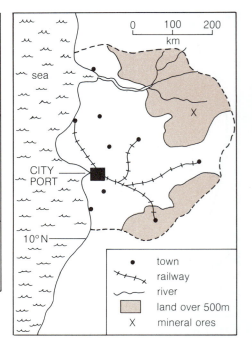

9.26

(d) Two types of manufacturing industry are described. Explain how each might benefit the country.

(e) Such projects eventually build up capital for future development. But they *can* commit the country to crippling debt-interest repayments. How might MDCs help LDCs in this respect?

27 Fig. 9.28 represents a newly-constructed multipurpose dam.

(a) What circumstances may hasten the silting-up of the reservoir?

(b) Why are some reservoirs in hot, dry regions deliberately covered by a fine oil film?

(c) Water hyacinths which grow rapidly over tropical water surfaces have been cleared as a weed; but they protect

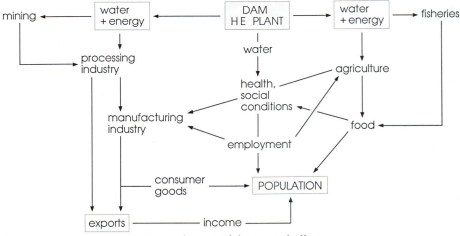

9.27 A new multi-purpose dam and some of the spread effects.

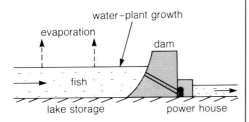

9.28 A multi-purpose dam and its reservoir.

against evaporation. Giant perch were put into Africa's Lake Kariba to provide food, but they have destroyed other aquatic life, and now eat each other. What experts, other than engineers, should be consulted when such projects are considered?

28 Look carefully at the statistics in Table 22.

(a) Find out what you can about the agriculture, mining, and manufacturing in these countries.

(b) These figures tell us nothing about the physical or social conditions. What information *do* they give about the economic circumstances?

(c) What other data might give a more realistic picture of (i) the stage of development of each country; (ii) the physical conditions; (iii) whether the GDP figure indicates living standards throughout the country?

Consider the terms used

A retailer sells goods direct to consumers, mainly in relatively small amounts (as opposed to bulk sales).

Consumer durables are goods that can be used over a long period of time, such as furniture and vehicles.

Mass consumption occurs when a population can afford to buy consumer goods on a large scale, and so there is an incentive for industries to manufacture to satisfy the demand.

In a labour-intensive industry a large proportion of the total production cost is made up of wages for the workers.

In a capital-intensive industry the costs involved in the plant and processes are high compared with those for the workforce, which may be quite small.

A footloose industry is one which is not tied to a particular location, but could easily be established in a large number of suitable places.

Agglomeration is the close clustering of industrial units which make common use of the infrastructure and local services. It allows capital, goods and labour to circulate between them.

Infrastructure (Latin *infra* – below) originally referred to a foundation. It is now used for the 'foundation' of an organisation (factory, industrial estate, and so on) in the sense of the basic lay-out of buildings, roads, pipes, power-lines, etc., needed to allow it to function properly.

Industrial inertia is the tendency for industries, firms and their industrial population to remain in a particular place when the reasons for their original location there no longer apply.

A high-technology park is a cluster of industries which use modern techniques and employ skilled scientists in fields such as electronics. There they can draw on each other's resources and skills, and on those of local research establishments and university departments.

A cash crop is one grown primarily for sale.

Import substitution occurs when a state produces for itself commodities which it has been importing (or would have had to import).

Neo-colonialism describes how certain MDCs control independent LDCs and LLDCs through economic and political actions. Aid, trade and investments can lead to a powerful state, or group of states, dominating the country which receives them.

Table 22

country (1988)	GDP/head ($US)	GDP % for:		area ('000 km²)	popn. (m)
		manufg.	agric.		
New Zealand	11544	21	8	269	3.3
Ecuador	691	17	17	224	10.2
Jamaica	1298	16	8	11	2.3

PART III

Social conditions

Theme 10   Populations and their characteristics

10.1 The rapidly increasing world population

There are about **five thousand million of us in the world, and *every hour* that number increases by some 10 000.** Ten thousand **more** people have been born than have died within that hour; and all add to the pressure on the earth's resources.

By the time the **extra quarter of a million** who appear **each day** are grown up and looking for work, our numbers will have increased by over a thousand million.

The period of long slow growth

Such rapid growth is recent. For thousands of years agricultural populations have been scattered about the globe. Yet, overall, their numbers have increased very slowly. In the two thousand years up to AD 1750 the world population grew from about 300 million to 800 million.

As farming families clustered in their villages and small towns, they contaminated soils, water, and food. Unable to cope with disease, as we *should* be able to

today, they suffered a high death rate (**high mortality**). The failure of crops, through drought, floods or destructive warfare, could bring famine. Life was short, and many women died before their child-bearing span was over.

Natural population growth occurs when the birth rate exceeds the death rate. So on average populations grew very slowly. Even when a stable, settled period allowed certain populations to increase considerably, natural disasters could quickly reduce their numbers.

The rapid increase with industrial development

From about 1750 the development of mass manufacturing brought a change in the newly industrialising countries. A rural population, with an average life span of under 35 years, and largely illiterate, became an increasingly urban, literate one. The life span was gradually extended. Today the newly born can expect to live over 70 years.

To begin with their populations soared, as a high birth rate continued while the death rate fell. Despite grim conditions in industrial cities, piped water, sewage dis-

posal and advances in medicine enabled people to live longer. Food supplies were more assured. The railways were opening up land in the Americas for large-scale cultivation (p. 118).

Colonies were exploited for new sources of industrial materials and became markets for cheap manufactures. In Europe's rapidly industrialising countries increasing foreign trade (helped by new forms of transport) brought a rise in living standards, despite their growing populations. There were, however, great gaps between rich and poor.

List those everyday things which *now* make for good health, but which were not available in the early 19th century.

Find out when mass vaccination and innoculation began to protect people against disease.

One can compare the results by looking at medical innovations in the LDCs. Look at Table 23 and say when you think DDT was introduced to destroy the malaria mosquito.

Table 23

country	death rate (per thousand)				
	1926	1936	1946	1956	1966
India	36	31	30	22	18
Sri Lanka	28	26	20	12	8

The rate of increase declines in the MDCs

Towards the end of the 19th century the birth rate in most of the MDCs began to fall. By the 1930s some had almost no *natural* growth of population.

Birth control, with modern methods of contraception, has enabled people to plan their families. As most people wish to give their children what *they* consider reasonable living standards, and find this expensive, they opt for smaller families. **Family planning** has undoubtedly produced a lower birth rate in the MDCs; though some people, notably Roman Catholics, have reservations about contraceptive methods.

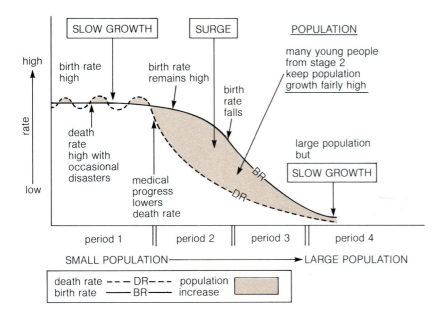

10.1 Changes in birth rates and death rates, with consequent effects on the rate of growth of population. Remember that even a low growth rate makes a large population much larger.

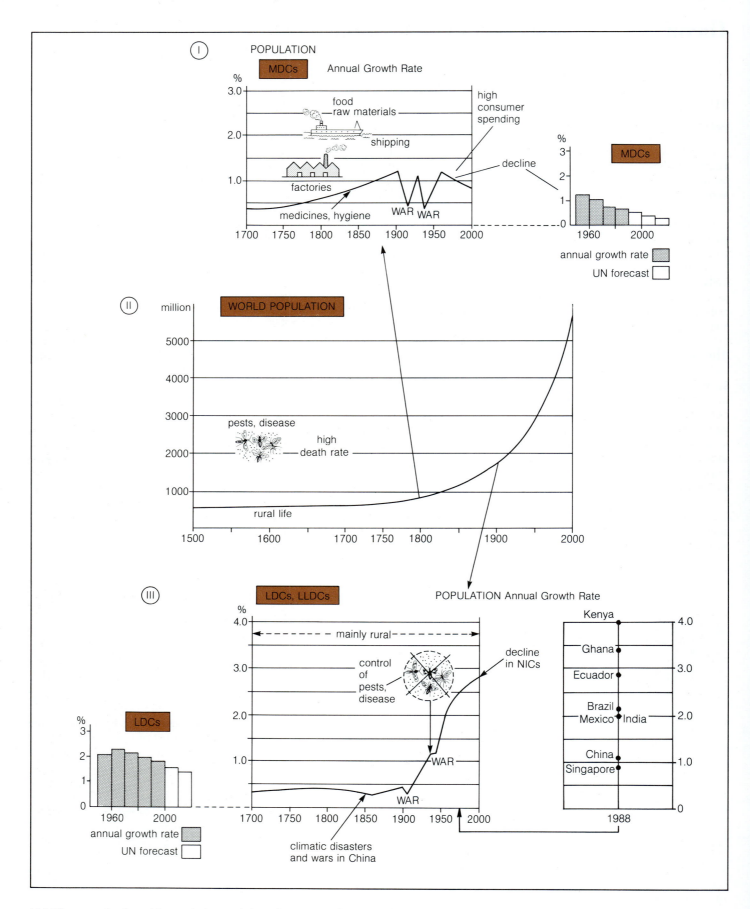

10.2 *The growth of world population and the relative contributions of the MDCs and the LDCs.*

Birth rates in most LDCs remain high, which contrasts with the low and declining rates in the MDCs. However, it is signicant that the birth rate has been falling in the newly industrialising countries of Hong Kong, Taiwan, and South Korea, and among China's huge population.

Fig. 10.1 shows how population growth has changed with the stages of development. But, of course, not all countries will necessarily pass through these stages, nor may they wish to.

The LDCs and the population explosion

There are a number of reasons why poorer peoples in the LDCs prefer large families. Children do useful work about the home and in the fields from an early age. For this reason some societies prefer boys rather than girls. They produce more children to ensure that there are boys (and so men) for manual work. Religious beliefs often favour large families. Thus Hindus try to ensure that a son will survive to perform rites at his father's cremation.

Yet during the 19th century most LDCs did not at first experience the rapid increases in population of the industrialising nations. Agricultural improvements and the introduction of new foods, such as maize and sweet potatoes, saw populations rise sharply in India and China. But various climatic disasters, and China's civil war (which by 1860 had cost 20 million lives) caused an overall dip in the populations of the LDCs.

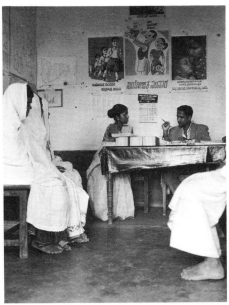

P 10.1 An Indian clinic giving specific advice on child health and welfare.

P 10.2 A direct appeal to limit population growth.

But then the effects of colonisation, and the introduction of medicines, reduced the death rate (a reduction in mortality). Better communication allowed foods to be moved to famine areas. During the 1920s, '30s, and '40s the populations of the poorer nations soared.

Two world wars held back the growth of world population. But **after World War II**, while the populations of the MDCs sharply increased, those of the LDCs became explosive. The rise was more rapid than in the industrialising nations of the 19th century. **Medical technology was now available, and soon insecticides and antibiotics increased life expectancy by over 50 per cent.**

Fig. 10.2 shows how the LDCs are contributing to the rise in world population. By the year 2000 more than 90 per cent of the increase will be in the less developed countries – in lands desperately trying to raise their living standards.

One of the reasons for such growth has been the reduction in infant mortality, in some cases from over 60 per cent to under 10 per cent. Before this, it was common for babies, while weak and less immune to infection, to die within a few months.

There are still distressingly large numbers of undernourished people, and a shortage of medical facilities in many parts of the world. Sadly, this is partly due to the rapidly increasing numbers. **The overall fall in infant mortality and the**

greater expectancy of life are combined with a continuing high birth rate. The rapid population growth makes it more difficult to raise living standards.

10.2 Problems for the future: checking the growth rate

If the present birth rates and death rates were maintained, the population of the world would double as each 35 years pass, and increase a thousand-fold each 350 years (and a million times each 750 years).

Remember the old legend of the king offering his daughter to the man who could supply a grain of wheat for the first square of his chess board, two grains for the 2nd, $2 \times 2 = 4$ for the 3rd, $4 \times 4 = 16$ for the 4th, and so on. Work out what he would have contributed for the 64th square!

It is obvious that these kind of increases cannot take place. Falling birth rates or higher death rates must reduce the rate of growth. The questions are how and when? **The pressure on the earth's food and other resources mounts with each hour.**

The population growth rate has declined in the MDCs, but remains high in many of the less developed countries. Some at least are aware of the need to restrain growth.

P 10.3 In China young people contribute to the earning power of a rural family which takes responsibility for particular production. Here boys sell leather goods and baskets in a small town market.

The most populous country, China, with more than one in five of the world's people, has a vigorous campaign to reduce the birth rate. The methods vary:

(a) commonsense advice to make people realise that if the population outstrips resources, they will not maintain their present improvements in living standards;

(b) aiming for a one-child family; though realising that there are 800 million rural people, who feel they will benefit from having more hands to work the land;

(c) emphasising advantages for the single child, and greater opportunities;

(d) providing incentives, through state benefits, for families with only one child;

(e) spreading knowledge and means of family planning and birth control;

(f) putting pressure on young couples through local social workers.

The rate is already falling steadily. But remember that, under normal conditions, it takes a long time for population numbers to decrease. The present large number of young people are the next generation of parents.

The large family, with the young looking after the very old, has been a stable part of social life in China over the ages. How will this be affected by the one child family? Some look on this policy as a harsh one: but have the people of China any option? What are the alternatives? Why are China's solutions of particular importance to the world as a whole? Discuss each of these points.

China is not alone in trying to reduce the birth rate. But it has a long history of social controls through local officials; so that its present central planning is having greater effect than in other large countries. The campaign in India is hampered by the many languages and different religious beliefs. In Latin American countries many people are illiterate, and there are wide gaps between rich and poor. There is also religious opposition to birth control.

10.3 The structure of the population

The proportion of young people to old people is very important for any country; not only for the future, but also for social reasons. Besides the working members of the population, there are the very young

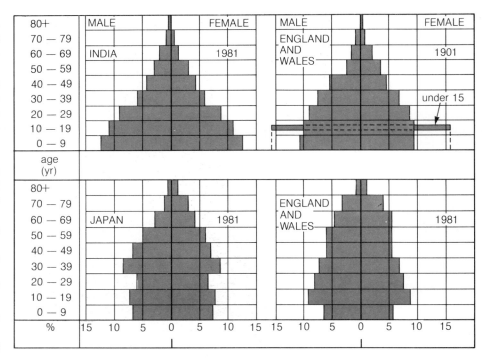

10.3 Population pyramids. What had the population structure in England and Wales in 1901 in common with that in India today?

and very old, who must be supported. **These proportions can be seen in the age-sex pyramids** (Figs. 10.3 and 10.4), which also indicate the relative numbers of males to females at any age.

Consider the populations to be made up of the following groups: (**a**) the very young (0–9); (**b**) youth (10–14); (**c**) the working population (when most become parents); (**d**) the older working population; (**e**) the elderly (over 60), mostly retired.

Look at the pyramid for India (1981), with the broad base and tapering upwards.

Which age-group (**a**–**e**) is the largest? What proportion is under 10 years old? Can they support themselves? What burden does this place on the groups **c** and **d**? What proportion is under 20 years old? Consider the general effect on living standards. Are there likely to be problems with education? Why does the graph taper so sharply after the 40–49 group?

Now look at the pyramid for England and Wales in 1901. What do you notice about the shape: is is somewhat similar to the Indian one? What percentage was under 15 (dotted line)? Most people had left school by the age of 15; what proportion between 9 and 15 was still at school?

Remember that this was the height of the British Empire. Despite class differences, it was possible to provide almost everyone with a basic minimum education. India, too, has many social divisions; it also has a much bigger population. Both of these work against equal opportunities. Also the GDP per head, in real terms, is very low by comparison, making it difficult to help India's very large youthful population.

Next look at the pyramid for England and Wales in 1981.

How does this differ from the 1901 pyramid? Has the rate of population growth increased or decreased? How is this indicated by the pyramid shapes?

How does the population under 14 compare with that in 1901?

By 1981 there was a much higher proportion of elderly people, and of older people to be supported. Which public services feel the strain as these proportions grow? Explain.

The birth-rate in England and Wales increased after the Second World War (see Fig. 10.2), so that for several years the population became greater than usual. This 'bulge' will continue up the age-scale. How and why does such a bulge affect schools and classes, and materials needed: (i) as the extra num-

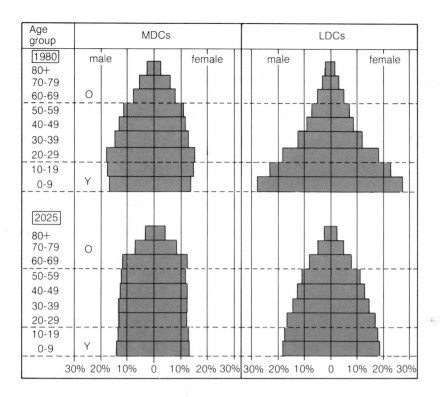

P 10.4 Large population increases act against educational opportunities. Few children in the LDCs have the advantages and facilities of those in this Kenyan classroom.

10.4 How the structure of populations is likely to change. Notice particularly the proportions of young people (Y) and old people (O).

bers reach school age, and (ii) as they begin to leave school?

Think of other ways in which changes in birth-rate and death-rate can affect social planning.

Japan's population pyramid once resembled that of India; but a campaign of strict birth control has successfully cut back the rate of increase. **Look at the shape in 1981.** When did this policy *begin* to take effect? Explain the differences in shape. What will happen if this policy continues?

Fig. 10.4 shows the age-sex structure of the MDCs and LDCs as a whole, with forecasts (from United Nations sources) for the year 2025.

Give reasons why the pyramid for the MDCs in 2025 has almost lost its shape.

What are the main differences between the pyramid shapes and structures for the MDCs and LDCs?

Do they suggest that the world's population is getting younger or older? Check with the bar graphs in Fig. 10.5.

What do Figs. 10.4 and 10.5 suggest is happening to the life expectancy of people in the LDCs? Is this an optimistic or pessimistic forecast? On what grounds?

Give approximate proportions, for each pyramid, of those most likely to have children (group **c**, 15–39). Say how this will affect future populations.

P 10.5 In all societies the young and old need special care. China has a long tradition of providing this, on a family and neighbourhood basis. Notice how the proportions of young and old in a population can change (Figs. 10.4 and 10.5).

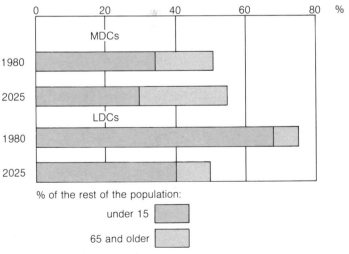

10.5 Likely changes in the proportions of young and old in the populations of the MDCs and LDCs.

Immigration

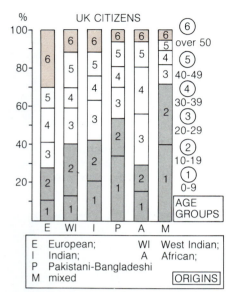

10.6 The origins of people who make up the population of the UK, showing the proportions in the various age groups.

Legend for figure:
- E European;
- I Indian;
- P Pakistani-Bangladeshi
- M mixed
- WI West Indian;
- A African;

ORIGINS

AGE GROUPS:
- (6) over 50
- (5) 40–49
- (4) 30–39
- (3) 20–29
- (2) 10–19
- (1) 0–9

Most large countries contain different racial, religious and language groups. For various reasons these may have different rates of population growth and age structure. This is seen in that country of notorious inequality, South Africa, with its policy of separate development. There the annual natural growth rate is much greater for blacks than for whites.

Where immigration results in a variety of peoples living side by side, their age structures may be quite different. This affects what they require in the way of schooling, housing, old people's homes, etc.

Fig. 10.6 shows the age groups of people living in the UK.

Which group has the highest proportion of old people, and which most young folk?

Not all were born in the UK, but have immigrated at various times. Sometimes large groups arrived after personal disasters abroad. Young families tend to migrate rather than older people.

Suggest how the age structure might show which of these groups has been in the UK longest and which are recent arrivals.

Why, do you think, are most of those of *mixed* parentage in the lowest age groups?

Discuss how educational opportunities and youth employment may be affected by these proportions; also why you should know the actual numbers in each group.

10.4 The distribution of world population and the irregularities

Look carefully at Fig. 10.7. You will see that parts of the world support dense populations, while large areas are virtually unpopulated. Notice also the many smaller concentrations, notably about the edge of the continents.

The reasons for the sparse areas are largely physical, especially climatic. How does this apply to each of the areas **A,B,C,D?**

Literally thousands of millions of people live in mainly agricultural regions of ancient settlement (O), developed on river plains and deltas, fertile basins and coastlands, especially in China and India, and in a more restricted environment in Egypt. Each has great cities, but their populations are still mainly rural.

Which are the main river valleys which support such large numbers?

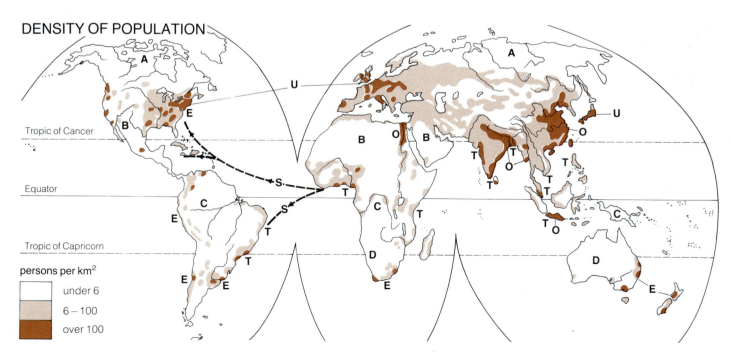

DENSITY OF POPULATION

persons per km²
- under 6
- 6 – 100
- over 100

10.7 The distribution of the world's population.

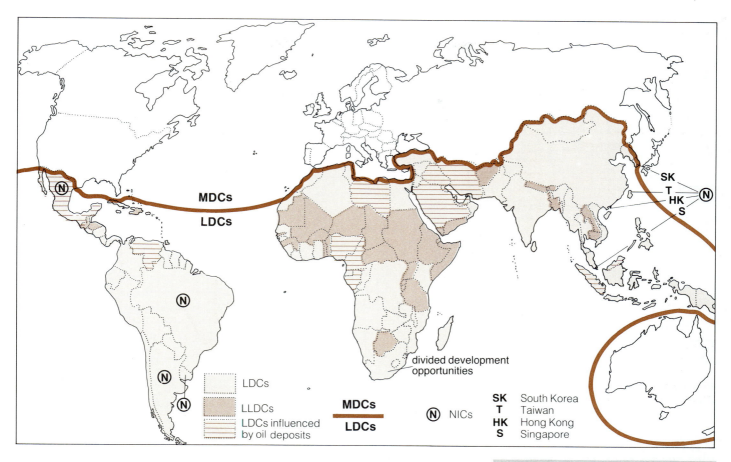

Key:
- LDCs
- LLDCs
- LDCs influenced by oil deposits
- **MDCs** / **LDCs**
- NICs

divided development opportunities

SK South Korea
T   Taiwan
HK Hong Kong
S   Singapore

10.8 The divided world, showing the relative development of individual countries.

More recently, European influences on agriculture, and the establishment of trading centres and communications have affected these and other old civilisations like those in Indo-China and Indonesia (in Java in particular). **During the period of European colonisation new population concentrations developed and have expanded.** The need for tropical produce created particular growth about the main ports on tropical coastlands (**T**).

The infamous **transportation** of over ten million slaves across the Atlantic in the 17th and 18th centuries established the large black proportion of the populations of the Caribbean lands, Brazil, and the USA (**S**).

Direct European settlement (E) led to the growth of the great city-ports of eastern USA, Australia, New Zealand, South Africa, Argentina, Uruguay, and along the Pacfiic coast of South America.

Name one city-port in each of these countries. What were its principal exports when it first began to develop? Where were these commodities sent?

These world-wide colonisations were boosted by demands for food and raw materials from the large expanding urban populations of the mass-manufacturing countries of north-west Europe. **Other urban-industrial regions (U) developed in eastern America and in Japan**, also with concentrations about the main ports.

Locate three large city-ports which have long served each of these urban-industrial populations.

In North America and Euro-Asia the population spread towards the interior of the continent, with rail links leading to centres of population on distant coastlands. Name ports at each end of the trans-American and trans-Asian railways.

Finally, look at two other groups of settlement. First the older ones, where Spaniards in Central and South America occupied ancient settlements, ranging from the Mexican plateaus through the length of the Andes. Many of these are now densely populated centres of Latin American peoples.

Suggest why most of these countries have at least **two** large cities, one inland, one coastal: such as Santiago-

Valpariso, Quito-Guayaquil, Bogota – Barranquilla – name others.

There are also ancient areas of civilisation about the Mediterranean, in the Middle East, and along the old trade routes of central Asia, where traditional and modern forms of settlement are combined to different degrees.

Then there are the interior settlements in Africa, where the distribution of people, of many differing cultures, was affected by colonisation. Most are now part of independent states.

The 'two worlds' of the MDCs and LDCs

Figs. 10.8, 10.9, and 10.10 look at the world distribution of population in different ways. They all emphasise the 'two worlds' of the **more developed and less developed countries.**

Looking foward, you will see that Fig. 10.9 is an unusual map: it is scaled to show the size and relative location of countries, rather than their shape. It therefore gives an immediate impression of **inequality**, showing that most people live in the less developed parts of the world.

Fig. 10.10 shows the expected growth

189

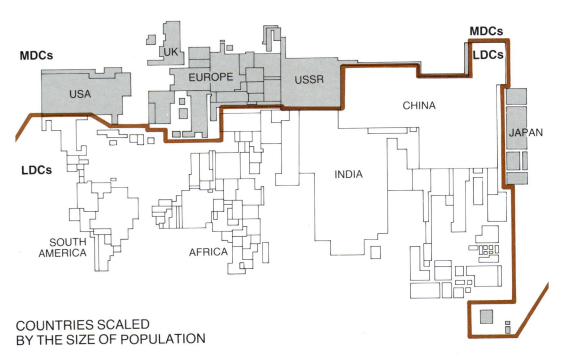

COUNTRIES SCALED
BY THE SIZE OF POPULATION

10.9 Where do most people live: in the more developed countries, or in the less developed?

of population. It stresses the increasingly large number of people in the less developed countries.

Fig. 10.11 overwhelmingly confirms how unbalanced our numbers and possessions have become. **Clearly the majority of the world's wealth is still being produced by the industrialised countries of the northern hemisphere.** Look again at

Fig. 10.8, which shows the actual distribution of the MDCs and LDCs, and notice how the location of the LLDCs emphasises the band of poverty across parts of Africa.

The wealth of some countries in the less developed world is boosted by the exploitation of their vast petroleum deposits. Other countries have oil reserves

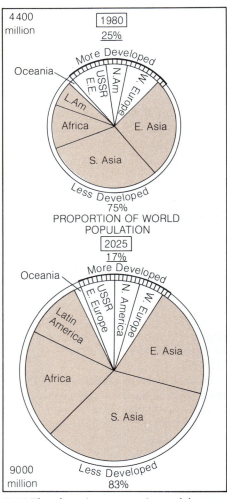

10.10 The changing proportions of the world population by continental areas, and also by stages of development.

P 10.6 The centre of Sydney reflects the wealth and continuous development of cities in the MDCs. Generations of commercial buildings soar above the old City Hall.

COUNTRIES SCALED BY PROPORTION OF WORLD'S ANNUAL PRODUCTION OF WEALTH

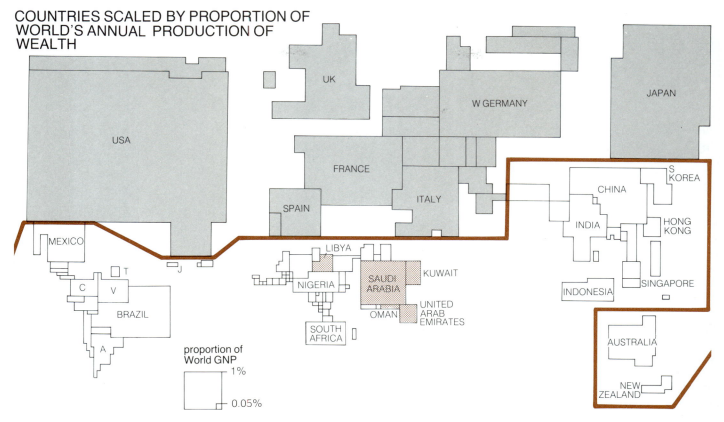

10.11 Compare this scaled map of the wealthy and less wealthy with that of world population distribution (Fig. 10.9). Notice the oil-rich states in North Africa and the Middle East (brown stipple)

and benefit from mineral production. But all of them, especially the poorer with large populations, like Nigeria, are seriously affected when oil prices fall (p. 247).

It is difficult to classify developing countries accurately. In Brazil wealth and poverty lie side by side (p. 101). Argentina and Uruguay, populated by white immigrants, have large industries, and are very different from the Asian group of NICs. These Asian countries produce consumer goods by using both manual skills and new technology. Many of their factories have developed from small workshops (p. 230).

> Fig. 10.11, comparing the wealth created annually, gives an almost crushing impression of the advantages of the mass-manufacturing countries.
>
> Look first at this map and then at Fig. 10.9. One is top heavy, the other bottom heavy. Explain exactly why this should be.

There are some omissions in Fig. 10.11. It does not show countries with less than a million people. For some GNP figures were not available. In countries with **centrally planned economies**, like

the USSR, where production and markets were state-controlled, the figures were not comparable. In China, which *is* included, large quotas are bought by the state, and prices and services carefully controlled; so that figures, again, may not

mean quite the same as in **market controlled economies.** There is also less of a gap between rich and poor, and families have advantages which are not suggested by the GNP figures.

P 10.7 A West African village reminds us that for most people in the LDCs economic development is very different from that shown in Photo 10.6.

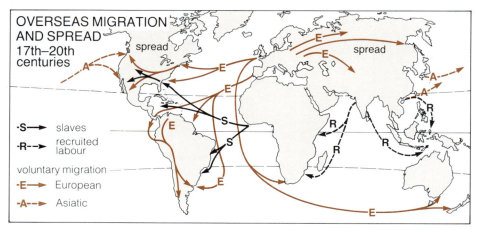

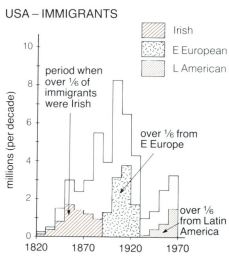

USA – IMMIGRANTS

10.12 Over the past four centuries hundreds of millions of people have voluntarily migrated overseas (though hardships often pushed them into going). Besides the forced traffic in slaves, large numbers of Asian families were recruited to work in other Asian countries, and in Africa and the West Indies, mostly on plantations.

10.13 Showing the millions of immigrants, who arrived in the USA in successive ten-year periods, and where they came from.

10.5 Population migration

Apart from natural growth, populations may fluctuate in other ways. Since the earliest times people have moved, or have been moved, from one part of the world to another. There have been migrations by family groups, mass movements after disasters, and peoples carried away into slavery, like the Africans to America, or made refugees by persecution, as in Nazi Germany. There was mass recruiting of cheap Asiatic labour for overseas tropical plantations in south-east Asia, Africa, and the Caribbean.

revolutionary upheavals in eastern Europe brought millions of peasants and urban poor to America. Many came from other parts of the world – Chinese and Japanese in large numbers – until the USA restricted immigration. More recently, most people have come from Latin America, especially Mexico.

Of course, pull has come into it. With little to lose, the *apparent* attraction of life in a new country offering opportunities is strong. As the USA developed, there was the 'bright lights' image, which pulls rural people towards the city in most lands.

The prospect of quick riches also sent millions abroad. Few succeeded, but many remained as settlers. The California gold rush of 1849 brought people to the American west (to the state where in-migration still continues, though the pull is now the sunny climate and modern industries). In 1851 a quarter of a million people flocked to goldfields in south-east Australia. In a few years Victoria had more people than the whole of Australia up to that time.

International migrations

We can view migrations in terms of push-pull factors. Some move away because they want or have to. Some are attracted by advantages and opportunities (or what they *think* are advantages) elsewhere.

The coming of the industrial age and the steam ships was a great spur to migration. As European populations grew, and their large, crowded cities expanded, their more remote rural areas became poorer. Many looked for better opportunities abroad. Overseas migration by Europeans was at its height between 1840 and 1930. They went mainly to the under-populated temperate parts of the world – North America, Australia, New Zealand, Argentina, Chile, South Africa.

Fig. 10.13 shows migrations to the USA which owed much to the push factor. In the mid-19th century large numbers were escaping the potato famine in overpopulated Ireland (Fig. 10.12). The

P 10.8 The mingling of European and Amerindian cultures. Andean Indians in Ecuador hold their local market in the plaza before the old Spanish cathedral in Latacunga. Potatoes, in the foreground, native to this part of the world, have long been an established crop in European countries.

Great migrations also took place in other parts of the world. **After slavery was abolished, millions of migrant workers were recruited from southern China and India and transported to work on plantations and in mines in south-east Asia.** Their decendants form a large part of the population in both Malaysia and Indonesia. Indians were also recruited for work in East Africa and South Africa — hence the large numbers in Kenya and Natal.

Today many migrate from the LDCs to the more developed countries. The numbers are small compared with their own large population increases; but **they have considerable impact on the host country,** which we will look at later (p. 219). The ease with which they settle in depends a great deal on opportunities for employment in the MDC. When unemployment is low, most can at least start in unskilled jobs; in times of high unemployment the hopes for the new life can turn sour.

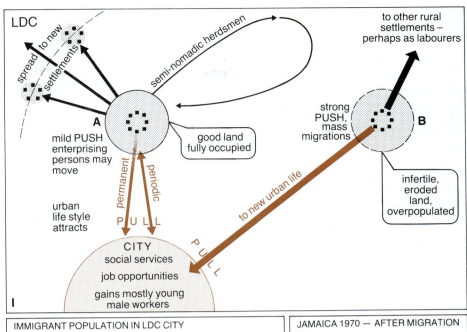

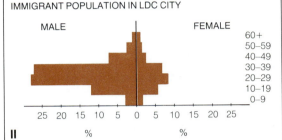

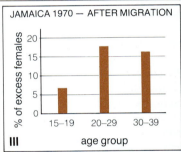

10.14 I shows the push of young male migrants from fertile but over-crowded lands, and the strong pulls attracting them to the city; the migration of whole families from infertile over-populated land; and other migrations in the rural areas. II shows the high proportion of young males among LDC city immigrants. III shows one result of predominantly male migration from Jamaica.

Migration within a country

In the LDCs there is much movement within the countries themselves, from one rural area to another, and from rural villages to towns and cities.

On the face of it, rural people migrate when their growing numbers put pressure on their local resources, and living standards remain low. But, in fact, improvements and innovations in rural communities can also cause migration. When, say, a new cooperative (p. 128) raises local living standards and provides better education, young people become *aware* of advantages elsewhere; so they think of moving. It is usually those with initiative who go; and so their drive is lost to the local community. In some cases new agricultural machinery means that fewer are needed on the land.

The loss of those with initiative can happen in the MDCs. Highly qualified, trained persons, attracted by better op- portunities and higher salaries in foreign countries, create a 'brain drain'.

A population may become unbalanced by migration. In the LDCs it is usu- ally the men who migrate to the cities, or leave the country, in greater numbers than women. Fig. 10.14 shows some of the consequences.

P 10.9 Nairobi, like other capital cities, is an attraction for rural people.

P 10.10 Another face of Nairobi is these slum dwellings, with make-shift shops and houses.

Where people live

What we have been doing is to look at the distribution and general characteristics of whole populations, static, or partly on the move. **What we will now do is to look at the individual people: at social groups, rural and urban, in their own particular settlements.** We can try to understand their particular advantages of living where they do; their problems; what the future holds for them; and how they affect that future by their present actions.

Short-term 'mobility'

People are now generally more mobile. Though they may not emigrate permanently, they regularly travel from place to place (Fig. 10.15). **They affect the economy of both the place they go to and where their home is.** Some, such as tourists (p. 172), move long distances for short periods. School pupils and commuters move short distances for even shorter periods.

Many, particularly within Africa, find employment in a city, perhaps in another country, but support a family at home.

For commuters and temporary migrants alike, the labour they put in, and the money they spend benefit industry and commerce at their work-place. But most of them bring back salaries, or remit money, to the home base.

Sometimes the mobility is part of an occupation, as with semi-nomadic pastoral people, farmers practising transhumance (p. 104), seasonal fruit pickers, fishermen.

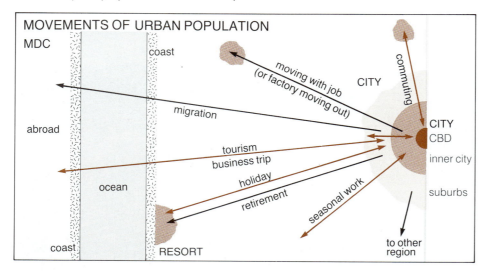

10.15 City-dwellers in a more developed country take part in a range of regular and irregular, permanent and non-permanent migrations.

Theme 10
Back-up section

Statistics and social conditions

Now consider social conditions in various countries in more detail. Those which cause infant deaths, or affect the health of the people, are **reflected in the population statistics**. So these figures are also related to medical facilities, to what people eat (nutrition), and to less obvious things like levels of education and unemployment.

We can present statistics to show the extent to which such things do or do not relate to each other. We may also see that some countries appear out of line – for instance being apparently prosperous but having a high death rate. So we should try to find out why this is.

It is helpful to observe how things change with time. Fig. 10.16 shows graphs drawn to compare figures before and after a 10-year interval. This allows us to spot trends. The cluster of dots *below* the diagonal shows that the death rate has *fallen* in most countries. Why not, we wonder, in the others?

All but two of the countries have a high birth rate, very high in four cases. In these four cases it has actually increased. The clearest decline is shown by industrialised countries (Japan and Italy), and by a newly industrialising country – Brazil. What this does *not* show is the circumstances *within* a country. The poorer tropical coastland north of Brazil's core area (Fig. II.2, p. 101) is noted for rapid *growth* of population.

> Now combine what you can glean from each graph, and make predictions about the size of population in each of these countries.

As industrialisation appears to affect population behaviour, so presumably should the greater wealth produced. A higher GDP per head ought to mean better conditions and fewer infant deaths. We can see if there *are* such direct relationships either by a statistical test (**the Spearman Rank Correlation test**) or by plotting such figures against each other on a graph, those, for instance, in Table 24.

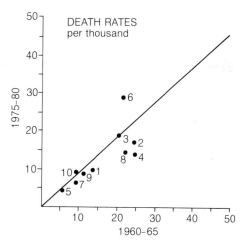

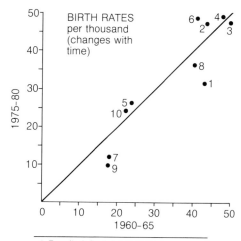

1 Brazil; 2 Bolivia; 3 Sudan .
4 Ghana; 5 Hong Kong; 6 Gambia
7 Japan; 8 Indonesia; 9 Italy
10 Argentina

Table 24.

country	GDP/head ($US) 1988	rank	infant death per '000 born	rank	d	d²
Nepal	160	1	139	1	0	0
Malawi	186	2	130	2	0	0
Nigeria	287	3	114	4	1	1
Kenya	309	4	80	6	2	4
Sri Lanka	423	5	30	9	4	16
Indonesia	473	6	84	5	1	1
Ecuador	691	7	70	7	0	0
Colombia	1280	8	50	8	0	0
Greece	5244	9	12	11	2	4
Oman	5500	10	117	3	7	49
Barbados	5840	11	13	10	1	1
Singapore	10580	12	10	12	0	0

number of countries (N) = 12

					total	76

In the Spearman test we rank the countries, first in order of increasing GDPs per head, and then in order of infant deaths per thousand births (highest to lowest), as in Table 24.

The correlation coefficient R is calculated from the formula:

$$R = 1 - \frac{6\Sigma d^2}{N^3 - N}$$

N is the number of countries, **d** is the difference in ranking. The sum of the squares (Σd^2) in our case is 76.

$$R = 1 - \frac{6 \times 76}{12^3 - 12} = 0.74$$

The coefficient **R** always lies between +1 and −1, so that our figure fits in as shown:

+1	+0.74	0	−1
complete positive correlation		no correlation	complete negative correlation

(A table will show that when **N** = 12 we can be 95% confident that any value of **R above** 0.506 indicates that correlation could not occur by chance.)

What we really do is to make a null hypothesis: 'There is **no** correlation between GDP per head and infant mortality'. Our calculation has shown that there *is* positive correlation, so the null hypothesis is rejected.

10.16 (left) For each country read off the average rate during 1960–65 and see how it had changed by the 1975–80 period. Which had increased and which decreased? Which countries had high rates and which low ones?

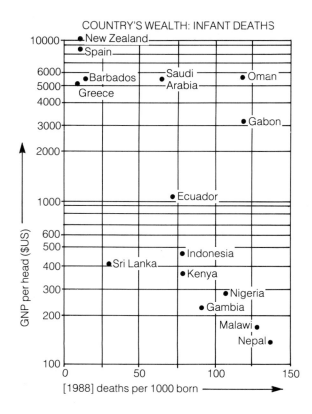

COUNTRY'S WEALTH: INFANT DEATHS

10.17

Theme 10 Making sure

1 What is meant by: mortality rate; age structure; population pressure?

2 A peasant family in an LDC may well see many advantages in having a large number of children. (a) Discuss their points of view in relation to: security; care in old age; life expectancy; infant death rate; lack of agricultural machinery; inheritance of land. (b) What are the main disadvantages?

3 It is natural to aim for improvements in health and general welfare in a less developed country. As more children survive, and more people live longer, what happens to the population? What factors *may* act to prevent a population boom?

4 In 1990 India's population was 830 million and the growth rate 2.0% per annum. On this basis alone, how many extra mouths were there to feed in 1991?

Caution

We should always be aware of the limitations involved in assessing human activities by means of statistics, and of the value of any test. Some GDP figures are not particularly precise. The fact that some of the figures in Table 24 differ only slightly makes our rank order rather a dubious one if we are going to use it in this kind of test.

Now look at the graph in Fig. 10.17, where the GNP per head is plotted on a log scale. It would be reasonable to suppose that the greater number of deaths per thousand born would occur in those with the lowest GNP figures. If this relationship were nearly perfect, the dots would lie close to a line drawn from the cluster of wealthy countries with low mortality figure (top left) to the other extreme (bottom right). In fact, there is a considerable scatter over the graph. This in itself can be useful, for it makes us **look for the reason** for apparently unusual positions.

Which two oil-exporting countries appear to have greater mortality figures than one might expect from their GNP per head? What may be the reason? (See p. 100)

Sri Lanka has a surprisingly low figure for the number of infant deaths. This should lead you to look at its size, communications, colonial history, and recent health precautions. The graph has highlighted it, so try to find out why.

Consider the other countries in turn and see what justifies their positions as plotted.

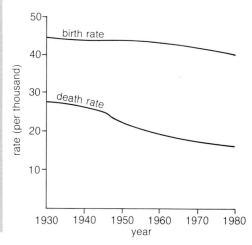

10.18

5 Fig. 10.18 shows causes of natural population changes in an LDC.

(a) Compare the rates of population increase in 1930 and 1980.

(b) How has the pattern changed since 1930?

(c) How will this have affected the population structure?

6 What, in any country, may cause a *sudden* decline in (a) the population, (b) the rate of population increase? Give examples of where and why this has happened.

9 Explain how an exceptionally large age-group will affect social services and employment within a country: (i) during childhood; (ii) as they pass to adult life; (iii) when they are past normal working age.

industrialised, and have a high GDP per head. How might the causes of death relate to these different circumstances?

Table 26

Illiteracy %

age-group:	15–19	35–44	54–64
Indonesia	13	38	60
Sri Lanka	10	13	24
Pakistan	66	76	89
Mozambique	49	84	92
Peru	6	20	33

Hong Kong population

year	population ('000)	increase during year ('000)	death rate (%)	birth rate (%)	natural increase (%)
1979–80	5040	160	0.5	1.7	1.2
1980–81	5150	110	0.5	1.6	1.1
1981–82	5230	80	0.5	1.6	1.1
1982–83	5310	80	0.5	1.5	1.0
1983–84	5380	70	0.5	1.5	1.0
1984–85	5460	80	0.5	1.4	0.9
1985–86	5530	70	0.5	1.4	0.9
1986–87	5610	80	0.5	1.2	0.7

7 Hong Kong's population has increased as shown in Table 25:

(a) What, roughly was the average increase in population each year between 1981 and 1987?

(b) Calculate the gain in population **due to natural increase** in each year.

(c) Compare the population **due to natural increase** during 1979–80 and 1986–87. Which statistics show the reason for the difference?

(d) Suggest why the total increase in population each year is different from that due to natural increase.

(e) In which years were there particularly large increases due to causes other than natural ones? Suggest why.

10 The figures in Table 27 show the differences in the medical attention available in countries at different stages of development, and how long a person might be expected to live at birth.

(a) What relationships can you infer about medical help and life expectancy?

11 Look carefully at the proportion of those in each age-group who can neither read nor write (Table 26).

(a) How do these seem to reflect the state of development within each country?

(b) How do the figures show the progress that has taken place over the years?

(c) Try to find what particular advantages/difficulties each country has in developing standards of education – consider the size of population; whether scattered or concentrated; historical background; advantages of location; economic circumstances.

8 China's annual rate of population increase is 1.2%. The numbers increased as follows: **1950** 550m; **1970** 830m; **1980** 1000m; **1990** 1100m.

80 per cent of the population is rural, 20 per cent urban.

(a) In 1990 how many lived close to the land?

(b) How many lived in towns and cities?

Its **urban population** alone is three/four/five/six times greater than the entire population of the UK (57 million) – which?

Why does China opt for a strict policy of controlling the rate of increase? What would happen otherwise?

Table 27

country (1990)	population (m)	doctors per million	*life expectancy (yr)	
			male	female
Ghana	14	58	52	56
India	860	373	58	58
China*	1134	839	68	71
UK	57	1615	72	78
USA	250	2035	72	79

*China also has para-medical assistants in almost all rural/urban communities

(b) Might not population size (and therefore the ease, or difficulty, of organising things) come into it? Why might doctors and hospitals be more concentrated in some places, rather than spread over the country?

(c) **Commonest causes of death** in India and Ghana are connected with childbirth, infant diseases and infection. Those in the UK and USA are connected with heart disease, cancer and tension. India and Ghana are tropical or subtropical, with large rural populations and low GDPs per head; the UK and USA are in temperate zones, are highly

12 Explain, with examples, how push–pull factors affect migration.

13 In an LDC city, which age groups are likely to be affected by large numbers of immigrants? How will this affect the future structure of the urban population?

Consider the terms used

Mortality refers to the number of deaths (over a particular period, or in a certain area).

The infant mortality rate is the number of deaths of infants under a year old per 1000 live births (in any given year).

Life expectancy is the average number of years to be lived, either from birth or from a particular age. That at birth is usually less than that after the first year, because of infant mortality (risks facing very young children).

Mobility is the ability to move easily from one place to another.

Innovation is the introduction of something new.

Correlation is the relationship two or more things have to one another – the degree of association between them.

An hypothesis is a statement put forward (proposition) as a basis for reasoning. It focuses the attention on what one should establish in order to accept or reject the statement.

Desirability; desirable image. These describe the picture built up in people's minds of a highly attractive place, so that it becomes a powerful factor in migration, a 'pull' factor. Often this is imaginary, as in Dick Whittington's London, with streets paved with gold, or the 'bright lights' attraction of a city for rural people, who find it very different in reality.

People clustered together. Theme 11

P 11.1 A nucleated settlement . . . *an Indian village on the northern plains, amid a patchwork of small fields. Here the hierarchy of regional town, market towns, and small villages is much as described in Figs. 11.2 and 11.3.*

Theme 11 Settlements and their functions

11.1 Why most people live in clusters

Consider again people's basic needs – food, water, clothing, shelter, companionship, security. **A peasant family depending on the land for survival wants** fertile soil; water for drinking, cooking, washing, and for plants and animals; fuel for cooking; and a roof over their heads. They need protection from outsiders – not just a stockade, but help from people around them. If they are clustered about common facilities, a well, stream, a well-drained site, so much the better.

A family living in an inner city in a developed country will certainly not get their necessities *direct* from the land. They will have to pay for facilities provided – piped water, gas, electricity, sewage disposal. They have daily access to food counters, and shops selling clothing and shoes, or to a general multi-functional store. Their security comes through arrangements made by their whole society – the law and policing.

Both these groups, rural and urban, belong to a settlement that occupies a particular place. They and fellow villagers or townsfolk are clustered about a centre, or nucleus, of a village, town, or city – **a nucleated settlement.**

11.2 Choice and location of site

City dwellers looking for somewhere to live have to consider distance from work, schools, shops, etc. In fact their choice may be limited by a housing committee, or estate agent, or their income. Whether they select an apartment or house within or close to the city, and what influences their decision, are part of urban geography (p. 213). But first we will look at how settlements are formed and grow.

Whenever, over the centuries, people have moved into new territory, they have had to decide where to locate their homestead. They weigh up the possible advantages and disadvantages.

Fig. 11.1 shows unoccupied territory in which a group aims to settle. A river winds through a closely wooded landscape, with steep slopes to the north. The lower hills to the east have coarse grasses

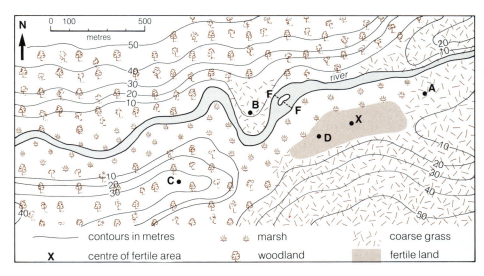

11.1 Where to settle?

on poor, thin soils. The valley is marshy, though there is a well-drained river terrace with deeper, fertile soil on the south bank.

The river is deep and fast-flowing, but fordable at **F**. The forest harbours animals likely to attack livestock, and perhaps people.

Now make a simple mathematical assessment as to which of the four possible sites (A,B,C,D) is the most suitable. First give each of the necessities a weighting (**W**) – a number 1–10 – depending on its importance to the settlers. Consider how regularly they will need to go to and from each resource. Measure the shortest practical distance between site and resources, taking the centre of the fertile land as **X**.

Record these, and for each site and resource multiply the distance (**d**) by the weighting (**W**). **Add together and find the site with the lowest score.**

> Work this out for yourself from Fig. 11.1. Follow reasonably gentle slopes,

and remember that firewood and full waterskins are heavy!

As always, statistical methods may not resolve the whole problem. What else would the settlers bear in mind, apart from distance?

Thinking of defence, would **A** be the best site? What particular strategic advantages have **B** and **C**?

What is the main disadvantage of site **D**? Consider space taken up.

Why in time may wood have to be carried over greater distances?

Put forward any other site which might prove more suitable than those indicated, and argue your case.

This may be just a game, but such considerations must have passed through the minds of countless settlers facing unknown country. There will have been much trial and error, and many disappointments.

Here settlement would be restricted by physical conditions. A settlement pattern

Table 28

site:		A		B		C		D	
resource	W	d_a	$d_a \times W$	d_b	$d_b \times W$	d_c	$d_c \times W$	d_d	$d_d \times W$
fertile land									
water									
wood (fuel)									
wood (timber)									
total		–		–		–		–	

must be influenced by the natural environment. We have only to look at differences between settlements on the dry savannas of northern Nigeria and those in rural north-west France.

Yet there are surprising regularities, especially in the distribution and pattern of settlements on long-established arable farmlands, whether on the plains of northern India or in the English midlands. This is because **economic factors, marketing in particular, play an important part.** So we will consider these strong influences before returning to location and site on p. 203.

11.3 Marketing and patterns of settlement

Regular patterns develop from everyday activities being repeated over and over again. Peasant farmers work the land within a few kilometres of their settlement (village). Over extensive level, fertile land, the villages have tended to become evenly spaced, some six or seven kilometres apart. These small settlements therefore serve roughly the same area about them, the shaded area in Fig. 11.2.

> Why, with settlements forming an evenly-spaced, triangular pattern over the landscape, would the boundaries of village land form these roughly regular hexagons? Why not circular boundaries?

While villagers might exchange excess produce or hand-made goods with people in other villages, **one well-sited settlement, a convenient meeting place, usually becomes their main market, a central place**. For people travelling on foot, or by animal transport, time would limit their journey to about 5 kilometres each way. So another market, some way from the first, would serve another ring of villages.

This is not quite true, for, as you can see in Fig. 11.3, **the villagers would have a choice of markets**. Notice that the village (5) is equidistant from *three* markets (**M,E,D**), and so are the other villages. The broken line encloses the shaded catchment area of the market town **M**.

A market town would expect, therefore, to have a third of the custom of each of the six surrounding villages, plus that of its own people. It would also have **more functions than the villages** – not just

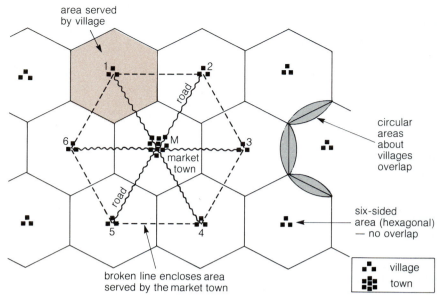

11.2 *Market town* **M** *serves six villages (1–6).*
Each village farms land about it (shaded for village 1). You can see (to the right) what might happen if each tried to farm a circular area, and why a hexagonal boundary pattern tends to develop.

marketing, but inns, shops and stalls, workrooms for saddlers and other craftsmen. People would go there not only to buy and sell, but also for services. **So, obviously, the market town would have a much larger population than a village.**

> If the working population about each village were 450, how many people from surrounding villages might regularly use a particular local town market?

With this triangular village pattern, notice how the number three remains significant as the **market pattern of settlements** develops in the countryside.

> How many villages surround the market town? How many sides form its catchment area? How many roads run to the town from the villages? What is its share of custom from each village area?

Fig. 11.3 shows how, on the same market principle, the towns grow and serve increasingly larger catchment areas.

> If the distance between each village is 7 km, what is that between market towns **A** and **B**? How far apart are the towns **Y** and **Z** (Fig. 11.4)?

Even in western Europe the market functions of the villages and small towns persisted into the 20th century. Their small shops sold mostly **convenience goods – the type people need most days of the week.** Villagers still travelled on foot or by horse-drawn vehicles to the weekly market in a local town, and visited its shops, or perhaps the doctor.

Occasionally they made a longer journey to **a larger town, a central place with a greater variety of functions, and more of them. Its shops sold more expensive, durable comparison goods.** They displayed furniture, or fashion clothes, or household goods not stocked in the smaller settlements. There were bookshops and a library. There were administrative offices, lawyers, accountants and a hospital.

Each of these larger places had a similar catchment area. This gave them a third of the custom of the regularly spaced, smaller towns about them. Thus **M** in Fig. 11.3 has gained in size and importance. Its functions will have increased as improved communications have enabled it to receive part of the custom from **A,B,C,D,E,** and **F**. For it now serves an area about three times that of the smaller towns.

As the hierarchy of villages, small market towns, and larger towns continues to develop, M expands further, as towns **U–Z** come under its influence (Fig. 11.4).

If the market influence is the main one,

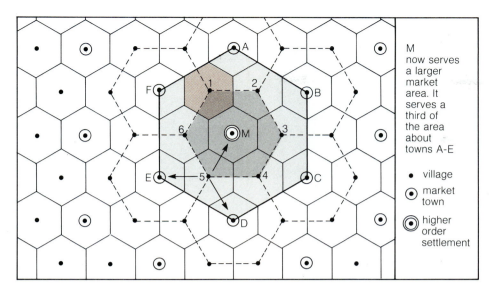

M now serves a larger market area. It serves a third of the area about towns A-E

- • village
- ⊙ market town
- ◉ higher order settlement

11.3 The market town **M** has become a larger central place, with more functions, and serves people in the towns **A–F** (each of which also serves nearby villages).

there is a regular increase in catchment area and spacing (distance apart) from village to city — and the number of functions grows accordingly.

The German geographer Christaller found that in southern Germany market central place settlements corresponding to those in Fig. 11.4 were spaced as follows:

Table 29

market settlements	distance apart (km)	popn. (approx)
villages	7	1000
small towns	12	2000
larger towns	21	4000
next largest	36	10 000

You will find similar spacing between villages and small towns over many parts of lowland Britain. But modern communications allow goods and services to flow more easily, so that by now rural towns have acquired new functions and more people.

Supply and demand

Large places offer more services than the smaller ones; because in order for any function to be present there must be suf-cient **demand**. A shop-keeper, garage owner, or building society branch has to be sure of attracting sufficient customers.

The minimum population needed to support a particular service is called its market threshold. This applies to a pub, shop or large store. The pub may get along by serving several hundred locals and the odd passer-by. Whereas a large chain-store, such as Marks and Spencer, will need a threshold of 50 000 – 100 000 people in its catchment area before setting up a branch.

Some towns will obviously have several shops or offices of the same kind. If a shoe shop has a threshold of 5000 people, then, theoretically, the large town *could* support 4 of them, and the regional town 24 of them! But, in fact, other considerations are involved:

(a) The goods sold by a small shop may also be sold by large stores and supermarkets, which can compete with shops in nearby towns.

(b) There are wholesale depots whose warehouses supply goods direct to super-

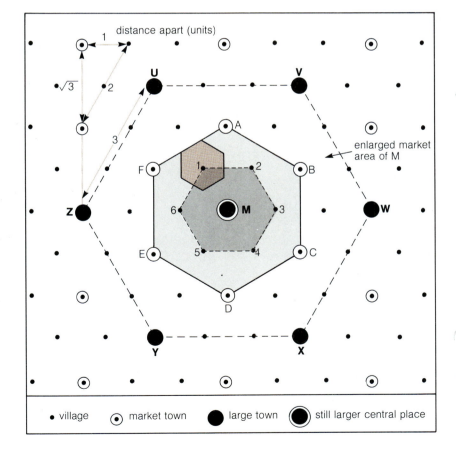

distance apart (units)

enlarged market area of M

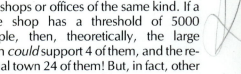
- • village ⊙ market town ● large town ◉ still larger central place

11.4 **M** is now a very large town. Its market area includes customers from towns **U–Z**. The brown lines show the relative distances between different order settlements (1 unit between villages).

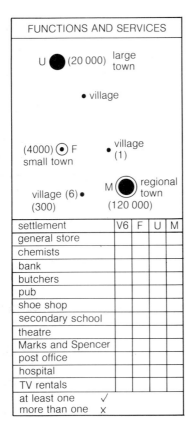

FUNCTIONS AND SERVICES				
U ● (20 000) large town				
● village				
(4000) ◉ F small town	● village (1)			
village (6) ● (300)	M ● regional town (120 000)			
settlement	V6	F	U	M
general store				
chemists				
bank				
butchers				
pub				
shoe shop				
secondary school				
theatre				
Marks and Spencer				
post office				
hospital				
TV rentals				
at least one	✓			
more than one	x			

11.5 Likely functions and services to be found in village (6) and the towns F, U, and M (shown in Fig. 11.4).

markets and village shops alike (if they are accessible). On the other hand, a village may be without a particular function because it is supplied by a mobile shop, or a travelling library, from a nearby town.

(c) Much depends on the lie of the roads, motorways and railways, which may favour particular centres. This makes it difficult in practice to work out a realistic catchment figure for a central place.

Fig. 11.5 is a segment of countryside taken from Fig. 11.4. It shows the number of people likely to be served by each order of settlement. Mark off in the box below it which function should find sufficient custom for its market threshold in a particular settlement.

The effects of market threshold can be demonstrated with the help of a local map and Yellow pages telephone directory. Plot places with over, say, 1000 people in the area covered by the directory. Look up well-known supermarket chains, insurance companies, travel agents, gas or electricity showrooms, etc., in the directory, and record where they are in the area.

P 11.2 The main street in Scone, a small stock-market town in rich farming country in New South Wales. Lines of shops stock convenience and comparison goods, food, medicaments, clothing. The adjoining block has jewellers, a furniture shop, a post office and two banks.

P 11.3 The other side of the main street in Scone, where functions cater for local and through trade . . . vehicle servicing and a motor inn (notice the long-distance truck). Scone has a theatre and golf course. What other functions will it have, not mentioned here?

You can use symbols to indicate where they occur on the map. Or make a table of settlements and functions, showing the number of each chosen function to be found at each place. Note the population of each settlement. This will *not* be a catchment population, but acts as a guide to where there are clusters of would-be customers. (Table 29 on p. 201 shows how different orders of settlements may be distinguished.)

11.4 Variety in settlement patterns

We have been looking at service centres set in a more or less uniform countryside, where the smallest and largest settlements are regularly spaced. We have seen that patterns do evolve because of economic activities. **But many things interrupt this over-simplified pattern of market central places.**

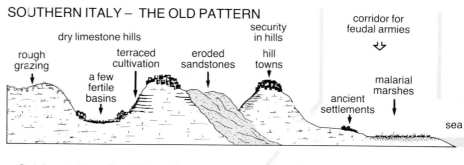

SOUTHERN ITALY – THE OLD PATTERN

● deforested from Greek/Roman times
● sandstones, especially, eroded
● water sinks into bare rock
● storm-water carries particles to coast
● sheep and goats graze scrub vegetation
● hill towns overcrowded – terraced slopes and basins hardly support people

● colonized by Greeks (400BC)
● particles from hill erosion choke seasonal streams
● water seeping from limestones forms swamps
● mosquitoes cause disease
● feudal armies disrupt settlements

SINCE 1950 ● chemical sprays eradicate malaria, swamps drained
● planned cooperative farming with rural industries on coast ● many hill people re-settled ● afforestation projects

11.6 Changes in the landscape and settlements in southern Italy from ancient Greek colonisation to the present-day development projects.

P 11.4 The hill-top town of Massafra in southern Italy, protected by deep gulleys in hard limestone, which produces poor upland soils.

P 11.5 A canal system built to drain the once malarial Sele plain in southern Italy. The tractor powers a pump to supply the irrigation channel.

Location and site

Physical features can make journeys to market long and difficult. They can also concentrate settlement in particularly favourable places. But the whole pattern of settlements is usually due to a *combination* of how people respond to their physical surroundings, and how they set about changing their natural environment.

The changing settlement patterns in southern Italy show this admirably. You can see in Fig. 11.6 that physical, biological, historic, economic and political factors are all involved.

The ancient Greek colonists cleared much of the wooded hills behind their coastal settlements. Slave-run Roman estates took over. Their cattle, sheep and goats grazed fast-eroding, cleared slopes. As a result, sandy particles choked the stream outlets. So the lowlands became swampy and insect-ridden. Malaria was a scourge.

By the Middle Ages disease and armed marauders made the lowlands too hazardous to occupy. People sought the security of hill-top villages. There they had to maintain themselves by farming the poor inland country. Increasing population put great pressure on the soils: so erosion increased.

Since 1950 an organisation for the development of southern Italy has used government funds, international loans and private investments to assist agriculture, forestry, industry, commerce, public works and social welfare in these poverty-stricken lands.

Many hill people migrated to the north, or overseas. But many others have moved back to the coastal lowlands, now drained and made free from malaria. **Fig. 11.7 shows land near the Sele river which has been transformed by drainage, land redistribution, and the building of family farms.** Here. today, local cooperative factories process tomatoes, citrus fruits, sugar beet and tobacco.

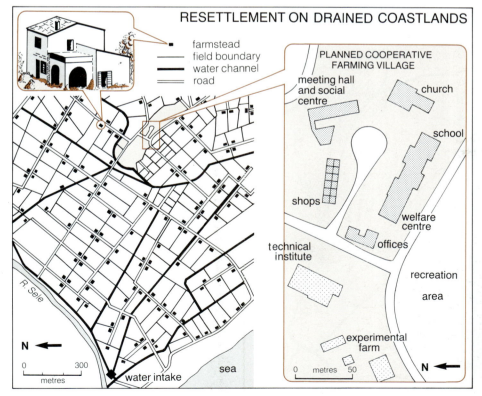

RESETTLEMENT ON DRAINED COASTLANDS

■ farmstead
— field boundary
━ water channel
═ road

PLANNED COOPERATIVE FARMING VILLAGE

meeting hall and social centre

church

school

shops

welfare centre

offices

technical institute

recreation area

experimental farm

R. Sele

N

0   300
metres

water intake   sea

0   metres   50   N

11.7 The lay-out of a coastal re-settlement area in southern Italy, based on cooperative farming.

P 11.6 A prosperous re-settlement farm on the Sele plain in southern Italy. New houses built on once abandoned land.

SMALL CENTRAL PLACES ON THE INDIAN DECCAN

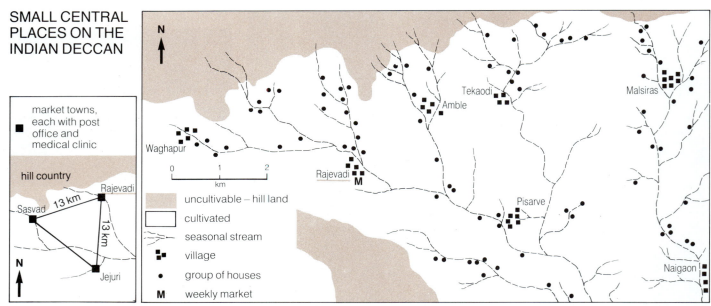

11.8 Central places on India's Deccan plateau serve small farming communities living close to the seasonal water channels.

Elsewhere, local physical conditions strongly influence settlement patterns, if less dramatically. **Fig. 11.8 shows how in central India the distribution of population clusters responds to the stream patterns.** Near the water courses wells can be used all the year round.

Yet market influences established the pattern of the central places long ago. Rajevadi, Jejuri and Sasvad include a weekly market, post office and medical clinic in their functions. The largest, Sasvad, has administrative offices and a local lawcourt. The overall pattern of settlements, as always, is influenced by a combination of physical conditions and people's behaviour.

There are innumerable examples of settlements taking advantage of a hill site, a river bend, or a source of water. In many towns these sites remain as the historic centre. The remains of walls and old buildings are embedded in the later spread of buildings.

A favourable site is important, but **a town must perform particular functions in order to prosper.** In each case the later developments will have depended on the town's ability to support a growing population and perform functions common to most large places.

Some acquire new functions which produce sudden expansion. Fig. 11.9 shows **Oxford**, which has seen two major functions overshadow the others. It began as a small settlement on a patch of gravelly terrace between the Thames and

Cherwell. It was the only place in twenty kilometres with a good ford across the marsh-edged rivers. Long after came the university. For six hundred years or more it could claim to be the biggest 'industry' in the city. You can see the heart of the city in 1500, a few hectares of walled land, but crammed with university functions.

> Consider why a university can claim to be an 'industry'. Consider not only those engaged in education, but college servants, clerks, landladies, printers, stationers, builders, local retailers, etc.

In 1801 Oxford's population was 12 000. A century later, after Britain's great urban expansion, it was only 50 000. But a local entrepreneur (William Morris) shifted from making bicycles to cars. He moved his works from the city centre to the village suburb of Cowley. **During the 1920s and '30s huge new estates for car worker's families developed beyond the Victorian buildings about the old city. Radiator works and various vehicle subsidiaries were set up in other parts of the city. Oxford had added a whole new cluster of functions to its traditional ones.

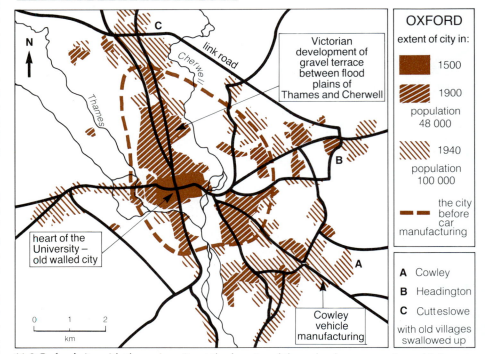

11.9 Oxford city with the university at the heart and the suburban expansion which followed the development of vehicle manufacturing.

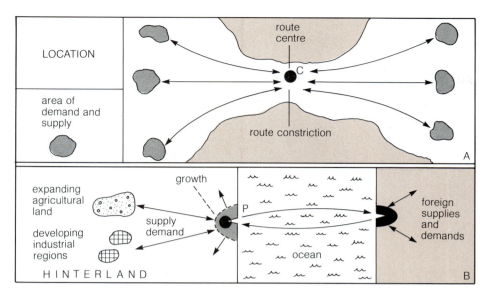

11.10 The growth of a well-sited port **P** suitably located between a flourishing hinterland and busy trade routes. **C** benefits from the concentration of communications.

The university function influences modern industries, however. Cambridge has already become a centre of **new high-technological industries, combined with its scientic research.** Now a high-technology park (p. 181) is developing at Oxford.

Advantages of location and site may be there to start with, but growth is often due to many other factors.

Locational advantage can work in other ways. **Many towns have flourished by being located** *between* **other powerful centres of demand and supply** (Fig. 11.10A). Sea ports and inland centres of

communication become **bulk-break points,** where goods and passengers are transferred. If their site is also suitable for urban expansion, they are likely to prosper.

Fig. 11.10B shows such a port. In early stages, **P**'s prosperity obviously increases as its hinterland is developed.

> Find how this applies to the establishment and later growth of New York, Sydney and Mombasa.

Some major cities owe their whole growth and development to their location

where routes converge: sea routes in the case of Singapore (Fig. 11.11), or land routes in the cases of Chicago and Winnipeg (Fig. 11.12).

If these places are to continue to grow, their site must allow for: (1) room for its main functions to expand, and for those it will acquire; (2) the development of efficient inland communications; (3) adjustments to modern techniques (roll-on/roll-off, containerisation, etc.).

Fig. 11.13**A** shows some of these requirements, and how in time the site itself may have disadvantages (as the city spreads). So though the location in terms of trade routes may still be good, a new or additional site may be required, as in the case of Tilbury (Fig. 11.13**B**).

You will be able to find endless examples of places, large and small, which have developed at road or railway junctions, or the head of navigation. This advantage increases with the number of passengers and goods interchanged there.

The pattern of market settlements can be disrupted by the growth of specialist settlements. There are mining settlements, manufacturing towns, resorts, ports, and others. These have grown and expanded because of a particular advantage.

Settlements grow as people cluster about particular things they can use. In the Yorkshire Pennines small textile industries along the streams used the local wool, soft water and water-power. Then

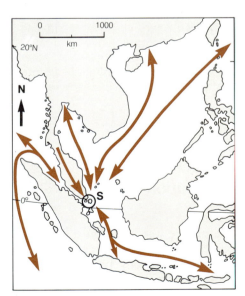

11.11 Trade routes focus on the island city of Singapore (**S**), located close to the Malacca Strait, linking the Indian and Pacific Oceans.

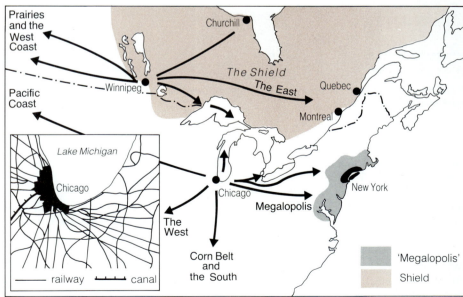

11.12 Routes focus on the cities of Winnipeg and Chicago. Notice the density of railway lines about Chicago (inset) and its canal link with the upper Mississippi.

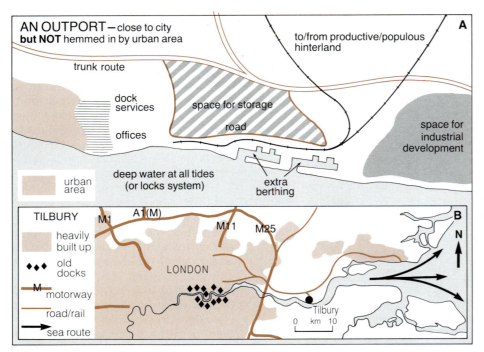

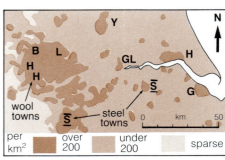

11.14 Population concentrated in an industrial conurbation, in rural central places, and in major ports.

11.13 (A) An outport beyond the main city, with an uncluttered site linked to major communications and accessible to large ships. (B) Tilbury, an outport for London: notice the road routes.

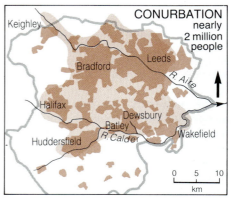

11.15 Towns located by early manufacturing requirements–resources and energy–merged to form a continuous conurbation.

P 11.7 Singapore's high commercial buildings rise beyond a container terminal . . . a small part of its extensive docks.

Specialist towns may owe their growth to a particular economic activity; but they have functions in common with other large places. Many industrial towns have less than half their population employed in manufacturing. Give examples of other occupations which will employ considerable numbers in these towns.

energy from nearby coal deposits powered the numerous factories, which now imported wool. They attracted many thousands of employees (and those who served them in shops and offices). The towns rapidly expanded, to form almost continuous urban areas.

Fig. 11.14 points to the contrasts between the concentrations of population among the groups of woollen towns and steel towns and the rural areas. Notice York (**Y**) as a central place in an agricultural lowland; also the growth about the ports.

Name the textile towns in the main conurbation, the steel towns (**S**), and the ports **H**, **G**, and **GL**.

Fig.. 11.15 shows in more detail how the woollen towns have merged to form a conurbation of almost two million people. There are, however, many other functions associated with these towns, especially since the decline of the textile industries.

11.5 Settlement size, character, and distribution

Industrial conurbations, great ports, and other specialist towns and cities obviously upset the order of central places, from market village to city. **Fig. 11.16 emphasises that specialist settlements stand apart from such central places** which form clusters of roughly the same size and population, and whose functions increase regularly with size.

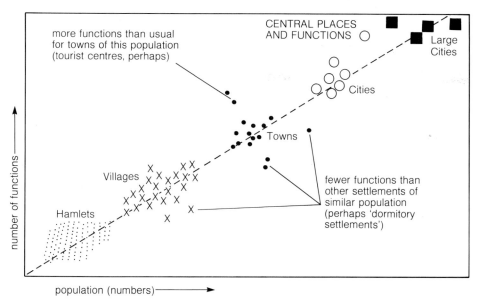

11.16 Central place settlements grouped according to the number of functions and services they offer.

Explain why, in theory, settlements performing marketing functions *should* be grouped in such clusters on one graph.

The diagram shows that some villages close to towns may have more people but fewer functions than one might expect. Consider why commuters might not look for goods and services in the village itself.

It also shows that a town of historic interest, or a resort, may appear out of place on a graph like this. Explain why.

Many large cities have more functions than the plot would suggest. Also a single population figure may disguise mini-conurbations, or towns such as ports, which acquire a great many functions peculiar to themselves.

When the settlements in a country are plotted in terms of population-size and ranking, the population of the second largest city should, in theory, be one half that of the first, the third city population a third that of the first and so on.

If the statistics are plotted on a log-log scale, this rank-size rule will produce a straight line, at 45° to the horizontal (Fig. 11.17a). Countries with a long history of urbanisation, such as Great Britain, tend to have this kind of rank-size settlement distribution.

Rank-size plotting is useful in indicating how a country's development and social conditions affect the size of the settlements. Thus the tendency for people in the LDCs to migrate to already large cities

is partly responsible for what you see in Fig. 11.17(c) and (d).

Notice that in **Nigeria** the city-port, Lagos, is by far the largest settlement. After the second city, Ibadan, there are many sizeable, growing regional towns; but they do not attract population from all over Nigeria as Lagos does.

This kind of city, which dominates others, and continues to attract investment, commerce, industry and population, is known as a primate city.

In Australia, as you can see, after the larger city-ports and the federal capital, there are few places with more than 50 000 people. Most of the towns are scattered central places with some 10 000 to 30 000 people.

11.17 (**a**) shows the actual rank–size relationship; (**b**) the population size of numerous long-established towns in a developed country; (**c**) an LDC where a few large commercial cities – Lagos for example (**d**) – grow rapidly compared with other settlements; (**e**) the dominance of Australia's city-ports.

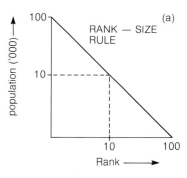

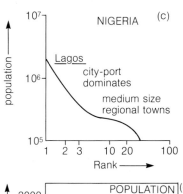

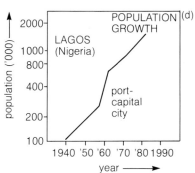

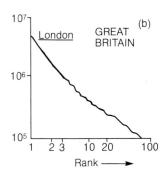

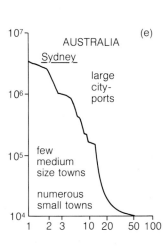

Introducing urban environments

Urbanisation took place rapidly in Western Europe and North America during the late 19th and early 20th century. It is now occurring in the less developed countries, though in a somewhat different way.

Urban geography is not just about the situation and size of towns and cities, however. It is concerned with their structure and how and where people live within them. As more than two-thirds of the people in the MDCs are urban dwellers, and about a quarter of those in the LDCs, we will treat this as a separate theme.

Theme 11
Back-up section

The sphere of influence and tributary area

Local studies should be concerned not only with location and site, but also with the sphere of influence of a settlement.

A town has a great effect on people living in the area about it. They use it for employment, schooling, shopping, recreation and other services; and also for information from its newspapers, or perhaps local radio.

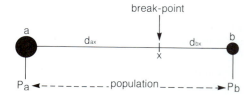

*11.18 The relative attractions of two settlements of different size (**a** and **b**).*

How far does its influence extend? We can regard it, again, as in competition with other settlements. A simple calculation indicates where one town's influence

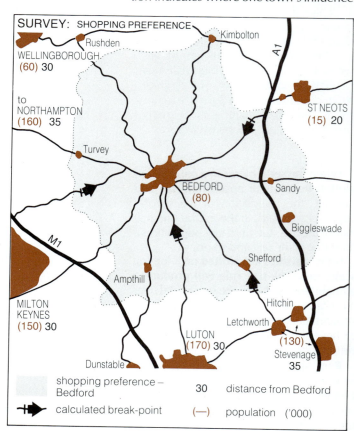

11.19 The results of a survey of preferences for places to shop, with breakpoints calculated from urban populations.

takes over from another's, based on their populations and distance apart.

In Fig. 11.18 the distance between town **a** (population P_a) and town **b** (population P_b) is d_{ab}. The distance from town **b** to the **break-point x** between them is:

$$d_{bx} = \frac{d_{ab}}{1 + \sqrt{\dfrac{P_a}{P_b}}}$$

If P_a is 80 000 and P_b 20 000 and they are 12 km apart, then

$$d_{bx} = \frac{12}{1 + \sqrt{\dfrac{80\ 000}{20\ 000}}} = 4km$$

By determining breakpoints between the influences of a town and comparable settlements nearby, a tributary area may be drawn about it.

What this really compares is whether people would go to one place or the other for a particular service. But size alone may not determine this. One place may have a particular speciality, or be a more pleasant place to go to. More detailed surveys are required.

It should be possible to draw a line which separates towns which offer the same range of goods or services, simply on the basis of shopping preference. **Fig. 11.19 shows the result of a preference survey, and also some calculated breakpoints between Bedford and towns about it.**

> Calculate where the breakpoint should be on the roads to Northampton and Wellingborough.
>
> Would the use of time rather than distance be a more suitable basis for calculation?

It is useful but time-consuming to sample the preferences of people for a particular town. We try to find who regularly come to it to obtain goods or services, or to whom deliveries are made.

Another useful indication of a town's tributary area, however, is that covered by its local newspaper. This might be found from a combination of local enquiries – from wholesale distributors, newsagents, or the newspaper itself – or from a survey of shoppers. One way is to jot down all places in the surrounding area mentioned in the paper's births, deaths, and marriages columns, advertisements, or in letters from readers.

Locate all these places on a map and draw a line from each of them to the town centre. This is relatively easy, and makes an immediate visual impact (Fig. 11.20). A similar survey in a neighbouring town may show an overlap.

This method may be used to compare spheres of influence of central places in other respects. By visiting settlements over a wide area and asking 'where did you obtain your....?', **desire lines** can be drawn from each survey point to the town involved – for, say, groceries or shoes, or services by dry cleaners.

Spheres of influence strictly depend on what you are considering. If it is notoriety, it may be extended to places visited by the local football team! If it's information, then this is extended over a wide area by a local radio station.

Table 30 shows how information from a local telephone directory may be used to compare towns as central places and to relate functions to higher and lower order places.

Some of these functions, found only in larger, more important places, can be seen as high-order functions. We can indicate this by giving them a **centrality value, C = 100 ÷ n**, where **n** is the number of places where they occur.

By adding all the centrality values for each place, we can give it a **centrality index**, as shown. You can see that the towns can thus be grouped in order as central places.

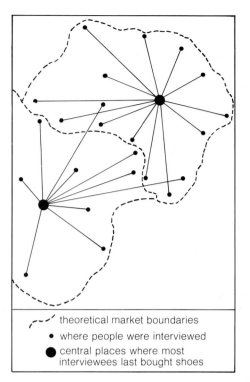

- - - theoretical market boundaries
• where people were interviewed
● central places where most interviewees last bought shoes

11.20 Desire lines.

While this is a useful indication, it may be misleading in a few respects. For instance, although Milton Keynes ranks lower on account of the absence of British Home Stores, it has other large stores with much the same functions.

Table 30

place	British Home Stores	British School of Motoring	British Red Cross Soc.	Marks and Spencer	W H Smith	Currys Domestic Elec.	Halifax Building Soc.	Woolworth	Boots Chemists	British Gas Showroom	Total Functions	Centrality Index
Bedford	1	1	1	1	1	1	1	1	1	1	10	201
Luton	1	1	1	1	1	1	1	1	1	1	10	201
Milton Keynes		1	1	1	1	1	1	1	1	1	9	151
Dunstable			1	1	1	1	1	1	1	1	7	93
Huntingdon		1			1	1	1	1	1	1	7	93
Letchworth					1	1	1	1	1	1	6	68
Leighton Buzzard					1		1	1	1	1	5	55
Hitchin						1	1	1	1	1	5	54
Wellingborough						1	1	1	1	1	5	54
Newport Pagnell								1	1	1	3	30
total places (n)	2	3	4	4	7	8	9	10	10	10	—	—
Centrality (100 ÷ n)	50.0	33.3	25.0	25.0	14.3	12.5	11.1	10.0	10.0	10.0	—	—

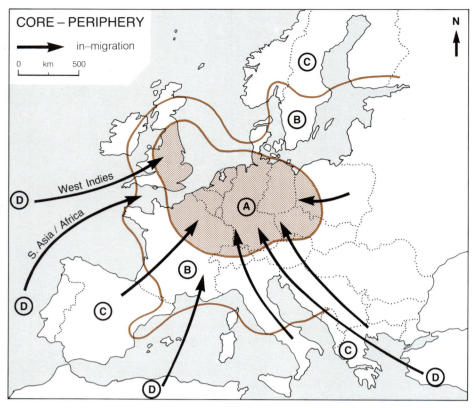

11.21 Migrations into western Europe's industrial core (**A**).

Theme 11 Making sure

1 The area on which a settlement is built is its: (a) location; (b) position; (c) source; (d) site; (e) zone; which?

2 The smallest number of people needed to support a service is its: (a) catchment; (b) threshold; (c) tributary; (d) breakpoint; (e) potential; which?

3 Which are bought more frequently – comparison goods or convenience goods? Which will need the higher threshold in order to be stocked? Explain.

4 The extensive urban area formed by towns expanding and joining up is: (a) a conglomeration; (b) an urbanisation; (c) a conurbation; (d) a collective; (e) a central place; which?

5 What functions may a town perform besides providing goods and services?

6 People have found it advantageous to live in a compact, nucleated settlement for a number of reasons. Explain, with examples from different forms of settlement.

7 Fig. 11.22 shows the Roman road to York, following the Lincoln Heights at some 40–60 metres above the eastern lowlands. Lines of villages to the east and west are linked by minor roads, following ancient tracks. Look carefully at the map and its key.

(a) Which are the spring-line villages to the east or west?

(b) Which lie about old wells near dip-slope streams?

(c) Suggest why the western villages are closer to Ermine Street than those to the east.

(d) Each village lies in a long east–west parish. In each parish people found dry sheep pastures; well-drained soils for cultivation; heavier, wetter soils for cattle. Explain why.

(e) Why did the Roman road, and modern main road, *not* follow the more ancient tracks?

Urban regions

We have seen where towns and cities expand until their urban areas form a large conurbation. **Fig. 12.27, p. 234, shows where some 50 million people form a megalopolis in eastern USA,** stretching from Boston to Washington though interspersed with rural countryside.

Western Europe has a large urban-industrial core, which includes the early industrial regions based on coal energy, in the UK, northern France, Belgium and West Germany. Within this are the great city-ports of London, Antwerp, Rotterdam, Amsterdam, Bremen and Hamburg.

The distribution of the urban population is mainly related to the degree of industrialisation. In Fig. 11.21 (**A**) is a densely populated industrial core; (**C**) the more sparsely populated outer areas (**periphery**); and (**B**) a zone where urban development intermingles with forms of intensive agriculture.

(**A**) is a 'pull' region, while from (**C**) people with less economic opportunity have been 'pushed' towards the industrial core, especially in the period 1950–70.

Strictly, there is an **outer zone** (**D**) – the countries from which immigrants have

arrived. Many have come from former European colonies to take, at first, low-status jobs in services and industry. Their part in urban society is discussed in Theme 12.

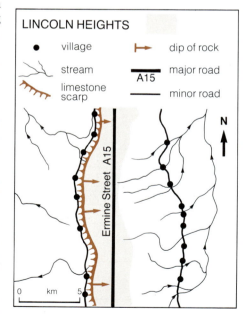

11.22 Villages located in relation to the scarp face and dip-slope of limestones which form the Lincoln Heights.

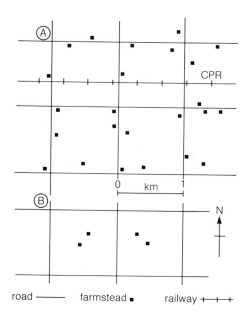

11.23 (A) Settlement pattern in Manitoba. (B) A suitable alternative location for farmsteads?

8 Fig. 11.23A shows settlement in an area of intensive farming (cattle and hogs) close to the Canadian Pacific Railway in Manitoba.

(a) Account for the pattern of the roads and the positions of the farms.

(b) What advantages does this position give farmers compared with those of the farms in **B**? Consider access, farming activities and costs, water and power services.

9 Fig. 11.24 shows the distribution of settlements about Aberdeen in South Dakota, USA. Look carefully at the communications.

(a) How do settlements relate to the roads and railways?

(b) What shows the influence of railways on early settlement?

(c) A survey has related the number of functions in central places in this part of the state to the order of settlements (Table 31):

(i) Why are there gaps in the population figures of these groups?

(ii) Which of these places is likely to have at least one – street corner store; real estate office; barber's shop; vehicle showroom; dentist?

(iii) Why are the settlements more dispersed than those in Table 29, which also have market central place relationships?

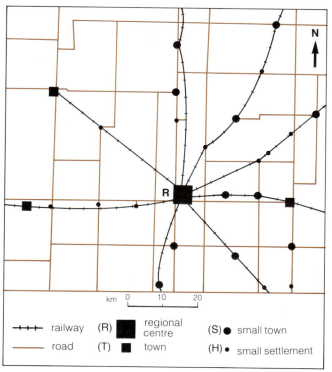

11.24 Central places near Aberdeen (R), South Dakota. See Table 31.

Table 31
central places

	population	functions
R	20 000	105
T	1000–4000	40–75
S	200–1000	10–40
H	under 200	1–10

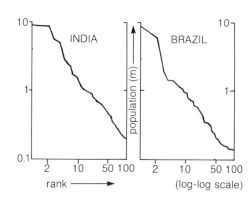

11.25 Rank-size plots, showing urban populations in millions.

10 What is meant by a 'primate city'? Give an example, and say why it differs from the other cities.

11 (a) Look at the plots in Fig. 11.25. Describe the numbers and sizes of the cities of over 100 000 people in India and Brazil.

(b) Which conforms more nearly to the rank-size rule? Suggest why.

(c) What are the main differences between the two?

12 'The status of an urban centre depends less on its size than on the number, range and order of the services it provides.' What exactly is meant by this? Find two places of the same size which are markedly different from the point of view of providing services.

13 Suggest why the coming of the family car has affected the clear distinction between town and countryside in the more developed countries.

Consider the terms used

A nucleus is a central part around which other things are grouped, or around which things develop.

A nucleated settlement is closely clustered, usually about a specific central feature – a well, crossroads, square, etc.

A regular hexagon is a six-sided figure with equal angles and sides of equal length.

A central place denotes a settlement from which goods and services are provided for the surrounding area.

A hierarchy is a ranking in a logical order. Thus a low order central place provides low order services for a limited area, and a higher order central place provides higher order services for a larger market area.

A catchment is an area from which a market settlement collects its customers – as a river collects its waters from its catchment area.

A threshold is the minimum level of population required to make it worthwhile establishing a particular function, or stocking particular goods.

Convenience goods, such as basic foodstuffs, have a low threshold. Those you are prepared to shop around for and compare for price and quality, known as **comparison goods**, require a higher threshold population.

The function of a thing is the way it works. The proper activity of something can be seen as its function: a shop sells goods, a shoe-shop provides shoes, a travel agent a service for travellers, a law-court justice, a school education. The number of functions within a settlement is closely related to its size.

A conurbation is an extensive urban area formed by the expansion and running-together of neighbouring towns and cities. Some conurbations are defined and described, as, for instance, the West Midland conurbation.

A primate city is the largest in a country or region. According to the rank-size rule, it should be twice the size of the second largest city, though it is often much larger than that. Being the largest, it tends to have special functions which cause it to increase at a greater rate than the rest.

The location of a place is its position relative to other things – the rest of the country, or an estuary, or between hills. It can be located by lines of latitude and longitude. This is not quite the same as its **site**, which is a specific area on which a building or settlement stands. It may be sited there, for instance, because that area has a well, or fertile land, or a defensive position.

Centrality is the degree to which a town serves its surrounding area. One of several indices used to measure centrality is shown on p. 209.

A preference survey is one which asks and records whether people prefer one thing rather than another.

A desire line is a straight line between a point of origin of a journey and another particular place. It shows the direct route people would prefer to take to their chosen market, for example. Desire lines mapped together can thus indicate preferences, and focus on particular points.

Theme 12   The towns and cities

12.1   More cities – bigger cities

In Fig. 12.1 you can see large cities, each of which in the mid 1980s had more than a million inhabitants. Many more were on the brink of becoming **million cities**. And, of course, in many other places hundreds of thousands of people are crowded together in an urban environment.

You can see those which have been growing exceptionally quickly. Which group of countries, the MDCs or LDCs, do most of these belong to? How many of those in the LDCs are tropical or sub-tropical? (See II.1 on p. 100.)

Urbanisation means an increasing proportion of people living in urban areas. The growth of urban population is caused by people moving from rural areas to towns and cities; and also by population increase *within* the cities themselves.

The rate at which this as been taking place is illustrated in Figs. 12.1 and 12.2. **By the year 2000 at least half the world's population will be living in towns and cities**.

Modern industrial urbanisation began in the last century. What was the period when urbanisation really took off? Look at Fig. 12.2. and suggest where most of the urban growth (and problems) are likely to be in the future.

The growing number of city-dwellers is much greater in the LDCs than in the MDCs. Their towns are growing more rapidly than the villages, the cities more quickly than the towns. Even their fifteen super-cities, with over 5 million people each, are expanding rapidly. Two, Mexico City and São Paulo, will each have more than 20 million people by the turn of the century. In Egypt urban growth has already covered the equivalent of all the land gained by building the Aswan

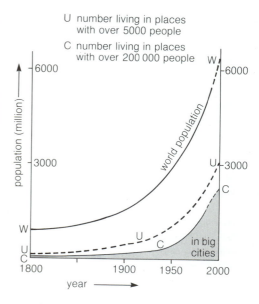

U number living in places with over 5000 people

C number living in places with over 200 000 people

*12.2 The world's population is growing alarmingly (**W**); and more and more live in huge urban clusters (**C**).*

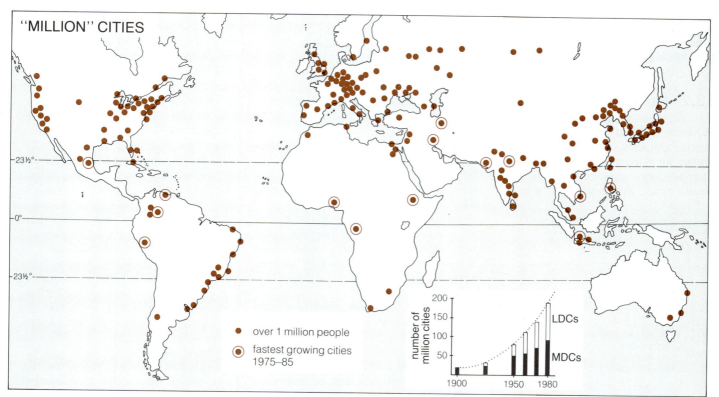

"MILLION" CITIES

● over 1 million people

◎ fastest growing cities 1975–85

12.1 Cities with a population of over a million in 1985 (some with over ten million). In the LDCs the number of million cities, and the population of already large cities, are increasing rapidly (inset).

dam. By contrast, the eleven super-cities in the MDCs are growing more slowly, or declining in population.

It is important to realise that urbanisation means a change in the way of life for rural people moving into the cities. Their values, attitudes, and the ways they behave are bound to alter. What happens to them depends not only on who they are and what *they* can offer, but on the city itself, and whether *it* is prospering or not. The people's problems usually reflect those of the city, and what it can, or cannot, offer them.

Urbanisation and its problems are different for people in the LDCs than they were when Europeans first began to abandon the countryside and live together in the mass-manufacturing areas. In western Europe their migrations left many outlying rural areas (the periphery, p. 210) depopulated and run down. City life was often squalid; but it offered employment in manufacturing and services.

In most LDCs the rural population is still increasing, despite migration to the cities; while the cities cannot offer sufficient industrial employment.

To begin with, we will look at the cities of the MDCs, where industrialisation first accelerated. By 1900 over half the people in Great Britain had become urban dwellers. **In most western European countries over three-quarters of their populations now live in towns.**

12.2 The city as a system

We have seen that large cities have a variety of functions. As the functions increase, there are more jobs (Fig. 12.3). So there are more wage-earners demanding goods; which favours industrial growth.

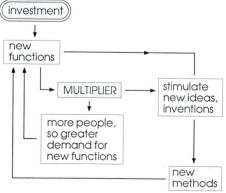

12.3 *When investment in new functions and new methods stimulates growth and creates new demands.*

Should functions decline, unemployment increases. The city ceases to attract, or even hold its population. Though people with exceptional needs, such as homeless immigrants, may continue to move in.

The functions in a city tend to be separated. There are business districts, shopping centres, industrial areas, poor and rich residential neighbourhoods, and so on.

As particular functions prosper, or otherwise, so do certain parts of the city. A city does not stand still. Its functions and opportunities for employment are always changing, one way or another. When in decline, unfortunately, it is the poorer citizens who experience the greatest problems. As we look at the character of different parts of a town or city, you may understand why this is.

12.3 The structure of a city

Pre-industrial development

Many pre-industrial towns lay about a central market place. There was a High Street nearby. In the adjoining roads were shops, craft industries and small businesses. Working people lived close about this inner area. But the more wealthy, with their own transport, occupied larger houses in more spacious districts away from the centre.

With industries and commerce the town expands

As the industrial age proceeded, the value of a central site increased. Here offices, banks and larger shops benefited by clustering together to form a **central business district** (CBD).

Manufacturing industry began to develop beyond the inner housing, often near a railway, with newer working class housing nearby. The wealthier citizens formed neighbourhoods even further out, so extending the suburbs.

The zones have continued to expand outwards. Many people (**commuters**) now move to work by car, bus or train from outer suburbs or villages close by.

In the 1920s E. W. Burgess proposed a model of urban structure for American cities. Its **rings of land-use** (Fig. 12.4A) could also be seen in many towns and cities in Europe. However, the towns and cities are more complex than this. Particu-

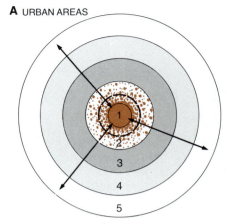

A URBAN AREAS

1   CBD（T–zone of transition)
2   factory zone
3   working men's homes
4   outer residential
4A outer residential (wealthy)
5   commuter route

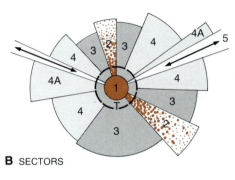

B SECTORS

12.4 **(A)** *The development of zones with different functions, and, more realistically,* **(B)** *outward-growing sectors. In each a transition zone* **(T)** *lies about the CBD.*

lar functions cluster in certain districts – light industries, parks, recreation areas, etc. So a model combining both rings and clusters seems more appropriate.

H. Hoyt's model (1939) shows how sectors develop along routeways (Fig. 12.4B). As industries continue outwards along railways or main roads, working-class districts follow suit. The richer neighbourhoods also extend outwards along the more favoured stretches.

The CBD retains its importance. It expands as some of the older housing about it is replaced, or converted to business premises. People with low incomes occupy some of the older inner property, where larger buildings are converted into lodging houses.

Notice how Bedford's expansion (Fig. 12.5) shows this sector development. You can see that it continues out in one direction as suburban residential areas, with shopping centres, and outer industrial estates (p. 163).

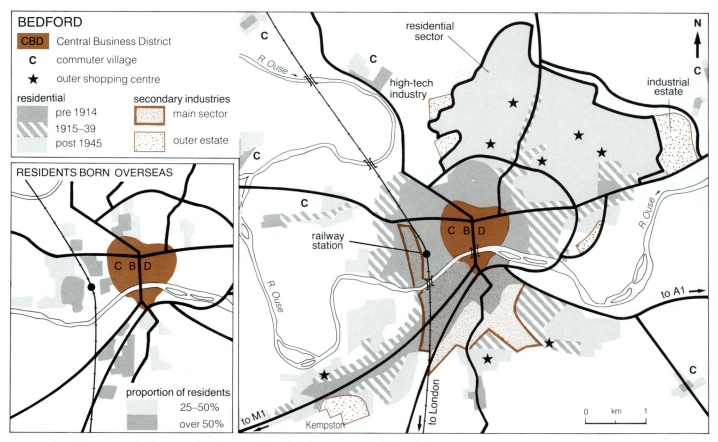

BEDFORD
CBD Central Business District
C   commuter village
★   outer shopping centre

residential
     pre 1914
     1915–39
     post 1945

secondary industries
     main sector
     outer estate

RESIDENTS BORN OVERSEAS

proportion of residents
     25–50%
     over 50%

12.5 Bedford shows marked sector development. Notice the new outer industrial estates. The recently developed CBD (photo 12.5) is fringed by a transition zone. The town has received a large number of immigrants from overseas.

In Fig. 12.5 notice the location of the railway station and the ancient bridge/ford site across the river Ouse.

(a) Comment on the extent of the pre-1914 town and its shape.

(b) Did functions occupy distinct sectors at this time?

(c) What is likely to have influenced the location of the main industrial sector and its continued expansion?

P 12.2 In the foreground the Punjab Continental Stores and Vitello D'Oro, butcher, tell of the large Asian and Italian communities in Bedford. What age is the housing? Where might this be within the town (Fig. 12.5)?

(d) What kind of industries have developed there in recent times? Suggest reasons for their location.

(e) Where would you expect the following to be located: the market square; the High Street; the main bus station; Marks and Spencer?

(f) Bedford has a large immigrant population, concentrated by the early 1970s in the areas shown. What type of housing did most of these foreign-born peoples move into? Notice where they live in relation to the town as a whole. Suggest reasons for this.

P 12.1 Part of the high-rise flats (T in Photo 12.5) with small terraced houses (served by the milkman delivering at the door) about to be demolished. Consider the social advantages/disadvantages of such changes.

Land values affect the zoning

The more desirable sites will be the most valuable. Bid-rents are based on land values; that is, people will bid more for sites with particular advantages

The bid-rents for the CBD are high. For here commercial offices, banks and government functions benefit from being close to one another. Central shopping areas, where large stores offer a wide

P 12.3 The transition zone: substantial family houses near the centre of Bedford converted for insurance offices and banks.

P 12.4 *The white line encloses Bedford's centre in 1960. Its businesses focus, as through the ages, on the market square **M**, near the church to the north of the bridge **B**, and in its high street **H-H**.*

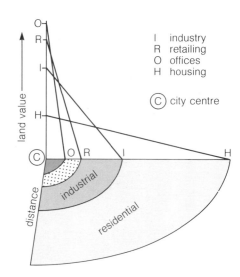

I   industry
R   retailing
O   offices
H   housing

Ⓒ   city centre

12.6 The relationships between high land values and zones of urban land-use.

choice of consumer goods, maintain their advantage of 'centrality' with the help of railway stations, bus depots, and multi-storey car parks.

> Bid-rents will also be high for favourable residential areas. But why should a high land rent make for high-density housing?
> Why do wealthier neighbourhoods, with large single houses in their own grounds, occupy districts further out? Consider land values.

Fig. 12.6 shows simple bid-rent relationships which help to create zones of urban land-use.

The influence of land values is strong. But other influences make for distinctive districts. There are concentrations of certain functions (**nuclei**) in certain parts of a city.

Things which disrupt the zones and sectors

1 **Industries occupy particular sites** where they can carry on their activities most efficiently and competitively.

2 **Governments control industrial location**. They can prevent manufacturing in some places, or favour industrial estates in others.

3 **New routes and ring roads** can improve accessibility to a district, and so attract industries and businesses.

4 **People's social class** and what they can afford affect their choice of where to live. Working people live in a mixture of owner-occupier and local authority housing (or rent accommodation privately). Cars and public transport enable people to live a long way out; but **different income groups tend to occupy different**

*P 12.5 Notice how by 1980 the white line encloses a very different CBD. Look at Photo 12.4. The old terraced houses west of the high street have been replaced by shopping complexes and a bus station. There are two multi-storey car parks (**P**), and tower blocks (**T**) have replaced other small houses (Photo 12.1). Further out are new high-tech industries (**E**) and trading estates. The CBD has also extended south of the river Ouse (bottom left).*

parts of the suburbs. The really poor have less prospects of leaving cheap inner-city accommodation.

5 **Many cities have districts with strong ethnic minorities**, particularly in the inner zone. (We will look at these and other social-political problems after considering the general characteristics of the various parts of the city.)

6 **The larger the city, the more recreational and sporting/cultural functions** — parks, playing fields, sports centres, concert halls, etc.

7 In all settlements the **terrain** itself may interrupt the spread of any functions.

It has been pointed out that the **density of population** declines with distance from the city centre, as in Fig. 12.7 **I**; though **II** shows that the density curve is more likely to have peaks and troughs.

(a) Say what you consider produces the central dip.

(b) Account for some of the other peaks and troughs (in the light of 1–7 above). Consider industrial nuclei; suburban parks; sites near major road junctions; and places once on the fringe but engulfed by further spread.

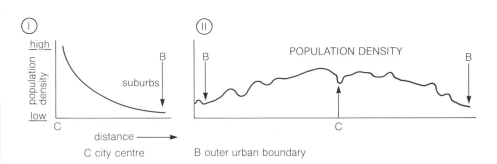

*12.7 Changes in population density with distance from the city centre (**C**).*

P 12.6 The clustering of large retail stores in the town centre, with people passing from one to the other.

12.4   The city centre

The functions of the city centre include: 1 retailing; 2 commercial, financial, and administrative functions (offices); 3 leisure facilities and tourist amenities; 4 hotel services and some expensive residences. And other activities are generated there because of these functions.

1 **The shops** cater for people in the city and from its catchment area. The type of shop will depend on the size of this market (remember the importance of **market threshold**).

People want to shop around and compare goods for quality and cheapness. So **there are clusters of stores selling similar goods** – groups of shoe shops or clothing shops, offering differing styles of what we call **comparison goods**. Special shops – jewellers, bookshops, and travel agents – are usually fairly close together in the city centre.

Chain stores offer a wide variety of commodities, consumer goods and durables, clothing, toiletries and medical goods, books, furniture, electrical appliances, and foods, but also cluster, so that people may wander from one to the other.

Some of the larger stores operate on many floors of a high-rise building. Others have street-level premises in multi-storey buildings, with offices and other functions at higher levels.

They occupy major thoroughfares, or squares, with ready access from underground stations (tube/metro), bus stations, and central car parks. Today some central roads may be for pedest-

rians only, or have restricted traffic. In many places parts of the central area have been re-built as **shopping complexes**. The old streets are often replanned to allow rear-delivery to stores; otherwise, delivery times are a problem for large retailers.

2 **Offices** range from those of local firms to branch-offices of national or international companies. Wherever finance is concerned there is office space for insur-

P 12.7 Eaton Centre, a vast shopping complex in central Toronto, has a wide range of clustered shops, sheltered from weather extremes and served by the adjacent subway.

ance, advertising, management consultancy, lawyers, council departments, and, of course, banks. **These, too, cluster as far as possible,** though some less obviously, being above ground-floor level.

Being close together shortens the linkages between them. Despite phone, telex and electronic links, direct contacts may be invaluable. They are essential in the case of stock exchanges or commodity markets in the big cities, where banking or insurance districts can be identified.

The offices themselves generate other service functions in the city centre, providing regular custom for restaurants, cafés and pubs. Their own caterers and office cleaners are usually provided by firms from outside the CBD.

3 **Leisure and tourist facilities** may well go together. The attractions of parks, museums and historic buildings are shared by citizens and visitors alike.

Theatres, cinemas and nightclubs also tend to cluster in entertainment districts, either within, or just on the edge of, the city centre.

In state-controlled socialist and communist countries, the city centre became a prestige area, an **historic-cultural centre**, with open space for parades and mass meetings, like Moscow's Red Square, or the Tian-an-men square in Beijing (Peking).

4 **Large hotels in the centre** can serve tourists, businessmen and conferences. There are usually many **smaller hotels on the edge of the CBD,** in old, converted inner-residential properties. **Here, too, some of the run-down houses are expensively reconstructed** for those wealthy people who wish to live as close to the centre as possible (**'gentrification'**). This brings us to the problem area for most large urban sprawls: the inner city.

What sort of historic features might attract tourists to the centre of a large old town? Give examples.

Why are clusters of *similar* types of shop so important to retail businesses?

Why are clusters of offices with different functions important to commercial and financial businesses?

What kind of shops are office workers in the CBD likely to visit regularly, apart from cafés and restaurants?

P 12.8 The high-rise financial and commercial centre of Toronto, by day the focus for office and retail workers, and shoppers. One attempt to ease congestion, by dispersing offices to the suburbs, can be seen in the high buildings of 'office parks' stretching out along the line of the subway and rail network.

12.5 The inner city

The expansion of any large town leaves a ring of old buildings close about the business centre. They usually include working-class terraced houses of the early industrial period. In Britain these give way to taller, detached and semi-detached houses of the prosperous middle class of the late Victorian and Edwardian periods, once on the outskirts.

In time these became outdated. As newer suburbs spread outwards, those who could afford it left the inner city belt, selling to speculators. The old properties were expensive to maintain, so landlords recouped costs through rent, by letting them as rooms or flats.

Such housing was occupied by lower-income groups. As they could not spend enough to support once-prosperous local shops, these either closed or stocked goods of a lower order. Whole districts thus became run-down.

Instead of single-family homes, there is now a dense population in tenement accommodation. Into these areas of increasing 'urban blight' come the immigrants. If employed, they have poorly paid jobs and little capital.

Groups of immigrants tend to congregate in districts where at least they know people of the same origin, with similar cultural or religious background, who can speak their own language. There is also the fear, often justified, that they would be unwelcome in other parts of the city.

The result is an area of above-average poverty and unemployment. It is also congested, with large families in a few rooms, often sharing water, cooking and toilet facilities.

Apart from this, **many industries have moved out from the former ring about the CBD.** While they were there, the small terraces housed families conveniently near their work. Today these have either moved out, or become part of the 'twilight zone' of old housing, or live in **tower blocks** of replacement flats (which take a lot of family rent from a small ground space).

Parts are cleared for offices or car parks as central city firms extend the CBD. But this does not increase local employment. Once there were small labour-intensive industries – printing, light metalworking, specialised clothing. But new techniques, and mass production using few operatives, have put many of them out of business, or forced them to cut the workforce.

We return to social problems and possible remedies later (p. 224). First look at a cross-section of the city in terms of how and where people live. **Fig. 12.8 summarises the outward movements which help to create the conditions described, and some in the other direction.**

12.6 The suburbs

These are the largest part of the city. They are mainly residential, a mixture of private housing and large council estates (subsidised by local or central government). As they spread, they enclose older settlements, sometimes a whole village.

But they also have other functions. **Suburban industries have developed along main roads from the centre, and along ring roads.** As land values in the CBD have risen, more and more firms have located offices and warehouses in the suburbs, choosing **accessible sites**.

Today most towns have outer industrial estates. There firms take advantage of low rents, a prepared site, good floor space, and easy access for transport, which can avoid the city.

Offices and light industries are not the only functions in the suburbs. There are schools, branch libraries, social centres, post offices, local contractors, garages, pubs and, of course, retailing. So many suburbanites work locally, apart from those who commute to the CBD.

Suburban families wish to shop as locally as possible for food and convenience goods (Fig. 12.10). **Along the busier roads are lines of shops with a service pull-in.** The newer estates include similar

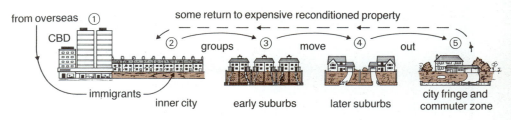

12.8 Movements of people into different types of accommodation within a city.

P 12.9 Towering council flats in Glasgow overlook lower housing, closer to the green spaces. The high buildings replace old slum areas, but create other problems, for isolated persons depending on the precarious life-line of a lift, for example.

shopping centres or **service centres**, selling lower-order goods. They also offer a few services, such as a branch post-office or launderette.

The increase in family cars and the development of ring roads have encouraged larger shopping centres with a car park. In these, shops and **small supermarkets** are located about a pedestrian precinct. They offer a wider choice of goods, and

P 12.10 Suburban housing for middle-class families, who obtain their convenience goods by car from shopping centres sited along the outer ring roads.

P 12.11 A small suburban shopping centre, with parking space.

P 12.12 Cowley's large shopping complex on the eastern outskirts of Oxford, with parking facilities and comparison shopping at leisure.

perhaps include a café or library. Chain stores may set up their own large branches and also provide a wide range of consumer goods. ·

P 12.13 Access by ring road is also important for delivery vehicles, like this truck serving Sainsburys at the Cowley centre.

DUMBELL SHOPPING CENTRE

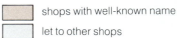

☐ shops with well-known name

☐ let to other shops

12.9 A major shopping centre, sometimes enclosed, sometimes with seats and landscaping in the pedestrian area (Photo 12.12).

On a different scale are the **hyper-markets** and **covered air-conditioned shopping centres**, open for late custom (Fig. 12.9). These enclosed shopping centres (ESCs) may include several hundred shops, and are **located where they can serve suburban families within half an hour's drive.** As Fig. 12.11 suggests, they are prepared to bid high for a suitable site (at junction **J**).

Of course, the suburbs contain many other shops and sub-post offices built in earlier periods. But these struggle to compete where newer shopping centres are within reasonable driving distance.

CONVENIENCE SHOPPING

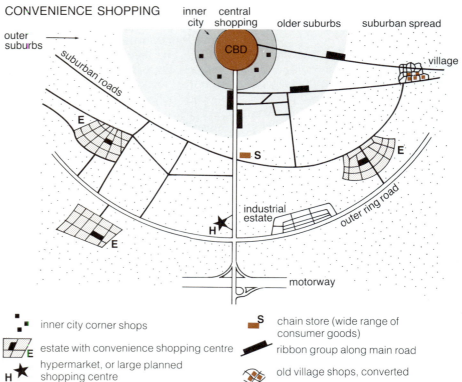

■·· inner city corner shops

▱E estate with convenience shopping centre

H★ hypermarket, or large planned shopping centre

S chain store (wide range of consumer goods)

◣ ribbon group along main road

⬨ old village shops, converted

12.10 Different opportunities for convenience shopping in the city suburbs.

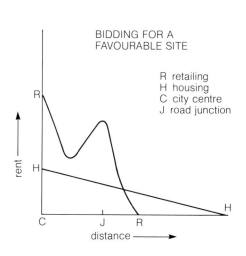

BIDDING FOR A
FAVOURABLE SITE

R retailing
H housing
C city centre
J road junction

12.11

Certain small shops survive by serving particular needs. Some provide special foods for foreign immigrants, as well as low-order convenience goods. They are particularly successful in the inner zone.

As we have seen (p. 219), there is a move outwards from the inner parts of many large cities in the MDCs, not only to the suburbs, but to rural sites and smaller towns. **In the suburbs themselves the outward movements are reflected by the variation in land values** (Fig. 12.12).

Instead of falling steadily from inner city to outskirts, the land value/distance graph, like that of population density, shows rises and peaks. The siting of offices and stores are influenced by junctions and ring roads and desirable sites may increase in value, while remaining cheaper than inner-city locations.

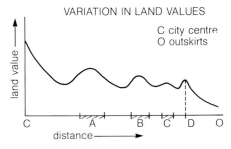

VARIATION IN LAND VALUES

C city centre
O outskirts

12.12 Changes in rental values with distance from the centre.

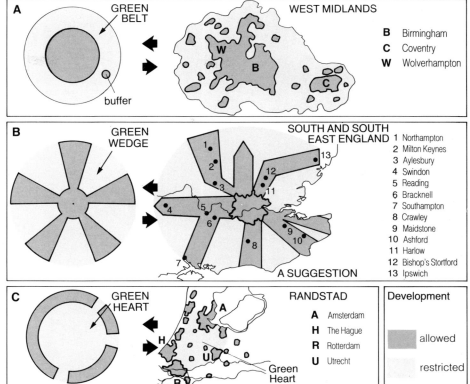

12.13 Ways of preserving a green area with restricted land-use, while allowing desirable urban-industrial development.

12.7 Beyond the suburbs

How far should the suburbs be allowed to spread? Too often the MDCs have allowed rural and urban settlement to intermingle, with disastrous results for the countryside. Some ways of containing the urban growth are illustrated in Fig. 12.13.

In Britain it was decided, nearly half a century ago, to enclose large urban areas with **a green belt**, in which further urban-industrial growth would be restricted. (**A**) **shows how this has been developed about the West Midlands conurbation. Notice that it also acts as a buffer between large towns.** Government permission is sought to modify the belt from time to time; in this case it has recently been extended.

Another scheme (B) restricts development to certain zones radiating from the city, and so leaves **green wedges.** In the case of Geneva the green wedges extend right into the city, forming **green corridors**. It has been suggested that such wedges might be preserved in south-east England. London already has a green belt about it, though the pressures on it are great.

In the Netherlands an almost continuous urban area has spread around a green, mainly pastoral countryside with historic towns and villages. **Inward spread is restricted, to preserve the green heart.**

When a green belt is adopted, the area just beyond it is at risk from what is known as 'leap-frogging'. Work out what is meant by this and what effects it has.

Suggest what land uses might be permitted within a green belt. Consider recreation and hospitals.

Notice how the restricted area acts as a buffer between Birmingham and Coventry. Look in your atlas at the Ruhr industrial area of West Germany. Why have **green buffers** been adopted there?

Why may the **green wedge system** be difficult to maintain in south-east England? Consider London's ring roads, airports, and the future Channel tunnel. Consider also the need for industrial expansion to give more employment, and the advantages a green belt could have for new industries (see Q13 p. 234).

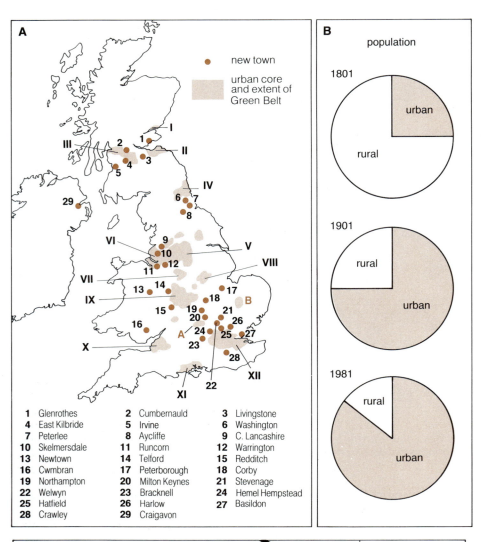

A

new town

urban core and extent of Green Belt

1	Glenrothes	2	Cumbernauld	3	Livingstone
4	East Kilbride	5	Irvine	6	Washington
7	Peterlee	8	Aycliffe	9	C. Lancashire
10	Skelmersdale	11	Runcorn	12	Warrington
13	Newtown	14	Telford	15	Redditch
16	Cwmbran	17	Peterborough	18	Corby
19	Northampton	20	Milton Keynes	21	Stevenage
22	Welwyn	23	Bracknell	24	Hemel Hempstead
25	Hatfield	26	Harlow	27	Basildon
28	Crawley	29	Craigavon		

B

population

1801

urban

rural

1901

rural

urban

1981

rural

urban

12.14 (**A**) *New Towns in relation to cities, conurbations, and their surrounding green belts. In some of these, and in places as far apart as Invergordon, Derry (Londonderry), Tyneside, Milford Haven and the Isle of Dogs (London), enterprise zones aim to attract firms by exemption from local rates and allowances on capital expenses.* (**B**) *How urban population has increased.*

12.8 New towns

In the last forty years Britain has also carried out a unique programme of locating and building **new towns**. The government provided funds for Development Corporations to create housing, industries, and amenities.

The great urban areas were becoming congested and unable to provide housing and newer industries. Most of the new towns were to be located close to these conurbations. They could thus take the overspill of population, ease urban congestion, and encourage new industries with employment prospects.

At the same time they would limit urban sprawl. They would provide urban functions in a more pleasant setting, with higher living standards.

Others were not so much overspill towns as centres to encourage growth in areas of declining industry.

Look at Fig. 12.14. Identify one city or conurbation at the heart of each Green Belt I–XII. Notice their nearby clusters of new towns. Suggest where new towns were built to help areas with declining industries. Which university cities are surrounded by the Green Belts A and B?

Some new towns were based on existing ones; some included both towns and villages. A number were created virtually from scratch. But all had carefully located residential, commercial and industrial areas.

In most of them people live in small **neighbourhood units** with local shopping

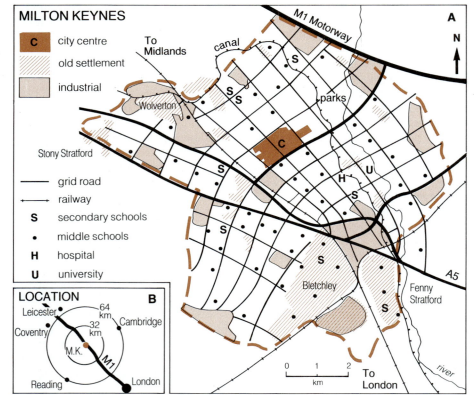

MILTON KEYNES

C city centre

old settlement

industrial

—— grid road

+++ railway

S secondary schools

• middle schools

H hospital

U university

LOCATION

Leicester, Coventry, Cambridge, M.K., 64 km, 32 km, M1, Reading, London

12.15 (**A**) *The grid pattern of Milton Keynes in relation to existing urban areas with established industries (Wolverton and Bletchley). Notice the major routeways, and (**B**) its location in relation to London and other cities.*

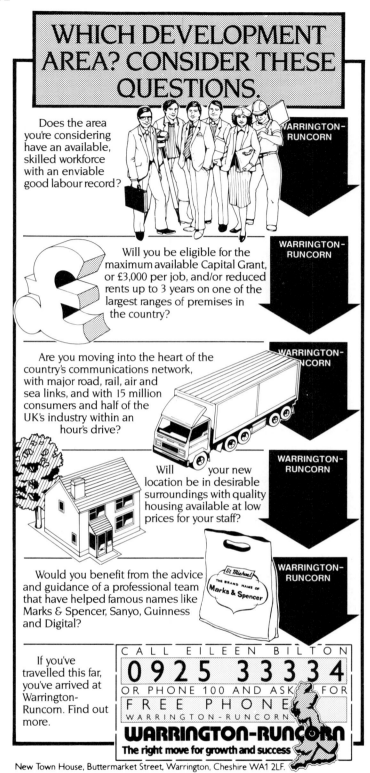

P12.14 Warrington–Runcorn, like other New Towns wished to attract firms, and so advertised its labour record, employment allowances, communications advantages, market possibilities, and desirable location.

centres, welfare facilities, and perhaps a primary or middle school. The towns include larger schools and colleges, and a central shopping complex. They are by no means all alike; but Milton Keynes gives an idea of how such a town is located, sited, and planned (Fig. 12.5).

Milton Keynes is in a rural setting in north Buckinghamshire, some 80 kilometres north of London, from which many of the people have come. It took in 40 000 people in Bletchley, Wolverton, Stony Stratford, and some villages. The density of population is low. Newcomers

have included young families, rather than older people. There are many skilled workers. Housing is owned or rented, and various neighbourhoods, or 'local areas', have different styles.

It lies alongside the M1 motorway, and is served by the A5 and the London–Birmingham railway. It took in railway industries at Wolverton. Now many technologically advanced industries, and high-level service firms have moved in. It also houses the Open University.

About a fifth of those working find jobs outside the town; some commute to London. About a third of those working in the town come in daily from outside.

Fig. 12.15 shows the network of roads that serves neighbourhoods of 500–600 people (notice the schools). There are cycleways to avoid traffic. A park follows the flood-plain of a small river. The centre with shops, offices and amenities draws people from far afield.

Besides such new towns, there are **expanded towns**, like Swindon. They plan developments in agreement with a nearby city (Greater London in this case).

The new town Development Corporations are now being wound up. Houses, factories and shops have been sold to associations or cooperatives, or privately. One aim is to use the huge sums received to improve inner city areas.

12.9 Urban problems in the MDCs

Such plans are admirable. But conditions in a city vary with what happens in the country as a whole. Such things as oil crises (affecting prices), political changes (new governments), changing technology (new industries), changing population structure (age-group bulges), cause some functions to prosper, others to decline.

Decline in manufacturing affects some cities more than others. Between 1971 and 1983 UK employment in metals and textile manufacturing was halved. Cities such as Coventry suffered particularly badly. Large vehicle and electrical firms decided to concentrate on a few locations in the UK. They closed their Coventry works; so the city lost half of its manufacturing jobs in eight years.

Even in less vulnerable industries, firms have been moving out to rural locations (p. 219). Fig. 12.17 shows the population changes within Greater London and the higher rates of decrease in the older parts and city centre.

P 12.15 The CBD's combination of office and retail functions attract people to the point of congestion, but only during working hours. At night it is almost deserted.

where help is most needed. **Table 32 shows some of the variables used as guides**

From these a **level of living index** may be found, whose values indicate where the problems are worst.

This list of 20 variables mixes both the **causes** and the **results** of the conditions they reveal. Take each in turn and consider which might strongly indicate a cause or a result of poorer than average living standards.

P 12.16 Inner city neglect in the zone of transition, with low-cost rented apartments, creates immense social problems.

The inner areas

Despite these losses, the inner urban areas remain congested and deprived of advantages available elsewhere. **The deteriorating environment and the poverty trap** (Fig. 12.16) are to some extent due to human greed, while many social problems arise from prejudice, ignorance and misfortune. Funds *have* to be made available to reduce the inequalities. They come partly from central government and partly from local authorities. But these often fail to agree exactly what should be done, and where. First, however, the people in need must be identified.

Identifying the needs and needy

In most cities such problems are concentrated in particular districts, but also exist in others. **Statistics can point to**

Table 32

1	% households with more than 1.5 persons/room
2	% households without hot water, fixed bath, inside toilet
3	% households sharing a dwelling
4	% dwellings with only 1 or 2 rooms
5	% dwellings owner-occupied/rented
6	new dwellings/1000 households
7	infant mortality rate
8	spending by local health services/1000 people
9	average number of doctors (GPs) load
10	(a) % students aged 15–19
	(b) primary school pupils per teacher
11	% professional workers
12	% unemployed
13	% aged 0–14; % over 65
14	% population change due to migration
15	% households without a car
16	rateable property values
17	public libraries (amount spent/1000 people)
18	population per social worker
19	children in care/1000

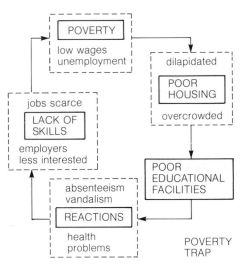

12.16 The cycle of urban poverty, and inner city problems.

Other statistics can point more directly to the results: those needing welfare assistance, or free school meals; poverty-related diseases, malnutrition; difficulties in rent payments; school absenteeism; crime.

What needs to be done

The broad aims, in no particular order, could be as follows:

1 Rehouse the worst accommodated; restore dilapidated houses; introduce new forms of housing to cope with overcrowding.

2 Improve the environment; provide playgrounds, social centres; landscape park areas on derelict sites.

3 Tackle unemployment; encourage firms to locate there; persuade people to take up training schemes.

4 Give a subsidy for insurance of property for firms prepared to locate and remain there; insurance premiums are very high in socially disturbed areas.

5 Give special help for education, and improve local schools.

6 Improve community relations; encourage people with different backgrounds to deal with social welfare together.

7 Involve local people in local planning.

The problem, of course, is how to go about it.

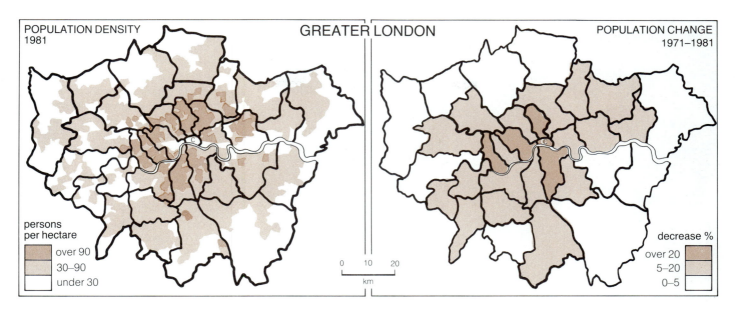

12.17 Inner London and outer suburbia, showing changes in permanent residence.

Attitudes, priorities and difficulties

Different authorities and political groups will tackle these praiseworthy ambitions in different ways. Some see it simply as a matter of providing sufficient funds. Some aim to remove the causes by pressurising politicians. They focus on conflicts of interests between social classes. These two groups alone would probably disagree about priorities.

Think about your own attitudes to the following, and to the difficulties which arise. What would *you* aim to tackle first? Consider the drawbacks.

Some would put re-landscaping and improving the whole environment first. They may think of run-down industrial districts in Lancashire and Staffordshire which have been made into green recreation areas. But is this possible in many densely populated inner areas? Might it not absorb funds needed for housing?

If house improvements come first, would this just be 'patching up'?

Inner-city tower blocks can be built to house many families in a small area. But won't different problems arise? Consider the drawbacks of families isolated in a high-rise building: lifts subject to vandalism; children far from ground-level and play areas (if provided); old people isolated; long treks for welfare services. These suggest that tower-blocks may not be the answer in problem areas; or could a particular design and siting help?

Providing employment may be even more difficult. At best, this is a semi-skilled part of the population. With established firms already moving out, would some other form of employment be possible? (One exception to Coventry's job losses has been increased employment by small firms making garments; these have recently been set up by local Asians.)

Education problems arise both from attitudes and lack of facilities. There is a high turnover of school staff, who find conditions unattractive – a 'chicken and egg' situation.

Remember that as rich people and firms leave the central areas, the revenue raised through taxes falls. **In these zones of change the improvements are required by those least able to pay for them.** Even when new large industrial units arrive, like the newspaper industry at Wapping, employees with the necessary qualifications are mostly imported.

12.10 Cities in the LDCs

From a rural to urban life

The cities in the LDCs are very varied; but in each country the urban population rapidly increases, with **a high rate of migration into the larger cities.**

What makes people leave the land to move into a city with inadequate housing and public services? Turn back to page 193. Describe separately the 'push' and 'pull' factors.

The movements of families to the cities may be direct or in steps. In Latin America immigrant families move directly to the big cities. They seek acquaintances or fellow villagers in inner city slums. Some join those who have already moved out to build a house of sorts in a shanty-town on the edge of the city.

In south-east Asia many impoverished rural families move from the land to a nearby town. After experiencing local urban life, they are perhaps unable to establish themselves. So they make a further move to look for jobs in a large city. Improved transport has reduced this **step-migration**, but it is still common. Remember that in each country young male migrants are a majority.

As immigrants pour in, the city population soars, especially as urban death-rates are slightly less than those in the countryside, and birth-rates still high. In Dacca, Lima, Kinshasa and Seoul it has been increasing by well over 10 per cent per year. **Table 33 shows these two main causes of population growth. Notice especially the high rate of movement into the cities.**

Table 33

region	% increase of urban population (1970–1980)	
	natural growth	by immigration
S E Asia	48	52
Latin America *	42	58
West Africa	56	44

* tropical

225

P 12.17 Congestion is also a feature of Indian city centres. Yet the very bustle, the advertising, the apparent job opportunities attract young men from over-populated villages with few opportunities.

Cities in the LDCs are very vulnerable to economic changes. São Paulo, in Brazil, is a huge, highly developed industrial-commercial city, and so attracts immigrants. **In boom times** there is much employment in manufacturing, and plenty of office jobs. Service industries prosper, for the wage-earners are spending. But **in times of recession** a large part of the workforce returns to unemployment in over-crowded suburbs or squatter areas, far from the high-rise city centre.

The huge buildings and traffic in the centre of cities like São Paulo and Lima are due to the concentration of large companies, international banks and government offices. In almost all LDC cities there are glaring contrasts between this kind of urban life, with intensive modern activities, and that of the sprawling suburbs with zones of real poverty

Urban conditions

As in the MDCs, **migrants tend to move to parts of the city where people from their own region are concentrated.** These may provide shelter and support while they try to fit into a different kind of life. With the rates of immigration you see above, their housing is makeshift or overcrowded. There is often a lack of sewerage and limited piped water.

Every so often, natural disasters, or political unrest, swell the numbers.

As has happened so frequently in Calcutta, this brings in tens of thousands of destitute, homeless families. Calcutta's bustees – groups of shacks of any available materials – are notorious. They house literally millions of people. Lacking sewer-

age and adequate piped water, conditions are appalling. In 1986 the United Nations reported that a third of the population was in temporary huts shared by an average of five families.

In most of these cities job prospects are slim. In the MDCs the cities grew as people sought and found jobs in manufacturing industries. **But in most LDCs there is insufficient industrial employment**. It is unlikely that modern industries can do much to lower urban unemployment. Even in Brazil, with its industrial core region, and two-fifths of the people living in cities, less than a fifth of the urban population works in manufacturing.

People first look for manual jobs at the bottom end of service industries – carrying, sweeping, and other casual employment. Many become small street traders, in competition with thousands of others.

P 12.19 Even low-level tertiary employment is scarce for migrants to the city. Here in central Lima people share a shoe-shine site, each for a few hours at a time.

Shanty towns as the first step

The scales are heavily weighted against the new arrivals and the poor within these cities. Yet many migrants improve their chances in life by moving to a city. Despite the shacks and dreadful conditions that do exist, the city has many forms of quite substantial housing, occupied by millions of people. Many of them have

P 12.18 Rural disasters bring people from village homes to the city. Here, as cholera followed flooding, villagers fled to a temple compound on the urban outskirts.

Suggest why modern technological industries are less likely to solve unemployment problems than the older types of industry. Consider the types of jobs and how many are employed in each.

'Unfortunately the urban areas are gaining people who cannot contribute to the economy, but require the services provided by it.' Consider carefully what is meant by this.

P 12.20 The barriadas of Lima on the outskirts of the city, where self-built housing is being continuously improved. Street stalls become small shops; street repairs move to small workshops; and urban amenities are gradually introduced.

12.11 The structure of cities in the LDCs

The cities differ greatly, but we will look at three categories.

1 **Those where colonial occupation created particular activities** (the majority). We have already considered both major exporting ports, and inland adminstrative-commercial cities (p. 134). Investments during the colonial period caused them to increase in size and importance. Settlement patterns established within the city still remain.

2 **Colonial cities with exceptional advantages**, of location and political importance (e.g. Singapore and Hong Kong).

3 **Cities whose development is controlled by state planning**, notably in China. There are many cities evolved over a long period, but which have changed in character with modern commercial and industrial developments.

Colonial contrasts persist

The huge cities of Latin America, outside Brazil, have grown from Spanish colonial bases. The Spaniards planned their cities as a grid of streets about a main square, with a cathedral and administrative buildings, even on sites of earlier settlements.

moved up the scale from squatting communities. **Shanty settlements can represent a form of progressive improvement.**

Shanty towns are usually on the edge of the expanding city. Though built illegally and without right to the land, some are well organised in terms of space. Many families continuously improve their housing, and some buy the land from private owners.

In a number of Latin American cities the authorities have, under pressure, recognised shanty suburbs. They have eventually provided water, sewerage and power.

Where such self-improvements are recognised, they may, in time, attract commercial and industrial activities. In some parts of outer São Paulo the authorities have *first* provided the water, sewerage and power, and offered a site to those who will put up their own low-cost house. This has partly prevented property-developers from acquiring land cheaply, evicting families, and putting up housing beyond the pockets of the shanty population. But the forecast of a city population of 24 million by the end of the century shows the scale of the problem.

There are forecasts that by the year 2000 there will be 22 cities with over 10 million people and many LDC cities will have over 15 million. So the alternative to arranging legal rights to land, and giving aid to self-help families, is vast areas of unplanned shacks, with all the social and health problems that would follow.

P 12.21 Do-it-yourself housing on dry ground provided by local authorities in the outer suburbs of São Paulo. A charity organisation provided the brick-making machinery.

12.18 (right) Spanish colonial Influences in Latin American cities, with contrasts between the old city and outer squatter areas.

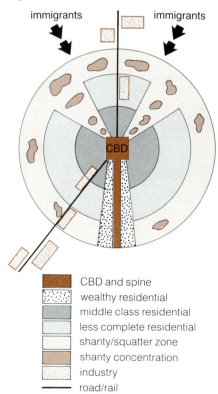

immigrants   immigrants

CBD

CBD and spine
wealthy residential
middle class residential
less complete residential
shanty/squatter zone
shanty concentration
industry
road/rail

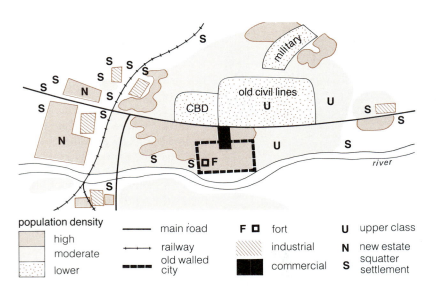

12.19 British colonial influences in Indian cities, with contrasts between the pre-British core, inner suburbs, outer housing estates, and squatter communities.

This old Spanish power centre has become the CBD of today's cities. Usually a commercial avenue extends from it. This has become the spine of a sector with open areas and parks. It also houses upper- and middle-class professional people (Fig. 12.18).

About this colonial centre are well-established middle-class suburbs, with good streets, schools and public services. These give way to a spread of newer suburbs, with more haphazard housing and fewer established services.

On the urban fringe the poor live in makeshift squatter housing. They struggle to establish some kind of ordered settlement; and may form shanty villages.

Fig. 12.18 shows that sectors of poverty extend into the inner city. There many of the older buildings are overcrowded with poor families, including recent immigrants.

Industrial areas are scattered along major transport routes, with newer developments on the outskirts of the city.

The actual layout varies with topography. In Venezuela, the spine of Caracas stretches along a valley. The shanty settlements (*ranchos*) spread along the hillsides. In Peru, Lima's suburbs extend to the coast; but inland the shanty towns (*barriadas*) line the roads and spread over hill slopes. Piped water is often scarce, so people queue at standpipes.

In many of the large cities of south-east Asia the densest population is still in and about the old city, with its maze of streets and small craftsmen's shops. Fig. 12.19 shows, diagrammatically, how in cities developed in colonial times the density falls where more spacious areas once housed Europeans involved in administration and commerce (the civil lines), with the military cantonment beyond. Close by, the area of imposing government buildings and offices has become part of the CBD. The commercial area runs out from the old city bazaar and links these two contrasting zones.

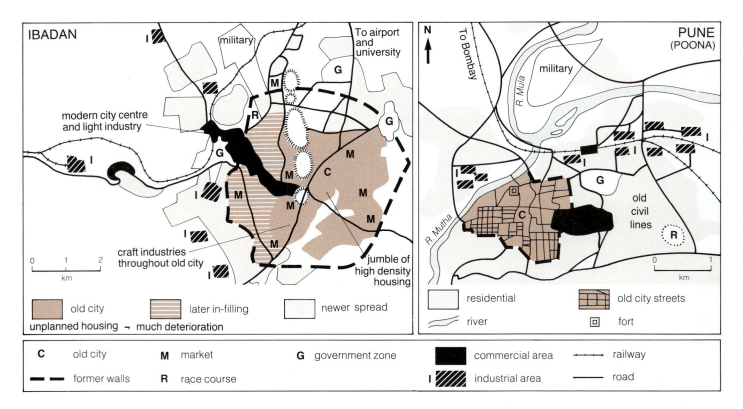

12.20 Similarities in former colonial cities in West Africa and India.

In India parts of the city close to the centre house separately the higher caste and upper-class Indian families. They now occupy much of the old civil lines. As the high-class residential areas are still mostly central, there is zoning; but not with the pattern seen in the MDCs.

New industries are mostly where the old ones were established, near the railway. Private estates of low-cost housing extend the city outwards, while **streams of immigrants form squatter settlements near factories and railway yards. They also occupy open spaces and slum housing within the city itself.**

While discussing patterns of urban settlement, we must not forget reality. The Indian Council of Medical Research predicts that 300 million people will be living in India's city slums by the year 2000. They point to the present surge of diarrhoea diseases, infections, and malaria amid this disorderly, unplanned urban housing, lacking filtered water and sewerage.

How do historic and social factors help to explain the distribution of people in a city?

In the great city-ports of south-east Asia the population density is low in the central area about the docks, but then rises sharply immediately inland. Consider why this is. Are the districts with business, commerce and administration likely to be densely populated?

Fig. 12.20 shows striking similarities between Ibadan in Nigeria and Indian towns with the European influences described above. What similarities can you see? Suggest reasons for this.

Why do conditions in the rural parts of a country have a bearing on settlement patterns and life in the cities?

Why is the fact that soon half of India's urban population will be living in slums particularly alarming? Why is it difficult to prevent this? Consider population growth rate.

Some exceptional cities

By contrast with most expanding cities in the LDCs, those of the NICs, Hong Kong, Singapore, Seoul and Tabei (Taipei), have achieved rapid industrial growth.

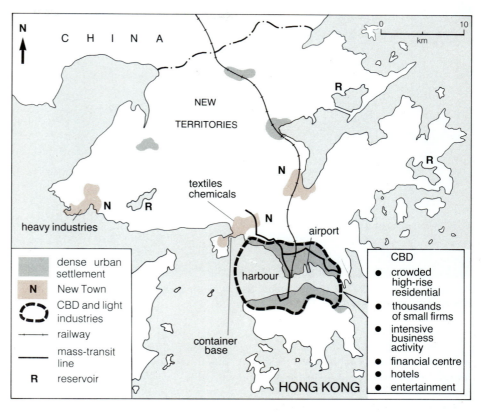

12.21 Hong Kong, with its central hive of financial, commercial, and industrial activity, and its new urban settlements. It will be returned to China in 1997.

In crowded Hong Kong people's enterprise in creating small industries has been backed by the government. The state has provided industrial floor space, together with housing, roads, and docks. At the same time **new towns** and larger industries have been established on the mainland part of the city, the New Territories.

From the dense mixture of small factories, family businesses, high-rise flats and squatter areas has come this rapid industrial expansion. Continuous immigration causes problems; but **the birth of small enterprises creates chances of employment, even if, at first, low-paid.**

The government re-houses make-shift workshops set up in squatter areas. It has found room for over ten thousand small firms, each employing five or six people, in blocks built on land cleared of makeshift housing. These produce clothing, shoes, jewellery, small plastic and metal goods, and light electrical equipment. The larger mainland industries receive government loans.

Hong Kong differs from the other LDCs by having been founded on 'Treaty territory' in 1842. (It will revert to China in 1997.) Under British control it became a great **commercial/financial city**, with multi-national companies and banks. In these circumstances enterprises are more likely to find backing than in most LDCs.

Make a simple sketch of China's coastline. Mark in the mouth of the Xi river and Guangzhou (Canton). Locate Hong Kong and mark the *direction* of sea-routes to Singapore, Manila, Shanghai, Tokyo, San Francisco, Vancouver. Why has its *location* been so important to Hong Kong?

The CBD is split by the harbour, but linked by road and rail tunnels. It is a mixture of spectacular high-rise offices, stores and hotels, and cavernous side streets bustling with activities. Traffic congestion and pollution are problems. Raw materials and much of its food, energy, and even water have to be imported. Yet there are lessons in planning, and cooperation between a state and its enterprising citizens, for other developing countries.

P 12.22 Part of the CBD in China's capital, Beijing, with its innumerable bicycles and plentiful public transport.

In Hong Kong two-thirds of the manufacturing establishments employ less than ten people, and only a tenth have over fifty employees. These small firms employ forty per cent of all manufacturing workers.

What advantages are such small workshop industries to people in the LDCs?

What is needed to start them up, apart from family savings?

What about markets for the products?

Which countries might find it difficult to develop manufacturing along these lines?

Which foreign interests have been mainly involved in the developments in South Korea and Taiwan?

Tax concessions and cheap labour have brought many foreign firms to Seoul and Taibei. Would such firms be as interested in setting up in remote places to spread development in an LDC? Why are they more likely to choose a port or large city?

Singapore's population is also mainly Chinese in origin. It, too, is a commercial-industrial city with advantages of location (p. 205). **Again, the government has backed both labour-intensive and capital-intensive industries.** It has created industrial estates and rehoused over 100 000 squatters. About half the people live in state housing.

Its industries include oil-refining and highly skilled precision work such as watch-making and the manufacture of optical goods. Much of its electronics industry is foreign-owned, however, unlike Hong Kong's.

In Singapore and Hong Kong, European interests laid the foundation for the present economic growth.

Urban developments in China

China's inland cities have served and controlled particular rural areas over thousands of years. The northern walled cities, once carefully planned, had social districts. The southern ones were more like those in southern Asia, with commercial centres and a maze of small streets and craftsmen's houses.

During the 19th century European intrusions created the CBDs of Shanghai and Guangzhou (Canton) to serve their commercial interests. They also financed railways which enabled industrial cities to develop on the coalfields and iron ore deposits of the north-east.

Today urban-industrial growth is carefully planned. In the last half-century the alarming population increase has threatened to swamp the already crowded cities. So the government has restricted migration into cities, to prevent what is happening in most LDCs. At one stage, young people from urban families were directed to employment outside the city. Today's more moderate policies still control employment and housing within the cities. Also, the one-child family policy is reducing the rate of increase of urban populations.

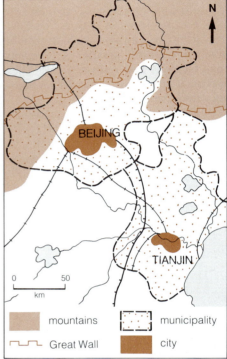

mountains

Great Wall

municipality

city

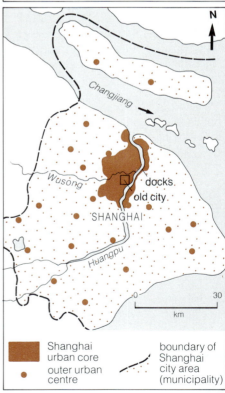

Shanghai urban core

outer urban centre

boundary of Shanghai city area (municipality)

12.22 Three Chinese municipalities which include planned rural and urban settlement beyond the main city itself.

P 12.23 In Kunming city, in south-west China, village-style housing remains amid the flats and offices, with intensive vegetable-growing and posters telling children how to look after their green environment.

Now positive urban planning aims to prevent overcrowding in the really large cities. Beijing (Peking), Shanghai and Tianjin are each part of a planned municipality (Fig. 12.22). Each includes thousands of square kilometres of adjoining rural land where villages supply the city with vegetables. **New satellite towns are developed in these areas, steering people and industries away from the city.** Reservoirs in the municipality control water supplies.

In Beijing the CBD lies about the vast central assembly square, with a great avenue threading through massive blocks of administrative office buildings. About this is a dense area of small streets with old, but renovated houses.

China has recently created Special Economic Zones (SEZs), based on urban centres with privileged industrial investment and joint ventures with foreign firms.

Shenzen, just across the border with Hong Kong (12.21) has developed into a modern city with high-tech industries within a few years. In 1997 it will link with the industrial towns of the New Territories and Hong Kong's CBD.

Most of China's booming economy is in the east, but also about selected inland cities, with the object of creating wealth which will spread to the less-developed areas.

In the suburbs industries alternate with intensively farmed fields and greenhouses. There is cultivation in open spaces about villages surrounded by the spreading city. These village-suburbs retain much of their old character.

The Chinese cities vary according to their history and present functions. But, in each, groups of streets, or blocks of flats form neighbourhood units. Their committees organise health services, social work, nursery classes, and so on.

City structure is by no means uniform and conditions vary in different districts. **But there are no predictable poverty zones that occur in so many cities (in the MDCs and LDCs alike).** Controls are strict. The authorities are anxious to avoid the urban problems which beset so much of the world.

It is worth remembering China's policy of 'walking on two legs'. They try to ensure that the growth of new technology and urban industries is matched by improvements in standards of living throughout the rural areas. How might this reduce the push-pull forces which cause urbanisation? Growth in medium-size rural towns is being encouraged. How does this help to control large city growth?

Theme 12
Back-up section

Urban fieldwork

Students in urban surroundings have an advantage where practical urban fieldwork is concerned. But some of the data sources given below may be used either to back up practical surveys, or to provide substitute statistics to test hypotheses.

In urban fieldwork it is as well to prepare copies of the OS 1:2500 plan which covers the area.

For practical reasons the work needs to be done by a group, usually split into pairs. **Hypotheses may be made and tested to a depth appropriate for those carrying out the survey, and for the time available.**

Take, for instance, two which are best carried out in moderate-size towns, rather than large urban areas:

The number of storeys per building decreases with distance from the centre.

The type of land use changes with distance from the centre.

The streets running away from the chosen central place (**CP**) are marked off in a number of lengths (or number of buildings), to be surveyed by particular pairs. The observations are recorded on a sheet, as below, noting the number of storeys, and the main function of each floor of every building. It may be necessary to limit the observation of function to a number of floors, say three.

The functions chosen are recorded as symbols, and can be simply: **A** residential; **B** offices; **C** retail store; **D** retail service; **E** other.

Or, in more detail:

A1 private housing; **A2** flats; **A3** hotel. **B1** legal/financial office; **B2** commercial office; **B3** government office. **C1** convenience goods shop; **C2** durable goods shop; **C3** retail service (e.g. hairdresser). **D1** service industry; **D2** manufacturing industry. **E** public service (church, school).

This is recorded as shown in Table 34.

Maps are prepared to show the number of storeys of each building. Others show, by letters or colour, **the functions on each floor** (on separate maps). Even their visual impression may suggest relationships.

Table 34

observer.	street.		
building number	120	121	122
number of floors above 2nd floor	2	3	–
2nd floor	B2	A2	A1
1st floor	B1	B2	A1
ground floor	C2	C3	A1

A scatter graph can be plotted to show the number of storeys against the distance from CP. The distance can be taken from the map, using the shortest route along the street. By inspection, groups may comment on general trends and variations. They may try to account for them by discussion related to the particular area.

To examine the functions, the streets can be divided into 100 metre lengths away from **CP**. The length of frontage occupied by each type of land use can be measured and expressed as a percentage. It may then be plotted, as in Fig. 12.23.

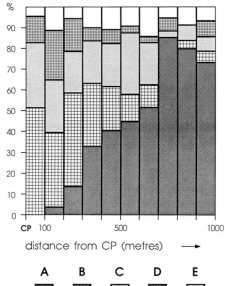

12.23 How urban functions change away from a selected central point.

Another hypothesis which may be tested by teams visiting properties in streets extending away from a central point, is that: **land values decrease with increasing distance from the centre.** (Side streets may be brought into the survey.)

This also calls for initial preparation. **The rateable value of a property** (which is an assessment of a fair annual rent, not a market price) can be obtained from the local authority rates office. This will show something like this:

Table 35

rateable value (£)		
House	21 Northcliffe Avenue	240
Shop and premises	23 Northcliffe Avenue	425
Shop and premises	2 Station Rd	2850
Offices and premises	12 Station Rd gnd floor	500
	12 Station Rd 1st floor	230

It may be necessary to add figures together for the total value of a multi-floor, multi-function building.

To have a standard for comparison, the area of each property should be calculated to give the rateable value per square metre. However, a reasonable substitute is to **measure the frontage of each building and calculate the rateable value per metre of frontage.** The distance of the property from the **CP** is found from a map, or paced as a pavement length by direct distance.

The rateable value per metre is then plotted as a scatter graph against the distance from the CP. If the values for the buildings are ranked, a correlation test can be made (p. 195), and related to the hypothesis.

If the place with the highest rateable value does not coincide with the centre itself, this could be considered as the central point from which to test the hypothesis.

For those unable to carry out a comprehensive urban survey, Kelly's Directory or Yellow Pages may be used to test the hypothesis:

establishments providing higher-order (luxury) goods will be concentrated near the city centre, while those providing lower-order goods will be widely scattered.

The distribution of these establishments (such as jewellers, in Fig. 12.24) can be found from the reference books and plotted as points on the map.

If the grid is placed over the point pattern, the distribution may appear as in Fig. 12.24. The edges of the grid are used to give coordinates of the points. **The mean centre C of these may then be found:**

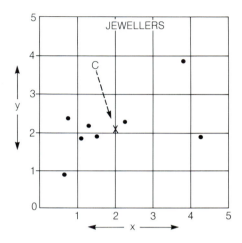

12.24 Concentration of a selected function within a city (in this case jewellery retailing). C is the mean centre of this activity.

Add all the **x** coordinates and divide by the number of points; in this case:

$$\Sigma x = 0.7 + 0.8 + 1.2 + 1.4 + 1.5 + 2.2 + 3.9 + 4.3 \ (= 16.0)$$
$$\bar{x} = 16.0 \div 8 = \mathbf{2.0}$$

repeat for the **y** coordinates

$$\Sigma y = 0.8 + 1.8 + 1.9 + 1.9 + 2.1 + 2.2 + 2.3 + 3.8 \ (= 16.8)$$
$$\bar{y} = 16.8 \div 8 = \mathbf{2.1}$$

C is thus located at **x** = 2.0, **y** = 2.1. The mean centre for the other establishments can be found in this way, and compared, together with their actual distributions.

The distribution of shops within a CBD may also be investigated. Plotting them as points may reveal clusters. It may be useful to use the map of shopping centres of the British Isles (for towns with over 50 000 people) – published by *Charles E. Goad Ltd (Old Hatfield, Herts).*

Ethnic distributions in urban areas – basis for discussion

As we have seen, part of the cities, mainly the inner areas, house distinctive racial groups of immigrants and their descendants.

The groups are sub-divided, not only between those of West Indian and Asian origin, but into smaller enclaves, based on language and religious differences. In Leicester, for instance, four-fifths of the Pakistanis and Bangladeshis are housed in two voting wards; whereas the same proportion of other Asians, though centrally clustered, are spread over six wards.

Fig. 12.25 shows how rapidly such clusters have strengthened in particular areas.

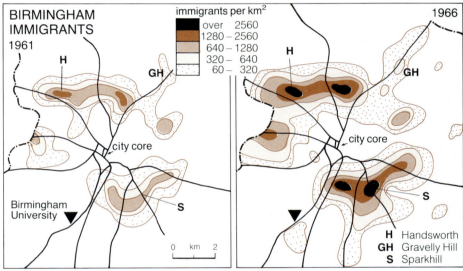

12.25 Notice the speed with which immigrant populations became concentrated in particular parts of the West Midlands (after P. M. Jones Trans. IBG vol 50 p. 199).

The distribution of the immigrant population is highly significant geographically. It calls for discussion, not only in terms of inner city neglect, touched on above, but in terms of national policies. **Such discussions need to be firmly structured,** in view of the emotions aroused by racial subjects. Here, then, are a number of points to consider:

1 Is segregation in a city voluntary or not? If voluntary, what are the advantages/disadvantages of people retaining their racial and cultural identity? Does it enhance their way of life? Does it serve them to be set apart? Do others gain by having a new, often lively culture in their midst?

2 Leading from this: what should be done to provide special religious centres, language teaching (their own and/or that of the adopted country), and unique cultural activities (festivals, etc.)? Is it good to emphasise their differences from other citizens?

3 If segregation is not voluntary, what causes them to remain in properties neglected by the majority? Should special aid be given? Might this be seen as racially one-sided? Should this aid simply be part of inner-city improvement?

4 Leading from this: is the problem one of class relations rather than racial ones? Is the coloured migrant simply one of the 'have nots'? Is it therefore really a matter of overcoming class differences and resource distribution which is needed? There are, overall, more native British than immigrants in the 'twilight' city areas.

5 What are the chances of immigrants filtering upward through the city housing zones, and so inter-mingling? This has happened with some immigrant groups. But it has also led to them clustering in more prosperous areas: just as the London East End Jewish immigrant community moved to Golders Green and other focal points.

Theme 12 Making sure

1 The CBD is likely to contain: manufacturing industry; department stores; hypermarkets; banks; bakers; solicitors – which?

2 A Green Belt is an area in which: dormitory towns develop; housing and industry are controlled; only recreation is permitted; no building is allowed; only agriculture is permitted – which?

7 What is meant by **gentrification**? When it occurs in the inner city, why is it reversing a social trend?

8 List some specialist activities which are located amid the housing of suburban areas and affect the concentric zoning pattern.

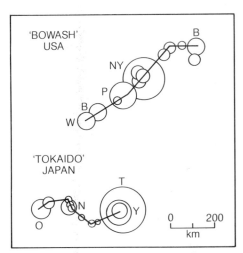

12.27 Megalopolis – in the eastern USA and Honshu, Japan.

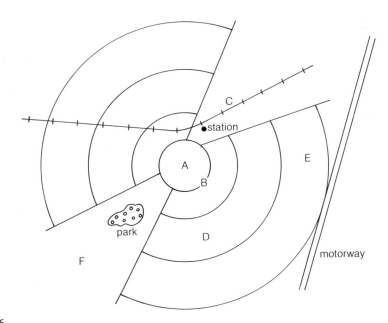

12.26

3 Fig. 12.26 shows zones of land use in a long-established town in the English midlands. In which location **A–F** would you expect to find the following: tower blocks of flats; a recent industrial estate; a tourist advice bureau; high-class residential housing; a one-way traffic system; old manufacturing industries; semi-detached housing with established gardens; department stores?

4 How could a study of rateable values be used to indicate the **limits of the CBD?**

5 Why do specialist districts (financial or entertainment) occur in large towns?

6 Which term describes goods offered by a cluster of shops selling similar products – commercial; convenience; durable; comparison?

9 How are push-pull factors involved in the following: (a) movements from inner city to suburbs; (b) movements from city to a new town; (c) movements to old inner city areas?

10 How may the following affect people's mobility (desire to move to another area and ability to do so): (a) income; (b) nature of employment; (c) unemployment; (d) skill; (e) car-ownership?

11 Suggest how the growth of new towns may be affected by: (a) a declining birth-rate; (b) concern about depopulation of the inner cities.

12 Large urban areas depend on the efficiency of their communications. A megalopolis develops with cities linked like beads on a string (Fig. 12.17). **This** shows 'Bowash' (USA); and 'Tokaido' (Japan), whose cities are linked both by expressways and high-speed railways.

(a) Identify the towns shown by initials.

(b) What other links are continuously in use in a megalopolis? For whom are they essential? How are they organised?

(c) To ease traffic congestion, office work and information-based work is increasingly being done at home. Why is this described as 'electronic cottage industry'? What other daily activities which once involved travel can now be home-based?

(d) What kind of countryside preservation should be planned for a 'megalopolis': Green Belts, Green Wedges, Green Buffers?

13 The M25 lies within London's Green Belt. Industries find its communication links attractive, and so wish to set up nearby. The government, facing large-scale unemployment, wishes to encourage industrial development. London's outer suburbs, and Heathrow–Gatwick airport links attract overseas industrialists.

Debate whether the government should relax Green Belt restrictions to help such industrial expansion.

14 Why are urban conditions in the less developed countries bound up with conditions in the rural areas?

15 How does the population explosion in the present LDCs differ from that in 19th century Europe? Would the enormous growth of urban population in the LDCs be best served by European-style industrialisation?

16 Shanty towns can be regarded in several ways:

(a) as parasite communities, best ignored or removed;

(b) as self-help areas, where people make an effort to improve conditions;

(c) as a temporary home for those moving up the social scale, helped by employment in the city;

(d) as places for local government to improve by up-grading housing and introducing services;

(e) as stressing the need for providing cheap self-help public housing to anticipate the arrival and requirements of more immigrants.

Discuss these and say what you consider are practical attitudes for authorities to take. What particular difficulties might there be?

17 What features of urban development and controls in Hong Kong, Singapore and mainland China seem worth consideration by other developing countries?

18 Why is it so difficult for many LDCs to emulate the spectacular growth of newly industrialising countries like Hong Kong and Singapore?

19 (a) How does the growth and structure of Ibadan and Pune (Poona) show that industrialisation may play only a small part in urbanisation? (Fig. 12.20)

(b) Why do some people call Ibadan 'a city village'?

(c) Why has Ibadan two central focuses?

(d) Can you point to three stages of growth which have influenced the size and structure of Pune?

20 (a) In Fig. 12.28 place the groups of countries I, II or III in one of the broad categories LDC, MDC, NIC.

(b) Does there appear to be a direct relationship between wealth per head and the proportion of city dwellers? Why is this?

(c) The 'in-between' position of Peru reflects both its mineral wealth and large urban concentrations. What is mined? Where is the population concentrated? Why does this separate Peru from the other groups?

(d) Greece is an EEC country. Why is it separate from Group I, which includes France and the UK?

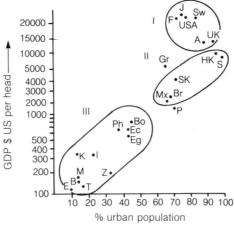

12.28 Although so many LDCs have rapidly growing cities, most still have large rural populations with low productivity. Compare **Group I** (USA, Sweden, France, Australia, Japan, UK), **Group II** (Singapore, Hong Kong, South Korea, Brazil, Mexico). & **Group III** (Ecuador, Philippines, Bolivia, Egypt, Zaire, Kenya, Tanzania, India, Malawi, Bangladesh, Ethiopia). Note Greece (Gr), Peru (P).

(e) How would you expect the proportion of urban population to total population to change in Groups I and III during the next 50 years?

Consider the terms used

Urbanisation includes the processes by which the number and size of towns and cities increase. It is changing the distribution of world population.

Central Business District (CBD) is the commercial and administrative core of a town or city. It is an area of the highest land values, where large offices and stores, and many high-rise buildings are concentrated. It has a large day-time population but a small night-time one.

Bid rent means what people are prepared to pay for land for a particular use; it is their rent-paying ability.

A service centre is one where a group of shops, banks and offices provides a range of goods and services for a surrounding area.

Convenience goods are those that can be obtained quickly for immediate use (p. 212).

A period of economic recession is one when businesses generally slump.

A tenement house is a building divided into separate rooms tenanted by separate families or individuals. It often describes a tall building used in this way in an inner city area.

Gentrification describes the way dilapidated, subdivided properties in the inner city are taken over by the wealthy to be reconverted to expensive, usually single-family housing. They thus acquire property near city-centre businesses, clubs and entertainment districts.

A satellite town is one located near a large city, and associated with it.

A municipality is an urban area which has local self-government. In China, several of the largest cities are part of a wider municipality which includes much open countryside.

Terrain refers to the natural features of an area of land.

A cantonment is the military quarters, or area of military family housing, usually associated with a British Army base overseas.

A new town is planned and built to provide accommodation, employment and various industrial opportunities, initially to relieve congestion in existing urban areas. Some are located so as to help economic growth in an area of declining industries.

An expanded town is an existing one whose planned growth helps to relieve over-population and congestion in large urban areas.

The overspill is the number of people who leave an over-populated urban area to be housed elsewhere.

Megalopolis (Greek: *mega* – great; *polis* – a city) is a huge area with large cities linked by communications, but containing open land.

An ethnic group is one whose members share common race, nationality, religion or culture, which distinguish them from others or, as an **ethnic minority**, from most of the population.

Theme 13   Unequal shares

13.1 How can we compare living standards?

It should now be obvious that the world's resources are unevenly distributed. Also the chances of an acceptable standard of living (let alone a luxurious one) are uneven. But how do you assess standards of living?

People have different views of poverty and affluence. There is **relative poverty** and **absolute poverty**. Even in a developed country there can be dire poverty, compared with the life style of the wealthier citizens. Yet this may be very different from the sufferings of the poor in the LLDCs. In a country like Ethiopia poverty can be absolute, where people have nothing to lose but their family or their life.

Development should be viewed first in terms of satisfying basic needs, and then of the quality of life. Which statistics should we choose to compare states of development? We can take certain pairs and look for relationships: compare the amount of nutritious food consumed per head and the mortality rates; the GNP per head and the possession, or not, of cars or radios; illiteracy and daily newspaper circulation.

These comparative figures can be revealing, but do not *necessarily* show cause and effect. Low newspaper figures may reflect difficulties in printing or distribution, or that the people speak many different languages, and not simply that they cannot read or write.

Figs. 13.1 and 13.3 (scatter graphs) give a good impression of 'haves' and 'have nots', but do not prove that one variable is responsible for the other. Nevertheless Fig. 13.1, which does not include the wealthiest countries, certainly shows that those producing little wealth suffer one sad result of deprivation, the death of many young children.

13.2 The cumulative effects of poverty

Nutrition, health, and medical welfare

In the less developed countries misfortunes are often cumulative: one thing leads to another. Look at the differences in food consumption and nutrition (Fig. 13.2) and the chances of medical attention (Fig. 13.3) in various countries.

P 13.1 In drought-affected Somalia supplementary foods are needed to maintain health.

Poverty means unsatisfactory water supplies, poor sanitation, and a small chance of effective treatment of illnesses.

The food energy needed for daily activities varies with people's age and build, with the climate, and with what they normally do. Very broadly, those doing light work should have at least 2400 calories from their food.

Protein is needed to build up and maintain the body; deficiencies can swiftly cause ailments. 80 grammes a day is a rough guide to the acceptable amount for health. **On this basis the figures suggest that large numbers of people are suffering from malnutriton.**

List those countries in Fig. 13.2 in which the diet of the average person does not approach the minimum requirements. In many of these there is only one doctor for 20 000 people or more. Which are shown in Fig. 13.3?

Most LDCs are in tropical countries. In many of them heat and moisture cause disease-bearing insects to multiply rapidly.

Find what you can of (a) the lifecycle of malaria-bearing mosquitoes; (b) the

13.1 The sad picture of infants dying in the poorer countries.

[Scatter graph: vertical axis "PRODUCTION OF WEALTH (GNP per head)" in $US, logarithmic scale from 100 to above 6000; horizontal axis "[1988] INFANT MORTALITY (deaths/1000 live births)" from 0 to 200. Plotted countries: Singapore, Venezuela, Brazil, Mexico, Paraguay, Colombia, Peru, Zambia, India, Nigeria, Niger, Malawi, Chad.]

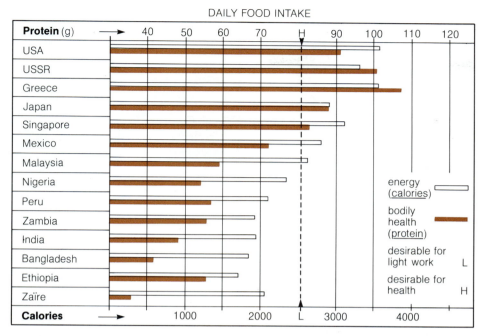

DAILY FOOD INTAKE

Protein (g) →	40	50	60	70	H	90	100	110	120
USA									
USSR									
Greece									
Japan									
Singapore									
Mexico									
Malaysia									
Nigeria									
Peru									
Zambia									
India									
Bangladesh									
Ethiopia									
Zaïre									

energy (calories) ▭
bodily health (protein) ▬
desirable for light work　L
desirable for health　H

| Calories → | 1000 | 2000 | L | 3000 | 4000 |

13.2 Notice the countries in which the mean daily food intake gives scarcely sufficient energy and insufficient protein for healthy living. These are not precise requirements, much depends on what people do and where they live. But there are obvious deficiencies and unbalanced diet in many parts of the world, and even within a country – witness food problems within the former USSR.

water snail harbouring parasites which infect people walking in watercourses and cause the debilitating disease *bilharzia*; (c) the tsetse flies which breed in bushes and transmit *trypanosomiasis* (sleeping sickness) to people and a wasting disease to cattle.

Just as investments in suitable crops (HYVs) improves the health and productivity, and hence the standard of living, so **investments in prevention and treatment of diseases must help the whole community.** It is not only equipment and chemicals which are needed. There must be publicity, then expert advice and supervision: for it needs discipline to keep spraying oil on stagnant water to kill mosquito larvae; to keep clearing snails from ditches, and removing vegetation which harbours the tsetse.

Fig. 13.3 shows the lack of doctors in the least developed countries. Unfortunately some LDCs have spent a high proportion of their medical outlay on large hospitals in a few places, whereas more widespread help at a lower level would benefit greater numbers. **China can point to medical success which starts at the village level.**

In China, with 800 million rural people, there is medical help at all levels and a long life expectancy. Large hospitals in

the major towns and clinics at smaller centres offer both traditional and modern forms of treatment. **Among the villages and urban neighbourhoods, suitable people are trained to a considerable level of medical skill.** They can diagnose and treat many ailments and, if necessary, pass on a patient to a medical centre.

In a country where all organic wastes are used for fertilisers and fuels, hygiene is insisted on, as the structure of the biogas converter (Fig. 8.4) shows. In schools, factories, and various meeting places decorated hand-posters advocate hygiene.

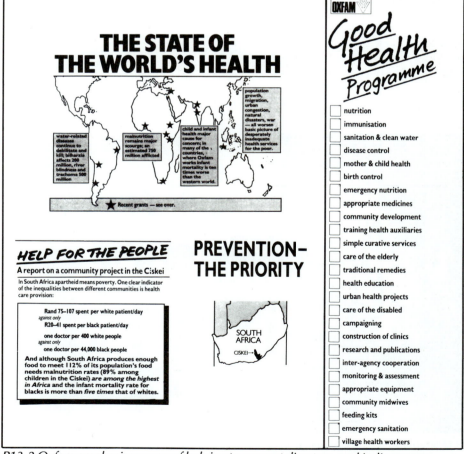

P13.2 Oxfam emphasises ways of helping to prevent disasters, and indicates one example of inequality in health care.

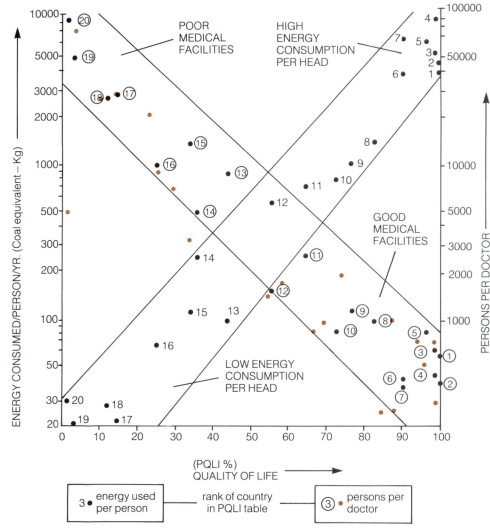

13.3 Comparing two things which affect the quality of life in countries in Table 36.

P 13.3 Families contribute milk at a dairy cooperative in Gujerat, western India. An assured family income raises the standards of nutrition, but the large number of children remains a problem for the future.

P 13.4 Paramedical help is very important where there are few fully-trained doctors.

Quality of life

It is difficult to put plans for health measures or agricultural improvements over to a largely illiterate population. So besides nutrition and health, **education should be regarded as a priority.** Understanding how to go about things is half the battle; and, of course, education widens people's outlook.

P 13.5 Schooling in rural Bolivia, with the minimum facilities. Funds for education are as necessary as funds for agricultural improvements, which need the backing of an educated population.

One means of assessing the quality of life in a country is to compare statistics of physical well-being and minimum education.

Three indicators are taken: (1) **infant mortality**; (2) **life expectancy**; (3) **literacy**. These simple characteristics at least measure well-being more effectively than the GNP figure. Together they give a **physical quality of life index (PQLI).**

The PQLI is calculated by listing the indicators separately. Each is given a score of 100 for the best condition and 0 for the worst.

Table 36

	country	life expectancy at 1 yr	scale	infant mortality (per '000)	scale	literacy rate %	scale	total	PQLI
1	Japan	78	100	5	100	99	100	300	**100**
2	Sweden	77	97	6	99	99	100	296	**99**
3	UK	75	92	9	97	99	100	289	**96**
4	USA	75	92	10	96	99	100	288	**96**
5	Hungary	71	81	17	92	99	100	273	**91**
6	Singapore	73	86	9	97	89	88	271	**90**
7	USSR	70	78	25	87	99	100	265	**88**
8	China	69	76	31	84	78	74	234	**78**
9	Malaysia	70	78	24	88	69	63	229	**76**
10	Colombia	65	65	46	74	85	83	222	**74**
11	Brazil	65	65	62	65	78	77	207	**69**
12	Peru	61	54	87	49	82	79	182	**61**
13	Kenya	59	49	71	59	60	52	160	**53**
14	Ghana	54	35	89	48	54	45	128	**43**
15	India	58	46	98	43	41	29	118	**39**
16	Bangladesh	51	27	118	30	30	16	73	**24**
17	Nepal	51	27	127	25	21	5	57	**19**
18	Chad	45	11	131	23	26	11	45	**15**
19	Ethiopia	41	0	153	9	33	19	28	**9**
20	Mali	44	8	165	0	17	0	8	**3**

Which PQLI figure would you say separated the MDCs from the rest? Point to one obvious newly industrialising country (NIC). What is its PQLI? Which are clearly indicated as LLDCs?

It is suggested that the PQLI gives a more satisfactory indication of wellbeing (or otherwise) for the bulk of the people than the GNP figure. Calculate the PQLI for Saudi Arabia and Hong Kong, from Table 37.

Where would Saudi Arabia and Hong Kong come in the scale in Table 36? Compare the GNP figures. Why is that for Saudi Arabia so large and that for India so small?

In which category of development would you place Hong Kong?

In Table 36 the statistics and the calculated PQLI relate to the late-1980s. Find up-to-date figures from the *United Nations Statistical Yearbook* from a local library – and use them to calculate what changes in position on the scale have taken place, if any.

You can see in Table 36 that for life expectancy Japan (78 years) merits 100 and Ethiopia (41 years) scores 0. The 100 points represent 78 − 41 = 37 years. So one year is roughly 2.7 points on the scale. Therefore Mali (44 years expectancy) rates 3 years (= 8 points) higher than Ethiopia.

Add up the figures for the three indicators, then divide by 3 to find the country's PQLI.

Table 37

Indicators (1988)	Saudi Arabia	Hong Kong	India
Life expectancy (at 1 yr)	63	76	58
Infant mortality (per 1000 born)	70	8	98
Literacy rate (%)	42	88	41
GDP per head ($US)	5311	9613	340

Communications and information

Statistics show a lack of machinery, vehicles and paved roads in many of the less developed countries. So it is not surprising that **radio and TV sets** are lacking. Yet **they can be of great value, educationally and politically.**

TV sets attract watchers of all ages, and in countries like China and India can be used to put across methods of cultivation, hygiene procedures and government policies. For this reason subsidised sets are widely distributed in China. Fig. 13.4 shows the numbers available in the countries listed in Table 36. you can see that some are virtually without them.

There are drawbacks to using TV in underdeveloped regions. In rural India there are difficulties with power supplies and set maintenance. The many languages and dialects also create problems.

P13.6 Schoolgirls among ricefields in Kenya. Practical agricultural fieldwork is a necessary part of education, but sadly lacking among so many rural communities in the LDCs.

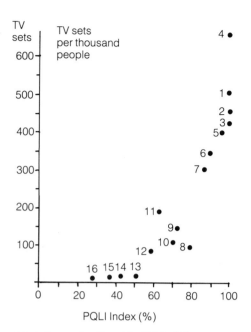

13.4 Countries listed in Table 36

P 13.7 The ambition: a commercial advertisement explains the methods of controlling pests. But it needs funds and careful supervision to ensure that Indonesian farmers can adopt them.

While radio and TV can make people **aware** of methods of improvement and self-help, this does not automatically **solve** their problems. Resources are still needed in sufficient quantities to improve conditions and to avoid disasters.

13.3 The poorer, the more vulnerable

One of the great differences between the MDCs and LDCs is their ability to cope with change for the worse – gradual changes which may lower living standards, or a sudden disaster, like an earthquake, which may create havoc. **The LDCs have few resources to prevent a dangerous situation, or to repair damage.**

Disasters in the long term or short term occur for a variety of reasons:

1 physical causes (droughts, floods, earthquakes);

2 biological causes (harmful crop viruses, locusts, disease);

3 human actions (political pressures, economic changes, overpopulation).

You have seen that **the lack of resources at family level can create a cycle of poverty and gradual decline.** In many countries, especially those with seasonal droughts, a lack of fuel means stripping woodland (deforestation). As wood becomes scarce, people turn to burning animal dung. Their fields are deprived of natural fertiliser, so the soil becomes exhausted. The land stripped of protec-

P 13.8 Reality: demonstrating the spraying of insecticide to kill cattle ticks to farmers in the highlands of Kenya, where it is easier to maintain good pastures than on the lower savannas.

tive woodland is eroded and gullies eat into farmland. Poverty increases. More than ever they need an input of funds or resources to check further losses.

But funds for improvement are not easy to come by. The apparent neglect and poor condition of the land can put off possible investors. In richer countries with more productive lands investors are found more readily; plans can be made to protect against possible disasters.

Drought is a major problem worldwide. But even permanent drought need not prevent productive settlement if the resources are there to overcome it, as shown by large scale irrigation in New Mexico (USA) and in Australia's Murray river basin. The way it is tackled, or not tackled effectively, in various parts of the world shows how the poverty gap can widen. **First consider the MDC.**

The problem of water shortage: (1) The British Isles

The British Isles lie where moist westerly winds prevail. Yet, as Fig. 13.5 shows, **large parts of England and Wales have insufficient water.** This, of course, is due to huge and increasing demands from densely populated areas, from industries and power stations, and from seasonal irrigation for intensive farming.

In 1976 prolonged drought caused reservoirs to dry up and water-tables to fall. Farmers suffered heavy losses, and in many places water was rationed. But **a country like the UK has capital and resources, and revives quickly.** It can confidently plan for future demands and the occasional very dry year. There was short-term loss and discomfort, but no national disaster.

The reservoirs are mainly in the highlands of Wales, the Lake District and the Pennines, where upland catchments benefit from high rainfall and impervious rocks. There relatively little settlement is lost by flooding. However, some agricul-

PLANS FOR INCREASING EXISTING SUPPLIES OF WATER

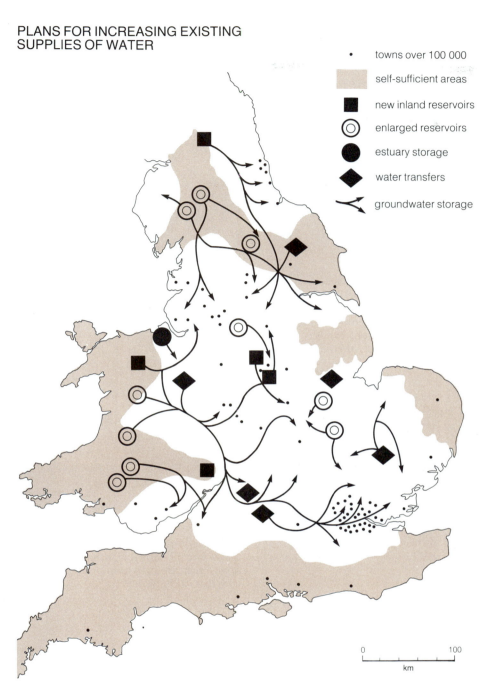

13.5 A country which can confidently plan and find the capital to tap, or create, sources of water for industry, farming, and people's daily use.

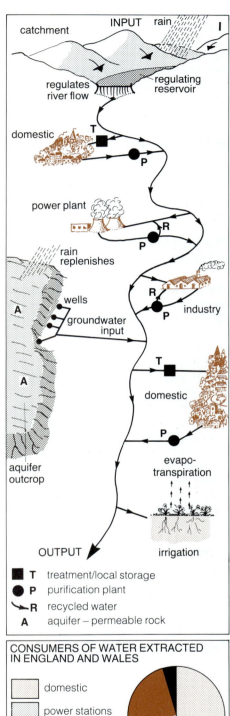

13.6 (I) Ways in which water can be stored, extracted, and supplied to different consumers (II); and ways in which it is re-used.

tural land disappears when dams are built; which is always a problem to be considered.

Pipelines run to large urban areas: from the Lake District to Manchester, from Welsh reservoirs to Birmingham and Liverpool. But notice that reservoirs are also built to hold sufficient water to regulate the flow in rivers (Fig. 13.6).

Water is transferred from high reservoirs by streams, aqueducts or pipes to the rivers, which act as transporters. It is then pumped from the rivers to local storages, and purified by filtering and chemical treatment. **Much is returned to the river after use, or recycled for industry and power stations after further treatment.**

Groundwater is an additional source, especially from chalk and limestone aquifers. In winter springs give a high yield, but in summer pumping is needed. In the London Basin pumping from boreholes reduces groundwater sources.

So the chalk aquifer, which receives insufficient water naturally, is recharged artificially.

It may be necessary to impound water in estuaries and basins, like the Dee and the Wash. **Undertaking large scale projects like these calls for huge investment.** But if schemes are necessary and feasible, funds are made available.

Now by contrast look at the problems of the 'have nots'. So often long-term planning and funding are lacking in lands where water shortages are predictable. Here droughts threaten not just the livelihood but the lives of millions of people.

The problem of water shortage: (2) Ethiopia

The country also suffers the prolonged droughts which affect the whole Sahel belt across northern Africa (Fig. 13.7).

Between which latitudes does the Sahel extend (a) in west Africa; (b) in east Africa?

In Ethiopia the south-western parts are the wettest, the northern and eastern parts much drier. Consider the reasons for this.

Look back to Figs. 1.13 and 5.5. Why does sinking air create such dry conditions across Northern Africa?

Now look at Fig. 13.8. What is the main difference in the northernmost advance of moist southerly air during normal summer conditions and during

P 13.9 Children help with ploughing in Chad's relatively moist inland basin. But the land suffers both from periodic drought and insufficient fertiliser. Compare the farming with that in Photo 13.10.

drought periods? How does this affect the nomadic pastoral zone just south of the Sahara (see p. 258), and the more settled farming communities in the savanna land of the northern parts of the west African states?

Describe the pattern of wetter and drier years illustrated in Fig. 13.9. Such variations can also be seen to have occurred far back into the past. Should not people have learned to plan to combat the extremes of drought? But who, and how?

P 13.10 A Scottish farmer spreads animal manure annually, immediately after harvesting his barley. This highly productive intensive farming contrasts with that in Photo 13.9.

THE SAHEL IN JULY

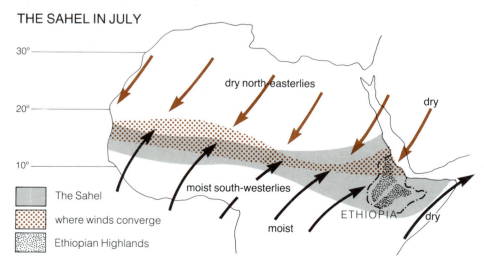

dry north-easterlies

dry

30°

20°

10°

moist south-westerlies

moist

ETHIOPIA

dry

The Sahel

where winds converge

Ethiopian Highlands

13.7 Africa's Sahel zone, where for years at a time the summer south-westerlies may fail to deliver sufficient moisture.

P 13.11 In the dry Sahel a well is a necessity for survival, as here in drought-stricken Mali.

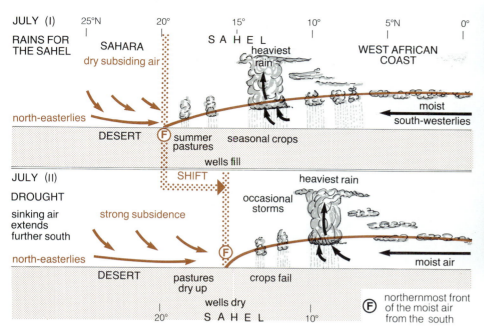

P 13.12 Aid in a practical form. A pump tapping deep water sources in the dry Sudan.

13.8 (I) The good years for the Sahel. (II) When the marginal lands dry up.

Now consider Ethiopia's problems in more detail.

Much of the Ethiopian highlands is made up of immense thicknesses of volcanic rock. These weather to give soils which are fertile when watered. Also at this altitude the temperatures are lower than in most of the Sahel. But the rainfall is erratic and water supply difficult.

The countryside is extremely broken. Seasonal streams in deep, steep-sided channels have carved up level surfaces into a jumble of flat-topped hills. Many of the villages are perched defensively on flat ledges. For, over the centuries, the people have suffered exploitation and persecution by rival warlords. Consequently many women spend a lifetime carrying up water from sources hundreds of metres below the settlement. The abundant waters of Lake Tana drain away to the Sudan through the spectacular gorges of the Blue Nile.

Most Ethiopians live in the highlands. But such terrain makes communications very difficult. The scattered farming communities grow vegetables and millet, which is threshed and stored locally. Farming methods remain primitive, and there are few cash crops.

There is poverty, with a cycle of declining soil fertility – a lack of fuel, deforestation, and erosion, much as described. Population pressure, overcropping, and burning organic wastes have reduced what should be fertile land to a poor condition. When drought sets in, hundreds of thousands face starvation.

The broken landscape even makes relief aid difficult to distribute. To add to the problems, the north is disrupted by civil war. **Aid has poured in, but what is needed is peaceful cooperation and long-term planning to balance food production and population numbers. Huge investments are needed for:**

1 **a widespread tree planting programme over the years**; to provide wood for fuel (leaving dung for fertiliser), and to check erosion;

P 13.13 The endless daily task of Ethiopian women carrying up water for family needs and for the fields about their high village.

SAHEL – VARIATIONS IN ANNUAL RAINFALL – standard deviation (selected places)

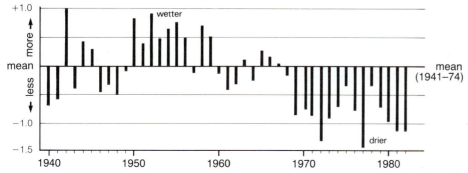

13.9 Periods with above average and below average rainfall. (After L. Musk, Geog. Mag. LV., p. 533.)

P 13.14 A village perched high on a volcanic tableland in northern Ethiopia, with sources of water, and some of its fields, in the valley far below.

2 **supplies of chemical fertilisers** to replace soil nutrients in the short term;

3 **large-scale water projects** (not easy in such broken country); groundwater surveys and equipment for local supplies are priorities;

4 **providing seeds** of drought-resistant grains;

5 **improving communications** and transport to market centres;

6 **some re-settlement** in the wetter south-west and rift valley;

7 **providing incentives** for farmers to be more than self-sufficient.

In 1974 the new communist government abolished land ownership and tenancy, and set up peasant associations. The urban poor enjoyed lower food prices, but the farmers received little benefit. Scattered farming families were re-grouped into communal villages, but this failed to increase production.

Civil war has disrupted aid from international and private organisations. Somehow political differences have to be overcome to allow them to accept immense investments from outside.

Are the problems of the LLDCs simply due to unfavourable climate or soils, or difficult terrain?

How much may be due to unwise actions by the cultivators themselves?

How much of this may be forced on them by circumstances?

How much is due to world politics and decisions they cannot control?

If help is offered from abroad, why may it be distrusted?

Why is there massive response from the outside world when things go wrong, but so little concern about preventing this in the future?

The answers are seldom clear-cut. But such considerations are every bit as relevant as asking whether the air temperature, rainfall and soils are favourable or not.

The problem of water shortage: (3) Tianjin, China

The rising demands for water for Tianjin, in northern China, have led to critical shortages in recent years. The city is rebuilding from the earthquake of 1976, which killed more than a quarter of a million citizens. The urban-industrial population is over 3 million, and its municipality (Fig. 12.22) about 8 million.

The precipitation, 570mm a year, is erratic. Much falls in summer, when run-off is great. The city is located on the Hai He, whose upper valley has a number of reservoirs. But these also supply Beijing (Peking), the capital. A mountain reservoir to the north (Maiyun) once supplied both cities, but since 1981 only Beijing.

Its rural lands once grew paddy rice. But water shortages have forced people to turn to dry land crops. So much water

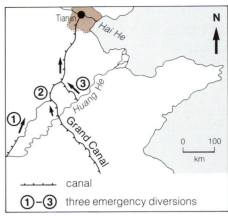

13.10 Channels through which local labour directed water northwards to Tianjin. Notice the scale.

was being raised from wells that the water-table had fallen by 30 metres in some areas. Deeper pumping only drew in water high in mineral salts, and seawater began to seep in under coastal lands.

By the early 1980s, water for irrigation, and for some factories, was rationed, and drinking water was salty. It was decided to bring in water from further afield: first by emergency schemes, and then by a long-term project. The following shows **a centrally organised state tackling water problems with urgent direction of both resources and labour**, in ways which differ from those used in an MDC (Britain) and an LLDC (Ethiopia).

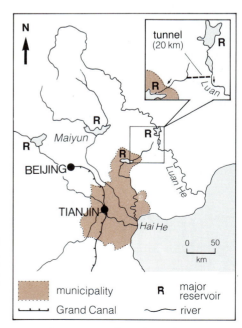

13.11 The Luan He diversion scheme (inset – the new tunnel).

Fig. 13.10 shows the emergency scheme of 1981–82. Three old canals were repaired, widened, and deepened, to transfer water north from the Huang He (Yellow river). Dams, sluices, dykes and bridges had to be built. But, because of the huge summer sediment load of the Huang He, water was only transferred during the *winter* months of 1981–82, and again in 1982–83.

This immense operation involved almost a million rural people. There were drawbacks: a check on their winter wheat production; and some land was lost near canals, for seepage brought up the water-table so that nearby soils later became salty.

So, far to the north, a reservoir was built on the Luan He (Fig. 13.11). Its water was directed through a tunnel south to a storage, and on to Tianjin. *In less than a year* a 20-km tunnel was cut, by sinking 15 vertical shafts into a mountain (giving 32 working faces). The whole scheme used 120 000 volunteers from areas which were to benefit from the project.

The long-term solution to the problems of the northern plains now involves transferring water from the Chang jiang (Yangtse river), along the line of the age-old Grand Canal. It means tunnelling under the Huang He. This will be part of an overall project for irrigation, drainage, power and navigation.

> Explain the processes touched on above: (a) the fall in water-table; (b) excess salts in water and soils; (c) the **summer** load of the Huang He; (d) water diversion in **winter** only.
>
> Give three reasons why Tianjin municipality was concerned with both short-term and long-term projects.
>
> Why did the vertical shafts produce **32** tunnel faces to be worked?
>
> In what ways does the **organisation** of supply projects in China differ from those in the UK? What advantages has China, compared with many LDCs in carrying out such projects?

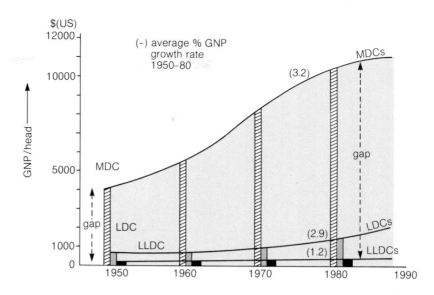

13.12 *The gap widens between the wealth created by the MDCs and LDCs – and in some African countries the GNP per head actually* fell *throughout the period 1985–1990.*

13.4 The gap widens

You can see that it is more difficult for low-income countries to cope with physical and economic problems (drought, hurricanes, and fluctuating oil prices) than for most of the MDCs.

If real progess is to be made, the gap between the MDCs and LDCs must be closed. But Fig.13.12 shows that the gap has been widening. Unfortunately many of the LDCs which have *increased* their gross national product have such high population growth that the **GNP per head** has *fallen.*

Also within the LDCs themselves the better-off countries are making much faster progress than the really poor ones, many of which are in Africa, south of the Sahara.

Recently the **growth rate** of some LDCs has been approaching that of the MDCs. But consider what this means:

> Take an MDC with a GNP per head of 10 000 $US in 1992, and an LDC with one of 2000 $US per head. These both increase by 3.3% per annum. (a) What will their figures be for 1993? (b) What was the *difference* in their GNP figures (in $US) (i) in 1992, (ii) in 1993? (c) What must happen for the gap in income level to close?

13.5 Ups and downs

There is no easy answer to problems of the 'gap'. It is also difficult to predict the future of any of the LDCs and LLDCs in a world where **economic changes benefit one group and cause distress in another.**

In 1986 there was a sudden *fall* in oil prices. This can benefit the LDCs by reducing oil import bills. It helps many MDCs, who may then buy more than the LDCs. It tends to lower interest rates on loans to the LDCs.

But for the oil-exporting countries, such as Algeria, Indonesia, Mexico, Nigeria, Gabon and Venezuela, this means a huge loss in annual income. These countries account for a third of the borrowing by LDCs, so they find it difficult to repay loans. Thus foreign banks and international lending organisations may also be troubled.

In 1986 Mexico owed some $10 billion **interest** for that year. Oil was to have brought in about $12 billion. The sudden price fall cut the expected oil income by about half. Even the OPEC countries, such as Saudi Arabia, can suddenly find themselves in difficulties (and remember that they have been giving aid to LLDCs).

The LDCs are also highly dependent on other countries buying their primary produce or raw materials. Most rely on exporting just a few commodities (some depend very heavily on a single commodity, Fig. 13.13).

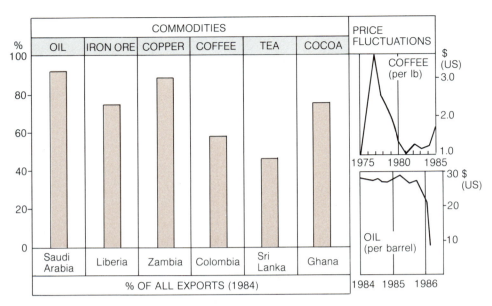

13.13 Dangerous dependence on a single commodity. Notice how price changes can affect the export income.

When the world economy is depressed, the demands for these commodities fall and so do the prices. A single country can also be affected by over-production in another, perhaps in a different part of the world.

> In hard times people cut back on luxuries. Which of the commodities in Fig. 13.13 may be regarded as luxuries?
>
> When the MDCs are closing factories and curtailing new engineering projects, which of these commodities will be affected?
>
> How do the graphs for oil and coffee prices show: (i) difficulties for planning ahead; (ii) the influence of world-wide economic and political decisions on the LDCs?
>
> There was a glut of coffee (over-production) in 1975: what exactly happened to prices?
>
> Do improving methods of production and increasing the yield of a crop *necessarily* allow an LDC to earn more through trade?
>
> Would the best way to make progress be to encourage production of many different types of primary products? What conditions might make this difficult? Give an example of a country, or part of a country, which could not easily diversify its exports.
>
> Should the aim be to encourage secondary industries in the LDCs rather than primary ones? What about com-petition with other manufacturing countries? What about the energy needed, and skills? Discuss this in more detail.
>
> It is said that Official Development Assistance (ODA) – provided by OECD, OPEC, etc. – and also funds received from private investments and charity donations end by being filtered back to the countries who provided it. How can this come about?

Theme 13
Back-up section

Political and economic understanding

Many of the issues covered in the last few themes are extremely complex. There is a danger that, by presenting them in a simplified way, we come to think that there are simple solutions. It is good to feel strongly about them. But however worthy our placards or charity donations, we have to try to find out why remedies to problems are not always easy to find: why wrongs are not easily righted.

Above all, we should obtain as much information about these issues as possible before taking a stance. Theme 14 acknowledges that a current cause for alarm is **acid rain**. But we should, at least, realise that almost all rain is 'acid'; that some forms of acid rain are most benefi-cial (nitrogen sources); that disasters attri-buted to acid rain may be found to be, at least partly, due to other causes (micro-biological ones). So that while we *should* be alarmed and investigate, we do best service to the issue by being as fully in-formed as possible.

In a wide-ranging subject like geo-graphy, issues can best be tackled in suffi-cient detail if various aspects are taken one at a time by individual groups and prepared for discussion. Returning to the issues of Theme 13, **there are a number of political and economic influences which cannot be dealt with simply in the text,** but which can form the basis for further group discussions. **The examples which follow show how a single issue can high-light such influences.**

Politics, oil movements and technology

Until 1967 the bulk movements of oil from the Middle East to the MDCs of west-ern Europe made use of the Suez Canal (Fig. 13.14**A**). Because of the restrictions on tonnage of vessels using the canal, **the tankers used were small**.

The outbreak of war between Egypt and Israel and **the closing of the canal** meant that within a few months the prin-cipal routeway from the Middle East had changed. Also, oil was now imported into Europe from other sources in greater quantities.

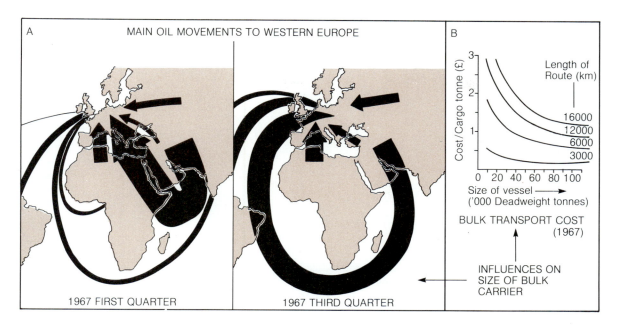

13.14 Long-term effects of closing the Suez canal.

What were the changes in routing? How did the volume of oil from the sources shown in Fig. 13.14 alter?

But **other important changes in technology and transportation followed.** Fig. 13.14**B** shows the relationships between the size of vessel, cargo carried, and distance transported. **Political action had triggered the change to supertankers.** The enormous increase in cargo–tonne–mileage had made it desirable to use a fleet of very large bulk carriers. The change was adopted world-wide, and affected the value of location of oilfields in far distant countries.

This then leads to *how* this could happen so quickly. **It is not just national political and economic decisions which affect us all today, but those taken by huge cartels and multinational organisations.**

Name four really large oil companies. Do they just explore for, develop, and market oil?

Find out about their control of shipping, production and marketing of chemicals, and engineering enterprises; and of the companies unconnected directly with petroleum which they acquire to increase their overall wealth (to carry out their activities), or to give them political influence.

Name multinational organisations other than oil companies; think of vehicles (motors), electrics, chemicals, foods.

The incomes of one of these huge corporations can exceed the gross national product of an LDC *country* many times over. **Huge vehicle corporations can have annual sales which exceed even the GNP of countries like Switzerland or New Zealand.**

When they invest in LDCs, those countries may benefit from introduced technology, and from taxes imposed on profits. But the corporations receive far more from untaxed profits. **They can control prices of the materials they acquire from LDCs.** They may use cheap labour to produce components for their more complex equipment manufactured in an MDC. **They can also damp down competition** in areas where it does not suit them.

Thus by considering one specific case (the Suez oil crisis), a number of vital issues affecting the relationships of MDCs and LDCs have been brought to light in a realistic way.

Balancing an economy

One further example enables us to see how the fortunes of an LDC may hinge on political and economic decisions rather than simply on being rich or poor in resources.

In the early 1960s Nigeria was what it had long been – a rural country depending on rural products. Seventy per cent of its export earnings were from groundnuts, oil palm products and cocoa; and others included timber, rubber, cotton and tin.

During the first five years of the '70s, its oil production increased four-fold, until it accounted for some 93 per cent of total exports. The government received a huge income from taxes and royalties.

Wages in the towns increased; so did jobs in marketing goods to meet new demands; so did services; so did industries based on *imported* materials. People flocked to the cities. Agriculture couldn't meet new demands for food. Imports increased. Domestic industries suffered from cheap imports.

By the late '70s a fall in world oil consumption cut sales; but expenditure continued to rise. During the early '80s both exports and prices for oil fell. Cutting back imports left local industries short of materials. Factories closed. Millions of immigrants from other West African countries, who had arrived during the boom, were sent back.

The World Bank then made loans with advice to invest in agriculture (to reduce food imports), and encourage industries using local raw materials.

The natural assets remain, and the oil-rich years have produced ports, roads, and airports (though a national network is far from complete). But the country has learned that reliance on oil makes it vulnerable. **The 1986 plunge in oil prices added to uncertainties about loan repayments.**

Theme 13 Making sure

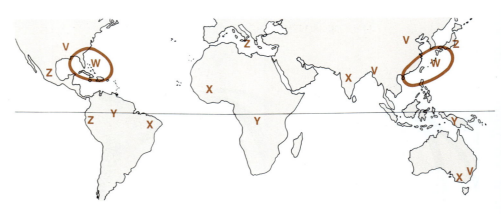

13.15 Places prone to natural disasters.

1 Explain the terms malnutritionm, infection, carrier-borne (vector-borne) disease. Which of these three forms of ill-health may result from: (i) a mosquito bite; (ii) lack of vitamins in food; (iii) fly-contaminated food?

2 Which of the countries in Table 38 are most at risk from one or other of these forms of ill-health (Q.1)? Explain why.

Table 38

country	daily protein intake (g)	doctors per million	access to safe water (%)	children dying under 1 yr (per 1000)
Philippines	53	138	65	44
Sweden	96	2743	100	6
Bangladesh	40	143	40	118
Ethiopia	42	11	38	153
Argentina	106	2506	67	32

3 Explain the reasons for choosing infant mortality, life expectancy, and literacy, as the three indicators of the quality of life in any community.

4 'Private investment is usually directed to those LDC's which can afford it.' Consider what this means. Remember that investors need a return on their investment.

5 Many LDC's have received huge loans from international organisations but are now crippled by annual interest payments. Discuss possible advantages (all-round) of regulating rates of interest or even setting aside the mounting debts of the LDCs.

6 Nissan is a multinational company. It has developed an assembly plant in the UK at Washington (Tyne-Wear). It builds trucks in the USA (Tennessee). It builds cars (with Alfa Romeo) in Italy.
(a) what is a multinational?
(b) What is meant by an 'assembly industry'?
(c) Competing countries have limited the direct imports of Japanese vehicles (by means of a quota). So what advantages are there to Japan and the country concerned of joint ventures like those mentioned?

Table 39

oil tankers

size	1940	1960	1975
length (m)	180	250	400
capacity (dwt)	40 000	70 000	500 000

7(a) What advantages and disadvantages have come with the changes in tanker size and carrying capacity indicated in Table 39?
(b) What do you think is meant by economy of scale?

8 What physical problems are there in distributing water to major consumers in Britain?

9 Why in some parts of Britain do demands for water increase considerably in summer? Where particularly?

10 What is meant by 'water recycling'? Why is the quality important for agricultural irrigation? In what sense is *all* water recycled?

11 In Ethiopia what physical problems are there in distributing water held in lakes, rivers, and as groundwater?

12 Why is the poverty cycle in highland Ethiopia so difficult to break?

13 (a) List the countries affected by drought in the Sahel (in the area shown in Fig. 13.7).
(b) At what time of the year are rains usually expected there?
(c) Explain exactly why changes of position of the front between dry and moist air (Fig. 13.8) are crucial to life in the Sahel.
(d) How did the period 1950–60 differ from that between 1970–80 in the Sahel (Fig. 13.9)?
(e) Why does the **combination** of these two sets of conditions (1950–60 and 1970–80) create potential dangers for people in the Sahel?

14 Suggest why schemes to encourage **settlement in arid marginal lands** may prove dangerous in the long term.

15 Give examples of successful large-scale settlement in very dry parts of less developed countries. What made this possible?

16 What natural hazards can affect the population of the areas marked **V, W, X, Y, Z** in Fig. 13.15? **Consider droughts, hurricanes, floods, eruptions, disease, and their causes.**

17 Discuss the following priorities for the distribution of voluntary aid contributions in drought-stricken lands:
1 provide food; 2 set up refugee camps; 3 provide medical assistance; 4 improve transportation; 5 improve roads; 6 explore for groundwater resources; 7 create propaganda for focussing attention on long term problems/solutions.

18 How does the way China has tackled Tianjin's water problems suggest advantages or disadvantages of: (i) its huge population; (ii) its rapid industrialisation; (iii) its central organisation?

19 Why is Nigeria particularly likely to have booms and recessions?
How does this also emphasise that LDC economies should be as broad-based as possible, and rely on their own resources as far as possible?

Most of the 120 million people can afford only a limited quantity of industrial products. Nigerian industries cannot easily compete with those in the MDCs. Why do these facts, together, make it difficult to broaden its economy?

Which group of countries can make decisions which affect Nigeria's whole economy? What will cause the price of a commodity to fall world-wide? Find out what particular facts led to the sudden collapse of oil prices in 1986.

Consider the terms used

A scatter graph uses dots to show the relationships between two sets of statistics, one plotted on the **x**-axis, one on the **y**-axis. If the dots are randomly scattered, no correlation exists. The closer the dots to forming a straight line, the stronger the correlation.

Paddy (padi) rice is unhusked rice which has usually been grown by irrigation (wet rice). Seedlings are transferred from a bed to a flooded field and water provided until the grain is mature; the husk is removed after threshing.

Microbiological action is that due to minute living organisms.

A cartel is an organisation which controls the commerce of a number of companies engaged in similar activities.

A multinational corporation is a huge organisation with production units in many countries and control concentrated at the top in the parent country. The individual factories have varying degrees of local control over their affairs.

Theme 14 Resources and the environment: conservation and protection

We are all in continuous contact, and conflict, with the natural environment. Sadly, through ignorance, greed or stupidity, we destroy much that should be preserved: so that in the end we are the losers.

People are also in conflict with each other: over the use of resources; over the circumstances which create the 'have' and 'have not' societies; and over their firmly held, but often very different political and religious beliefs.

14.1 Controls over our activities

Groups of nations which come together because of their similar political and economic beliefs take decisions which affect huge numbers of people.

The Commonwealth brings together over forty countries which were once British dependencies, part of a great empire. They use their common interests to foster trade links and development projects. They seek a common approach to world problems. They share cultural and sporting activities, such as the Commonwealth Games.

The links are voluntary. The opinions of individual members on various world affairs do not necessarily coincide. The ties between them are sometimes loosened, as when countries boycott the Games.

Britain is also a member of the **European Economic Community (EEC)**. After World War II certain Western European nations tried to rebuild their industries and agriculture together. They developed trade and tariff agreements with one another. France, West Germany, Belgium, the Netherlands, Luxembourg, and Italy formed the EEC in 1958.

Britain, concerned about the effects of EEC policies and trade links on the Commonwealth countries, did not become a member until 1973, when Eire and Denmark also joined. Greece joined in 1981, and Spain and Portugal in 1986.

Each country contributes to a common fund. Together they decide on ways of improving agriculture and industry, and assisting the poorer parts of the Community, where particular groups of people are at a disadvantage.

Agriculture receives by far the largest support, recently about three-quarters of the total funds. A *Common Agricultural Policy* (CAP) seeks to provide a relatively risk-free form of agriculture. Prices need not coincide with those on world markets. Many products are purchased from EEC farmers at fixed prices even when surplus is produced. This has resulted, however, in 'wine lakes' and 'butter mountains'. The export of such surpluses can be subsidised by EEC funds.

Certain EEC regions have come to specialise in a particular range of products. Their farming has generally become more intensive, with more factory-like systems of production.

> Look at Fig. 11.21 and suggest which parts of the EEC form mainly the poorer peripheral areas, and which the core.
>
> What kind of industrial–urban problems are most likely to cause concern in the core area (see page 163)?
>
> The EEC is also concerned with social improvement, and expects members to respect decisions of its Court of Justice. Do you think that matters like equal pay for men and women, or the abolition of corporal punishment should be decided centrally by EEC institutions, or left to individual countries to decide?

The EEC, like other economic blocs, also provides aid for many of the LDCs and LLDCs.

Some of the countries are also members of the political–military alliance with the USA, known as **The North Atlantic Treaty Organisation** (NATO). This means deploying each others' troops and weapons, and using joint bases in the member countries. This leads to disagreements from time to time when policies about nuclear weapons, or military actions, clash with the political beliefs of a member country, or groups within the country.

The most wealthy of the Western industrial countries belong to the **Organisation for Economic Cooperation and Development** (OECD). This, among other things, supplies a large proportion of the Official Development Assistance (ODA) given, or lent, to other countries.

The USSR and Eastern European countries, together with Cuba, Mongolia and Vietnam, formed a political–economic bloc known as COMECON. They shared common beliefs in state ownership and state controls over economic development, and the even distribution of wealth. Foodstuffs, industrial materials, manufactures, and energy pass between them. Others attended COMECON meetings as observers – including Angola, North Korea, Ethiopia, Mozambique, Nicaragua, Laos and Yemen.

The breakdown of this great bloc has seen individual ethnic minorities seeking greater control over political and economic issues. Yet, even as the former USSR is reshaped, regions are seeking to group together for mutual benefits, which only a bloc can achieve.

Blocs of countries are established in other parts of the world to assist one another economically (Fig. 14.1). The **Association of South East Asian Nations** (ASEAN) includes Indonesia, Malaysia, Brunei, Philippines, Singapore and Thailand. It has committees in their capital cities dealing with food and agriculture, finance, commerce and industry, etc.

The **Latin American Free Trade Association** (LAFTA) includes all South American countries (except Guyana), and also Mexico. Because of the great economic differences between the members, it has to give special tariff benefits to those of lesser and least development.

The **North American Free Trade Association** (NAFTA) aims to encourage a greater exchange of commodities – but opponents envisage many USA or Canadian firms locating in Mexico to take advantage of the lower wage costs.

The Caribbean countries and Guyana form a **Caribbean Community and Common Market** group (CARICOM).

There are other groups among the world's countries. Such grouping has the advantage of giving them common aims and allowing self-help. Where the countries have very different stages of development, however, a general policy (say towards tariffs) may benefit some but hamper others.

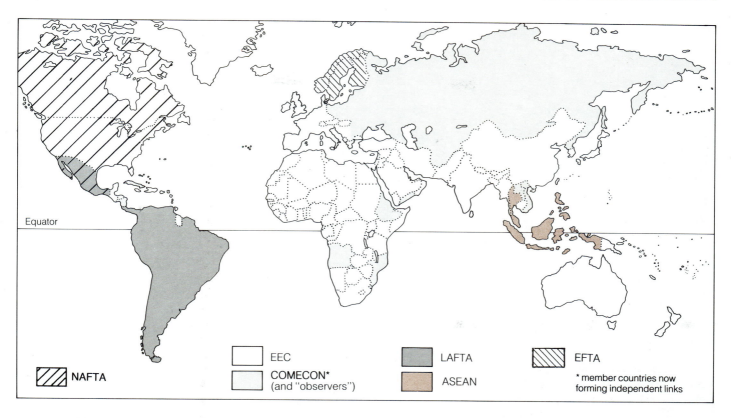

14.1 *Large blocs of countries with common economic interests. *The break-up of COMECON has led to the recognition of independent countries who seek new political and economic alignments.*

The United Nations organisation (UN) was formed in 1945. Its head-quarters is in New York. Apart from the meetings of its General Assembly, where members attempt to agree on common policies towards world problems, **its work is carried out through various Agencies**, for example:

FAO   (Food and Agricultural Organisation)
WHO   (World Health Organisation)
UNHQ   UNDRO   (Disaster Relief Organisation)
UNICEF   (International Children's Emergency Fund)
UNESCO   (Educational, Scientific and Cultural Organisation)

Other UN Agencies deal with particular situations and problems. Obviously the success of these Agencies depends on the cooperation of member nations. One difficulty has been the influence of the most powerful nations on the thousands of millions of people in the blocs mentioned above. In the Assembly one group may solidly vote to prevent actions which another group feels are essential for human progress or freedom.

Nevertheless, there is the machinery to deal effectively with many of the world's immediate problems. One of the main advantages is that it continuously makes people aware of what is happening elsewhere, and why.

Similarly, **groups outside the UN**, like the Save the Children organisation, and the organised fund-raising events like Band Aid and Live Aid may seem to be dealing with amounts which are small, for all their immense efforts, compared with those allocated by groups of nations, or the International Monetary Fund (IMF): but **they also do an immense service by focusing attention on particular situations.**

Ignorance of conditions outside our own immediate surroundings, and of other people's problems and points of view, is not just our loss but can be dangerous. Organisations like Live Aid help to make us aware. More disturb-ingly, groups of people use force to try to make us see social problems from their point of view. Discuss the whole topic of 'finding out' and 'other people's points of view'.

Apart from international controls, there are many ways in which people can be directed to act so as to benefit the whole environment. National governments act independently to assist their own deprived areas, to conserve their own resources, or create protected environments, such as National Parks.

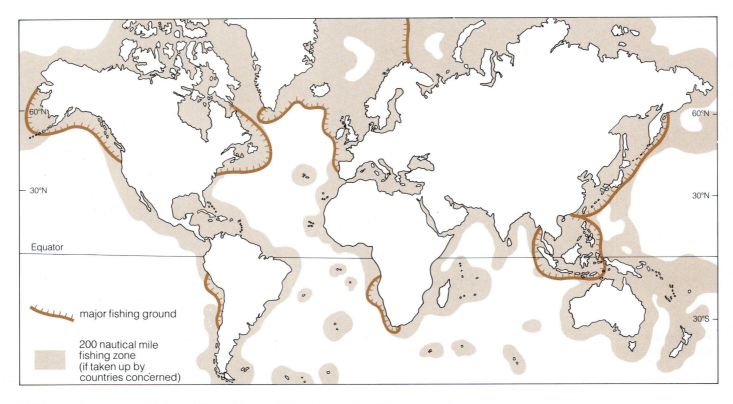

14.2 Parts of the ocean which could be subject to 200 nautical-mile offshore control over fishing resources. Many countries have declared such limits – in Canada's case over both Pacific and Atlantic waters. EEC countries have agreed exclusive fishing zones.

major fishing ground

200 nautical mile fishing zone (if taken up by countries concerned)

14.2 Conservation

Some resources, such as fossil fuels and metal ores, are non-renewable, on our time-scale. We already know roughly how long reserves of fuels are likely to last, so we consider alternatives. Other resources are renewable but need careful conservation lest they diminish to vanishing point. Fishing and the need to avoid over-fishing is a clear example.

Fish: a valuable food resource

Fish are a renewable source of food energy and protein. Sunlight and nutrients in the water cause a rapid growth of billions of the minute marine plants and animals known as **plankton**. Huge numbers of tiny fish feed on the plankton and are themselves consumed by larger fish. Thus a teeming fish population becomes concentrated where conditions favour an abundance of plankton.

According to habit, some fish, such as

herring, mackerel and anchovies are near-surface feeders (**pelagic fish**); others, such as cod and haddock, feed in deeper waters, some near the bed, like sole and plaice (**demersal fish**)

Fig. 14.2 shows favoured fishing grounds, where conditions promote plankton growth. Consider just four of them:

1 In the North Sea minerals from adjacent lands concentrate in waters over the shallow continental shelf, which allows both surface and deep feeders to benefit.

2 Off Newfoundland and Nova Scotia the shallow waters over submarine banks are penetrated by sunlight, and warm and cold currents meet and mix the minerals.

3 In the north-west Pacific, too, contrasting currents and a continental shelf produce an abundant supply of the many species fished by fleets from Japan, the USSR, and China.

4 Off western South America the cold up-welling waters and the Peru current favour dense shoals of anchovies. Millions of tonnes of fishmeal are processed each year from the catches off Peru.

Considering the North Sea fishing grounds alone, it is understandable that uncontrolled fishing to supply all the adjoining countries would soon prevent annual replacement of the shoals. **Agreements on permitted catches, size of the mesh of nets, and periods when certain types of fishing are prohibited, are essential.**

Nations are concerned to secure fishing rights over a given area off their shores. Accordingly, **EEC member states have an exclusive fishing zone (EFZ) of 200 nautical miles from their shores.** The boundaries are agreed internationally. (Rights over a few areas are still to be decided.) The coastal states manage the stocks and may fix periods of no catching for various species. **Each country has a total annual allowable fish catch.** If they cannot meet this themselves, they arrange access to other states' waters.

Beyond such limits are the High Seas. Here controls are more difficult. Here, too, national fleets are accompanied by factory ships with refrigerated storage, and ships are equipped with electronic aids for detecting shoals. But, as Fig. 14.2 shows, the waters of the major fishing grounds are now mostly in the control of nations who wish to safeguard stocks in their EFZ.

The growing world population puts increasing pressure on fish stocks. Fleets, especially those of Japan and the USSR, now catch huge quantities of **krill**, the tiny shrimps which sustain many species of whale. Conservation methods call for total international agreements, and these are difficult to obtain, as whaling has shown. **During the 18th and 19th centuries whalers all but exterminated five of the largest species.** Another seven species are now in danger of extinction. Most of the whale oil is made into margarine or soap. Most of the meat feeds domestic animals or is made into fertilisers.

Before World War II almost all whaling was in Antarctica. But during the 1950s yields from Antarctica rapidly declined. The large blue whales were almost fished out.

In the next ten years a quarter of a million of the smaller finbacks were killed, besides other species. The International Whaling Commission set quotas for catches, which were largely ignored. Attention turned to sperm whales in the north Pacific. Whatever our view of the cruelty of such slaughter, there is no doubt that we are bringing still more species to the point of extinction.

P 14.1 The introduction of cooperative fish farming in ponds prepared among the forest in Zaïre.

P 14.2 Scientific fish breeding has produced high yields from ponded water sources on the Brazilian plateau.

Recently a total ban on whaling, as a protective measure, has led many nations to give up whaling. Some still hunt whales; but these are now few, and under pressure from the others, and from organisations like Greenpeace, genuine protection is slowly coming about.

People still need food, and methods to increase fish supplies include:

(a) The stocking of available ponds and small rivers, as under China's policy of 'where there's water there's fish'.

(b) The use of tropical swamplands and flooded padis for fish farming. Some in south-east Asia have yielded more than 10 tonnes of fish per hectare each year.

(c) Scientific fish farming, both to provide fish directly, and to breed large numbers for release into rivers, ponds, and seas.

Mineral resources and substitutes

New technology has helped to counter the danger of non-renewable minerals becoming mined out, and so endangering our industrial future. We have been finding **substitutes:** using plastics or carbon fibres where we once used metals; using minute computer circuitry where we once needed vast rooms of bulky machinery.

Find as many examples as you can of: (a) direct substitution of modern

materials for traditional ones; (b) ways in which machinery, apparatus and gadgets have become more compact.

P 14.3 The recycling of precious metals from discarded computer parts and other electronic equipment at a works in Sweden.

But while some substitutes have helped to conserve mineral reserves, they have also put mining communities at risk. The Cornish tin miners, together with others worldwide, have suffered from a collapse in demand for the metal.

How and when did the use of tin change the nature of food production and distribution? What modern forms of food storage, packing and processing have cut down the use of tin? Suggest other reasons why the demand for tin has fallen.

Modern substitutes can have other disadvantages as well. Plastic bags may save metal and timber resources, but pollute the environment when thrown away, and endanger livestock when people discard them in picnic areas.

Scientists have enabled industry to produce bio-degradable packaging materials. These break down into soluble mineral and organic materials when dumped. But a further drawback is the amounts of energy and petro-chemicals needed to produce most of these substitutes.

The same applies to the conservation of our domestic and industrial wastes. **Many parts of north-west Europe now use urban wastes as an extra energy source,** and are concerned to **recycle** scrap metals for conversion into usable raw materials, in the way that old cars are crushed, and their iron and steel components extracted for re-use. But these processes also call for a large input of energy, so that careful costing is needed.

P 14.4 Refuse vehicles carry urban waste to a New England plant which combines recycling with heat generation and electricity production.

Consider softwood timber in terms of conservation. Among its uses are construction, furniture, paper, packaging, artificial fibres (in chemical industries), and fuel. Many hectares of forest are needed to provide paper for a single issue of a national newspaper.

(a) Is this a renewable resource? Why is it now referred to as a 'crop'?

(b) What kind of substitutes are available for the uses referred to above?

(c) Which use continues to exert a great, and increasing, demand for softwood? Explain why. (Consider literacy/illiteracy and population numbers.)

(d) Which alternative methods of spreading information may reduce demand?

14.3 Preservation

Besides the need to conserve resources, there is an urgent need to preserve much of our natural heritage. It is not just wildlife – individual plant and animal species – which are endangered, but also whole ecosystems. In these the living and non-living components achieve a unique, working balance, whether in forest, savanna or swampland.

We must not exclude the landscapes people have created over the years, including our farmlands. They form part of an ecosystem with delicate balances between plant and animal life, water, and soils, which are easily destroyed.

Historic sites and buildings also come in the same category, and we need to assess which should be preserved.

Parks, reserves and leisure areas

Many countries are creating wildlife reserves, where species can be preserved, for reasons stated. But the game parks also serve national interests. Those of east Africa, in particular, have become part of a tourist industry which combines the attractions of sun and shores with views of the wide savannas and their wildlife.

There are drawbacks, however. The attentions of conservationists and rangers on the spot create a new ecological balance. In places preservation has increased some species to the point of overstocking. Then, apart from the serious threat from poachers, in search of ivory and rhino horn, there are dangers from tourism. **People who are all for preservation and conservation may help to destroy what they wish to preserve.**

(a) vehicles, roads, camps, hotels and regular tourist circuits not only affect the local wildlife, but tend to create an open zoo rather than preserve a particular ecosystem;

(b) physical pollution from tourist wastes can include virus contamination as well as dumped materials;

(c) tourists undoubtedly disturb the seasonal behaviour and migratory habits of both wildlife and local peoples.

Turning to the **National Parks** in Britain, we find much the same hazards. **Conservation interests are in conflict with needs for leisure and recreation, and the life of local peoples.** The same applies to the **Areas of Outstanding Beauty**. There are also tiny areas of historic or wildlife interest designated **Sites of Special Interest**. Some visitors wish to ramble, some to bird-watch or explore the countryside; others wish to play in the open, set up camps, or simply drive, park and take photos. Also, the long-established inhabitants within the park wish to earn a living, improve their farming methods, and perhaps hunt over the countryside. **Many of these interests must clash.**

Choosing **Dartmoor** (Fig. 14.3), we find that there is a National Park Committee, with farmers, industrialists, housewives, etc., combining to serve public interests. There is a National Park Officer with a team of rangers, foresters, information officers, etc. Also keeping an eye on the environment is a Dartmoor Preservation Association.

What they all have to aim at is not just keeping what's there, but to make sure that the ever-changing features are treated

P 14.5 The impact of visitors on a Kenyan game park, where Maribou storks, vultures and monkeys scavenge among the litter.

in a sensible way. The most attractive valley woodlands of oak and ash, with hazel and rowan below, and carpets of herbs beneath, maintained themselves because in the past people coppiced them carefully. Today expert forestry attention is needed to maintain them.

The farmers want fields for silage and hay, but conservationists watch for any encroachment on wild moorland. Yet the silage and hay help to keep stock off the moor early in the year, when otherwise they might damage moorland plants.

Okehampton wanted a by-pass to ease the summer snarl-up, which pollutes the whole north-west corner; yet proposals to take a tiny part of the National Park for this purpose incensed many conservationists. Things are never as simple or as straightforward as they seem!

There are 8 million visitors a year (some returning many times). Some 30 000 people live in the Park. The Park has valuable china clay reserves. Its height makes it a good place for communications masts. The military want to use it for exercises. Some want a civil airport near Yelverton. Some want more coniferous plantations (including the Forestry Commission). **All these interests have to be considered and weighed up.** Some have been rejected outright – the airport, a new high mast; some are limited – china clay mining, military uses, more forestry plantation.

Besides these demands, think what the **tourists** are apt to need and what they may do. **They tend to flock to attractive sites** – outstanding tors, historic places, the prison, and so on, especially where

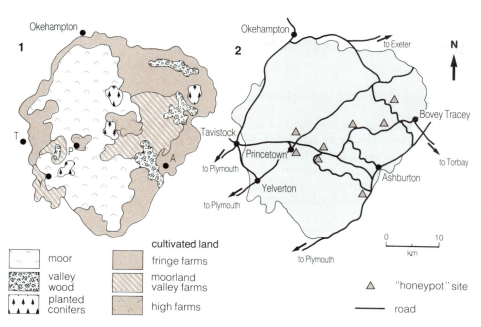

14.3 The Dartmoor National Park: **1** *cultivated areas;* **2** *'honeypot' sites easily accessible from a main road.*

these are near the road. They need car parks, public lavatories, places for refreshments. **Such sites are known as 'honeypots', and there many of the dangers lie.**

Visitors wear out river banks, widen bridleways, and make new foot tracks (for cars are restricted to hard surfaces). New tracks can lead directly to erosion as water follows their channels. Dogs interfere with livestock. Walkers carry germs on their boots, which also may endanger stock (so the farmers want more fences on the moor!). More notices appear, but these are not really desirable.

> Why do you think the number of visitors to the Parks has increased so much in the last 20 years? How would you try to prevent them clustering within the Parks? What do you think of more notices, and 'guided parties only' to certain parts?

Consider the way that social changes and population structure can affect the need for particular amenities – a larger proportion of old people, a higher proportion of unemployed, a shorter working week.

Spectator sports cater for large numbers, but only for short periods. People need to take part and participate in activities as locally as possible. In view of increasing urbanisation, **urban leisure**

activities are needed. Games fields, swimming pools and sports centres, as well as cinemas, theatres, clubs and social centres, are as much part of the urban environment as housing, factories and businesses. Public buildings, schools and libraries often share their facilities with the general public, providing games areas, lecture halls, music rooms, and so on.

> Looking at what you have seen of large towns (Theme 12), where would you expect to find: (i) public recreation fields; (ii) squash courts run for profit; (iii) a golf course; (iv) an amusement arcade: (a) in the CBD; (b) in inner urban areas; (c) in inner suburbs; (d) in outer suburbs; (e) close-by in the commuter belt?

14.4 Pollution

We make a mess of our environment in many ways: on different scales, with short-term consequences and long-term, perhaps permanent, effects. Street litter reflects a lack of care and organisation. This can be remedied, but many of our wastes can create lasting damage.

Freely circulating water can spread pollution over a wide area; while in enclosed or slow-moving water pollutants can build up dangerous concentrations. Many pollutants are not visible. Spillage

from oil tankers makes the headlines, and can foul beaches and harm wildlife. But more dangerous chemicals are continually poured into rivers as industrial and agricultural wastes.

Many metal industries, being large water consumers are situated along river banks and coasts. Strict control over their wastes is essential. Rivers such as the Rhine flow past so many heavy industrial areas and chemical complexes that they become chemical sewers, rapidly corroding the vessels which navigate them.

Agricultural wastes washed into streams, rivers and lakes include insecticides and pesticides. These can build up dangerously in animal food chains (Fig. 6.13). But even nitrogen-rich manure and artificial fertilisers can be harmful. Large concentrations stimulate such a growth of algae and small aquatic plants that they choke streams and lakes, depriving other life-forms of oxygen.

Air pollution affects even the upper atmosphere (p. 259). While the air about us becomes dangerously polluted, by fumes from industries, vehicle exhausts and chemical works. **Air circulation carries pollutants far afield. Industrial areas can release gases which increase rainfall acidity until it becomes harmful to vegetation.** The extent to which **acid rain** is responsible for forest destruction is debatable, but the danger is there.

The effects of acid rain and other air pollutants are due to their continuous transport by a prevailing wind. Places hundreds of kilometres downwind of industrial districts may be affected.

> Why do Scandinavian countries in particular blame Britain for air-borne pollution, which has affected their ponds, rivers, and vegetation?·

P 14.6 Student volunteers cleaning the mess of oil pollution from the beaches of Brittany.

Radioactive wastes are a different matter. Their ability to harm remains for a very long time, and their harmful effects can be hidden for many years. The 1986 disaster at Chernobyl emphasised that radioactive particles can be distributed over a very wide area. Unusual concentrations can be built up locally by sinking air or polluted rain. Radioactivity can also be passed on through food chains.

The type of pollution varies with levels of development. People in the more developed countries suffer not just from lead in traffic fumes, or chemicals from aerosols, but create noise pollution. There are houses under the flight path of aircraft, hotels whose upper storeys open onto motorway fly-overs (England's soccer squad, Mexico '86!), the rumble of heavy goods vehicles, the shattering noise of low-powered scooters, and high-volume transistors. Sadly, most of the large cities in the less developed countries have come to suffer much the same noise and congestion.

Pollution takes many forms. It is distributed in particular locations and can be examined geographically, like any other component of the ecosystem.

14.5 The large-scale problems

We should rightly be alarmed at many of the things we are doing to the planet. Often people's actions have unintended and disastrous effects on soils, water resources and the atmosphere. It is hoped that the various themes presented here will give a clearer understanding of how one action can trigger off others.

To understand this, look again at the effects of rainforest clearance and the problem of increasing desertification.

Rainforest clearance in Amazonia

Look in the atlas at the huge area of the Amazon basin covered by rainforest. It has developed over millions of years, unaffected by glaciation or desert conditions. it is immensely rich in animal and plant species. It is a balanced system:

1 The forest vegetation, with shallow root systems, recycles plant nutrients so quickly that the soils have few reserves.

2 The tree canopies and the steady percolation of water into the soil prevent surface erosion.

3 The vegetation returns (recycles) about half the rainfall to the atmosphere by evapo-transpiration.

4 The large number of plant and animal species have their own particular ecological niches; but each is part of the whole balanced rainforest system.

But now, from the foothills of the Andes to the lowlands of eastern Brazil, the rainforests are suffering large-scale cutting and burning. They are being replaced by agricultural land-use and cattle pastures. These have often proved unsuccessful, with the result that huge areas have been abandoned. But the original rainforest is lost forever.

Deforestation changes so much of the natural balance:

1 Stripping the forest allows nutrients to be washed out by rain.

2 When large areas are used for crops or grazing, the nutrients pass into the plants and animals, and so are removed from the area (exported). In Amazonia ranches have replaced tens of thousands of hectares of forest. They have mostly been turned into poor grassland.

3 Cattle trampling produces bare soil, which increases run-off and erosion.

4 Heavy rain washes away fine clay particles and produces a coarser sandy soil. Dust appears during dry periods.

5 The forest may survive local clearances; but large-scale deforestation means that much less water is recycled, so the local rainfall decreases.

6 With drier conditions, the shallow-rooted trees cannot reach the deeper soil water, so many die.

7 When cut, rotting and burning release to the air about four-fifths of the carbon in the vegetation. If all Amazonia were cleared, the carbon dioxide in the atmosphere would increase by about 8 per cent. This could cause a rise in atmospheric temperature, due to the 'greenhouse effect' (p. 259).

P 14.7 Heavy equipment clearing rainforest in Central America.

P 14.8 Final clearing of the area shown in Photo 14.7, by firing the felled branches and lower vegetation. The plant–soil balance is destroyed, and nutrients retained in the ashes are quickly lost.

8 Clearing destroys many of the unique living species, which have evolved over millions of years.

9 The native peoples have been part of the forest ecosystem; but their ways of life are being destroyed by peoples who live in industrial countries, far from the forests. Their life-style will change, but there is little effort to allow them to progress in a protected environment.

Six years after rainforest clearance, the artificial pastures in north-east Brazil could support only a third of the cattle they could to begin with. Suggest reasons for this.

Rainforests in Africa and south-east Asia are under particularly great pressures from timber extraction and clearance for settlement.

P 14.9 A poster in rural India stresses the effects of deforestation in parts of the country which have suffered badly from the removal of protective woodland.

P 14.10 Preparing the beds for many thousands of tree seedlings to be used for planting in an afforestation scheme in Ethiopia. Each is set in a cylindrical container.

257

P14.11 Overstocking with poor cattle, and goats which rapidly destroy low vegetation, is one of the causes of desertification in this Sahel belt. Rain temporarily fills hollows, but can sweep away what is left of overgrazed soil. The following drought turns the surface material to dust.

Desertification

The spread of deserts can be due to climatic changes (Fig. 13.9), but also to the way people treat the desert margins.

Few people live in absolute desert unless there is an assured water supply. But on the fringes of the desert a period of sufficient rain may support a dry savanna, which attracts herdsmen with their cattle, goats and temporary dwellings. During prolonged periods with adequate rainfall, the stocks are increased.

Dry years inevitably follow, when there is insufficient grazing on the overstocked marginal land. Herds then concentrate on the more favourable areas with waterholes. There over-grazing and trampling rapidly reduce, and destroy, the vegetation. Trampling loosens the surface, and wind erosion removes the remains of the thin top-soil.

Once lost, the vegetation is difficult to re-establish. Even when the rains return, the bare surface is immediately exposed to gulley erosion. Much may recover; but some remains as wasteland.

This displaced population then puts pressure on the more closely settled dry farmlands beyond. There have recently been conflicts in the Sudan between poor farmers and the herdsmen, whose animals have not only trampled, but grazed their crops.

Good soil can become infertile in marginal lands which depend on forms of irrigation. Irrigation water brings up salt minerals, and continuous evaporation can cake surfaces with salts harmful to plants.

Irrigated cultivation is often precarious. The land suffers when fertiliser does not arrive in time, or if there is mechanical trouble. Pumps supplied for deep wells can fail, and spare parts be unavailable, leaving no alternatives when the water-table is low. Mechanical ploughs (also subject to repair problems) can cause soil to lose too much water during dry periods.

In fact, developments in one area can lead to problems in another. In the Sudan, serious erosion has also occurred in land abandoned by people attracted to move to better-irrigated areas.

In regions where the soil-vegetation stability is precariously balanced, desertification can be rapid and on a huge scale. The USA dust-bowl of the 1930s showed what can happen when marginal land is mismanaged, even in the more developed countries.

14.6 A balanced view of environmental problems

Global environmental problems are seldom straightforward. **It is right to be concerned, but harmful to panic.** Remember that alarmist statements sell newspapers, and it may pay a politician or supermarket to be seen to be 'greener' than

P14.12 Heavy machinery is not necessarily the answer to agriculture improvements in lands where rainfall is unreliable. Deep ploughing in dry, dusty soil can be a step towards desertification.

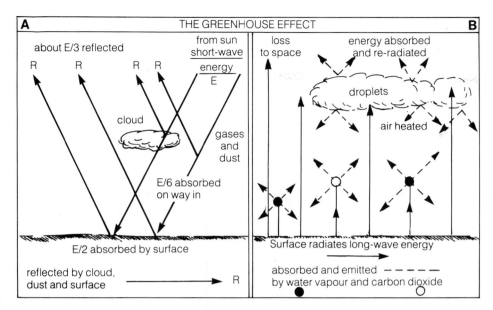

14.4 A: short-wave energy from the sun readily penetrates the atmosphere, though considerable amounts are reflected from clouds and dust particles and then from the surface. B shows the parts played by water vapour and carbon dioxide in heating the lower air. CFCs absorb and emit long-wave energy even more effectively, though their concentration is relatively small.

competitors. Here are two global issues with which we should be concerned, and about which we should be fully informed, in order to assess likely dangers, possible benefits, and priorities for action.

The Greenhouse Effect

Fig. 14.4 shows that about half the incoming short-wave energy from the sun is able to penetrate the atmosphere and heat the surface; the rest is absorbed or reflected by the gases, droplets and impurities it encounters, and, especially, reflected from the surface itself.

Energy from the earth's surface heats the air above; for water vapour and droplets, and carbon dioxide (CO_2), in particular, can absorb this long-wave energy and so heat the rest of the air about them. Many of the gases with which we pollute the atmosphere, such as nitrogen oxides and chlorofluorocarbons (CFCs), have a similar heating effect.

The system acts rather like a greenhouse: the sun's radiation penetrates the lower air, which is heated from below. A cloud cover, preventing loss of heat from ground to space, and itself absorbing and radiating long-wave energy, increases warming.

Over the last hundred years the CO_2 in the air has increased by about a quarter, mostly from burning fossil fuels and vegetation (for land-use). Methane, released by vegetable matter decomposing in swamps, ricefields, and in cattle, is also increasing and adds to the 'greenhouse effect'.

During this period the average global air temperature has risen by some 0.5 C°. Should the CO_2 content double, computer predictions suggest a further rise of some 1.5 C°–4.5 C°, though this is far from certain.

Alarms

Possible consequences might be:
1 Climatic zones shifting (p. 75), with some areas drier and warmer, others wetter. This could affect crop distributions and yields.

2 Increased melting of Antarctic ice sheets; which could raise sea-level and endanger coastlands.
3 Arctic sea-ice melting; which could affect ocean currents and thus climates.
4 More erratic and more extreme weather conditions, related to warmer air and increasing amounts of moisture.

Consider other facts:

(a) The actual rise of 0.5 C° over a century is *less* than the CO_2 increase would suggest.
(b) In the Northern Hemisphere mean air temperatures rose from 1860 until 1940, but then *fell*; fluctuating since 1970.
(c) Recently, the volumes of snow and glacier ice in the Northern Hemisphere have *increased* at high altitudes.
(d) **Fig. 14.5A shows how mean temperature has fluctuated during recent centuries.** Low sunspot activity seems to coincide with falls in average temperatures. What *might* happen during the next century? (Fig. 14.5**B** shows greater variations over millions of years).
(e) The rise in temperature from 1860 may have been partly a recovery from periods of unusually low temperatures during the 17th–19th centuries.
(f) Periods of excessive volcanic activity can lower air temperatures; followed, naturally, by a warmer period of recovery.
(g) Ocean temperatures, and the behaviour of currents, respond to variations in the heat input from the sun. **Changes in the position and temperature of ocean currents have marked effects on climate.**
(h) The burning of vegetation for land clearances is likely to decrease, with less CO_2 from this source.

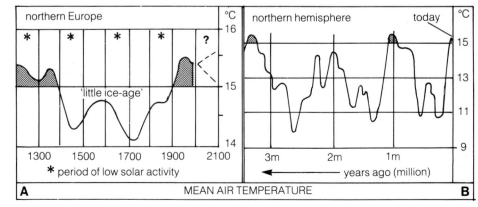

14.5 A: Sunspots are associated with great outbursts of short-wave energy. Periods of cooling have followed times of very low sunspot activity. B shows temperature decreases sufficient for 'ice ages'. Notice how rarely temperatures have been as high as in recent centuries.

Feedback

(i) If ocean surfaces warm in response to a greenhouse effect, they will absorb *less* CO_2, making for further atmospheric warming.

(ii) Warmer oceans mean greater evaporation. More water vapour and low cloud may add to the greenhouse effect: though high cloud acts to cool the surface.

(ii) More atmospheric moisture, however, is likely to mean more snow, so *increasing* the volume of glaciers and ice sheets. (It is by no means certain that a warmer atmosphere would cause a significant reduction of the main Antarctic ice covering).

Could the Greenhouse Effect be a good thing?

1 **Extra CO_2 can stimulate plant growth.** A doubling may increase wheat, rice, and cassava yields by 10–50 per cent, and millet, maize and sugar yield by up to 10 per cent.

2 **Extra CO_2 partly closes plant stomata (leaf pores)**, conserving water. Less is taken from the soil; irrigation is more effective.

3 A climatic shift may see parts of the deserts being invaded by grassy vegetation.

4 Warming in temperate latitudes may mean producing new crop varieties and farming new areas: but developed countries could cope with such gradual changes.

The Ozone Layer

In the rare atmosphere, 30 km or so above the surface, **the sun's ultra-violet (UV) radiation creates ozone from oxygen molecules** (Fig. 14.6). Various gases from earth have long been destroying some of this ozone. These include chloromethane compounds and nitrogen oxides released from fungi and as bacteria break down rainforest debris.

A natural balance has been achieved – with sufficient high-level ozone to act as a shield and prevent excessive UV radiation damaging life-forms, long-adapted to survive at the surface. **Today, however, we are releasing enough ozone-destroying gases to upset the balance**, so that dangerous amounts of UV radiation can reach the surface. This could make for an increase in skin cancers and peculiarities in plant organs.

Among our emissions reaching the upper air are the chlorofluorocarbons (CFCs)

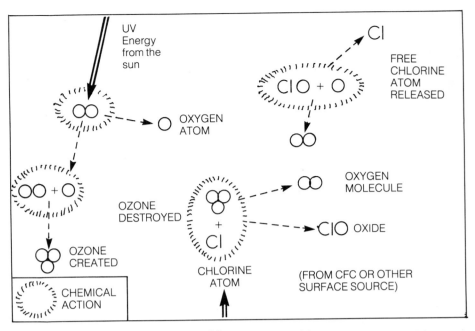

14.6 In the upper air CFCs release chlorine. Here a chlorine atom reacts with ozone (O_3) to form an oxygen molecule (O_2) and an oxide (ClO). Here, too, the sun's UV energy splits an oxygen molecule into atoms. You can see that when ClO combines with an oxygen atom chlorine is again released, capable of destroying more ozone.

which, besides contributing to the greenhouse effect, release chlorine, which destroys ozone (Fig. 14.6). Nitrogen oxides and methane are also destructive, though they are relatively short-lived: but CFCs can remain for centuries, and, as you see, chlorine can be regenerated in the upper air.

Ozone concentration has apparently become unusually low over Antarctica,. This so-called 'hole' in the ozone layer is seen as a warning to what *may* be occurring elsewhere.

Consider other facts

1 Ozone is continuously being produced in the upper air by incoming UV radiation. Our contributions, therefore, do not completely destroy the 'layer'. But **we must cut back these emissions**, to restore a satisfactory balance.

2 The thinning over Antarctica waxes and wanes with the seasons, and varies from year to year. Most of the loss occurs during early summer; however the concentration increases again by autumn.

3 Advances in technology and satellite observations have only recently made possible a detailed study of the Antarctic thinning. The part played by the varying energy inputs from the sun is not yet clear, but it seems that major volcanic emissions, like Pinatubo's massive output since 1991, add destructive chemicals.

Concerned, but informed

We *should* be concerned about possible disasters, and be wise enough to take action against them. **By considering the many factors which might affect such problems we get a broader view, and can focus our attention on the most urgent problems.** We can direct resources to where they are most needed. We should, in this way, avoid attributing every climatic oddity to 'the greenhouse effect'. We should also, for example, realise that DCs and LDCs, alike, have got to cut back on dangerous chemical emissions. Also that the DCs should help to contribute to the cost of providing suitable clean apparatus and technology for use in the less developed parts of the world.

Theme 14
Making sure

1 Between 1960 and 1980 nearly one-sixth of all English hedgrows were removed.

(a) Give reasons why this was done:

(b) give reasons why hedgrows should not be removed.

2 On what grounds might a preservation society object/not object to the following proposed activities in a National Park in England or Wales:

(a) siting a nuclear power station;

(b) an extension of farmland for fodder crops;

(c) building a kiosk to sell souvenirs related to the Park;

(d) building a large new car park;

(e) damming a lake for a reservoir.

3 (a) Make a list of dos and don'ts for people using an upland National Park. Give reasons for each of them.

(b) Should such notices be posted as widely as possible throughout the Park? What objections could there be?

4 Why are the major fishing grounds concentrated in certain parts of the oceans?

5 A female fish produces over a quarter of a million eggs, from which 200 000 may survive in a fish farm, but only 2 or 3 in the open sea. Why? What does this suggest about necessary fishing restrictions in the oceans?

6 Why may the mesh of fishing nets not be *below* a certain size?

7 (a) What is krill, which is now caught in huge quantities, especially by Japanese and USSR fishing fleets?

(b) What is the advantage of taking a food source lower down the food chain than a whale?

(c) What could be the effects of large-scale krill fishing?

8 Explain how vegetation exchanges oxygen, carbon dioxide and water vapour with the atmosphere.

9 (a) What might bring about a large increase in atmospheric carbon dioxide?

(b) How might this cause a global rise in air temperatures?

(c) What effects *could* this have (i) on areas under ice; (ii) on sea-levels; (iii) on low-lying land areas?

10 A recent publication has described the advantages of beef cattle ranching in western Amazonia thus: 'The climate is ideal for grass; there are constant high temperatures and abundant rainfall evenly spread through the year. Beef cattle can be driven through the forest to collecting points on a highway. The demand for meat is increasing and the cattle can be sold in highland markets.'

Comment on this in relation to the effects of forest clearance, and its replacement with grass. Discuss possible consequences: what may occur immediately, and after a few years.

11 Many wandering herdsmen in the Sahel, and other parts of Africa, regard the numbers of livestock as a form of wealth, irrespective of quality.

(a) Why should this alone tend to lead to desertification?

(b) Income for herdsmen comes from hides rather than meat. (i) What might be the reaction to slaughtering cattle to reduce numbers during drought; (ii) does their way of life favour a switch to meat production; (iii) do the natural conditions favour meat production?

12 A massive tree planting scheme to produce a 'green belt' with billions of trees along the southern Sahara has been proposed. What are the natural and practical drawbacks to such a scheme?

13 (a) Explain what might cause a general warming of the lower atmosphere.

(b) What natural events might act to counter such warming?

(c) Why should we be concerned about what happens to the upper atmosphere?

(d) Why does ozone continue to be produced there if so many other gases are able to destroy it?

14 As they develop, the poorer countries will use more energy and need more cars, refrigerators, etc. as living standards rise. How might developed countries help to ensure that pollution from such sources is kept to the minimum while development goes ahead?

Consider the terms used

Plankton is made up of very small animal and plant life, making use of the sun's energy in the surface layers of the ocean. It is the most important source of food for fish.

Pelagic refers to the surface and middle waters of the ocean.

Demersal fish are those that live on or close to the sea-bed.

Fishmeal is made from ground, dried fish and is used as fertiliser and animal foodstuff.

A nautical mile (one minute of latitude) is about 1853m (6080 feet); this is the standard British nautical mile.

Bio-degradable means being capable of being broken down by living organisms into products that will not harm the environment.

A virus is a sub-microscopic organism which enters living cells and causes disease in life forms. Visitors to an area can unwittingly introduce viruses to which wildlife have no natural immunity.

China clay (kaolin) is a fine white clay formed by the breakdown of granite minerals; so there are accumulations bordering the granite moors of southwest England. It is used to make fine porcelain and china, and as a filler in paper manufacture.

Honeypot is the name sometimes used to describe a place with so strong an attraction that it draws large numbers of sightseers.

Greenhouse effect refers to atmosphere warming by long-wave radiation from a surface heated by incoming, penetrative solar radiation.

Ozone layer is a zone, some 20–50 km up, where atoms from oxygen molecules split by incoming UV radiation recombine to produce a particular concentration of ozone.

Abbreviations

ASEAN	Association of South East Asian Nations
CAP	Common Agricultural Policy
CARICOM	Caribbean Community and Common Market
CBD	Central Business District
CFC	Chlorofluorocarbon
CMEA	Council for Mutual Economic Assistance (COMECON)
COMECON	Economic Union of Communist Countries (formed as the CMEA)
CPE	Centrally Planned Economy
DALR	Dry Adiabatic Lapse Rate
EEC	European Economic Community
EFTA	European Free Trade Association
ECOWAS	Economic Community of West African States
ESC	Enclosed Shopping Centre
FAO	Food and Agricultural Organisation
GDP	Gross Domestic Product
GNP	Gross National Product
GP	General Practitioner
HGV	Heavy Goods Vehicle
HYV	High Yield Variety
IEA	International Energy Agency
IMF	International Monetary Fund
ITCZ	Inter-Tropical Convergence Zone
LAFTA	Latin American Free Trade Association
LDC	Less Developed Country
LLDC	Least Developed Country
MDC	More Developed Country
NAFTA	North American Free Trade Area
NATO	North Atlantic Treaty Organisation
NIC	Newly Industrialising Country
ODA	Official Development Assistance
OECD	Organisation for Economic Cooperation and Development
OPEC	Organisation of Petroleum Exporting Countries
OS	Ordnance Survey
PDR	People's Democratic Republic
PQLI	Physical Quality of Life Index
SALR	Saturated Adiabatic Lapse Rate
STJ	Sub-Tropical Jet Stream
UNDRO	United Nations Disaster Relief Organisation
UNESCO	United Nations Education, Scientific, and Cultural Organisation
UNICEF	United Nations International Children's Emergency Fund
UN	The United Nations
WHO	World Health Organisation

Subject Index

Physical Features, Physical Processes (AT3)

Investigation – Measurements, Techniques, Apparatus (AT1)

Place Index